Our Sciences Ruled by Human Prejudice

Humanly Necessary Causal Blindness Persisting Even in Sciences

Books by D. G. Garan

The Paradox of Pleasure and Relativity, 1963

The Relativity for Psychology, 1968 (Reprinted by Nippon Shinrigakkai, Tokyo, 1970)

The Key to the Sciences of Man, 1975 (2nd ed. 1976, and reprint by Nippon Shinrigakkai, 1978)

Against Ourselves: Disorders from Improvements Because of the Organic Limitedness of Man, 1979 (2nd ed. 1981)

OUR SCIENCES RULED BY HUMAN PREJUDICE

Humanly Necessary Causal Blindness Persisting Even in Sciences

by

D. G. GARAN, Ph.D., J.U.D., LL.D

Philosophical Library
New York

Library of Congress Cataloging-in Publication Data

Garan, D.G.
Our sciences ruled by human prejudice.

Bibliography: p.
1. Values. 2. Causation. I. Title.
BD232.G28 1987 121'.8 86-2495
ISBN 0-8022-2507-1

Philosophical Library
200 West 57th Street, New York, N.Y. 10019

Manufactured in the United States of America

TABLE OF CONTENTS

PREFACE

The central idea of this book is the causal relativity of value experiences, which ultimately constitute the universe of man or everything he feels and knows. That relativity results from the fact that our inner values derive from their opposites. This is not difficult to understand.

We experience the pleasure of eating or drinking to the extent that we have felt the displeasure of hunger or thirst. Any organic value is a similar satisfaction coming from equal need, or a restoration of organic normalcy after its equal disturbance. And even our loftiest inner values derive from our organic values. Survival or existence itself acquires the great value of highest pleasure to the extent a threat to it has been experienced as an equally great displeasure.

But relative or opposite-value causality is unacceptable in normal, wholesome human thinking. Men could not survive with relativistic value attitudes. Therefore ideas of value relativity are as repulsive to man as are inedible foods.

Moreover, the opposite causality is contrary to the logic of our exact, technical sciences. These sciences have evolved, and achieved miraculous successes, precisely because they do not have to deal with the inner values, with their impossible causal logic. Yet because of the success of these sciences their logic and methods are applied totally, axiomatically also to the sciences about man. These human sciences, however, have to deal with inner values, governed by exactly contrary, relative or opposite causality.

Our inner values decrease through addition and increase through subtraction. Addition in satisfaction leads to decrease in satisfaction, to satiation. Subtraction as decrease in satisfaction, through added needs as non-satisfactions, increases the potential of satisfaction. But presently no scientist, in any field, would proceed according to this paradoxical causal logic in his "scientific," experimental calculations or thinking.

The decisive fact is that the whole human universe derives from value experiences. Our value feelings determine what we do, how we behave, react, have motivations, evolve capacities, incur the chief modern, stress-related diseases, work culturally, or build our civilization. And all our human sciences, from medicine to economics, deal only with this human universe, with these matters and problems.

Consequently, all sciences of man will remain unscientific, causally confused, until the "impossible," relative causality of values is recognized. Typically, the human sciences are lost in thousands of controversial causal theories, as many as there are scientists, whereas in the exact sciences the causal principles are few and uniformly simple, understood by everybody in the same way.

Even the physical universe of man, as he knows it, is ultimately a product of his value experiences. In the final analysis knowledge derives from value differentiations. The higher theory of physics will, therefore, continue struggling with causal uncertainty as long as the causal, opposite or "negative" sources of man's physical universe are not recognized.

This book can be viewed as offering a novel causal explanation, particularly in the fields of sciences dealing with man and with his knowledge. Of course, causal understanding is the basis or beginning of any science. But the explanation that this book offers is not due to any superior insight. On the contrary, it is due to a "degradation" of outlook.

The role of this book could be compared to that of somebody making an important discovery by rummaging in a refuse heap that respectable people are avoiding as repugnant. What this book has to offer is humanly unattractive, though important for a causal, scientific understanding. The attractiveness of the book is not improved by its seemingly disrespectful treatment of what presently deserves highest esteem in our sciences.

This book uses the best, most certain scientific findings of facts to verify the causality it expounds. There are enormous amounts of such findings, by the best authorities. But this book must reject the causal logic by which such findings are interpreted, under the universal human prejudice indicated above.

We all like gracefully written, sophisticated books, in which the authors downplay their own views and extensively explain those of others. This book offers little of that, and not only because it is written without such a high degree of talent or knowledge.

What this book has to explain is so different from present approaches that it amounts to a different general outlook, however repugnant to natural, healthy human thinking. The point of view on causal, scientific facts in this book is contrary to the usual point of view. And with a new, totally different universal view you do not have to go into detailed analyses of previous explanations.

Also, since it is explaining a new general view, this book has to verify it for almost every field of knowledge. Not much space is left for extensive explanation, in graceful detail, of differing views.

Parts of this book are merely theoretical. Generally, theories are easy and not helpful. But this book only explains a self-evidently simple, universal human prejudice. Think here of what happens even with really great scientific explanations. The Copernican or Darwinian theories are so simple that they need no experimental proofs. In fact Copernican mathematics are now found to have been erroneous and facts of Darwinian evolution are being continuously revised, as will be explained in the book. But these theories became self-evident as soon as the corresponding prejudices were overcome.

Probably the main handicap of this book is the simplicity of its causal explanations. Most of the fundamental causal principles in sciences are simple. Scientists know that. But they would hate, more than anything, to entertain simplistic ideas.

Indeed the idea of relative causality is simple and known to everybody. We all know that a return to an ordinary state of feeling from that of pain brings pleasure. Equally simple are the other truths of value relativity, such as the dependence of every satisfaction or value on its opposite.

No originality or difficult, ingenious discovery is necessary to understand the causal relativity of values. Insistence on such a simple causal fact, therefore, can seem to be a rather simplistic attitude.

It may be noted here that I will repeat the explanation of relative causal logic through this book at several important points. The various phenomena of relative causality treated in the book are paradoxical, seemingly illogical. They may remain incomprehensible unless the paradox of opposite-causality logic is made clear repeatedly, in its various aspects.

The book has not been edited by anybody, except myself. The usual editing of books improves them. But editors tend to make the copy more acceptable to readers. That would hardly improve what this book has to say. The consistency of the "impossible" ideas of this book is, in my view, more important than matters of language or style.

By the way, I am using the pronoun "he" instead of "he or she" after nouns like "person" and "man." This seems easier, more concise to me. It does not reflect an attitude about women's rights, which I fully respect.

In general, the explanations in this book are simple and brief. They may be even spotty and scientifically untechnical. After all, the book merely explains a simple, universal human prejudice, which happens to be causally, scientifically decisive.

The book is mostly critical, as exposure of a prejudice requires. Usually criticism is easy and not constructively useful. In this book, however, the intention is to demonstrate how incredibly extensive are the effects of this prejudice in our present human sciences. Then it becomes concretely clear what scientific changes can be thought of.

The book may not be interesting to read. This, probably, could not be helped. The relativity of values is humanly too unacceptable to be made attractive. And it is too simple to be treated in the context of exciting or sophisticated discoveries.

In compensation, the book offers the presently missing, scientifically necessary, causal explanations in the sciences dealing with man. In these sciences the key factors are inner values, which follow a simple yet presently "impossible" causal logic.

Indeed, the only merit of this book is that it explains what seems impossible because of a natural, universal human prejudice. True, this requires less talent and more readiness to accept what is repugnant to human thinking. But our explanation happens to be scientifically relevant. It makes possible a simple but decisive causal, scientific understanding generally prevented by a human prejudice that is necessary for man's survival.

D. Garan
New York, 1987

I

HUMANLY INEVITABLE CAUSAL PREJUDICE

Man did not recognize the role of his planet in the universe or his place in evolution because of his value prejudices. We have overcome these prejudices. But man still lives with a prejudice that is the most decisive of all.

Man still does not recognize that his inner values derive from their value opposites. In fact, this opposite or relative-value causality is exactly contrary to the beliefs man still holds, even in his scientific thinking.

This prejudice is all-important because the universe of man is ultimately a result of his experiences of values, deriving from opposite causal sources. Moreover, to know something essentially and scientifically is to understand its causal source, since the cause of a phenomenon determines what it is or how it works. In short, man presently sees or knows his universe in ways exactly contrary to what it is and does causally, scientifically.

All our inner values derive from their opposites, just as satisfactions come from needs which are non-satisfactions. But man would not have normal motivations if he believed that his values, for which he lives, cannot come without their equal opposites, which he does not want. He would not survive if he accepted nonsatisfactions or disturbances as necessary sources of satisfactions or values. Consequently, man must live with inherent prejudices against the truth of how his values derive causally.

But the universe of man is, in the final causal analysis, that of his value experiences. His value feelings determine what he does, how he behaves, reacts, avoids the chief modern, reactive diseases, evolves his capacities, or builds his material civilization and his cultural world. Even his knowledge, and therefore his view of the physical universe as he knows it, results from value experiences. Knowledge comes from value differentiations, however minute or complex.

In sum, the decisive causes in the universe of man are inner values, but any inner value derives causally from its opposites, which determine what effects it has. These opposites, the "negative" causal sources, however, are not recognized or understood as such causal determinants. In fact, the causal logic of opposite-value causality is exactly contrary to universal human thinking, and to the causal logic of our technical, exact sciences.

As a result, all sciences dealing with man, and even the higher theory of physics, remain unscientific. Causal understanding is the only possible basis of a science. But scientists, as all men, have not recognized the "impossible" causality of values deriving from their opposites. This is particularly so because scientists proceed according to their strictly "scientific," experimental methods. Experiments are conducted only with the usual mathematical logic, even in the sciences dealing with man. It is critical that the very logic and methods of our exact sciences are contrary to the relative or opposite-value causality.

The only true, exact sciences are presently the technical sciences. They have nothing to do with inner values. They therefore evolve and progress without any difficulties of causal understanding. In contrast, the human sciences could not become exact sciences, because the causal reality in these fields has remained hidden or repugnant to man.

The technical, exact sciences have achieved marvelous successes. Consequently, their logic and methods have been accepted as axiomatic by scientists in all fields, including human sciences. The causal logic of the exact sciences is the humanly "right" logic under which man strives to increase his values in themselves, not through their opposites. Thus, the real causal sources of values, their opposites, are totally disregarded under this logic. It is the logic of values increasing by addition.

This is exactly contrary to the actual logic of value causality, under which values increase with the addition of their opposites—that is, by subtraction. Satisfaction increases with addition of needs as non-satisfactions. It decreases to zero if added up to the fullest extent, to satiation. Pleasure of eating a food diminishes and finally ceases as more of the food is eaten. That pleasure returns through accumulation of its opposite, the hunger or nonsatisfaction of the need for food.

No wonder all sciences dealing with man, and with his universe as he knows it, are struggling with a vast and admitted causal confusion. There are as many controversial theories in the human sciences as there are noted scientists.

Causal understanding is missing in these fields. They are not yet scientific. In the exact sciences the fundamental causal principles are few and simple, understood by everybody in the same way. In contrast, every one of the thousand theories in the human sciences such as psychology has its own causal principles or fundamental forces, different from those in the other theories.

The greatest miracles in the future of man will become possible when all fields of his universe become scientific, through the overcoming of his universal causal prejudice. Man is created by nature under a simple causal principle or "design" (explained later). Nature does not know or invent complex causal principles.

Causal, scientific understanding of what man is and does is therefore possible. And the presently scientific, technical sciences show that virtual miracles become realities through sciences. Our present technical capabilities—say, of watching something that happens a thousand miles away—are so miraculous that even a century ago they would have been attributed to divine powers.

Far greater miracles will result from scientific, causal understanding of how to change man himself, how to increase his capacities, the sources of further capacities. Man will indeed become a seemingly godlike self-creator, changing himself in presently unimaginable ways. Our past shows that true, causally understood sciences can create miracles.

The "Impossible" Causality of Values Deriving from Their Opposites

The causality of values deriving from their opposites governs the human universe. This causality is due to the organic limitedness of man. Our value feelings derive from organically relevant changes, such as needs or pleasure releases. But the organism has to conserve its essential organic sameness. Consequently, each change that creates a value or feeling derives from or leads to equivalent opposite changes, creating opposite-value feelings.

We shall use the term "value reactions" for such value feelings, deriving from relevant organic changes, within the conscious world.

Mostly, an organism finds satisfactions, to restore organic normalcy or sameness, after experiencing needs as disturbing changes in this sameness. Evidently, the restoration of normalcy is as great and organically significant as was the disturbance. Further, an organism imposes restrictions after enjoying pleasure releases, to restore its normal reserves of living energy. The restrictions have to be as great as were the releases. The result is equivalent opposite-value experiences. This is clear from aftereffects of all over-enjoyments. The simplest example is the aftereffect of drugs.

The conservation of their sameness by organisms is the fundamental law of organic existence. This law makes all men as organisms causally, scientifically understandable in the same, simple way. Everything that is organically essential, causally decisive, is governed by this law.

The rule of this law is all-inclusive because organisms are limited to remaining the same, not only in their forms but also in their dynamics. This organic limitedness is universally important causally, though it is humanly unacceptable.

The principle of the conservation by organisms of their sameness derives from the simple, universal fact that only that exists which is able to persist. Organisms are able to survive only by conserving to the tiniest detail their evolutionary adaptations.

This is as important as it is self-evident. Man's heart, eye, or hand has to remain essentially the same as it has been evolved through millions of years. This is equally true for all his functions or dynamics—in his circulation, metabolism, physical exertion, or any other organic activity.

Scientifically, the whole and only "purpose" or reason of being of the organism is to conserve its organic sameness or normalcy. Higher, human values or purposes are conditioned elaborations of this organic reason of being. Consequently, all human values are merely results of the organism experiencing changes and meeting them with equivalent opposite changes.

This opposite or relative-value casuality has many aspects. First let us mention what may be the most important one.

Man as a conscious, planning being wants to improve his organic reactive functions beyond their natural limits. He wants to obtain more release of living energy, more pleasure, in spite of the organic requirement of equal releases and restrictions. Thus *a person may "improve"* his heart function or metabolism. Inevitably the organism has to counteract such abnormal changes by opposite processes. These are felt as diseased restrictions or stress.

If this stress is overcome by still more "improvements," then even more restrictions have to be imposed. As these "improvements" require more of the release of living energy, *the result is functional exhaustion* or impoverishment that deepens in a *vicious circle.* Under a person's continued drive for such improvements, this vicious-circle exhaustion can reach almost any degree. It thus causes a "chronic," functional disease such as heart disease, hypertension, or diabetes.

In the same way every kind of functional impoverishment or disease can result from man's planned efforts to "improve" and sustain his feelings of well-being. Modern man is prodigiously resourceful, as well as free of restrictive traditions. He vastly and ingeniously improves his reactions or feelings, by intensely exploiting the underlying functions that yield the feelings.

The result is the epidemic of functional diseases such as heart disease, as well as functional mental disorders. Motivational and behavioral impoverishment is caused by similar "improvements" and leads to problems like those of education, crime, and drug addiction.

It is revealing that modern science admittedly remains incapable of understanding these diseases and disorders causally.

Scientists cannot accept the causal logic that directly clear improvements can bring equal worsening.

Doctors admit that our principal, functional diseases, and functional mental disorders, have remained mysteries causally. We shall explain later how unbelievable the persistence of these mysteries can be. Each of the functional diseases is uniform in its effects; it therefore must be caused by one, totally simple, natural causal principle, since nature does not know complex principles. Yet doctors here remain mystified by what can be only simple.

Our behavioral and motivational problems—of crime, maladjustment, hate, or violence—have increased through similar reactive impoverishment. This is happening in spite of unprecedented improvements in our conditions of life as well as in our scientific skills and resourcefulness.

Not much can be done presently to help these problems efficiently, scientifically, in our scientific era. For, as everybody knows, no true science, and therefore no efficient policy or scientific "engineering," is yet available in fields like education or crime. The reason is that the very logic of causal thinking of scientists is exactly contrary to the causality of value reactions which determine human actions and behavior.

The same is true in other fields. For instance, we live with all kinds of addictions. They are clearly products of the vicious circle of worsening through improvements of feelings. But scientists have not explained addictions causally, because opposite causality is "scientifically" impossible. Theories on various addictions are as many as there are investigators, but the cause of all addictions is one and simple—the reactive worsening through overimprovement.

Relative or opposite-value causality is less decisive practically for the experiences of cognition or knowledge. In such *cognitive experiences* the value reactions, as organic changes, are infinitesimally minute. It is therefore only natural that cognition, ideas, reasons, knowledge, or cognitive learning has little effect on behavior and motivations.

We all can know, understand, or learn easily how we can be successful with more positive reactions, more interests, or more satisfactions for what we intend to do or wat is desirable. But such knowledge or understanding cannot really help us. Otherwise we would become perfect and successful after reading a good book on positive thinking. Why not espouse positive reactions, which are also pleasant? Yet our modern thought and psychology accept as causally decisive various cognitive factors such as ideas, perceptions, cognitive attitudes, or learning.

In reality, only our value reactions can determine our behavior. But positive reactions, our satisfactions or pleasure releases, are possible only through the equal accumulation of conditioned restrictions, which is the most difficult thing for man to do.

The relativity of values is more easily recognized in regard to experiences that are practically less important, where such insights do not relate to our emotionally weighty value attitudes. Thus the *relativity of sense perceptions* is generally recognized.

This indicates that the value relativity of all experiences and reactions could be easily understood if it were not for the universal and practically important human prejudices against value relativity—which are necessary for wholesome motivations.

The relativity of sensations and perceptions is illustrated in many ways in books of psychology.[1, 2] Even more often, the relativity of perceptions, while not expressly recognized, underlies explanations offered in psychology. The whole field of Gestalt psychology is a good example, as will be explained later.

Standard illustrations in psychology show how, for instance, gray appears light against a dark background and dark against a light one.[2] A line or circle appears longer or bigger when placed together with shorter or smaller ones.[1] Above all, according to the Weber-Fechner law, sensation capacity decreases as stimulation increases.[1, 2] Any experience of value or satisfaction decreases the potential for its further experience.

But such illustrations imply that values are relative only to a degree. Actually, the value relativity or value dependence on opposite-value backgrounds is total.

It is true that feelings of, say, cold or hunger do not disappear entirely even if no opposite causal background, or relief, is offered for a long time. Here we have to realize that many, deeper and deeper, organic standards, take part in such experiences. If the last of the standards becomes effaced, by the relative extinction of sensation through its intense continuation, then the feeling of cold or hunger would indeed disappear. But at that stage the person would be unconscious or dead.

Other facts may obscure the totality of value relativity. When you go from a very hot room into a moderately warm one, you feel cool. But one could feel a hundred degrees as cool only if his range of heat experiences was, say, a thousand degrees and he went to a hundred degrees from a much higher temperature.

In a word, interference from persisting and deeper value standards prevents values from becoming totally relative in the short run. And the limited range of our sense experiences makes it impossible for us to feel relative reactions beyond that range.

But no such standards or limitations apply to our psychological world of inner values, where we can create in our minds value experiences without limits. Also, our values of perception, such as vision, can be fully relative, while the physiologic process of perceiving is not a value experience, not an essential organic change subject to the rules of relativity.

Here as in many organic processes the reactions are endlessly multiple and minute. They repeat or renew themselves continuously as in the action of nerve connections or of sensory cells and organs, such as the cones of color vision. Thus, the physiologic reactions here are repetitively continuous and tiny. Instead, interrelations of whole masses of such reactions are felt as the actual values, which then are governed by value relativity, fully and clearly, as all organic changes are.

In experiments on vision the subjects wore glasses that slanted the world in one direction. After the subjects discontinued wearing the glasses, they saw the world as slanted in the opposite direction. The same was observed about the sense of touch.

Now, assume that the whole world, including ourselves, was generally distorted in some even more complex way. We would not know that anything was so distorted. Values derive from relative comparison, and change only as their relationships change.

Alice in Wonderland saw herself as becoming smaller when actually the size of the world around her was increasing. Spatial measurements are more clearly relative because space is more simply a result of relating spatial values. Time intervals are as clearly relative because they also result more simply from the relation of changes. Imagine that a time period equivalent to a thousand years had passed without change in the universe, and in yourself, after you had finished reading the last sentence and started this one. You would not know that any time, even a minute, had passed.

The values of vision are fully relative where they can be isolated from interfering standards. In a room where everything is red, only shades of gray appear. When you put on green glasses, after a while everything regains its natural colors—actually relationships of colors—though in fact you are seeing only differences in green.

Aftereffects of light and color reveal the relative causality even of physiologic processes. The afterimage of a bright cross is a dark cross, or, of red color, green color. Here organic mechanisms have been altered by a stronger-than-usual experience as organic change. Normalcy then is regained by equal changes in the opposite direction.

Generally, in color experience, a spatial or temporal background of one color makes the opposite color appear. After you have read a page printed in red, you find the normal, gray print on the next page to be greenish. In a bus with all sides, except its front, enclosed by green glass, the images glimpsed through the front seem reddish.

A similar relativity of values can be observed in our experiences with smell, taste, sound or touch. Again, our persisting, deeper and deeper, organic standards may prevent total relativity—until they also become extinct. Or the limitation of the range of values that we can normally experience may make the relativity limited. But as a general law, all values, including the cognitive ones, are relative. There are *no values in themselves*. They all derive their meaning from relative comparisons, from *their opposites*, in the final analysis.

Does the opposite-value comparison involve all our experiences? A tree is recognized as an object even apart from its distinctive color or other values. The explanation is that the *nothingness* everywhere offers the universal contrast against which things are perceived.

Without nothingness we could not perceive anything. If everything, including ourselves, consisted of one universal stuff—say, of uniform clay—without nothingness, we could not differentiate or know anything: no things would exist for us. Every form derives its distinction against the background of nothingness. And the dynamics of things derive from instantaneous successions of forms.

We should start realizing that the world as we know it derives as much from nothingness as from our material reality. This causal fact becomes important for understanding the causal, "negative" source of the physical universe as man knows it, to be explained by the theory of physics.

Before we conclude, we may look at the most important general values, *pleasure and pain*.

It is not difficult to see that feelings of pleasure are relative. The deepest experience of general pleasure, provided by drugs, brings in the end an equal torture. Over-enjoyments bring negative reactions, just as strong pain brings pleasure upon transition to a pain that is less strong.

Here we should remember that all value relativity is due to organic limitedness. An experience of value or disvalue is organic change. If the change mounts up to the organic limit for it, the value experience inevitably ceases. Then the opposite process of returning to the normal state or balance becomes inevitable and brings opposite feelings.

Pleasure is best understood as the release of living energy or acceleration of life. Evidently, every release or acceleration requires equal restriction or deceleration, so that normalcy or sameness is conserved in organic dynamics. This opposite process, the restriction, is as unpleasant as the pleasure was enjoyable.

We have seen what happens when such unpleasant restrictions are overcome by a further increase in the release of living energy, by functional "improvements." The end result is a vicious-circle exhaustion in the function, leading to functional disease or disorder.

Other practically important facts become understandable from the relative causality of pleasure. Our positive motivations and capacities, such as interests or enthusiam, are pleasures. Should they be condemned? Not at all. They can be increased, to any extent, without negative aftereffects, if equal restrictions are increased first. Within the organic limitedness only equal *restrictions can create potential for releases*. The restrictions, of course, are as difficult as the motivational pleasures are enjoyable.

It is generally decisive to realize that restrictions are the ways to positive adjustment. The effect of restrictions can be thought of as the "damming" up of living energy so that reserves for motivational pleasure-release become available.

Practically, restrictions are imposed by educational and cultural conditioning. Natural needs, mostly those of survival, are conditionally kept unsatisfied. The accumulated non-satisfactions or needs then are sources of satisfactions, released when the person behaves in the desirable, conditioned ways. All traditional education and culture, by which people have progressed, is restrictive and difficult.

Of course, according to the "scientifically" self-evident logic, restrictions and non-satisfactions are to be eliminated as much as possible in order to have more of the pleasure-releases or satisfactions, the clear causal sources of positive behavior and motivations.

Pleasure is functionally identical with the success of organic survival. Organisms survive by doing what we consciously know as pleasant. Survival is the ultimate pleasure. When survival is threatened no other value has any meaning. But survival becomes synonymous with boredom itself if it continues without disruptions. Only to the extent that survival is threatened or its needs have not been satisfied does it acquire its supreme value.

Pain is the opposite of pleasure and is equally relative. It comes from disruptions or negations of existing organic satisfactions. Somebody born without the full satisfaction of a function—say, in circulation—with a defect in it, feels no pain from it. A normal person with such a defect arising during his life would feel excruciating pain. Everybody has inborn defects, to various extents, in some functions. Another person suddenly acquiring similar defects would feel pain, whereas the person born with them does not.

Pain is relative even in its shorter-range effects. The sensation of pain decreases with its duration, as the Weber-Fechner Law predicts. Experiments have shown that pain from heat stops increasing after the temperature reaches 152 degrees. A state of pain may be even pleasant, if it comes after the experience of a stronger pain.

Organically important pain, however, does not cease completely even after a longer duration. We have explained the reason. The general and deeper organic standards, as requirements of satisfaction, continue as long as the person lives. Thus, the full, relative extinction of pain is reached only as such standards cease, as death ensues.

Schematically, what has not given rise to or brought satisfaction can not bring pain. But every growth, as organic satisfaction, has to bring equal pain when it is disrupted and, finally, terminated by death.

Here it can be said that *one's life can bring him only as much pleasure as pain*. It is like a ride in a plane that starts and ends at ground level. However intricate the ascents and descents of the plane, they inevitably cancel each other out exactly in the end. You can have a higher ascent, or make it last longer by making it less steep. But the up-and-down movements, the decisive factors of value, will even out.

Finally, we have to emphasize that *relative-value causality is totally unacceptable* in general human thinking.

The relativity of inner values implies that human pursuits are futile. We always strive for a gain or ascent in our feelings of value. Actually we get only equal ups and downs in our feelings. But men cannot survive with convictions that their existence is futile. Ideas contrary to our normal pursuits of survival have to become as repulsive as unhealthy foods. Such ideas are inevitably ridiculous. The very essence of what is laughable is non-seriousness as the opposite of the restrictive seriousness under which we live; laughter is a release from the restrictions sustained by that seriousness.

Objectively, value relativity is self-evidently clear. In nonpractical, philosophical thinking this has been often recognized.

Plato explained how pleasure follows pain.[4] Aristotle recognized value relativity, though he argued that general value standards remain; he was not inclined to go so far as to analyze the standards themselves.[3] Many modern philosophers, including Hobbes, Hamilton, and Whitehead, have abstractly accepted the relativity of values.[3, 4] The modern pragmatic philosophical movements recognize the dependence of cognitive satisfactions on pre-existing needs, in the world of knowledge.[4] Value differentiation as the method of cognition is recognized in most philosophies.[3, 4]

Recurrent movements of thought and religion such as stoicism or Buddhism recognize the relativity of enjoyments and their futility. Such movements urge the abandonment of immediate, natural human drives, with the final, objective realization that pursuits of values, or pleasures, are futile. But men cannot remain resignedly objective, uninvolved in value motivations. Thoughts and cultures that reject value relativity always win.

In our scientific era, most important is the fact that the very logic of our present sciences is contrary to the logic of opposite or relative causality. *This prevents causal, scientific understanding* in all fields dealing with man, and even in the theory of physics, studying the cosmos as man knows it.

But first we have to establish that in these fields, in the universe of man, the causal factors are indeed his inner values, governed by the opposite causality.

Man's Universe a Result of His Value Experiences

Our feelings are our most direct value experiences. And they determine our behavior, motivations, reactions, perceptions, "reasoning," and capacities.

Men are inclined to think that they proceed according to their reasons or ideas based on facts. Actually, our reasons and ideas serve either as justifications for what we feel or as the intellectual tools for attaining what we want according to our feelings or wishes.

We can establish, perfectly, by plain reasoning or perception that we need only positive reactions to succeed. If you have satisfaction or pleasure as the motive for what you intend to do you cannot fail. Reasoning all this out is easy, and the positive reactions or satisfactions are pleasant. Then why aren't we all supermen? Evidently our behavior is determined by our value feelings, or simply by pleasure releases; and their source is equal restrictions, the hardest things for men to bear.

Man's universe is mostly the world he builds around himself. He builds it for his various satisfactions, present and future. Our important cultural and moral satisfactions derive from conditioned needs, as conditional non-satisfactions or restrictions.

In a word, the external world as the civilization that man creates and controls is a result of his value goals and feelings, of his inner values, governed by relative or opposite-value causality. Our intellect, working with facts, is only the tool for the creation of that world in compliance with our value feelings.

Our inner world is even more clearly a product of our value feelings. Motivations come from the pursuit of satisfactions, or simply of pleasure in its various forms. All our behavior is thus determined by value reactions. Of course, most of our useful, cultural pleasures or inner values are conditioned satisfactions.

The main problems of behavior come from the lack of such conditioned, cultural, or "rational" motivations. Everybody knows clearly what his behavior should be in order to have a perfect individual and social life. The only difficulty is the insufficiency of motivations, of the potential of conditioned satisfactions for behaving in the desired ways—the lack of "will power."

Behavior *difficulties and disorders* come from the over-enjoyment of pleasures, in unrestricted or non-conditioned ways. The ultimate cause of man's difficulties is his organic limitedness and the opposite causality that follows from it. Reactions opposite to an enjoyed pleasure are inevitable if the enjoyment goes beyond normalcy, above previously accumulated needs or restrictions.

The inexorably limited, organic pleasure potential is easily exhausted. Then restrictions become necessary to restore that potential. If the restrictions are prevented by further, deeper enjoyment, the restrictions have to become more intense in order to re-establish the normal pleasure potential. The vicious circle of deepening over-enjoyment and restrictions thus continues. Through it the reserves of living energy, felt as pleasure, can be exhausted to any incredible degree, as each increased enjoyment amounts to exploitation of the living energy.

Mental disorders, psychoses and neuroses, are expressions of the extreme exhaustion and impoverishment of the satisfaction or pleasure potential. The neurotic or psychotic has not lost his other mental capacities.[5] He merely behaves in the way we all would under extreme emotional negativity, fear, and depression, which are inevitable aftereffects of over-enjoyed opposite feelings. Psychosis or neurosis disappears, temporarily, after administration of a drug, such as chlorpromazine,[6] that has the effect of releasing pleasure as positive reactions.

Physical diseases are even graver problems in man's world. Three-fourths of our fatal diseases today are caused by what man does to himself. Physical factors, such as infections, injuries, or organic defects now cause less than 20 percent of deaths.[7]

The other 80 percent of deaths now come from diseases and disorders caused by our way of life, our reactions, motivations, and behavior—determined by our value feelings.

In the final analysis, these diseases are caused by man's strongest drive, the pursuit of pleasure enjoyment, to excess. As a planning, conscious being man wants to improve his feeling of well-being as much as possible. He can do that by "improving" or intensifying and accelerating his organic functions.

Modern man attains such improvements to extreme degrees. His skills and resourcefulness are extraordinary. He is "scientific" enough to reject restrictions and to strive for as many of the reactive functional improvements as possible. The result is excessive functional "improvements" leading to a vicious-circle functional worsening and final exhaustion.

Men are ingenious. They learn, intuitively, that to derive feelings of well-being they have to "improve" the various underlying organic functions. This is the only way to do it successfully. In nutrition alone we resort to thousands of more stimulating, richer foods and ingredients, as well as culinary skills, to get such improvements. Of course, in doing all this man merely wants to enjoy more of the pleasure release and the feeling of well-being, which he also associates with good health.

Consequently, the opposite functional reactions, arising to restore the normal release reserves, are felt as extensive and tormenting restrictions in our organic functions. This creates organically painful stress in endlessly varied deepening forms. That explains why *stress has become the scourge of modern man.* It has been blamed as the cause in the confused etiology of heart disease and as the main reaction in the other functional diseases.[2, 5]

By the way, the term "functional" diseases may be the best since it indicates that these diseases originate not from physical, organic causes or defects but from the way the person exploits the underlying functions to obtain increased feelings of pleasure and well-being. Of course, our whole way of life determines how much we strive for and attain such feelings, through our functional self-exploitation.

As to general human motivations and capacities, they are evidently the sources of what man does and creates because of his feelings, his pleasure drives which determine his value goals. If man has sufficient forces of motivation or "willpower" to carry out what he intends, his world can be transformed in various wondrous ways. Motivations are conditioned pleasures, which as drives of living energy itself are effective, while purely cognitive factors are not.

We have to note here an important fact. Cognitive experiences also derive from value reactions. But these multiple reactions are so infinitesimally minute that they have no organic weight.

Generally, we are motivated by our value reactions as pleasure drives while we use our cognitive capacities as instruments to serve our motivations. Of course, our primary aptitude for developing motivations, bearing restrictions is inborn, as are our cognitive capacities. But it is not decisively important. A greater aptitude can help do more harm than good if used with wrong motivations. The decisive influence is the educational and cultural conditioning that turns innate emotional capacities into desired motivations. With positive motivations even less intelligent people perform well.

All in all, the internal as well as the external world, mental and physical, that men create for themselves results from their value experiences, particularly from their management of their inner value reactions. Of course the strongest, universal organic force, the pleasure drive, practically determines all behavior; and pleasure is causally synonymous with value in human reactions.

Now we may look at some general, practically important phenomena of the human universe that are not noticed or are misunderstood because the relativity of value experiences is not recognized.

First, we may explain the paradox that *the more universal a fact or condition is, the less it is noticed or "known."* To the extent that a condition or value is universal or omnipresent it offers no possibility of differentiation, no way of knowing it. The discovery of air as a substance took a long time; that of atmospheric pressure even longer. The force of gravitation was not "noticed" because it is so universal.

Modern scientists have failed to discover some of the most universal and therefore most important causal facts for the same reason. We shall see later in discussing admitted mysteries in physics how the most universal causal source or field is still not recognized—how the force itself is never perceived by man though it determines everything in the universe.

But at the moment we may mention some "unnoticed" universal facts in the sciences dealing with man.

The universal principle or "design" by which all organisms exist is their preservation of their organic sameness. This principle has not been recognized, precisely because of its universality. It is too commonplace, too obvious, to be noticed as anything in particular. But that "design" makes inevitable the organic limitedness and thus the universal law of the opposite causality of value reactions, which derive from organic change and are the sources of man's universe. An understanding of that law could serve as the simple causal basis, with a new scientific logic, for dealing with practically everything in the human sciences. We saw that indeed everything in these fields is determined by value reactions.

Another *universal, "unnoticed" fact is pleasure as causal factor.* We live every moment of our lives for and by pleasure. Pleasure is the universal organic mechanism that makes man tick. But pleasure as a causal factor is too commonplace to be "noticed". By being so universal pleasure is not concrete enough in our perception, not real enough for scientists to bother with. Pleasure is hardly mentioned in the sciences as the universal, determining causal factor it is.

Actually, pleasure can serve causal, scientific understanding perfectly. It is totally mechanistic and simple in causal terms. If the pleasure of taste did not show us the precise causal meaning of each food we would not survive. Similarly, pleasure reveals the precise mechanistic, causal meaning of all organic events, which are also the sources of our mental world.

The universal organic needs are also not real enough for scientists. The most universal need, from which practically all other needs derive, is that of survival. Subordinate to the survival need are the universal needs of growth or of exercise of one's capacities, and of superiority. But scientists and educators do not "notice" the survival needs, the non-satisfaction of which is the basis of educational conditioning. They see as important the more "real" needs such as those of food or shelter. Or they assume the pre-existence of intellectual needs, which are actually results of the conditioning of survival needs.

In fact, conditioned non-satisfaction of the all-powerful survival need, of the need for security, is the very gist of educational conditioning. It is the source of cultural or intellectual interests as satisfactions. But the conditioning itself here is also too universal to be noticed as a concrete reality.

Educational scientists, consequently, are missing the very sources from which education grows. Rather they are seeing as decisive the seemingly more concrete acts of conditioning, such as the physical handling of infants or the toilet-training of children. Thus, neither the universal, most decisive needs nor their universal minute-by-minute conditioning are recognized as the decisive causal realities by scientists and educators.

The universal facts of value relativity itself are hardly viewed as worth noticing. Men can see such facts all around them. They can easily observe how their valuable motivations require effort; how satisfactions lose their pleasure value after they are attained; how a continuous happiness or enjoyment is impossible; how satisfactions require needs; how a mere relief from pain becomes a pleasure; how ordinary existence acquires great value upon its disturbance; how something to be noticed has to be different; or how a value experience requires organic change while the organism has to remain the same (which makes the opposite or relative-value causality inevitable).

But man dismisses such universal facts as meaningless because they are commonplace. Actually by being so universal they are causally the most important, scientifically decisive.

Other universal, "unnoticed" conditions or facts of human behavior and existence will be discussed throughout this book. But we may mention now that the very first universal human condition for understanding the world is not "noticed."

The human mind is inherently limited. It can deal only with one thing at a time; nobody can think of two things simultaneously. This limitedness of mind makes it unbelievably inferior to living mechanisms, which work purposively with myriad elements at every instant. Obviously, if this universal fact were "noticed," the causal, scientific insights would change completely, not only about our understanding of living phenomena but also about our mind and reactions as living processes. And man's universe is a product of his mind or reactions.

Also, the very first universal aspect of the *existence of man as a material being*, is similarly not recognized. Man is a being of matter, created by principles and mechanisms of matter. That is why the principles or laws of nature are simple to man; he exists in the same way as nature does.

These laws are "meaningless," poor in mental content precisely because they are so universal. Similarly, a person's existence does not seem to have in itself any concrete meanings to him, because it includes everything for him.

Ultimately, the natural laws of matter are most truly "divine" or "spiritual," because they create and causally manage not only nature but also man and his mind as a form of his existence. Yet the confused, piteously limited human mind has created delusions about a spiritual reality superior to the material world. There is no reason to deny the immanence of God in our world. But His work is evident right here in the simplest material, mechanistic laws—which create man and mind—if we know how to look beyond human delusions.

A practically important universal phenomenon, originating from the relativity of values, is *fixation.* Its universal prevalence and causal origin are not "noticed" or recognized.

Values derive their meaning and strength from relation with a value background; no value has meaning in itself. As a value object is enjoyed, at first even accidentally, the background for its experience expands, becomes richer; more or stronger need and satisfaction pathways become established. Such a background makes easier the enjoyment of the same value, and as it is enjoyed the background is enriched still further, making the value still more enjoyable.

This vicious circle can turn an initially insignificant value into the strongest value for the person who started to enjoy it. To the extent that any value can be enjoyed repeatedly, the vicious-circle fixation for it deepens automatically and can increase it to an incredible degree.

The decisive factor here is the ease of enjoyment of something for which the background of comparisons, of needs and satisfactions, is already there. Even as the value of the enjoyed habit starts fading, the fixation deepens. For it is easier to perfect, in some way, the old enjoyment source than to establish a new one; a new satisfaction requires a previous accumulation of needs.

The repeated watching of baseball games does not become boring because it is continually perfected and improved, by glorified visions of particular teams or players. As expectations increase, the games are watched even more, which increases the capacity for enjoying them. Of course, any increased, fixational enjoyment brings opposite value feelings. Then more enjoyment is sought to overcome them. This strengthens the vicious circle.

Fixations are strong around socially created value enjoyments. Natural, varied, organic needs prevent fixations on some one organic satisfaction. Such controls are lacking in social enjoyments.

Once a social enjoyment is started, even by mere chance, it deepens automatically, at each turn, and may become a national cult. Conditions that merely permit repetition of the enjoyment keep the vicious circle running. Scientific experts try to find some deeply significant meaning for such strong and "sacred" cults, which are meaningless in their substance.

Fixations are as varied as our ways of enjoyments. Everybody has his preferred chair, a way of eating his breakfast, a pattern of daily leisures, hobbies, and special interests. They may be as deeply valuable to him as they may seem meaningless to others. Even commerical advertising exploits the human tendency to fixate on names or on the recognition of products and on their valuation or use. Political sloganeering as well as party affiliations are similarly fixational.

Fixations are, at best, nuisances. But the compulsive force of the vicious circle of fixations is not causally understood. Such understanding would require the recognition that the strength and meaning of a value experience can derive merely from its background. Social scientists always seek for deeper, important causes of the sacred, complex customs and institutions of peoples. Theories expounded in humanistic thought are here particularly misleading. They stress the verity of deep or rich value experiences, and nowhere are values deeper, more sacred than in fixations.

The result is that our social scientists and learned experts are viewing as revelations of highest truths or wisdoms the "sacred" customs and institutions that are substantially as meaningless as neurotic mannerisms.

Another general phenomenon of relative-value causality is the *intense and "ingenious" way in which men seem to turn against themselves* in pursuit of greater enjoyment or improvement of their value feelings.

As a person tries to enjoy a feeling perfectly, the opposite reactions arise. If these are suppressed with even a stronger, ingenuous enjoyment of the feeling, the opposite reactions return in equally "ingenious," stronger ways. Then it may seem that some inventive, forcefully persisting agent inside the person is acting against him.

Such opposite reactions are inevitable with the enjoyment of "improvements" of various organic functions and feelings. Thus men everywhere seem to be ingeniously bringing on themselves negative mental reactions as well as physical, functional worsening, the opposite of the "improvements." The vicious circle of worsening through added improvements deepens such self-defeating efforts into grave and fatal diseases.

But the relative-value causality also permits man to attain *unlimited positive reactions or capacities.*

Though it is difficult, one can impose to any degree restrictions on his enjoyments, on the flow of energy of life. By doing so he can accumulate "reserves" of such energy to any amount needed. Pleasure releases or satisfactions are made available through previous restrictions or non-satisfactions that create needs. This is regularly achieved by our restrictive educational conditioning, which transforms natural survival needs into desired useful or cultural needs.

Positive motivations are clearly pleasures or satisfactions. They are also the sources of our positive behavioral capacities. You can have satisfactions and capacities as extensive as the corresponding non-satisfactions you have accumulated. Of course, if our positive capacities, as satisfactions or pleasures, came without the difficult non-satisfactions, we would be limitlessly capable and perfect.

Sciences Still Bound by Causal Prejudice

Our present sciences dealing with man, and even with his knowledge of reality, are causally prejudiced, scientifically misleading. The very logic or way of causal, scientific thinking in these sciences is exactly contrary to the opposite-value causality that actually governs the universe of man. For that universe is a result of man's value experiences.

It should be emphasized that under the actual, opposite or relative causation of values they derive from their opposites. Addition in a value decreases it. The fullest addition of a value, such as satisfaction, leads to its extinction, by satiation. Subtraction in a value, as an addition of opposite value—say, need—leads to increase in the value. The greater the need, the greater the satisfaction.

But the only *causal logic* known and used in all present sciences is that of *our exact, technical sciences*. It is the mathematically precise logic of the increase of values by addition and decrease by subtraction. This logic determines the very way of thinking and proceeding in all modern sciences. It is automatically applied in every experiment, observation, recording of data, calculation of results, or correlation of causal factors. The possibility of a different, opposite causal logic has not yet been even mentioned in the present human sciences—or in any other field.

We should keep in mind two evident facts. First, inner values are the determining causal sources in all sciences dealing with man, and even in those dealing with his knowledge of physical reality. Secondly, inner values are governed by the "impossible" relative or opposite-value causality.

And no science can be true or congruous without causal understanding. Still less so when its causal logic is exactly contrary to the causal phenomena it has to deal with. In other words, *the human sciences, dealing with the human universe, are precluded from becoming scientific by the only scientism that is presently known.*

The human prejudice against recognizing the relativity of

values still holds men bound, even in their scientific, causal thinking. We may recall here that the exact, technical sciences have evolved precisely because they have nothing to do with value reactions, with their impossible, humanly unacceptable causal logic.

The depth of human prejudice against relative-value causality should be emphasized here as well. This causality is due to the limitedness of man as an organism. Man lives by and for the pursuit of his inner values. But his efforts here are like those of a squirrel running on a wheel in its cage. Men, simply, cannot start thinking of the relative-value causality.

If they could, they would have evolved exact scientism in the human sciences more easily than in the technical sciences. For it is easier—with the right causal understanding—to analyze or observe causally our own feelings than to deal with technical complexities, to control physical phenomena outside ourselves, or to analyze the processes inside matter.

But people holding relativistic beliefs would be unable to compete with stronger believers in pursuit of their value goals. Movements of thought permitting relativistic ideas, or sciences requiring relativistic insights, have not been able to develop. By cultural and social selection ideas of relative-value causality are precluded in all human thinking.

Explaining value relativity is nothing to be proud of. We do not intend to convert anybody to relativistic value attitudes. But can we disregard the relative-value causality that governs everything in the fields of human sciences, the whole human universe? Such a disregard would amount to perpetuating a human blindness and missing the causal, scientific understanding in the sciences of man. Potentially these sciences could be even more miraculous than are our present technical sciences.

We now shall outline briefly how the prejudice against the relative or opposite-value causality has been decisive in the main fields of human sciences. (Detailed explanations, for each field, are offered in separate chapters of this book.)

Medicine is surely the most important science dealing with man. It is scientifically exact and tremendously successful in the treatment of infectious diseases, in surgery, and in its other causally understood or technical fields. But, as we have seen 80 percent of modern men die of diseases caused by the way they live and react, even independently of conditions such as pollution. Here belong heart disease, hypertension, diabetes, arthritis, peptic ulcers, emphysema, all kinds of disorders such as headaches or sleeplessness, and—by most indications—cancer.

And all doctors admit that the *causes* of these most important diseases are *not yet understood*, as we shall see in detail later. This causal mystery is a very revealing, *incredible* fact in modern medicine. Each of these diseases is uniform. It therefore must be caused by one causal principle; and natural causal principles can be only *totally simple.*

As we have indicated already, the simple cause of our chief functional diseases is the exhaustion of organic functions through the enjoyment of excessive "improvements."

The source of the modern epidemic of the functional diseases is fairly obvious. An organism is inexorably limited to its normalcy or sameness. But the functional "improvements" enjoyed by modern man are prodigious. They easily exceed the limits of the preservation of organic sameness. The organism has to return, after such "improvements," to its normalcy or sameness by oppposite processes, by an equal "worsening." As this is met with more "improvements," the progressive, vicious-circle exhaustion of the over-enjoyed, over-exploited function easily deepens into a functional collapse.

But only the paradoxical opposite causality can explain how the experimentally clear "improvements" turn into equal functional worsening.

We may note here that experimentally every functional "improvement" can only appear as beneficial. Experimenters proceed only by a direct, mathematically exact, causal logic. If a drug improves a function, it has to be accepted as beneficial. The subsequent opposite effects are so totally different from the improvement that they cannot be logically related to it. Indeed, medical scientists use the term "side effects" in all such cases—except where the causal relation is flagrantly clear, as in the case of narcotic drugs.

Even if the experiment is extended, at each phase the "improvement" shows to be, again, beneficial. There simply is no place for an insight into the paradoxical opposite causality, which has seemingly unrelated and continuous parallel effects.

These effects logically seem to belong to some different causal process. Opposite causality is paradoxical throughout: the negative effects accumulate concurrently with the increase of the positive effects. Also, the opposite effects from an over-enjoyment may appear through an organ or part of the body different from that which served as a channel of over-enjoyment. In the organism everything is causally interconnected.

Our drugs are rated only by their "logical," direct effects. Negative, opposite effects always follow the "improvements" from drugs, but they are considered as not directly related, side effects to be remedied by still further "improvements." A deepening, vicious-circle, functional exhaustion becomes inevitable.

The modern means of improvement become dangerous precisely through their effectiveness. They are so powerful and subtle that the organic restrictive mechanisms are soon overcome; all living mechanisms can be easily stopped. Moreover, the constantly added "improvements" prevent the disease from appearing until final functional collapse or irrevocable exhaustion. This is typical of the chief functional diseases, heart attacks and cancer.

The cruder narcotic drugs are far less effective in providing progressively increasing "improvement" and in hiding its aftereffects. These drugs, though, show that perfect, logically and experimentally clear improvements do bring an incredibly strong, even fatal worsening.

In sum, modern medicine, never recognizing the actual, opposite causality of organic reactions, unintentionally helps man in his self-destruction, in his over-enjoyment of the now prodigiously effective, almost limitless functional "improvements." The result is the modern epidemic of functional, reactively induced diseases, which have remained mysteries causally while causing 80 percent of our deaths.[7]

Psychiatry and psychology are sciences in which the inevitable prejudice against relative or opposite-value causality has results similar to those in medicine. The causes of our principal, functional mental diseases are still unexplained and controversial.[5] These diseases are increasing together with improvements of modern life and medicine, as will become clear in detail later.

The logic of the modern treatment of mental diseases is practically senseless. Modern psychiatry tries to make patients enjoy what they could most easily enjoy by themselves or do what they have done too much already.

Mental patients suffer from extreme restrictive negativity in their emotional reactions.[2, 5] In directly logical, experimentally "scientific" terms, all that the patient needs is a free, effective acceptance and enjoyment of more positive reactions. Such reactions are pleasant. Nothing would be easier than to enjoy them.

The mentally undisciplined and weak psychotic or neurotic yields more than anybody to what is pleasant. In fact, he suffers from restrictive mental exhaustion exactly because of previous excessive enjoyments or improvements in his mental reactions.

But psychiatry knows only one logic of treatment: to improve or make more positive the emotional reactions of the patient. This amounts to intensifying what the patient has been doing to excess already and what has made him mentally ill. However involved the psychiatric treatments may be, they are governed by the seemingly axiomatic direct-improvement logic.

The paradox of reactive worsening through improvement is, in fact, clearer in mental disorders than in other functional diseases. Practically any one of the symptoms of mental diseases has been observed to result also from the most liked and used drugs.[5, 6] Of course, such drugs are sought exactly for relief from negative mental reactions.

But the paradox of opposite causality, of worsening through improvement of reactions, is still the last thing that psychiatrists as scientists could accept.

Psychology should be a science providing uniform causal laws for the engineering of behavior. All exact sciences must and do have uniform and simple causal laws. Psychology could have similar laws, because the causality of value reactions, which determine behavior, is uniformly simple.

But presently no such a science in the field of psychology exists. Instead, each psychologist has his own theory about causal laws, principles, and fundamental mechanisms.[1, 2] Professional psychologists, in education or industry, ignore or hardly ever mention the various psychological theories and proceed according to accumulated observations from practical experience.[8]

The contrast between the sciences and psychology is conspicuous. Causal certainties or laws are as simple and few in the sciences as they are controversially complex and infinitely numerous in psychology.

The only uniformly accepted truth in psychology is the "scientific" logic, of values increasing through addition or deriving from sources of the same nature. Satisfactory or pleasant causal backgrounds are expected to create positive, pleasant behavior.

You cannot read one page of a book or article in psychology without finding direct or implied acceptance of the logic that positive adjustments and capacities derive from positive experiences. Psychologists are merely accepting here the like-from-like causal principle of our exact sciences, which is exactly contrary to the causality of value reactions.

If positive reactions derived from positive experiences, we would start with a pleasant, positive feeling and derive from it more positive reactions that would create even more positive feelings. This increase would be progressive and inevitable. We all start with, and pursue, positive and pleasant emotions on the slightest justification, at every moment.

Psychologists safeguard their "scientific" methods by generally ignoring the emotional causal factors—particularly their central source, pleasure. Instead, psychologists deal mostly with *cognitive factors*, such as learning, perceptions, thoughts, reasons, faulty reasoning, ideas, insights, understanding, cognitive attitudes, or conditioning in its classical sense of animal learning.[1, 2]

Now, the cognitive factors can indeed be treated *with exact-science causal logic*. Opposite causality applies only to the behaviorally decisive value reactions. We have seen how causally weightless are the cognitive factors, exactly to the extent that they are different from emotions.

But conveniently, the results of cognitive activities, such as learning, perception, or understanding, are not governed by opposite-value causality. The value processes as organic changes are so minute in cognitive reactions that they have no practical effect as value factors. The perceptual or cognitive reactions and capacities merely serve human value goals and are not values in themselves.

The cognitive capacities, as instruments for value drives, are suited for dealing with the external environment, with the things around us, which are governed by physical, non-relative causality. The cognitive world is thus parallel causally to the physical world. For instance our learning or understanding is causally "logical," non-relative, and increases through additions in it.

Confusion about the importance and causal limits of cognitive factors is inevitable. Man's tremendous successes in dealing with the outside world are due to his *cognitive powers*. Everything here works under the direct scientific logic. *Man is forever impressed by these powers* and convinced by their direct logic, as he is by our marvelous technical sciences. Everybody wants to follow reason and believes that he acts only according to understanding and reasoning—which in truth only serve his value goals or feelings.

Cognitive factors are *easy and causally ineffective* in behavior.

One can decide in five minutes to work hard in the future or to quit smoking. Similarly, any positive behavior can be fully espoused cognitively, by reasoning, insight, or learning. Emotional or value factors are decisive but difficult to have, since positive reactions as satisfactions require accumulation of conditioned needs as non-satisfactions.

By disregarding these simple but paradoxical truths and dealing mostly with the "scientifically" logical cognitive factors, modern psychology accepts as causally decisive what is easy and ineffective, as well as confusingly complex. Psychology thus easily turns into a modern alchemy in its theories and methods.

Our positive reactions, our precious capacities, would be acquired with alchemic ease if cognitive factors were decisive. Yet modern psychology accepts as decisive conscious and unconscious insights, perceptions, reasoning, or learning, as well as other cognitive and ideational factors such as identity, identifications, projections, roles, and the self- or ego-concept.[1, 2, 5]

The inherently alchemistic scientism, imitated from our exact sciences, becomes a pivotal, practical fallacy. Our precious positive capacities are positive reactions or satisfactions and pleasures, such as interests or love. Under "scientific" logic they should be increased by direct additions in them, by added enjoyments. This could be done most pleasantly, with total alchemic ease. But everybody knows that this cannot work. Even though psychologists theoretically see promotion of satisfactions as the goal, they would not favor increased pleasure enjoyments in practice.

Here we come to *the most important psychological truth: pleasure as the universal organic drive* and its impossible, paradoxical causality. Pleasure is the source of all decisive feelings and thus of all motivations. But it clearly decreases through increase and acquires its potential through restriction or non-satisfaction. Understandably, pleasure is never treated as a causal factor in formal scientific psychology.

In practical reality, however, pleasure determines everything that man does, feels, or exists by. Even the minutest mechanism in us is governed by pleasure. If our organisms did not select our food according to pleasure, we would not survive. Our other organic functions are similarly determined by pleasure; and all our value reactions ultimately derive from organic functions. It is not difficult to see how we live every minute only for and by pleasure, mostly our conditioned and future pleasures.

Moreover, pleasure is *causally mechanistic or scientifically precise* to the tiniest detail, if its paradoxical causality is understood. You cannot have even a minute pleasure release without a precise, strict organic reason that is mechanically determined. Primarily, each pleasure or satisfaction requires an exactly equal restriction or need. If man proceeds against this rule, the organism corrects him by imposing the restrictions.

Pleasure may appear to be a scientifically vague factor because it seemingly cannot be measured, since it cannot be treated by physically experimental methods. But the inner values, as pleasures, which determine what man does, have to be treated on their own causally meaningful, rather than physical, terms.

Merely physically similar reactions, by organs or muscles, can have the completely different causal meaning of exciting, pleasant benefit or of disturbing, painful harm. A physically structured experiment cannot show whether a subject's heart pounds intensely in love or in hate. The same is true for all psychologically meaningful value reactions.

In psychologically relevant instead of merely physical terms, pleasure can be perfectly measured and dealt with. You can manage your pleasure reactions precisely by accepting equal restrictions. Measuring always amounts to comparing or relating what is meaningfully comparable. In these terms, pleasure can be precisely measured, by exactly equivalent opposites.

Above all, this is the only measurement here practically needed or useful. If you know that you have to impose on yourself as many restrictions as you can, then you do not need precise measurements. Practically you just exert the maximun effort possible for you. This is what people with good common sense are doing in their practical behavior.

Physically precise measurements are useful and required in the technical sciences. There you gain advantage by using precise arrangements or formulas. But you can never invent easy arrangements in your motivational, inner-value management. It would be alchemistic to expect mental enrichment through inventive formulas, though psychologists see cognitive skills as decisive.

If formulas or skills worked in our motivational economy, they would long ago have been discovered, since organic, causal principles are simple. Then such formulas would have generated a gigantic engineering of man's most valued treasures, his motivational and behavioral capacities.

We are viewing here *pleasure as the source of all behavior* and motivations, simply because it is such a source. If you manage your inner values so that you have plenty of pleasure or satisfactions and interests, you can attain practically everything you want. Positive reactions are pleasures and they are remedies for all problems of behavior as well as of health. In particular, our main functional physical and mental diseases are caused by the mismanagement of pleasure reactions.

Pleasure is the affective indicator and drive for everything that happens in the organism. As such, pleasure becomes in human behavior equal to a totally and precisely integrated understanding and control of everything that the organism does, of all its unfathomably complex mechanisms. Of course, even our higher values are merely elaborations of organic mechanisms.

In a word, pleasure determines and "explains" causally whatever we do practically throughout our lives. It is *the only bridge, of understanding and control, between your mind and the ungraspable myriad processes in your organism.*

In nutrition, you "understand" what your body requirements are, and you determine what foods will meet them, by simply following the pleasure of your taste. In reproduction, sexual pleasure provides the "insight" about reproductive purposes and determines the precise operation of their mechanisms. In the survival drive, which integrates all organic mechanisms, pleasure ensures all the "understanding" and corresponding operation of such mechanisms. We fear and avoid death or seek security in a thousand precise, causally extensive, and deeply meaningful ways, in accordance with our feelings of pleasure and displeasure.

Pleasure is, in every way, the most significant causal fact of human, conscious existence, including our psychological life.

Man's mind can never grasp the astronomical complexity of his innumerable organic mechanisms. A mind can only work with one thing at a time, while an organism works with countless elements at every point and instant. Therefore, as men evolved into beings controlled by mind, their organically integrated mechanisms had to unite further to act as one supermechanism that the mind can understand and control—as the conscious pleasure that gives the simplest yes-and-no answers.

Pleasure is thus the mechanism by which man causally "understands" and operates the otherwise ungraspable, myriad operations of his organism. *The mechanistic and total causal precision of pleasure* is what makes organisms survive. This causal precision is truly miraculous, and therefore can be most revealing and useful scientifically.

When you taste a piece of food you learn, in a few seconds, how the various ingredients in the food will meet your countless biochemical requirements, through precise digestive and metabolic processes. Your survival depends on such "understanding" of every one of the requirements and processes, as they have been evolved and perfected through millions of years.

Or, in the reproductive function, the pleasure mechanism provides an "understanding" of even vaster requirements and future effects decisive for procreation, in strict accordances with countless adaptations in the evolutionary past.

When a man looks at a woman and finds her beautiful, his pleasure mechanism provides him with unbelievably complex "insights." These include his "knowledge" that the woman is able to conceive, bear, and bring up his progeny, in functionally satisfactory ways, through the endless organic processes of reproduction—such as pregnancy, birth, or breast-feeding—perfected by the dictates of a million-year evolution.

If such "insights" were missing, the human reproductive function would become chaotic. For here again, the "understanding" through the pleasure mechanism also guides the operation of all the countless processes and performances required for reproduction.

The "insights" and operations provided by the pleasure mechanism may be even more involved and exquisite when a person fulfills some other human function, like avoiding harm, insuring his safety, exercising his capacities of functional development, meeting competition, or striving for superiority. Further, even the highest human activities are only conditioned elaborations of lower functions.

In decisive, practical behavior, nothing is more powerful as well as certain and precise for man than his pleasure reactions. Every moment of his existence man is aware of pleasure, compares or measures it, and follows it as the only guide in what he does. Even when he resists pleasure enjoyments he does so by way of his conditioned satisfactions, conditioned pleasure, or for sake of future pleasures.

We also have to emphasize the miraculously detailed and multiple precision of pleasure when we look at *scientific experimental observations*. Pleasure, governing all our causal mechanisms, is incomparably more precise than anything that is now experimented with or experimentally observed in the sciences dealing with man.

The decisive fact here is that pleasure reactions, as feelings, causally represent and account for all the endlessly multiple determining factors of a given organic response, in a precise and simple way. When you taste a food, the pleasure indicates and accounts for every one of the innumerable causal factors, even in their evolutionary causal meanings. It can be said that the whole causally decisive past and present are here accounted for by the pleasure reactions.

In contrast, the usual experiment as presently conducted can account only for one or few isolated causal factors. Yet, in organic responses, every one of the uncountable causal factors, even from their evolutionary past, is causally decisive. And experiments that leave out causally decisive factors are useless.

Indirectly, pleasure is commonly recognized as causally decisive in behavior. Psychologists usually proceed under the implied assumption that people will do what they wish, like, want, are interested in, find satisfactory or pleasant. But the underlying and paradoxical pleasure causality is never recognized.

Consequently, the implied pleasure factors here become more misleading than helpful. Restriction of pleasures is a clear evil in the usual scientific logic. Release, not restriction, of pleasure is indeed the source of our capacities; but only restriction can make the potential of release available.

To conclude, it is truly unbelievable that scientists have causally, scientifically ignored pleasure, the central causal source of what organisms do. Pleasure is the *mechanism that determines what man does or becomes* every moment of his life. We simple mortals know this as we pursue only pleasure or happiness. But psychology as a formal "logical" science ignores these facts

When we turn to other *behavioral sciences*, we find that they are ruled by causal fallacy in the same way psychology is. They also have accepted as axiomatic the causal logic and methods of the exact, physical sciences. Thus, they proceed by a causal thinking and experimental mathematics exactly contrary to the causality governing human behavior, determined by value reactions.

The central fallacy in the imitation of the physical sciences is, of course, the acceptance of the "scientifically," mathematically true, like-from-like causal logic, acccording to which values increase through addition.

In the behavioral sciences, as in psychology, positive reactions are assumed to originate from positive causal backgrounds. This assumption underlies the very way of thinking in everything written or said in behavioral sciences. All experimental demonstrations or conclusions are still made according to the mathematics used in physical-science experiments.

Of course, the *immediate, direct,* experimental effects may confirm the mathematical logic, as the paradoxical, later aftereffects are disregarded—because they are never anticipated or thought of. The immediate effects of any reactive "improvement" are positive.

In any case, the actual opposite-value causality of behavior has not been even mentioned in the behavioral sciences. The results are predictable. The behavioral sciences produce enormous amounts of studies and research. But they lack the only thing that could turn them into exact sciences: *causal understanding.*

As in psychology, in the behavioral sciences each scientist has his own theory about the causal principles or fundamental causal forces. Compare this with the exact sciences. Can you imagaine physicists having different laws of motion or knowing many more causal forces such as gravitation and electricity?

We have to emphasize that the causal laws of human behavior do not have to be multiple or complex. Everything man does, the whole human universe, as we have seen is a result of his value reactions. And only one, simple principle, the law of opposite-value causality, governs all value reactions.

This is to be expected because man is created by nature, which does not know complex causal principles. The only "design" or purpose of organisms is to preserve their sameness. Opposite-value causality derives from this preservation of organic sameness, from the organisms' inexorable limitedness.

It can be said that our behavioral sciences, just as psychology, are at a stage of development comparable to scholasticism and alchemy. Behavioral scientists have imitated, accepted without questioning, the causal logic and methods of the currently authoritative physical sciences. This imitation is as misleading causally as was the acceptance in scholasticism of the authoritative, philosophical science of that time.

The *alchemistic logic* of our behavioral sciences is equally complete. Positive reactions are, rightly, seen by behavioral experts as sources of behavioral enrichment, of what is most precious in behavior. And positive reactions are pleasant. Then why not increase them directly, logically, without difficulties? Indeed, every noted expert on behavior has advocated a "logical" increase in positive attitudes or "positive thinking" in one way or another.

Of course, most theories of behavioral scientists are highly intricate, sophisticated enough to sustain their ideas with scientifically structured quite involved explanations. But the inherently alchemistic logic is always underlying their theories. This is inevitable as long as opposite-value causality is not recognized. And no self-respecting behavioral scientist has ever suggested that negative causal backgrounds or non-satisfactions are the necessary sources of positive reactions.

This unawareness of the affectively hard and paradoxical causes of behavior, combined with the imitation of physical sciences, has led to an *emphasis on cognitive causal factors* in the behavioral sciences as well.

We have seen how cognitive factors, such as perceptions or learning can indeed be dealt with by the logic of increase through addition, or by the methods of the physical sciences. The cognitive, easy causal sources seem believable if it is not realized that a difficult "payment" is necessary for each positive, pleasant behavioral reaction.

Indeed, the behavioral sciences have gravitated toward emphasis on cognitive causal sources, such as learning, perceptions, reasons, faulty reasoning, ideas, identifications, projections, identity, or the self.[2, 9] We have seen how easily one can espouse cognitively the most positive reactions, by learning, perception, reasoning, identification, or any ideational reaction.

As to the *social sciences* , we find that the belief in cognitive or ideational causality there is more pervasive than in any other science. Further, whatever place is left for the consideration of value factors, they are treated with the same "scientific," like-from-like causal logic of the physical sciencies.

Both these fallacies are inevitable under scientifically logical thinking, as we have explained. They are more easily accepted in the social sciences because social phenomena are more extensive and complex. No place is left here for individual behavior, which quite often reveals personal contradictions and paradoxes of reactions.

Anyway, social scientists generally deal only with ideas, ideologies, perceptions, cognitive attitudes, points of view, reasons or similar factors.[9] And when emotional factors, or reactions to factual conditions, are considered, the scientific, like-from-like causal logic is never doubted. Negative social reactions are invariably attributed to negative factual backgrounds. The paradox that factual improvements lead rather to negative reactions is not recognized, though it sometimes is noticed in other human sciences. Social scientists follow the general scientism from the exact sciences totally and uncritically in their vast and complex field.

Consequently, causal confusion and the *multiplicity of causal theories* or of assumed fundamental causal forces and principles are even more extensive in the social sciences than in pyschology or the behavioral sciences. This indicates that the social sciences can not offer us any real causal, scientific understanding. Social theories then cannot be much better than mere social or political opinions, as controversial and multiple as are the people who care to express them.

Causal understanding constitutes scientific understanding. The behavioral and social scientists have adopted—even more thoroughly than the other human sciences—a causal logic, a causal way of thinking, exactly contrary to the actual causality, in their fields. The result is that in these "soft" sciences their colossal effort is in fact moving them away from true scientism.

Finally, in general *humanistic thought* the same causal prejudice is perpetuated with a particularly deep conviction. Here the belief in positive value sources of our positive inner values is accepted as sacredly true.[3, 4]

Consequently, the causal confusion is total in humanistic thought. This has been remedied in the past by the restrictive moral and religious, necessarily superstitious, traditions. But the more modern humanistic thought is freeing itself from such "backward," restrictive superstitions. It is becoming more "scientifically" logical, even trying to acquire the authority of advanced scientism.[3, 4]

It thus creates practical obstacles to our useful progress. Its intended progressive scientism leads to confused, degenerative attitudes, conflicting with what is causally right for practical progress, for the creation of human capacities, as value reactions. The restrictive, "negative," causal sources of positive value reactions are rejected in favor of more freedoms and satisfactions. The result is degeneration of behavior in our permissive society.

Before we conclude, we have to mention the effect of the causal human prejudice on thinking in *theoretical physics*. The higher theory of physics has to deal with the way man knows the physical universe. Theoretical physicists will continue struggling with unbelievable, admitted confusion if they, as all men, remain bound by the universal human prejudice against recognizing the actual, "negative" causal source of man's "positive" universe.

The physical universe exists for man in the way he knows it. But knowledge is a process of differentiation of values. We know things by differentiating them against nothingness. Without nothingness, with absolutely all space filled with matter, we could not know things or the physical, material reality.

In all differentiation the contrasted opposites have opposite values. Nothingness has for man a value of absolute unreality, because matter has for him the value of the highest, primordial reality. For he himself is a being of matter, existing by virtue and help of matter. He pays attention only to matter, not to its opposite. Now, imagine the world of matter as a pattern cut into a large sheet of plastic. If you concentrate only on the pattern, the sheet has no existence, no distinct form for you, though it actually has rather wider forms than the matter has, forms that are opposite to those of matter.

In a word, *nothingness* has no value of reality and no form for man, but in truth is *the causal source of material phenomena*, as they are known to him.

Nothingness determines the forms of matter, by variously outlining them. And it determines the dynamics of these forms by changing their outlines, or exchanging places with them. Where nothingness moves in, matter moves out, and vice versa.

But would not "nothingness" as such a reality or medium be felt by us or hinder our movements? If a medium—say, a uniform flow of water—moves an object, there is no hindrance, friction, or any other noticeable effect of the water against the object, which thus experiences nothing in particular from the water.

We shall later explain "nothingness" as a universal causal medium that we will call the Field. We shall see in detail that the Field inevitably remains unnoticeable, unregistrable because it is the Field itself that creates all phenomena of matter by moving it in various ways. You can move freely, without hindrance from the Field, because every molecule in your body is moved by the Field itself.

The Field and matter act as two opposite media of force. Matter is dynamically similar to force, though opposed to it causally. The famous equation of Einstein established that matter equals energy. This reveals straight interaction between matter and the Field, which as causal opposites define and equate each other. Of course, energy is merely the effects of force acting on matter. Men always see only various effects of force, not the force itself.

The Field is obviously the incomparably vaster, therefore much more effective or stronger, causal opposite as force, since it surrounds matter everywhere. The Field thus dominates matter, compresses and controls its atoms, and moves or causally determines it, in uniform ways, throughout the universe. But for man only matter is real, while its opposite, the Field as the universal force, remains unreality itself, a total nothingness.

Here we come to the most important fact in the universe as it exists for man and is understood by him. *Force determines everything in the universe but force is always a nothingness* for man. Nobody ever sees force in itself. In other words, man does not recognize the causal determinant of his universe because it has the opposite, "negative" value to his "positive" value of reality, of matter. Man never recognizes the actual, negative sources of his values.

A series of scientific as well as common-sense confusions results from the fact that man is inherently unable to recognize the reality of the universal causal source, the "nothingness" as the field of force, that determines everything in the cosmos. We shall discuss those confusions in the chapter on the admitted mysteries in physics. Here we only wanted to indicate that even in man's physical universe he fails to recognize its causal, "negative" source because of his prejudice about value causality.

For practical purposes the human causal prjeudice is not so important in theoretical physics as it is in the fields dealing with man. These fields can become exact sciences, potentially more miraculous than are the technical sciences, if that universal human prejudice is overcome and causal understanding becomes possible.

Miraculous Future through Science Free of Human Prejudice

Exact sciences can do miracles. What the technical sciences are doing now would have been viewed as miraculous, beyond human powers, a mere two centuries ago. Yet all that is needed for a science to become an exact, potentially limitless science is causal understanding. For the fields dealing with man, for our "soft" sciences, this is still to come.

As we have indicated, what man is and does is not too complex causally. Man, as a product of nature, exists by one simple causal principle, the conservation of his organic sameness, from which the law of opposite-value causality derives. This law governs all our value reactions, the causal sources of our human universe. With the understanding of the opposite-value causality scientists could engineer the behavior of man, his capacities, conservation of his health, and even the extension of his longevity, his most desired goal.

Schematically, by imposing restrictions on functional energies, by "damming" them up, we can create equal reserves for the release of pleasure as the source of our positive motivations and capacities. The same principle of extended capacities applies to our problems of health and human longevity.

Naturally, men will want, first of all, to be saved from fatal or disabling diseases. Causal understanding will enable scientists potentially to prevent our *main, functional diseases*, physical and mental. These diseases are caused, as we have seen, by the intense functional "improvements" favored in present medical thinking. Admitted causal mystery is the result.

Insight into opposite causality can provide a causal explanation of these diseases and thus a scientific understanding of how to deal with them. In fact, all that is needed here is, again, restrictions in the use of living energy, in its over-enjoyments. Practically, men know that already. They know that by stopping an over-enjoyment, such as smoking or overeating, they can prevent a chronic disease. Scientists can here turn simple truths into the bases of exact sciences.

Causal, scientific understanding will enable scientists even to control radically the *extension of human life*. Scientists will invent ways of slowing down man's rate of living and thus extending his time of living. The slowing down could be attained by restrictions on the deepest mechanisms of life.

Nature has done that with all species, particularly by increasing their restrictive brains. Restrictions on living mechanisms increase their elaborations; a "dammed"-up flow of living energy creates new, more extensive channels. More elaborate mechanisms bring more advanced organic performances and wider capacities. Also, a living process that has to go through more elaborations has to last longer. The causal principle here is simple, as are all natural principles.

It is possible that the sciences will increase our longevity to the potentially unlimited extent that they learn to impose restrictions on organic mechanisms. Even our present, primitive experiments point to such possibilities. Scientists have nearly doubled the life of animals by underfeeding them or retarding their maturity. The longevity of insects or plants has been increased by several multiples by preventing the organisms from maturing.

More immediate, practical human progress can be advanced by *overcoming various prejudices or fixations* by which men perpetuate irrational cultural and value beliefs. Such prejudices and inveterate beliefs bring stagnation in thought and social goals, with a deadening effect for creative progress. A true causal understanding of our value reactions and fixations will provide the necessary help.

It may be noted that the understanding of relative-value causality *does not lead to value relativism.* On the contrary, it shows that the same certainties about values are true for all cultures. Conditioned restrictions are sources of value enrichment in education and morals everywhere. This wisdom is indeed embodied in all cultural and religious, restrictive, traditions.

A main causal insight necessary to overcome value prejudices would be the understanding of the *insidious power of fixation.* People are unsuspecting victims of fixations in various ways. They become slaves to fixational "truths" and ways of life—to fixational ghosts they themselves have created.

Many goals of human progress are doomed by value fixations. People in affluent societies waste most of their surpluses on fixational fashions and customs, though surplus is the main source of progress. Even greater hindrances to progress are the "sacred" beliefs about existing values or unchangeable rights. In fact, they merely consecrate contemporary, inveterate customs, whereas progress requires radical changes in beliefs and customary values.

For instance, the *improvement of man himself,* by eugenic

means, should, rationally, be man's very first goal. But we still have deep, sacred feelings against such means.

Abortion is still felt as killing by many people. Artificial insemination and test-tube pregnancies or similar methods would be seen as unethical and shocking if they were intended for eugenic improvement. Men have attached, for ages, their value feelings to "normal" reproduction. Our sexual and reproductive habits have become fixationally sacred.

This has deepened our feelings about reproduction into fixations, primarily on biological or animal values and emotions. We should love our children deeply and unreservedly, as continuators of our spiritual heritage. But the present *fixational love* of children is that of man as a sexually compelled animal selfishly and stupidly wanting *only "his" sexual seed to be perpetuated.*

The fixational irrationality here is self-evidently clear in many ways. Parents, after conception, cherish the fetus almost in the way they love a child as a treasured continuator of their identities. By being so valued the fetus becomes a center of the highest possible love. But, rationally, the fetus is merely an organic growth; and if it is so viewed, it cannot become an object of distorted value feelings.

The decisive fact is that we are human by virtue of having consciousness. Animals are alive in the same way as we are. But, not having consciousness, they do not even know that they exist. They are nothing, non-existing, to themselves. The same is true of the fetus, or even for the infant before he starts acquiring consciousness.

After men learn to love children as conscious and potentially intellectual beings, that are more than mere living growths, many crippling prejudices will disappear. Methods such as artificial insemination will be preferred, in order to have more capable children. One's identity is best perpetuated by his education of his children, whereas biological conception is an accidental, animal event. More capable children make possible a better perpetuation of the parents' human selves. Even an adopted child becomes for adoptive parents a truly loved inheritor and continuator of their identities. A change in our fixational value feelings is all that is needed for the selection of better future humans.

As men free themselves from irrational value fixations, they will prevent *one of the most hideous present sources of human suffering: mental defectiveness and inferiority.*

We would find as unspeakably horrible a creation of defective children by, say, a promotion of damaged genes. But is it not equally horrible deliberately to permit births of infants with mental defects or low capacities? We are doing exactly that, as we remain more concerned about the inalienable rights of birth than about prevention of defective children.

Little scientific effort has been invested in the detection and abortion of mentally defective or undesirably inferior infants about to be born. This should be one of the most important human concerns. It would be a means of selecting better future humans. Criteria for the discovery of future mental capacities in a fetus could be developed, particularly through better insights into fundamental organic principles. Such principles, of natural "design," are generally simple; we have seen how the mere aptitude to bear restrictions can bring enrichment of capacities.

The problem is how far our irrational value fixations permit us to go. The love of children should be deep and sacred. Human survival and culture depend on it. But we can have such love without fixations about the "normal" conception and birth of children. Attributing sacredness only to one's own sperm or ovum, even where it may be a handicap to the future child, is cruelly selfish as well as self-defeatingly brutish.

Rationally, nobody should be concerned about human beings that could have been born but are not. Such a concern would be equal to worrying about every ovum and sperm. Similarly, we should not worry about non-births, or abortions, of defective or less capable children. Rather we should consider how much *suffering and shame* is brought by their birth, *for hundreds of millions* of them and those close to them.

The only *humane moral law* is to do onto others what you want done to yourself—to free men of humiliating inferiorities when this can be done without any suffering whatever. The most important rational human concerns should be not to create human suffering and to improve men.

These goals are attainable by *human eugencis*. Higher mental capacities are the most satisfying as well as creative human treasures. Eugenic selection of better humans can bring these treasures. Presently, however, the very idea of eugenic selection for men has remained abhorrent, associated with the handling of animals. Yet the gains could be immense, even from the primitive eugenic methods that are presently available. Men now can improve other species, to unrecognition, by simple genetic selection. Why refuse to improve ourselves?

Would such selection violate human dignity? Man's humaneness and spirituality are sublime. But they come with more positive reactions, with better, more restrictive brains. The ways of man's highest, humane progress here can be as simple as are the methods of, say, artificial insemination. Of course, future eugenics will be probably more different from ours than is a spacecraft from a horse buggy.

When human sciences become exact, through causal understanding, they will be far more miraculous than the present exact sciences. The very capacity of man to improve himself will be cumulatively and continually improved.

Man will become his own creator. He will change himself by an exponentially progressing "engineering." Imagine how *immense* will become such progress through centuries, as the abilities to increase more capacities accumulate at *exponential* rates. We cannot even try to visualize the future progress. But in terms that we can think of, it will have to be strange indeed. For instance, we can speculate that men will make themselves capable of living naturally in space or within oceans. Such men would be monsters by our standards. But is not the human sense of beauty or virility biologically imposed on us like chains of enslavement?

Value feelings do not help intellect, the only distinctive human attribute. They only oscillate up and down. Our great authorities, however, see values such as beauty or a sense of harmony as the ultimate goals in human destiny.

Such exalted present ideas about human progress can lead only to futility and confusion. Objective value reactions such as love or interests are very important. But they come by way of the imposition of "negative" value experiences, conditioned non-satisfactions as needs and as sources of satisfactions.

Direct, even the loftiest, *value enjoyments can lead only to mental exhaustion.* Drugs can induce the most exalted value experiences. But the results are mental disorders. And organically it does not matter by what means a higher enjoyment is created. Once it has been attained, as a special affective change, the organism reacts by an opposite change.

The man of the future will depend only on his intellect, which finally will have reached a full understanding of itself. It will be free of value delusions. But would not this extreme specialization by man become his doom? In a fully intellectual, causally understood world, the pursuit of values reveals itself as a mere delusion. Then why continue living?

Extreme specializations by species have often brought their extinction. The fate of the dinosaurs is the most discussed example of species' extinction. Overspecialization is probably still its best explanation, in spite of recent theories.

The specialization of dinosaurs was, evidently, that of feeding on the lush, fernlike vegetation that became extinct together with them. This vegetation up to then had been growing and accumulating, undestroyed by microbes, in profusion. Most of our oil deposits come from it. Revealingly, geological studies show that these sources of oil ceased at the same time, sixty million years ago, that dinosaurs became extinct. New microbes, capable of eating that lush and accumulating vegetation, must have been the simplest cause of its disappearance. After that, different vegetation evolved. Our living plants are inedible and poisonous to microbes.

Imagine what would happen if a microbe species evolved that was capable to eat our living plants, as the citrus canker does with orange trees. That would finish our flora and the "era of man."

In any case, overspecialization can quite understandably become the cause of extinction of a species. But *man's intellectual specialization* is as radically different from that of other species as mind is different from nature. The intellect enables man to foresee the future. That is its main, unique function. Man will not create for himself a blind, dead-end future by the use of intellect or reason.

Man's emotional or value reactions are a different matter. Even those who prophesy destruction by atomic bombs blame the irrational feelings of people. Unfortunately, the clamorous fighters for causes such as disarmament are mainly emotional youth who have little of the intuitive wisdoms, mostly acquired with age, about the paradoxical ways needed even for preventing a war. The best protection against irrationality, of either kind, is causal understanding of human value reactions. It will come with insight into the actual, opposite-value causality.

However, the intellect will have in the end a potentially destructive influence, in a way quite different from what people are thinking of now. As intellect progresses it is bound to deepen the inevitable understanding of the inherent futility of human aspirations. Men live for gain in value experiences, which is causally impossible. Everybody asks himself, more or less frequently, what is it all about. Man's life ends with a zero, and if there are no gains while it lasts, there seems to be no reason to continue.

But men do not live by reason. Abstract insights do not affect our motivations. As long as men live they will function as organisms moved by the pleasure drive, which they will follow and restrict or condition, minute by minute. The restriction is the necessary goal, since it brings behavioral enrichment. Here the insight into the relative-value causality will be decisive.

Men can establish restrictive, enriching institutions and culture by pursuing a scientific policy of new public goals. Science has already changed our culture, regrettably for the worse. A merely abstract scientific understanding will be sufficient for men to start imposing from above restrictions on themselves, in the miraculously ingenious ways that the sciences are capable of.

Still, human existence is, in the end, nonsensical—a pursuit of what men can never attain. It is possible that *intellect, reaching higher progress* and revealing more fully the futility of conscious existence, *might dictate its decease* eventually. Of course, the progress will reach dizzying, exponential speed at its later stages, even during mere centuries.

Incidentally, is this why we do not hear from intelligent beings in other star systems? Such beings would be highly intellectual at the point at which they developed the capabilities of interstellar communication. But in a thousand years or so from that point such beings would already have ceased to exist. Their higher intellect would hardly favor a continuance of their inherently nonsensical conscious existence. And a thousand years is a mere second in terms of cosmic time. There is little chance that such second-long flashes would coincide with the similar flash that we are about to live through.

Human existence does seem nonsensical. Perhaps it is not so in its ultimate terms? We do not know what unimaginable miracles are awaiting us in the end. We know that the possibilities are limitless. We have evolved from one-cell organisms, and the progress is already accelerating immensely.

The final existence of man could be as *unimaginably miraculous* for us as our conscious existence is unimaginable for protozoa. Could not such a progress offer, in some way we cannot think of, *a sense for our existence*?

It may be noted that our progress, from primitive forms to conscious, intelligent beings, has been mechanistic; and it will be so on the way to a presently unimaginable superconsciousness. But the course of future progress will be incomparably faster. Up to now men have progressed by unplanned biological and social selection. Those social groups survive better which happen to develop restrictive moral and cultural traditions.

This blind selection will be replaced by planned progress when the sciences of man gain insight into the causal sources of his capacities, particularly into the creative power of restrictions. Then self-creator man working by plan, instead of advancing through blind selection, will progress at unbelievably faster rates. Yet the planned progress will be attained through use of merely mechanistic methods, particularly organic restrictions. All progress has come mechanistically. This corresponds to the "meaning" behind cosmos.

Man is too limited to know much about God. But progress in the universe has followed a course of mechanistic opposition or restriction. This can be seen from evolution by selection, and from the development of the mind through the restrictive brain, or from human progress through restrictive morals and culture. Apparently this corresponds, in human terms, to the mysterious "will" of God. Above all, what is mechanistic or material is not of some lower order.

The philosophical contrasting of the "spritual" with the material comes from a lack of insight into the relativity aspect of knowledge. What is universal, and most meaningful, like existence or being, cannot be known or have meaning except as something one and simple.

The universal, mechanistic laws in nature are similarly simple while they universally govern an ungraspably multiple and complex creation, including that of man and mind. Evidently these *mechanistic laws* must be embodying the most meaningful, *most "divine"* principles of the universe.

II

UNBELIEVABLE, ADMITTED CAUSAL MYSTERIES IN MEDICINE

Our best physicians admit, without exception, that our chief "chronic" diseases have remained mysteries causally. The noted authority Dr. Lewis Thomas finds the lack of causal explanation of our chronic diseases to be a general and intolerable problem of modern medicine.[22]

This causal mystery is being repeatedly admitted in regard to all our "chronic" diseases—heart disease, hypertension, cancer, diabetes, arthritis, or peptic ulcer. Found to be similarly mysterious or paradoxical therapeutically are many other frequent disorders such as allergies, emphysema, Alzheimer's disease, insomnia, or chronic headaches.

The causal mystery of our chronic diseases is as revealing as it is unbelievable. Each of these diseases is so uniform in its syndrome that it can be diagnosed, by a computer, more readily than other diseases. This means that one natural causal principle governs each of these diseases; and natural causal principles can never be complex.

The simple cause of the chronic diseases is functional overimprovement. We would even prefer to call these diseases "functional" instead of "chronic" diseases.

The organism always has to remain the same anatomically and physiologically. But man as a planning, conscious being continuously tries to improve his organic functions, to derive more pleasure, felt as well-being. Of course, each such improvement amounts to exploitation of the function, to its abnormal intensification and thus exhaustion.

In particular, the prodigiously resourceful modern man attains such improvements in excessive, continuous ways. Naturally, the organism reacts by opposite processes to counteract the "improvements." These opposite reactions are felt as a restrictive, or stressful, diseased worsening. If this worsening is overcome by further, continuous improvements, the function is progressively exhausted, in a vicious circle.

Modern men have all the means, and a "scientific" attitude, to continue adding such improvements incessantly. The result is that the vicious-circle functional exhaustion can deepen itself under modern conditions to an incredible extent, through nothing more than continuously added enjoyments of "improvements" in organic functions. Our chronic diseases thus become inevitable and fatal. Think of how a person taking more and more of a stimulant to overcome the resulting and progressively increasing fatigue inevitably reaches a point of collapse.

The overimprovement etiology is clear in all our chief functional diseases. They are not due to any organic, physical defect or failure. They are caused by the way people live and react—by what men are doing to themselves. Of course the only thing that men really overdo is their pursuit of pleasure, of happiness in its most direct form.

These diseases have reached epidemic proportions in the more highly developed, wealthy countries. You can be sure that people who can afford it strive most of all to enjoy the improvements in their feelings, including those of well-being, which they also "scientifically" associate with improved health.

Such people avoid in the most effective ways the "diseased"

restrictions that they feel as stress. All men do so. But modern, scientific man enjoys the improvements or avoids the stress continuously and cumulatively to an extraordinary extent. The modern man is so resourceful that he always finds ways and means to improve the underlying functions that provide the most enjoyable feelings of well-being and freedom from stress. In all overenjoyments, as in the use of drugs, a continuous avoidance of stress increases it to extremes in the end.

In functional diseases, the skillful modern man "improves" excessively and thus in the end exhausts fatally his organic functions that bring the feelings of freedom from stress. Such improvements added continuously, for years, permit the vicious circle to deepen itself limitlessly, to its final, fatal effect. It has to be emphasized that the decisive factor here is not any stress in itself but the repeated, excessive avoidance of it through exploitation of the underlying organic functions.

The use of narcotics too creates extreme, even fatal stress through nothing more than clear, experimentally evident improvements. Morphine, the standard narcotic, is a good example. It provides such experimentally clear improvements perfectly. During its early use it was found so totally beneficial that the famous Sir William Osler called it "God's own medicine." Of course, our modern methods are far superior to any drug.

Our present improvement skills, and particularly medicines, are more dangerous than were the medieval methods such as bloodletting. The old, bizarre cures were ineffective, to heal or to harm, since they were hardly connected with organically relevant causes. In contrast, modern medical means of "improvement" affect the organic functions with enormous scientific effectiveness.

The very efficiency of modern skills increases the danger. The functional "improvements" provided by modern life and medicine are not only perfectly effective but also extremely subtle. The inevitable and equally strong opposite after-effects are insidiously hidden or delayed. Simpler drugs, such as narcotics, also provide clear initial improvement. But their effects and after-effects are simple and superficial in comparison; even so, progressively increased use of narcotics can lead to death.

In any event, the perfected means and skills of our modern life and medicine can provide functional over-improvements so refined and far-reaching that functions are affected at their deepest levels without immediately perceivable after-effects. Each "worsening" as pressure by the organism toward return to normalcy is overcome by an immediate and still stronger "improvement."

Thus the over-enjoyed functional improvements may seem genuine until the last moment of collapse, as in a heart attack. Or the over-improvements can be accumulated for years without perceptible ill effects until the exhaustion has become total, as in cancer.

The one thing men cannot change is the maintenance by the organism of its sameness, its normalcy. The phenomenon of excessive worsening resulting from equally excessive improvements is as inexorable as that maintenance.

Drugs and skills that man invents cannot alter organic normalcy. They are preposterously crude in comparison with the myriad purposive adaptations of the organism. Moreover, even if a new adaptive change were induced, the organism again would have to maintain this new sameness. Thus any further pursuits of improvement would have equivalent opposite aftereffects, as before.

Unbelievable Causal Mystery of Our Principal, Functional Diseases

Modern medicine is a superb, exact science where it proceeds with causal understanding. It does so in the treatment of infectious diseases, in surgery, and in its other technical or causally understood fields.[1, 2] But medicine totally and admittedly lacks causal understanding, and therefore is not even a science, in the field of functional diseases. Here it has to deal with diseases caused by what man does to himself—by how he functions and behaves because of his feelings or value reactions.

Medicine here is not only causally confused, but proceeds by the usual scientific causal logic, which is exactly contrary to what is causally true for the functional diseases. In fact, opposite-value causality alone governs our feelings and reactions, which determine what we do to ourselves or how we live. In the simplest terms, *we suffer extreme stresses because we avoid stress excessively.*

Three fourths of the most advanced modern men suffer and die from the "chronic," functional diseases[21] caused by the way they live and react, by the excessive improvements that turn into the vicious-circle worsening under opposite causality. The paradoxical stress causality of these diseases is plainly evident.

The functional diseases are always found to be connected with stress.[1, 2, 24] They also have become epidemic in the more advanced countries where people enjoy a richer and more resourceful existence. These people avoid stress—before they do anything else—most successfully, through the functional "improvements." Stress avoidance, as functional over-enjoyment, here becomes extreme.

Statistics show that less than 20 percent of deaths in this country are now due to infectious diseases, organic defects, injuries, or other such well-understood causes.[21] All the other deaths are caused by functional diseases, mostly heart disease and cancer, with other functional disorders and their direct or indirect consequences contributing to the toll.

Such disease and disorders remain mysteries causally because no logical disease-causing agents or anatomical, organic deficiencies are found. These diseases are clearly caused by the way we live, by our "style of life."

Physical factors, like pollution or hardships at home and work, cannot possibly be responsible for the epidemic increase of these diseases. The advanced, rich modern men who suffer from these diseases most can avoid all such difficulties, which are unpleasant. Any hardships here are tolerated only as trade-offs for greater enjoyments.

The cause of functional diseases is the self-perpetuating, functional exhaustion incurred to extremes by the *vicious-circle* pursuit of reactive improvements. But the ways these improvements are pursued seem logically to be totally unconnected with the diseases. The reactive and functional "improvement" is always the opposite of its final effects. That is the core of the mystery.

If the causal process here seems confusing, think again of what happens in the use of drugs. They are the simplest and clearest means of reactive improvement, through the *avoidance of stress.* But they increase stress to fatal levels. Modern people are driving themselves into excessive stress by avoiding it through the most effective ways and means, more perfect and refined for the purpose than any narcotic drugs.

In short, men are sinking into functional exhaustion felt as stress while they have the best resources and unrestrained will to overcome it—while they are avoiding it to extraordinary degree. This can happen only through the *opposite causality of reactions*. Of course, physicians as orthodox scientists cannot recognize it. The result is a *total lack of causal understanding* of our principal diseases. We may now look at the admitted causal mystery of the most important of them.

Heart disease causes half of the deaths in this country.[21] Physicians know that they cannot deal with it efficiently as long as they do not understand its cause. Efforts in the etiology of heart disease have been colossal.[3, 4, 5] Every possible cause has been explored.

But no final, decisive, etiologically understandable cause-and-effect relation for the various factors involved has been found.[3, 5] The causes here are simply "not yet known."[5] Practically, "no one knows why a person will get a heart attack."[3] Controversies and the variety of explanations offered in etiology of heart disease are endless.[3, 6] A foremost authority in the field, Irvine H. Page, thinks that the "breakthrough could come from a direction we least expected."[3]

Presently the only hopes offered are that some of the efforts will lead to a causal explanation.[5, 6] It is expected that future discoveries will end the causal mystery in the etiology of heart disease.[3, 5]

Of course, physicians know in detail the proximate causes of heart disease. They know that the heart muscle fails because it is starved of blood supply, or that coronary arteries become obstructed because of the accumulation of plaque, and so on. They can offer further excellent, detailed explanations of the physiologic processes involved. In fact, physicians are in perfect agreement about the details of the *syndrome* of heart disease, which are *uniform*.

But physicians cannot agree when it comes to explaining the primary or decisive, real cause of the uniform effects of heart disease. That is why there are controversies, with categoric yes-and-no answers, on every one of the methods of treatment and causal meanings of the factors involved in cardiovascular disease.[7]

In sum, heart disease is causally uniform but its cause is not understood. It should be clear that, as a uniform causal phenomenon, heart disease can be governed only by one natural and *therefore simple causal principle*. Then why are physicians, with their mostly higher intelligence, failing to understand heart disease causally?

The reason is that their *very logic of thinking*, the logic about experimentally clear "improvements," is *contrary* to what causally happens in functional diseases. Of course, with assumptions contrary to causal facts medicine can do more harm than good in the treatment of heart disease.

Cancer is the second most frequent modern cause of deaths.[21] It is particularly prevalent in the more advanced countries. Everybody knows that the cause of cancer is a mystery; we do not have to adduce references for that. Efforts to discover the cause of cancer have been as enormous as those concerning cardiovascular disease.

Again, physicians are in perfect agreement on the proximate causes of malignancy, on the syndrome of cancer. Uncontrolled multiplication of functionally unrestricted, less differentiated cells is here the main proximate cause.[8, 9] Of course, functional loss of control, through exhaustion, can result from various over-enjoyments affecting different functions and organs. This does not mean that cancer is several diseases in one, as has been sometimes argued.

The *uniformity of the cancer syndrome* proves that the cause of cancer derives from one natural and therefore necessarily *simple causal principle*. Of course, such uniformity would be general also if the cause of cancer was virus infection or some other one factor. But all indications show that, in the final analysis, the cause of cancer is something we do to ourselves in excessive ways, *which can be only our over-enjoyments*.

Animals, not knowing how to improve their functions, do not suffer from cancer in their natural state. Cancers are found most clearly to be caused by smoking, overweight, pleasant meat diets, alcohol, drugs, and artificial stimulants. The proof of functional over-enjoyments as causes of cancer thus is clearly there.

But the modern medical approaches are, expectedly, dominated by contrary views. Pollutants or similar environmental hardships have been accepted most often as possible causes of cancer. Such hardships are unpleasant and therefore readily seen as harmful. However, the resourceful and free, more advanced people who suffer from cancer most would hardly be exposed to many unpleasant environmental influences. They would certainly accrue to excess their enjoyments of life. These enjoyments easily exceed any environmental difficulties, accepted as trade-offs.

Above all, organisms are uncannily clever in overcoming even the most involved environmental difficulties. Poisons or injuries that are not immediately fatal lead subsequently to adjustments by the organism that are rather more resistant than was the previous protection.

Over-enjoyment as the cause makes it inevitable that cancer remains a mystery causally. Over-enjoyments are derived from logically clear improvements of our functions, their intensification or acceleration. The inevitable opposite effects are experimentally so totally different from the "improvement" that they are never causally connected with it.

A potential cancer victim may seem to enjoy perfect health because of the "improvements" he is adding. His life and health may therefore appear completely normal. Logically there seems to be no cause whatever for a functional abnormality to arise. But when the perfect enjoyments of the "improvements" are accumulated, by exploitation of the underlying deeper functions, the functional exhaustion becomes total in the end. Then cancer suddenly appears, after decades of seemingly perfect, healthy life, as if without cause or previous relatable condition.

Of course the over-enjoyments are sustained by continuous suppression of organic restrictions. Such suppression of restrictive organic mechanisms may gradually efface them completely. The result is uncontrolled, malignant growth of undifferentiated, organically unrestricted cells. Cancer is incurable because a function totally exhausted or lost in the past cannot be repaired. Prevention, along with early discovery of cancer symptoms, is the only remedy.

The functional over-enjoyments finally leading to cancer are as involved and numerous as our organic functions. Each kind of enjoyment can be different, inventively varied. The opposite effects, the forms of functional exhaustion, therefore, are also numerous and varied. Then it may be demonstrated that malignancy is not causally always the same.

Most scientists, however, know that the cause of cancer is single and fairly *uniform*, as the uncontrolled, undifferentiated growth in it shows. It would be understood as completely uniform causally if the functional over-enjoyment was recognized as the cause. Anyway, the overall symptoms or proximate causes and effects of cancer are uniform; everybody knows what cancer is. It all proves that the primary, real cause of cancer is some one natural causal principle—which can be only simple.

Yet the greatest, most intelligent efforts to discover that simple cause have failed. Evidently, here as in all functional diseases, the very way of thinking is never directed toward the real cause, the functional over-improvement.

Diabetes is another serious and frequent, though less fatal, "chronic" disease of modern men. It causes deaths mostly indirectly through various complications and infections that it brings on or contributes to. Diabetes is a general syndrome of metabolic exhaustion[13, 14] which also causes obesity and vascular disease.[15, 16] The cause of diabetes is admittedly "unknown," "not identified," "not yet understood," or an "enigma."[13, 14, 15, 16]

As with all functional diseases, the proximate causes or causal processes of diabetes are clear and uniform. This is generally recognized.[13, 16] Insulin deficiency seems to be the main such cause. But studies on use of insulin, especially the more recent research, have revealed that insulin levels are actually higher in the blood of diabetics.[13, 16] The insulin causality—particularly its opposite, "habituation" effects—has become as enigmatic as diabetes itself.[13, 15, 16]

In the confusion, some physicians are accepting the view that the causes of diabetes are multiple or heterogeneous.[13] This, again, is a convenient way of substituting the generally clear, uniform proximate, causes for the missing real cause.

Nobody would contest that the overall syndrome and the secondary causal mechanisms of diabetes are *uniform* in all cases. The uniform, definitely certain, and impressive effects of insulin on diabetes confirm this. Obviously the cause of diabetes is *one natural, simple causal principle.*

Diabetes is an important chronic disease often clearly caused by the way affluent modern men live. In less-developed countries diabetes never becomes a problem for those poor people who do not resort to some unusual means of reactive improvement.

We shall discuss the functional over-improvement aspects of diabetes in detail later. They reveal that diabetes is a chronic metabolic exhaustion. But a self-deepening functional exhaustion is possible only through vicious-circle over-enjoyment. Without added over-improvements organic functions cannot become chronically abnormal. The organism always finds the proper countermeasures, even for chronic, abnormal influences, unless they are increased as the vicious-circle "improvements."

Over-enjoyment as the cause here is clear from the *paradoxical improvement effect of insulin* on diabetes. In all functional diseases some wonder drug or hormone relieves all symptoms—to make them worse afterward. Insulin, in its first effects, relieves all the complex diabetes reactions, evidently coming from one cause, from metabolic exhaustion. The relief here is brought by increased functional "improvement." Opposite reactions therefore become inevitable, and more improvement becomes necessary.

Indeed, the abuse of insulin is a particularly grave and constant problem.[13, 14] Physicians, though, rarely recognize that the "abuse" becomes necessary for the insulin user because insulin's effectiveness decreases, in the same way as the effectiveness of heroin decreases for drug users.

Arthritis afflicts more people in this country than any other disease does.[17, 18] The "causative agent or agents of arthritis are not yet known."[18] It is a "chronic inflammatory disorder of unknown etiology."[17] Its "causative infective agent is still to be identified."[18] Research on arthritis etiology is extensive; but it is only hoped that the future will bring a causal explanation.[17, 18]

Predictably, physicians like to view arthritis as being caused by multiple factors. This permits causal explanations from the uniform, secondary reactions that all physicians agree on. The overall syndrome of arthritis is as uniform as such reactions. Everybody knows what arthritis is and a computer can diagnose it at once.

Since the effects of arthritis are *uniform*, its cause is necessarily *one natural causal principle*, which can be only *simple*. Of course the negative effects of arthritis are multiple, because the functional over-improvements here are as varied as are the mechanisms of body movements that are involved in the "improvements."

In its simple causal terms, arthritis is a system of aftereffects of a functional *over-enjoyment of body movements*. Man does not know what organic processes enable him to move. But he highly enjoys the vigor and suppleness of his movements. He is smart enough to attain such enjoyments through various means, such as foods or hormonal stimulation.

What he actually attains are "improvements" in the underlying mechanisms of the function of movement, which are the sources of his enjoyment of vigorous ease and suppleness of movements. The results of such over-improvements are corresponding *opposite effects*—painful difficulty and rigidity in the movement system. For a practically useful causal understanding here you do not have to analyze all the myriad processes involved in the enjoyment of movement or in arthritis.

A person sets all those processes in action by simply over-enjoying various functions of movement. His arthritis consists simply of various corresponding opposite reactions, of opposite processes. By stopping his over-enjoyment he could avoid arthritis, though the immediate reactions would be felt as a worsening. Analyses of the infinite processes involved can only confuse.

The point is that the cause of arthritis is one and simple: over-improvement of the functioning of varied movements, leading to equally varied dysfunction. This is confirmed by a general, remarkable fact about arthritis treatment. All the varied arthritis symptoms are miraculously relieved, at first, by *cortisone* administration. The improvement here is dramatic but the result is worse after-effects.[17] Such treatments have been abandoned as highly crippling after the great enthusiasm they had first evoked.

Over-improvement as the simple cause here is clear. But the paradoxical logic of opposite effects is inherently contrary to the experimentally logical tenets that physicians as scientists accept automatically, without questioning. Hence the general causal mystery of arthritis.[17, 18]

Peptic ulcer is a disorder typically suffered by highly resourceful, modern men. It afflicts mostly professional men and executives. Its primary, determining cause is still not understood.[19, 20] Expectedly, multiple factors are often viewed as its causes.[19] But none of the considered factors have, in themselves, been found to cause ulcers.[19, 20]

Stress seems to be a general cause of ulcers. Stress-relieving drugs offer, temporarily, clear relief from ulcer effects.[20] Of course, *avoiding stress directly only brings more stress* afterward. Indeed, ulcer-relieving drugs have side-effects that make the disorder worse in the end, and therefore are not recommended as a solution.[19]

Typically, under conditions of real, severely felt stress ulcer disappears,[20, 27] because over-enjoyment then has been stopped. Such *causal paradoxes* confirm that the cause of ulcer is reactive over-improvement governed by the paradoxical opposite causality. That is why the causal course of ulcer cannot be "scientifically" explained.[19, 20]

Other chronic disorders are also caused by functional "improvements" and consequently, have remained mysteries causally.

In respiratory disorders, such as emphysema, allergies, or asthma, the *over-improvement causality* is evident. Emphysema is caused by smoking, which is an important, typical functional over-enjoyment. Allergies do not afflict people living with the greatest amounts of natural pollutants. Antisensitization is the best way to treat allergies. Asthma is a typical disorder of pampered children, and disappears under real, acute stress.[20, 27]

Alzheimer's disease is a good example of the mystery of reactive, functional disorders. It is reportedly becoming the "disease of the century," already afflicting many older people. This disease is most clearly a *reactive* disorder, a total exhaustion of mental *reactive* functions. It is also a most mysterious disorder causally, with no discovered *primary causes* whatever.

This shows that the more clearly functional a disorder is, the more unexplainable remains its cause. Here we have a *total impoverishment of psychologic reactions* in our era of the *greatest stimulation* and enjoyment of such reactions.

The terrifying AIDS is so easily connectable with excessive, degenerating enjoyments that it is often viewed as a punishment of the sinners. The tendencies toward such "sins" may however be inherited, much like the syndrome of drug addiction is. Thus the excessive, inevitably degenerative pleasure indulgences of our whole era are to be blamed here.

Chronic *gastrointestinal* disorders are frequent with persons who fuss about their digestion, and not with people who cannot afford to do so. Typically, the *most effective drugs*, the laxatives, *make the disorder worse.* This is so clearly evident that no prudent physician recommends them, in spite of their perfect initial effectiveness.

A recently often-discussed disorder is *anorexia nervosa*, which causes excessive weight loss. It afflicts mostly youngsters, exclusively from richer, higher-class families. It has remained a mystery causally. Involved explanations have been proposed, implying that the disorder is somehow wanted or is incurred through perceptual confusions.

The cause here is simple, if you consider that a child in a rich, very solicitous family is *over-nourished* or made to grow faster than his organic normalcy permits. He then has to slow down, to live through *opposite processes*, or to stop eating, in order to regain the normal dynamics in his growth.

Chronic headaches and insomnia are typical and frequent modern disorders. Headaches are suffered most by medical students and doctors or other professionals, and least by farm laborers. Perfectly effective drugs against headaches are available. But the *opposite side-effects* are so inevitable that such drugs are not recommended in good medical practice as effective remedies.

Insomnia can be perfectly overcome by drugs. As perfectly *the same drugs turn insomnia* into a chronic *disorder*. Physicians have been pointing this out repeatedly.

In sum, all these minor chronic disorders are also caused by functional over-improvements. The causality is here paradoxical at every stage and in every aspect of the disorder.

Physicians therefore cannot understand these disorders causally, though they recognize the most flagrant after-effects of the "improvements" brought by drugs that relieve such disorders wondrously at first. The causal mystery is due here to the same functional-improvement paradox that prevents causal understanding of all our functional diseases.

Disorders from Improvements—Because of Organic Limitedness

Two universal facts have to be pointed out in the field of our most frequent, functional diseases. First, these causally unexplained diseases are caused by the way of life of modern men. Secondly, the improvements attained by modern men in their way of life are unique and most freely enjoyed. The inexorable limitedness of organic normalcy here conflicts with the prodigious powers of modern man striving to improve his most enjoyable feelings of well-being.

It is important to understand that modern man attains his improvements here by "improving" the *organic functions*, from which the feelings derive. Purely psychological reactions would not be grave. But organic exhaustion brought by continuous vicious-circle over-improvements in the functions that provide the feelings is bound to be fatal in the end.

The functional diseases that we have discussed are usually seen as "chronic" diseases. This implies a continuous suffering. Actually, the typical facts in the causation of these diseases are the persistent enjoyments of uniquely rich and scientifically efficient modern improvements, followed by unexpected, often sudden reversals in reactions and, more importantly, in the underlying functions.

That is why it is better to view these diseases as functional diseases. They are clearly results of extreme functional exhaustion resulting from functional vicious-circle over-improvements.

Such over-improvements are tenaciously added up to the final limit. The reversal is therefore often sudden. It may strike after years of excellent health. This is typical of a heart attack, or of cancer.

The physiologically grave causation here should be always kept in mind. True, we incur these diseases by seeking improvements of our feelings. But it is not the feelings or merely psychological experiences that are the real causes here.

Arguments about grave effects resulting from psychologic reactions or feelings are not convincing, however intricately they are made.[1, 2] Grave effects from light causes are as impossible here as is the alchemy of an expected enrichment of mental capacities from easy, cognitive reactions. Also, feelings reverse and thus equalize themselves continuously.

Yet the acceptance of psychological causes for the "chronic" diseases is general. The reason is obvious. Physicians do not see the real cause here, the paradoxical "improvement." But they see the restrictive, stressful aftereffects, felt reactively, psychologically. Therefore psychological stress is assumed as the cause for these causally mysterious diseases.

The decisive fact is that man succeeds in *"improving" his essential, organic functions* by seeking for a merely mental *reactive* improvement. He manages to reach the deeper, underlying functions that are the sources of the feelings which can be really sustained only in this way.

Here the ingenuity of man should not be underestimated. By endless trials and errors, in his pursuit of happiness, he intuitively learns the ways and means that provide the deepest, most sustained, physically real "improvements" as the sources of steady feelings of well-being.

Modern man, in particular, succeeds in directing his own physiologic functions. He then tries to overcome organic limitedness. He is aided in his efforts by modern methods provided by affluence and technologic progress, as well as by medicine and increasing psychological expertise.

In our affluent society, prodigious improvement means are all around us. We enjoy, continuously, delicious, rich foods, improved by recipes from hundreds of cookbooks. We are helped even more by smoking, coffee, alcohol, and various pills, as well as by the endless comforts of home and work. We have it so easy that we cannot go a few hundred yards without a car, or do anything without our wonderful appliances and machines.

Above all, the *avoidance of stress* has become the supreme preoccupation of modern man. This is only natural. Stress is the most tormenting reaction. You can see that from the incredibly compulusive force of narcotic drugs used against stress. Naturally, the modern man exploits his whole gigantic system of improvements, material and medical, or psychological and social, to overcome the excruciating stress that is overwhelming him. Exactly because he avoids stress excessively he suffers from it in the same degree; the law of opposite causality is inexorable.

It may be important here to understand the etiologic paradox of this general modern scourge, *stress*. What is designated as stress, in our modern era, is mostly the tormenting, restrictive reactions resulting precisely as the opposite effects of modern over-enjoyments.

Evidently, this modern stress is as "rich" or mysteriously extensive and physiologically deep as the over-improvements that modern man enjoys, on deepest functional levels. This stress becomes the most tormenting feeling because of the vicious-circle deepening by which it grows. We shall see repeatedly how important it becomes, etiologically, to recognize *that stress is the most unbearable and general of all feelings, and that it increases through its excessive avoidance.*

It is often argued that we suffer from stress because of the difficulty of decision between "fight and flight" or similar difficult alternatives. This explanation merely perpetuates the fallacy about decisions or reasonings and ideas being causally important. The fight or the flight is either stressful or pleasant. Why not simply decide or choose to avoid what is stressful and to enjoy what is pleasant? Difficulty of decision thus can never be here a problem.

Modern man in particular has the widest possibilities of choice. That is why he incurs excessive stress, by avoiding it prodigiously.

Etiologically, stress is felt as a general and strong fear or anxiety. These are feelings opposite to those of insured survival or security. Certainly, survival needs govern every human adjustment and improvement. All our enjoyments are ultimately survival satisfactions. Consequently, our every over-enjoyment, material or mental, brings opposite reactions felt as threats to survival, as deep anxiety and tension, which constitute stress.

This vast, general stress becomes the cause of our chief functional diseases as it is overcome by continuously added "improvements" on the deepest physiological levels. Of course, the causation here is paradoxical and presently not understood. But extensive studies and experiments have demonstrated, convincingly, that stress is causally decisive in the functional diseases.[1, 2, 3, 24]

Expectedly, some scientists point out that this is not so. Individuals such as the Type A personalities are shown to exhibit particular freedom from stress or from anxieties. Over-enjoyment in the behavior of the ebullient Type A personality can be easily observed, but the paradoxical over-enjoyment causality is not recognized.

Only incidentally is it realized that added improvements for the avoidance of stress are not helpful. A foremost authority on stress, Dr. Hans Selye, understood that stress should not be avoided. But even he did not recognize the paradoxical causation of stress. He merely argued that there is good stress and bad stress.[2, 3] He also assumed that stress is adaptive to a certain point but becomes harmful thereafter. Consequently, he theorized that the organism can poison itself. Which is contrary to the miraculous purposiveness of organisms.

Dr. Selye demonstrated in his noted experiments that "stress" from intense stimulation, particularly when induced by corticoids, at first strengthened organic defenses in animals, but later had opposite effects typical of diseased stress. Opposite causality was at work here because of overstimulation. Indeed, when animals were exposed to stresses induced without corticoid stimulation, no failures or reversals in defenses resulted, under regular conditions.

The fact is that stress, if not interfered with, is a natural reaction beneficial to the organism. It is not the cause of the functional exhaustion reacted to by feelings of stress. On the contrary, stress serves the restrictions necessary to "refill" exhausted functional reserves, by saving up the functional energy.

But this opposite-reaction causality is hardly understood, and the experts on stress have offered endless "logical" explanations. Since men always believe in the power of ideas and reasoning, doctors seek for causes, here as well, in various *cognitive or ideational* influences such as perceptions and learning. The inexorable organic rule of equal restriction for equal release is never considered.

Scientists may suggest as remedies merely cognitive corrections, in perceptual or learning experiences or in ideas and thoughts. Such corrections would be easy. Dr. Selye used the example of how a slight push on a phonograph needle can bring it into the right grooves.[3]

The vast field of psychosomatics rests on assumptions of ideational causality. The mere idea of a "burden on my back" becomes a backache. Or the idea of not being able to "stomach" something brings gastrointestinal disorder.

But even the less extreme psychological explanations accept as decisive cognitive factors such as thoughts, perceptions, reasoning, ideas, or learning. Positive thinking, more philosophical attitudes, or broader and more insightful views on life and peace of mind are considered as safeguards.[3, 4, 24]

Expectedly, many scientists have enough common sense not to accept such psychosomatic and psychological explanations. In the confusion, stress is sometimes viewed as irrelevant in the etiology of our chief functional diseases. Actually, the *stress is the cause* of these diseases, in the sense that they are *incurred through excessive avoidance* of stress. Of course, it should always be kept in mind that this avoidance is effected through the exploitation of the underlying organic functions.

If there were no stress we would not have these diseases. Also, stress is a precise causal indicator in these diseases, if its paradoxical causality is understood. Stress shows how far and in what way the functional disease has progressed, as functional exhaustion.

Generally, scientists are increasingly recognizing stress as the cause of our chief functional diseases.[3, 4, 24] Let us look in more detail at the generality as well as the paradoxical presence and absence of stress under various conditions of life.

The most revealing aspect of stress is its overwhelming, generally unpleasant effect. In fact, stress is *the generally integrated expression of all functional restrictions*, resulting from equal depletion of pleasure reserves overdrawn, in particular, to counteract stress. We should keep in mind that all our reactive improvements are ultimately enjoyments of the survival values, which govern everything. Drug-users seek relief from a general stress, and incur the torment of stress in almost every organic function.

Evidently, modern men suffering from stress are actually suffering from general, integrated functional restrictions due to exhaustion incurred through functional exploitative "improvements" for the avoidance of stress.

Of course, this is paradoxical, as is all causality of reactions, because of organic limitedness. But this casuality explains how stress, in its usually understood meaning, becomes the reason of why and how we bring on ourselves the functional diseases.

We have to emphasize that modern men can attain and enjoy almost everything they want. Naturally they want first and most of all freedom from stress, from this source of all torment. They attain this freedom by ways and means that are far subtler and more extensive than any drugs.

Consequently modern men incur a functional exhaustion that is much deeper and more insidious than are the often-fatal drug aftereffects. Though our usual over-improvement means are less dramatically effective than a drug can be, their impact accumulates continually in a *vicious circle*, through long years of life.

Modern men are far too intelligent not to recognize stress as the general source of their negative reactions. The stress of modern life is now blamed for most of the difficulties suffered by modern men. Supposedly modern man has made life more difficult for himself by *unfortunate strategies* in his efforts and behavior. The argument can *hardly be taken seriously*. It implies that men would torture themselves without noticing it.

No complexities, no calculations of involved strategies are necessary for avoiding stress or its effects. Clearly, stress is a general, integrated reaction that governs all other subordinate reactions and feelings. Thus, we can avoid stress by simply avoiding what is particularly painful, and nothing is clearer than the undesirability of pain. Even a dumb animal knows how to avoid what we know as stress, what is painful, though animals do not invent excessive avoidances of stress.

Surely, the life of modern man is full of stress. He meets with stress at every turn. But this is so precisely because he avoids stress as persistently, everywhere, to excess.

Complexity, speed, and change in modern life are mostly blamed. But they are here because we want them, because their immediate effects are pleasant. The complexity of modern life results from use of more extensive and varied means for our enjoyments. We are speeding because there is so much to enjoy. And we are seeking for what is new because it is exciting.

Even when we overwork or overdrive ourselves we do so by calculating this against the greater pleasures of future enjoyments that it brings. Future pleasures are as real for man as present enjoyments; and any enjoyment is primarily that of freedom from stress. Particularly is the "rat-race" competition for more of everything a pursuit of freedom from stress. Increase in wealth and power provide a sense of security to the highest degree. Competition for superiority, in various forms, amounts to striving for a particular, instinctive security in the pecking order. And all enjoyments of security, of whatever kind, are in effect enjoyments of the freedom from stress.

Also, when we are conditioned so that we become workaholics, *we work to gain more of conditioned pleasure*, more freedom from stress as guilt or need, in addition to insuring future benefits or security to be enjoyed. In the pursuit of conditioned pleasures as well, *men are too intelligent to incur more stress by some mistake*, while seeking for pleasure or relief, for freedom from stress as a conditioned demand of conscience. Particularly since conditioned pleasures are merely elaborations of organic pleasures.

Whatever the secondary complexities, the causal facts are clear and simple. Avoidance of stress is the dominant pleasure that integrates all other enjoyments. It is absolutely clear to man, in whatever he does, at every moment. There is automatic simplicity in evaluating this highest pleasure, the freedom from stress, against anything else.

In sum, man is too intelligent to make miscalculations in his trade-offs, when the values involved are as automatically clear and simple as in the avoidance of stress.

Of course, the paradoxical opposite causality of stress cannot be logically understood. The result is confusion and *untenable explanations*. It is argued, for instance, that stressful conditions are less prevalent in primitive societies, where diseases attributable to stress are surprisingly rare.

In reality, *primitive man* lives under a constant, immediate threat to his very survival. He is helpless against disease, starvation, or dangers from nature and other men. He is constantly surrounded by dreadful forces, malevolent spirits, witchcraft, and sorcery. In our terms his life is infernal. But he is indeed free of excessive stress—because he does not attain the functional over-improvements as sources of increased freedom from stress.

Animals do not suffer from the functional diseases, which are clearly brought by men on themselves. What are men doing here so persistently to themselves that animals are not? Obviously, men are accumulating enjoyments of pleasure; and the highest integrated embodiment of pleasure is the freedom from stress. Men plan this pleasure and increase it above everything else, as the integrated central source of their natural and conditioned inner enjoyments, of survival itself. Animals cannot increase their enjoyments at all. Consequently they are free of functional diseases incurred through enjoyments of the avoidance of stress.

Men too are free of functional diseases when they are prevented from enjoying this highest pleasure, the freedom from stress. *The Jews in Nazi concentration camps* lived under the highest constant stress. But they were singularly free of functional diseases, so clearly connectable with stress causally.

In the Warsaw Ghetto under the Nazi terror, Jewish doctors found that its inhabitants did not suffer from chronic diseases: heart disease, hypertension, diabetes, arthritis, peptic ulcer, asthma, allergies, neuroses, and psychoses. This is comprehensively documented, by Jewish doctors, in hospital records recovered after the war.[27]

Later, Jewish doctors, previous inmates of Nazi concentration camps, compared their observations in a conference in Israel. They found that they did not see "a single case of heart attack or angina" among camp inmates, including those who had previously been sick with heart disease.[27]

Generally, organisms act by drives which in human terms are pleasures. *The natural and usual pleasure drives serve to maintain organic normalcy or health.* They are kept in healthy limits by equal restrictions. It can be easily observed that the unrestrained enjoyment of pleasure drives brings organic exhaustion. In animal life the restraints imposed on pleasure drives, by environmental and inner organic restrictions, are automatic. But man as a conscious manager of his reactions tends to remove such limitations. This tendency has been kept in check by cultural or moral traditions and by the insufficiency of effective "improvement" means in the less affluent and scientifically less proficient societies of the past. Our modern progress has changed this, and the functional diseases have increased epidemically.

The insidious fact here is that the general natural role of pleasure drives is to maintain health. This can lead to a lethal deception in human adjustment.

Man, in his natural reactions, believes that he is healthy when he feels well, or that his health is improving when his feeling of well-being increases. *Then comes man's capacity to increase his feeling of well-being beyond natural limits.* Everybody can see that men have this capacity. There are thousands of drugs, not only narcotics, that can improve any feeling, any functional reaction, dramatically. So can the countless improvements and skills of modern life and medicine.

Experimentally or "scientifically," the evil to be overcome is the physiologically real restrictions—imposed by the organism to counteract over-improvements. These restrictions are incapacitating and painful. They clearly seem to constitute the disease.

Logically, these "diseased" restrictions are overcome, in scientific medical treatment, by the addition of improvements having, in some way, the same causal effects that the over-improvements had which caused the disease. This is the only directly effective way of stopping the restrictive, stressful reactions. An alcohol hangover or drug withdrawal is best "cured" by alcohol or the same drug.

Patients as well as their doctors proceed here according to the experimental logic that the improvements which bring direct, best relief or the feelings of well-being, as affective indicators of health, are to be used and increased to higher levels so that the improvement effects are insured.[1, 2]

But in functional diseases *the restrictive, "diseased" processes are the ways by which the organism regains its normalcy.* This may seem absurd: the experimentally clear disease is then to be accepted as cure.

However, this is causally true, and is evident by good common sense in the world of reactions. Clearly diseased reactions are felt and can be experimentally registered when the body purifies itself from the "improvement" stimulants accumulated by the use of drugs, smoking, alcohol, strong foods and drinks, or by any other habitual means of stimulation.

Of course, physicians, with their intelligence and training, recognize that distressing after-effects are necessary in clear cases of previously enjoyed stimulation. They do not prescribe more narcotics to relieve a drug-withdrawal syndrome.

But the point is that this causal paradox is true for the functional diseases in all their intricate details. Functional, experimentally clear, man-directed improvements, in all their endless variety and perfection, are here the causes of disease.

On the other hand, experimentally clear "disease" here is the organism's effort to regain normalcy. Every one of the countless, involved processes in this effort is restrictive, clearly incapacitating. If you consider how a person becomes "sick" when he faces a danger to be overcome, you can see how the organism copes under organic limitedness.

But for physicians all sickly incapacities and negatively felt limitations are a disease. *Opposite causality* and organic limitedness as its reason are *not even mentioned in medicine*, though they determine our organic normalcy and reactions. Under the paradox of opposite causality, "worsening" is the way toward normalcy in functional diseases, as it is in drug withdrawal.

No physician would, however, be inclined to consider this paradox when he faces experimentally clear "disease" to be counteracted. Simply, opposite causality, which governs the functional, reactive diseases, is contrary to the very way of thinking in modern medicine. We saw how this becomes the reason for the unbelievable, admitted causal mystery about our functional diseases, the causes of 80 percent of our deaths.

Over-Improvement Etiology of Our Principal, Functional Diseases

Our most frequent, functional diseases are disorders in our most enjoyed organic functions. Heart action and blood circulation are the primary, central sources of our functional enjoyments. Correspondingly, cardiovascular disorders constitute our chief functional disease. Man indeed over-enjoys his life through his "heart" and incurs the equal aftereffects.

Cancer is our next-gravest disease and it afflicts us through functions that we enjoy most, by way of smoking, overeating, alcohol, concentrated meat diets, and the enjoyment of sun, drugs, or other stimulation, including that of the most effective reproductive glands.

Metabolism is a function that is enjoyed, and "improved" extensively. A very frequent, corresponding disorder is diabetes. Similarly, vigor and suppleness of movement, of our muscles and joints, are a major source of enjoyment for man. Correspondingly, arthritis is a frequent disease, with a syndrome of effects opposite to such enjoyments. A general source of enjoyed youthful vigor is our digestive function, particularly its stomach and digestive activity. Peptic ulcer is a functional disorder in the management of stomach acidity and peptic reactions.

Let us look, in more detail, at the over-improvement etiology of these chief functional diseases, which cause three fourths of our deaths.

HEART DISEASE. Fifty percent of the deaths in this country

are caused by heart disease.[21] Supposedly, 40 million Americans suffer from the various cardiovascular disorders.[21] The typical heart patient has no organic, innate defect, nor injury, in his cardiovascular system. Environment or hardships of life, such as the pressures of a job, do not cause heart disease if the person responds to such stress normally.[3, 4, 24]

Heart disease is thus clearly brought by man on himself. The great authority Paul Dudley White concluded that "heart disease before eighty is our own fault."[3] Of course, *what man brings on himself to excess is always the reactive enjoyments.*

Heart disease is the "plague of the 20th century,"[6] of the era that has provided men with unprecedented improvements of life, scientific skills, and freedoms from restrictions. It has been estimated that heart disease occurred at only one-fifth of its present rate at the beginning of this century.[6] Increased *longevity is not the reason* for the increase in deaths from heart disease.[3, 24]

A typical heart attack strikes a man when he is otherwise still vigorous, even at the peak of his powers. Deaths from heart attacks start climbing at the age of thirty to forty, reach their peak at fifty-five to fifty-nine, and start declining at sixty-five.[3, 5, 6, 24]

Moreover, the causes of heart disease start accumulating from an early age. In the Korean War many autopsies were performed on young men. A "surprising discovery" was made. Three-fourths of our men with an average age of twenty-two already had the narrowed arteries, increased cholesterol, and other signs of incipient heart disease.[5]

It is now generally recognized that heart disease is caused by the way we live, by our *"style of life."*[3, 6, 24] Our times are, of course, the age of anxiety and stress, which are incurred through their excessive avoidance. Furthermore, stress is the quintessence of all negative, restrictive reactions and is the most unwanted of all feelings. Freedom from stress is the highest general pleasure for man, who moreover sees it as the source of health, particularly under our experimentally scientific views.

Modern life and medicine have enabled man *to enjoy this highest pleasure*, widely and continuously, through his central source of all enjoyments, *through his cardiovascular function.* The result is the vicious-circle exhaustion of this function, to the point of final collapse, as each "improvement" brings an equal worsening that is overcome by still more improvement, much as in the continued overuse of a stimulant.

Stress is recognized as cause of heart disease, in most studies.[3, 6, 24] But it is also generally recognized that stressful conditions in themselves do not cause pathological stress.[3, 6, 24] The decisive factor is how the individual reacts to various conditions of stress. In the widely noted study by Meyer Friedman and Ray H. Rosenman, behavior by a Type A personality was found to be the main cause of heart disease.[24] It has now been generally accepted as such a cause.[3, 5, 6]

But the Type A personality is, on a closer look, almost the exact opposite of people suffering under stress. He is full of energy, optimistically aggressive, competitive, expansive, readily excited, and always in an eager hurry.[3, 6, 24]

It can be said that the Type A personality is intensely pursuing the over-enjoyments of various kinds of aspired successes. It is pointed out that he is obsessed with time schedules, which supposedly impose stress.[24] But there is no other way for a person really to enjoy his successes than by measuring them and attaining them quickly.

Thus analyzed causally, Type A behavior is that of a person seeking exciting enjoyment at an intensified pace. Even Friedman and Rosenman had to admit that no external signs of stress could be observed in Type A behavior.[24] This has been a reason why stress has not been accepted as cause of heart disease by some authorities. But the study by Friedman and Rosenman was highly insightful to connect Type A behavior with stress, which follows such behavior.[24]

We may emphasize that the stress syndrome in heart disease only reveals the opposite, vicious-circle over-improvement effects in the heart's function. The over-improvement leads to restrictive reactions felt as stress. The decisive factor is the vicious-circle exhaustion of the function. To sustain the pursuit of *over-enjoyment, actually the overcoming of increasing stress*, the person *exploits*, to excess, the underlying mechanisms of *the heart's function.*

Modern life and medicine provide extensive, refined means for doing so. The main sources of over-improvement are, again, smoking, overeating, drinking, overindulgence of physical ease, pills or other stimulants, as well as "expert" psychological and behavioral assistance.

The inner mechanisms of the heart and blood vessels are infinitely refined, and protected against unnatural outside influences. A milligram of some reactively effective substance can alter their functioning. Man employs means that are a hundred times more extensive and powerful. He selects them for their greatest "improvement" effect, without realizing that each added improvement deepens the vicious-circle exhaustion to an equal extent.

Anybody can understand that use of an effective stimulant to sustain vigor, and taking more of it as fatigue follows, has to lead to a breakdown. But even the best analysis cannot reveal what happens in the myriad microscopic processes during functional over-improvement—particularly because the reactive mechanisms involved follow a paradoxical causal logic.

A person, however, knows what brings him a sense of improved health or vigor. Moreover, *the improvement appears as such* in any kind of experimentally "logical" treatment. If the improvements are skillfully sustained, the breakdown comes only at the very end of final exhaustion. Heart attacks strike suddenly, after long periods of seemingly excellent, actually "improved" health.

We read in newspapers every day how men in seemingly good health, enjoying the best medical care, die suddenly of heart disease. In fact, it can be said that our typical medical care is here a potentially dangerous factor. It provides the most powerful means of direct improvements, of sustained vigor. Typically, in the most critical stages of heart distress physicians use drastically stimulating drugs and techniques.

Nature is incomparably more refined in meeting organic exhaustion, even by attuning the involved functions to their lowest levels. The exhausted organism becomes "diseased" to the point of seemingly fatal functional cessation.

In its natural state, an *animal* suffers through its weakness fully, even sinks into a death-like state, upon extreme exhaustion, but does not die suddenly of a functional failure such as a heart attack. The human organism would do the same *if protected against our tremendously effective "improvements."*

Of course, modern people would have to start recognizing that the slowed-down, restrictive life of weakened old age serves us better than the pursuit of youthful vigor through the enjoyment of all kinds of inventive stimulation.

Organic restrictions do not decrease health or creativity, though they often seem debilitating. Even a deficient diet is better than stimulating foods enjoyed to sustain "normal" reactions for an aged or exhausted organism. Animals under starvation diets live longer and remain potentially vigorous.[22]

During the two world wars people in Europe lived through dreadful stresses or deprivations and suffered from malnutrition that, scientifically, would be expected to cause heart disease at extremly high rates. But, "unbelievably," these people suffered less from cardiovascular diseases as well as from the other chronic diseases than at any other period.[5, 6]

Deaths from heart disease decreased appreciably during the years of our recent recession and high inflation. No explanation for this decrease has been found in terms of scientifically analyzable logical causes. [3,6]

A simple insight in the paradox of restrictions and "improvements" would explain why a war or recession has such unexpected effects. People know that they can prevent the chronic diseases by stopping over-enjoyments such as overeating, smoking, using alcohol, or other pleasures. Such a general, simple wisdom could serve as a practical guide for scientific prevention and treatment of heart disease or other functional disorders if the paradox of "improvements" were medically understood.

In all functional diseases, *causal analysis would be practically more useful if it dealt with the integrated reactions of the simple enjoyment of pleasure.* Technically detailed analyses can confuse more than explain, particularly because of the causal paradox involved. Cardiovascular disease can be analyzed in its endless physiologic details, and this can be written down on two thousand pages or more. For instance, the hardening and narrowing of arteries can be studied in terms of countless molecular biochemical processes.

On a more generalized level, changes in cells can be analyzed. This would show how aging or loss of vigor, through overstimulation, leads to weakened responses. Still, the complexities to be dealt with would be endless. Reportedly, a hundred thousand kinds of proteins are involved in the building and operation of our organic cells.

The difficulties disappear when the hardening and narrowing of arteries is dealt with in terms of the integrated, simple aftereffects of "improvement" enjoyments. It is causally clear that our overall reactions of pleasure and displeasure integrate, to tiniest detail, the underlying processes in causally precise ways; without it the organism would not surive. (The myriad organic processes can, in truth, be causally understood only through such reactions.)

Under an analysis of such simple, integrated reactions it becomes understandable why and how our functional over-enjoyment, deriving from the suppleness and expansion of arteries, inevitably leads to their hardening and narrowing. Such causal understanding is simple, but all-inclusive, and practically useful. It indicates which enjoyment, such as smoking, provides the "improvement," the freer and vigorous blood flow in the arteries, and therefore leads to opposite aftereffects.

In contrast, even a vast analysis of microscopic detail can reveal here only a small part of what the disease does in the organism. Confusion is inevitable. Moreover, it leads to conclusions contrary to what is causally true. The experimentally "scientific" logic is inevitably, mathematically applied to the functional reactions revealed in analyses, but the reactions are governed by the opposite causality.

The *cholesterol* controversy is a good example of scientific causal confusion. Conflicting opinions on the role of cholesterol in heart disease are extensive.[5, 6, 7, 24] Cholesterol is high in the blood of heart-disease patients. Obviously, this amounts to a negative functional reaction. But negative reactions, such as high temperature, pain, or stress, are, first of all, *organic protective measures*. Thus, in regard to cholesterol as well, the "question is the old familiar one: how we distinguish a symptom or a sign from a cause."[24]

Various experiments at the National Heart Institute, and particularly by Dr. Stewart Wolf, have shown that exposure of subjects to stressful conditions dramatically increased cholesterol, fats, and coagulants in their blood.

This shows rather clearly that *cholesterol is increased to meet functional emergencies*. Its increase amounts to a restrictive, "diseased" stress. Restrictions are necessary to accumulate functional reserves. Cholesterol is known to be generally restrictive in its effects.[24] Organism usually imposes stressful restrictions to meet emergencies. This may turn a person, temporarily, into a weakling or partial invalid, but the organism is subsequently strengthened through it. The paradox of natural improvement through what seems like worsening explains how cholesterol can become so controversial. Cholesterol appears to be "the most enigmatic molecule in human biology."[5]

The role of lipoproteins becomes paradoxical and controversial. They seem to have bad and good effects on cholesterol accumulation. Theories are increasing about the role of high-density and low-density lipoproteins to explain the opposite effects of the same substance.[5, 6]

It would not be difficult to understand that cholesterol as a restrictive substance serves to accumulate functional reserves, and has the same "diseased" effects as all functionally necessary restrictions have. Indeed, the organism itself produces, regularly, up to 80 percent of its cholesterol and controls it precisely.[7, 24] More cholesterol is synthesized by the liver if less of it is supplied by food.[24] Animals that eat foods containing cholesterol, such as rats and dogs, showed no abnormal increase of it in their blood even when fed enormous amounts of it.[24]

The *cholesterol issue was not resolved* by the study sponsored by the National Heart, Lung, and Blood Institute on 3,806 subjects selected as prone to cardiovascular disorders. The program primarily imposed a strong restriction on our usually preferred foods.

Limitations of enjoyed foods can indeed make the whole difference. But they are irrelevant for cholesterol intake. Nobody eats too much cholesterol by preference. Cholesterol is one of the least tasteful ingredients. It is most plentiful in foods like pork brains beef kidneys or sweetbreads, which few people would prefer to eat. Similarly, low-saturated fats are least tasteful and are consumed at the minimum of body requirements.

The NHLBI program was right in emphasizing restrictions in foods that people may overeat. Practically, this amounted to a restriction in foods quite opposite, in their taste and therefore in their effects, to foods such as cholesterol or low-saturated fats. Of course, foods are very complex in their interaction with the body; and only taste indicates precisely their exact role, which is causally paradoxical for the "improvement" effects.

A strong, even sickening, drug called cholestyramine was used in the NHLBI program. The disturbing drug evidently interfered with the functional enjoyments of the subjects prone to heart disorders. That necessarily helped, as did the interference with food enjoyments. The sickening drug decreased the total overimprovement effectiveness. Therefore, the production of cholesterol by the body became less necessary. Here again the perennial problem is to "distinguish a sympton or sign from a cause"—to see the protective role of a "diseased" reaction.[24]

Any organic process is experimentally ungraspable. Particularly so is a reactive mechanism such as cholesterol production, because the causal logic of reactions is paradoxical. But our pleasure is precise in revealing causal meanings of reactions. It indicates that cholesterol is a restrictive factor, a dull, tasteless food ingredient.

Modern rich people avoid cholesterol in their foods. *Excessive avoidance leads to excessive increase of a restrictive factor.* Consequently, richer people have more cholesterol in their blood, for the same reason that they have the other restrictive or stressful, "diseased" cardiovascular reactions.

Poor people eat foods containing much cholesterol. Bedouins and Masai tribesmen have been observed to consume enormous amounts of it, through milk. But they are, in the words of Sir John McMichael, the "world's healthiest people."[24]

Physicians as logical scientists inevitably find cholesterol to be a cause of heart disorders, for *it does bring reactions of "diseased" stress.* We have always to keep in mind that stress comes together with functional diseases but increases through the excessive avoidance of it. Particularly on the more detailed levels of analysis, the increase in cholesterol as an experimentally clearly negative reaction has to appear to be a cause of heart disease. In all functional disorders, the "disease" is actually the organism's pressure toward normalcy.

Hypertension is another important syndrome of cardiovascular disease. Physicians have often argued that by prevention of hypertension heart disease would be brought under control. Hypertension has also remained a mystery causally.[3, 5, 7]

In the simple terms of integrated reactions the cause of hypertension is clear. Stimulation exhausts the circulatory system. Tranquilization induces it to abandon or decrease its more difficult peripheral functions. The end result is an exhausted system having to do more work to remedy neglected functional tasks. Both effects correspond to the syndrome of hypertension.

Probably the most interesting thing about hypertension is that *it can be miraculously relieved by a whole series of drugs.*[3, 5, 6, 7] Physicians have repeatedly demonstrated how hypertension can be controlled by some new drug which, supposedly, would help to prevent heart disease.

Certainly, drugs can add more stimulation and tranquilization. They thus can overcome hypertension, temporarily—and *bring worse after-effects.* Even an increase in salt intake has been experimentally proven as clearly beneficial. Most recently this has been demonstrated in a wide study by the Oregon Hypertension Program. But salt is the main cause of hypertension. If drug effects did not reverse, heart disease would have been wiped out by now for good.

The widest study so far on the effect of hypertension drugs is revealing. It was conducted by the NHLBI for ten years on 12,866 subjects. The study showed that "men who received drug treatment for high blood pressure actually had a higher death rate".[22] It pointed to "the disturbing possibility that the extra drug treatment contributed to the deaths."[25]

Hypertension is a natural organic reaction to the effects of previous functional over-improvements. If it is overcome by further improvements the disorder deepens into heart disease. People who lack or do not develop more perfect means of "improvements" *suffer from more hypertension but less heart disease.*

Statistics on the Japanese show that they have many more hypertension cases than we have but only one-tenth of our heart-disease rate.[5, 6] Their less affluent diet and their traditions do not permit the more efficient "improvements" that we enjoy. When the Japanese emigrate to California their heart disease rate increases tenfold.[5, 6]

Of course, *doctors have the most perfected means of improvements* at their disposal. They suffer from heart disease at rates three times higher than the general population.[5] Revealingly, they also commit suicides three times more often than other people.[25] This indicates to what extent they suffer from the highest stress. The organic cause of stress is, of course, functional exhaustion. In the famous Framingham project, physicians were found to suffer from stress at the highest rates; and stress was causally related to heart disease.[23]

CANCER. Discovery of the cause of cancer is probably the highest medical challenge. No easy solution can be expected here. Still, everything known about cancer points to over-enjoyment of functional "improvements" as its cause.

Cancer is quite clearly related causally to our main continuous, functional over-enjoyments. Smoking is statistically and officially proven to cause cancer. Overeating is equally clear as a cause of cancer;[8, 9] underfeeding of animals dramatically reduces the incidence of malignant tumors.[9, 22] The most frequent fatal cancer of the digestive tract, cancer of the colon, is causally traced to beer-drinking and the consumption of meat—especially beef,[3, 22], a particularly enjoyable food. Sex is a most enjoyable function and cancer in organs or glands related to sex is frequent. The use of drugs and the alcohol habit are other clear causes of cancers.[9] Stomach cancer is often caused by strong food-seasoning and spicing, enjoyed by many peoples.[9] Cancer of the skin is caused by sunbathing, which modern people enjoy so much.[8,9]

Thus it can be said that almost every form of cancer can be causally traced to some over-enjoyment, some functional "improvement" that people enjoy, in perfected ways. Animals in their natural state do not die of cancers, because they do not know how to increase or perfect the functional improvements enjoyed by man.

The psychological etiology of cancer is also revealing.[10] The relation of cancer to *psychologic causes* has been convincingly demonstrated by such authorities as L. LeShan, R. E. Worthington, G. Booth, D. M. Kissen, S. J. Kowal, W. A. Greene, and R. R. Grinker. They all agree on emotional negativity, expressed in continuous stress, as the causal factor.[10] But excessive, chronic stress is possible only as a result of the vicious circle of over-enjoyment.

Another typical phenomenon of over-enjoyment effects is clear in cancer etiology. In continuous over-enjoyments the *after-effects* appear, without warning, *after long delay*, after the exhaustion has become final and no further improvement is possible. This is typical of cancer, as it is of most functional diseases, particularly heart attacks and the chief functional psychoses.

Cancer comes from exhaustion of the deepest functions of life. Modern men "improve" these functions with everything they enjoy. And however skillfully the enjoyments are added, the after-effects become inevitable in the end. Continued additions or increases in all functions of life finally exhaust them—which is self-evident from what life is.

Also revealing is the fact that the same causal agents which can, temporarily, relieve a cancer can also cause it. The best noticed of these ambivalent agents are steroids, sex hormones, enzymes, various carbon compounds, mineral-enriched preparations, X-rays, ultraviolet rays, folic acid, and growth hormones.[8, 11] In all functional over-improvements, such *ambivalence of effects* is the rule.

Finally, prevention and the rare non-reversing cures of cancer show that prevention and cure are possible through the counteraction of over-enjoyments. Evidently if people stopped the enjoyments, such as smoking or over-eating, most cancers would be prevented. But all cancers probably cannot be prevented in this way, by consciously felt, psychologic controls.

The physiologic causation and control of cancer has to be considered. Organic cells, as all living forms, live by the drive for pleasure release, under equal restrictions. Then if the cells are somehow deranged even by a purely physical influence, they may start on the course of vicious-circle over-improvements and exhaustion that causes malignancy. The vicious-circle over-improvement process here makes the malignancy self-sustaining, comparable to fire.

Then a strong *restriction or shock* on the purely physiological level can be a means of control, as shock has been proven to be for physiologically caused psychotic depressions. As is generally known, infections by bacteria and fungi evoke the strong, alarming reactions of restrictive shock in the organism on the physiological level. This is evident from the various types of toxic-shock syndrome.

Revealingly, it has been long observed that *strong infections*, particularly of tuberculosis, *have stopped malignant growth*. The remarkable pioneer work by W. B. Coley may be mentioned here. Now vaccines from live TB strains are used by the National Cancer Institute and by doctors in a dozen countries. Interferon is also a typical alarm agent. It is produced by infected cells and acts as alarm to other cells.[8]

Thus immunotherapy can play an important role in the prevention of malignancy; and research here has progressed notably.[1, 11] Prevention of the total range of cancers can be insured after this physiologic prevention is added to the psychologic prevention, for the avoidance of the functional over-enjoyments. *Prevention, rather than cure*, is the way to deal with cancer, since a cancer, when it appears, is a syndrome of final functional exhaustion.

Of course, cancers from psychologically originating causes, from conscious over-enjoyments such as smoking, are overwhelmingly more numerous. Their prevention is as simple as it is hard to follow. Stop smoking or overeating and you'll not risk getting most cancers. The same is true for our other important over-enjoyments. They become our unnatural effort to overcome our functional limitations or organic normalcy. As we succeed, we finally efface organic restrictions on the deepest levels, and the malignant growth of unrestricted, undifferentiated cells follows.

Presently, *pollution* of environment is blamed most for malignant disorders. This fits well with the modern attitude of turning against the insidious restrictions and stresses that spoil our enjoyments everywhere. Pollution is generally unpleasant. Its felt effect is opposite to that of enjoyments, which are clearly causes of cancers.

The various pills, by themselves, that we take every day can be a hundred times more probably causes of cancer than is pollution. Several studies show that the Seventh-Day Adventists, who shun enjoyments such as smoking, have low cancer rates even while living in heavily polluted areas such as Los Angeles. By the way, air pollution inside homes has been found to be ten times higher than the unpleasant, outside air pollution.[25]

Of course, pollution, as any artificial influence on the organism, can be disturbing; we have mentioned the possible disorientation of cells. But pollution or a poison that has a direct, unpleasant effect cannot cause malignancy.

The first certainty about cancer is that its cause accumulates for years. Organisms are perfectly able to reject, immediately, what they do not like. Poisons and pollutants are painful or irksome. They would never be accumulated. Also, how and why should a poison remain latent in the body for thirty years? *Poisons and injuries actually make an organ stronger.* A healed broken arm has a stronger bone around the break. Hard work that seems to do injury to the heart strengthens it. Yet, generally, the directly logical "scientific" thinking dominates our modern attitudes.

A pollutant or poison is viewed as dangerous to the extent of its "logical" injurious or negative effect. Fear of dioxin has become so intense that the American Medical Association has had to issue a clarification to the public. Dr. Lewis Thomas finds the dioxin scare completely unfounded scientifically and unbelievably excessive, even in our governmental reactions.[22]

But don't *statistics show pollutants as causes* of cancer? Actually, a pollutant or trauma may merely become an identifiable condition under which the malignancy breaks out. This condition then shows in statistics, though the real cause of the malignancy is a general functional exhaustion. In all over-improvements the final collapse is precipitated by some negative, incidental factor.

Even in ordinary diseases similar confusions are frequent. It is now often recognized that contagious diseases afflict an organism only to the extent it is exhausted. Still, particular traumas or germs are generally blamed as causes, while the real cause is organic exhaustion. Particularly when medicine does not recognize a general cause of a disease, all kinds of accidental factors are bound to be blamed as causes.

For instance, black-lung disease is formally seen as caused by coal dust. In fact, it is due to functional exhaustion through over-enjoyment: its real cause is smoking. This has been perhaps best explained by Dr. W. Keith Morgan, of the West Virginia University Medical Center, and Dr. William Barclay, editor of the *Journal of American Medical Association.* They find black-lung assistance to be a mistaken program that actually subsidizes smoking.

Asbestos as a cause of lung cancer has aroused a general panic, fostering emotionally charged reactions. But "nonsmokers exposed to asbestos virtually never have lung cancer."[8] This has been confirmed in research studies by Drs. R. Doll, N. H. Hiatt, J. D. Watson, and J. A. Winsten.[8]

Even the most enraged medical critics here admit that lung cancer from asbestos afflicts smokers fifty-five times more often than nonsmokers. Could not those rare, one-in-fifty, cases of the cancer, for nonsmokers here, also be due to some lifelong overimprovement and be merely precipitated by the asbestos in the lungs?

It is a general problem in cancer etiology to distinguish between its real causes and the merely apparent or *precipitating, secondary causes.* In cancer research it is frequently realized that a factor like a virus appears as a cause although the real cause is different.[11, 12] Nobelist Howard Temin, has explained how in cancer etiology a secondary condition can precipitate the disorder that is causally due to a primary deeper factor.[12] A virus as the cause of cancer has been widely proved and disproved.[8, 9,11] Generally, all kinds of viral infections are facilitated by weakened condition of cells.

By the way, even the dreadful AIDS virus becomes effective only in organisms evidently suffering from extreme functional exhaustion through what moralists would call lives of sin. Millions of people have the virus but only few thousands of the "sinners" suffer the ravages from it.

Cancer is caused by exhaustion of the deepest living functions. Under such a general exhaustion any point in the organism can be the one to yield first. Usually it is the organ most directly affected by the functional "improvement." But even some causally unrelated yet intensely overactivated center of accidental injury or trauma may serve as the point of outbreak for the malignant growth. It was believed for a long time *on the basis of observations* that cancer can be caused by a single trauma, such as a physical blow.

In brief, a merely accidental, strong irritant—say, a pollutant such as asbestos—may appear as a cause of cancer, whereas the actual cancer cause is general functional exhaustion. This may be confirmed also by what is now explained as metastasis.

A cancer is a result not of incidental, transitory happenings but of a very general and *deep organic exhaustion, intensely accumulated by lifelong over-improvements* that are continuously enjoyed. Cancer is too deep and general to be caused by accidental traumas or by organically opposed poisons and pollutants. The organism overcomes, in miraculously purposive ways, even its most complex and dangerous attackers, including pollutants and viruses, if it is not exhausted by human over-enjoyments.

Generally, organic functions are the results of restrictive evolutionary specializations. Over-enjoyment as a continuous assault against restrictions exhausts the limited powers of a function and effaces its restrictive specialization. Then functional exhaustion is followed by a more primitive, undifferentiated growth, as a last, grossly inadequate, remedial effort by the organism to fill the functional vacuum caused by the exhaustion.

Of course, functional over-enjoyments can be complex, and may not amount to enjoyment in the usual sense. Somebody may live in unpleasant conditions and compensate for it by the over-enjoyment of some function. Limited to untasty foods, sufficient in themselves, people may use strong spices and thus contract stomach cancer.

Also, a particular racial group or some individual may be genetically normal at some different, lower level of functional stimulation, and therefore can be overstimulated by improvements that are merely normal for other people.

Inheritance of functional exhaustion as a potential cause of cancer may be important. Children suffer leukemia before they could have accumulated functional over-improvements. *Cancer risk from over-improvement can indeed be inherited.* Use of DES by mothers caused cancer in daughters later. The cases became too clear to be overlooked.

Cancer can be caused by chromosomal changes, which are inheritable. Pleasure controls deepest mechanisms of growth and genetic reproduction. The clearest pleasure-releasing enjoyments, from drugs, change chromosomes. Continuous enjoyment, for decades, of a drug such as aspirin would certainly affect chromosomes, and thus have corresponding, inheritable effects.

A medically strong or refined drug can have extensive as well as subtle effects. Aspirin controls prostaglandins that act through almost every cell and affect most organic reactions. That is why aspirin can relieve so many ills, temporarily. Of course, modern men have even more effective enjoyment means, not necessarily drugs, that can insidiously change the deepest mechanisms, including chromosomes, through decades of use.

The apparent, often merely precipitating, causes of cancer become increasingly confusing and numerous as the real cause is missed. *New carcinogens are seemingly found everywhere, in endless succession.* It is discovered that even our natural foods contain, normally, substances that have been found to be carcinogenic. In fact, "carcinogens" may be present in many foods at incomparably higher levels than in artificial pollutants.[22]

Probably any active material, if administered persistently or in gross amounts, can become the secondary or precipitating factor in cancer. A gross disorganization of cells, harmless in itself, may permit a tendency toward over-improvement to prevail, on the cellular level. This kind of tendency may be strong in the animals used in cancer research, as they are selected because of their innate proneness toward malignancy. We have mentioned the immunological ways of counteracting such tendencies in humans.

Various apparent causes are easily accepted as true when the real cause is not suspected. *Viruses* are persistently blamed as causes of cancer. Virus infection is also inferred from the fact that experimenters in cancer research have contracted cancers. But here we may note that cancer drugs, dealt with by experimenters, have the ambivalent effect of relieving as well as causing cancers.

Other kinds of causal confusion and mystery about cancer are inevitable. It has been sometimes pointed out that cases of cancer have been more numerous in *certain localities*. But localities may have their special, distinct ways and means for attaining "improvements" of life. For instance, a local doctor liberal in prescribing strong improvement drugs may create a pool of people with chromosomal distortions. Thalidomide, a particularly effective improvement drug, was discovered as genetically dangerous only because its genetic effects were so tragically evident from the defects in the infants affected.

But, generally, the paradoxical "improvement" influences are not even looked for—particularly since factors such as enjoyments or pleasure are not considered scientific, though they are the deepest causal sources of everything that organisms do or become.

The functional *"disease" is deceptive* throughout. A physician may conclude that a direct-improvement drug extended the life of his patient. The conclusion is made from comparison between the strongly "diseased" state of the patient and his subsequent improvement from the drug. There is no other way to make such conclusions. Nobody, however, can know how long the patient would have lived without the improvement from the drug, without the interruption of the "disease" that is actually the organism's pressure toward normalcy.

We should always remember that in functional disorders the "disease" is in fact a remedy, though it cannot help much in cancer, which is usually due to total functional exhaustion. The "disease" here is precluded from having its curative effect, before it is too late, by the uncessant addition of "improvements." This is also the case in heart attacks and in the main functional psychoses.

The very first problem in dealing with cancer is its *causal mystery*. Physicians know that discovery of the cause of cancer would be a breakthrough for its treatment. They also know, generally, that the cause here is principally one. This cannot be otherwise if the syndrome of cancer is uniform; and almost everybody can identify cancer from its uniform syndrome. Uncontrolled reproduction of undifferentiated, functionally unrestricted cells is the proximate cause of all malignant growth. This points to the removal or effacement of functional restrictions, through over-enjoyments.

All in all, the etiologic *uniformity* of cancer proves that *one natural, necessarily simple causal principle* is here at work. Of course, the effects of cancer are multiple, and confusing. That is typical of all over-enjoyments; one simple narcotic drug can create a series of negative reactions or complex after-effects.

The point is that medicine, in spite of its collossal, intelligent efforts, is *not coming here closer to discovering the one simple cause*. For as a uniform natural phenomenon cancer can only be governed by one entirely simple causal principle. Natural causal principles are never complex.

The reason for the unbelievable failure of medicine here may be that *the very logic of thinking*, throughout its enormous effort, is exactly contrary to what is true of cancer causally; and this causal fallacy is being institutionalized.

DIABETES. The immediate cause of diabetes seems to be insulin deficiency. But researchers now are discovering that insulin and insulin-like activity is actually higher in the blood of diabetics.[13, 14] We can refer here to research studies by Gerald Reaven, Lester Salans, and Lawrence Power, as well as to earlier work by Kreisberg, Sims, Farrant, Kalkhoff, Trohman, Kosaka, York, Olefsky, Rabinowitz, and Ziesler.[16]

Evidently, diabetics are individuals who are able to increase their insulin activity, to obtain a higher metabolism, as one of the most enjoyable functional "improvements." The opposite effects then become inevitable. Diabetes is a syndrome of the exhaustion of metabolism.

However, the paradoxical insulin effects are not causally understood. Physicians speak of insulin resistance and of habituation to it, or of its antagonists, and of its often-observed high degree of "inefficiency" together with its "striking elevation" in the blood of diabetics.[13, 15, 16] This reveals a general confusion as well as the *causal paradox* in diabetes etiology.

In some cases the amount of insulin in the blood of diabetics may indeed be found to be abnormally low. This happens when the islet cells themselves, which produce insulin, have been overstimulated. Genetic inheritance of the effects of such overstimulation in a previous generation is as possible as is that of the effects of drug use or alcoholism; we shall explain such inheritance later.

The over-improvement etiology of diabetes is equally evident from the way it depends on foods. As everybody knows, carbohydrates make diabetes, initially, worse. The more stimulating, protein-rich foods seem to prevent diabetes. Such rich foods become the regular diet in the more advanced countries, where people can afford them. They bring the enjoyment of metabolic improvements. In poorer countries food consists mostly of carbohydrates, which have the worst direct effect on diabetes. But diabetes is lowest in such poor countries and highest in the rich countries.[13, 15, 16] Of course, some poor people find other means of overstimulation to compensate for their non-stimulating foods or living conditions.

Effects of the treatment of diabetes reveal the same paradox. Insulin injections naturally relieve diabetes. But the action and effects of insulin have remained confusing. [13, 15, 16] Insulin "abuse" creates the worst diabetes reactions;[13, 14] and deaths of diabetics, mostly from heart disease, are often caused by diabetes-treatment drugs.[13, 15, 24]

Actually, the abusive doses of insulin become necessary for the diabetic when the insulin starts losing its effectiveness for him. Further, in functional diseases, death may finally come from failure of some deeper underlying function that is sharply "improved" by a treatment sustaining the vanishing functional enjoyment.

Diabetes-treatment drugs, often more effective than insulin, provide dramatic intitial improvement, but bring equally grave after-effects. Several studies have shown that the risk of deaths from heart disease was doubled by use of sulfonylureas—Orinase, Tolinase, Dymelor or Diabenese.[16, 24] Similar effects have been found for Phenformin. These drugs have been widely used by diabetics for decades. The FDA, AMA, and ADA have warned physicians of the risks.[16, 24] But such drugs bring temporary relief and the feeling of well-being which people associate with improved health.

Typically, diabetes is relieved also by the general improvement drugs—aspirin, antihistamines, sulfa compounds, or vasodilating drugs.[13, 16] Even smoking and alcohol may be enjoyed as immediately beneficial by a diabetic,[13, 16] though they clearly lead to opposite aftereffects.[15, 16]

It is perhaps even more revealing that diabetes can be causally *correlated with psychological difficulties*.[13, 14, 15] Of course, persistently disturbing psychologic difficulties can grow only through emotional vicious-circle over-improvements.

ARTHRITIS. Ease, suppleness, and vigor of our physical movements are, naturally, general sources of enjoyment. Modern life and medicine enable people to improve such enjoyments, on the deepest levels, extensively and skillfully.

The over-improvement aftereffects then are as extensive and intricately varied. Supposedly 50 million people in this country suffer from arthritis; and it affects physical movement in surprisingly varied ways.[17, 18] The numerous "improvements" for the enjoyment of suppleness and vigor of movement lead here to equally numerous opposite processes bringing the arthritic stiffness and exhaustion of tissues, joints, or muscles that create movement.

The over-improvement etiology of arthritis is glaringly confirmed by the *paradoxical effects of cortisone* on arthritis. The initial effects of the administration of cortisone compounds to arthritics can be virtually miraculous.[17, 18] But the subsequent result is opposite effects that bring equally extensive devastation and crippling.[17, 18]

A most revealing explanation of the cortisone effects has been offered by Dr. Philip S. Hench, winner of a Nobel Prize for research related to cortisone treatment.

In his later research he found that it is not the simple deficit of adrenal hormones that causes arthritic reactions, but a change in the circulating hydrocortisone from abnormally high to low levels. He observed that the disease flares up when the cortisone tide ebbs, and that the letdown in long-term cortisone treatment is due to the same phenomenon; obviously, continuous increase in the cortisone level is impossible.

As Dr. Hench commented, his observations required a theory so new that he did not expect other physicians to accept it. In truth, the relative descent, not any actual level, in a given improvement factor causes the negative reactions in all functional disorders. Reaching higher levels of improvement leads to opposite effects because a descent becomes inevitable.

As is now generally known, corticosteroid treatments have been dramatically effective but have led to equally strong negative results and have been abandoned as dangerous.[17, 18] Functional over-improvements by other means cannot succeed any better. Oraflex, a nonsteroid drug, also was wondrously effective, but its after-effects were even more dismaying. It caused sixty deaths in England and more than thirty in this country.[22, 25] In all functional disorders, a skillful pursuit of improvement in some function may exploit its underlying, deeper, living mechanism and thus cause its fatal failure.

The dependence of arthritis on *emotions* is generally noticed.[17, 18] Curious remissions and exacerbations in the arthritic syndrome come together with emotional experiences.[17] We may repeat that unmanageable emotional difficulties can result only from emotional over-improvements.

General improvement drugs, used as remedies for various kinds of pain, offer temporary relief from arthritis symptoms.[17, 18] *Such drugs provide reactive improvements* of a wide range because they affect more general organic functions, including those of movement. Consequently their after-effects can be extensively varied and confusingly subtle for the arthritis syndrome as well. Arthritis is a disease as frequent and varied for modern man as are the "improvement" means available to him.

It should be noted that functional over-improvements are possible even while a person lives through unpleasant hardships. In his efforts to lessen a hardship the person may over-improve the corresponding functional sources of reactions. This explains why people who work or play hard, or are exposed to rigors of climate, suffer more from arthritis.

But if hardships are met without over-improvements, with normal natural, painful reactions, no disorder is incurred. Animals in their natural adjustments do not suffer from arthritis. Moreover, no logically direct relation has ever been established between arthritis and physical exertion, climatic conditions, or any other factor.[17, 18]

Drugs, of course, are the most effective means of over-improvements, of avoiding natural unpleasant but necessary reactions. The widely used *aspirin* is found to have a specific affinity for relieving arthritic reactions. Consequently, it may be a cause of arthritic effects as results of over-improvement. No wonder that arthritis is so widespread.

Another etiologic confusion has to be mentioned. Generally, whatever the organic processes involved in a function, they are carried out by organic tissues. Therefore, aftereffects of intense functional over-improvement include some weakened or impaired tissues. Such tissues are taken care of, absorbed, by the white blood cells.

Particularly in our physical movements and their mechanisms, the involvement of organic tissues must be significant. Correspondingly, in arthritis, tissue impairment is equally extensive, and the white blood cells may remove significant amounts of the tissues involved in the movement mechanisms. In the absence of a causal explanation for arthritis in general, it may seem that the organism here is destroying its own normal tissues.

An auto-immune response thus has been blamed as a possible cause of arthritis.[17] Disagreement with this view, expectedly, has been strong.[18] Considering the virtually miraculous purposiveness of everything organisms do, it is inconceivable that they would have built-in mechanisms for harming themselves.

We do act against ourselves, as we drive ourselves into functional exhaustion. But we do so by pursuing enjoyments, not direct harm.

PEPTIC ULCER. Functional over-improvement etiology is evident in peptic ulcers. They clearly depend on emotions,[19, 20] which can have disordered, stressful effects only through over-enjoyment. Also, ulcers increase together with improvements of life.

Peptic ulcer is a typical disease of people in more advanced countries and of individuals enjoying more successful careers or affectively richer, more involved lives.[19, 20] Such people improve their reactions more perfectly and deeply, by exploiting the underlying functions. Of course, occasionally poorer people too find means of compensatory, affective improvement that are strong and subtle enough to cause ulcer.

Usually, however, ulcer is found to be a disorder typically afflicting executives and professionals.[19, 20] But proofs have been controversial. Here, as in all functional diseases, the personality is decisive, and the executives at the very top are mostly people of steady, balanced character, averse to overindulgences.

But generally executives and professionals are more resourceful in obtaining reactive improvements, and therefore suffer from ulcer more often. Revealingly, in experiments, the "executive" monkey who could avoid shocks by pressing a lever developed peptic ulcer, while the one who could not remained free of it.[20] Similarly, people do not develop ulcers when they live through unavoidable stressful conditions, of war, disaster, or deadly threat.[20, 27]

Drugs are recognized causes of ulcer.[19, 20] They of course are used for reactive enjoyment or relief, attained through improvement of underlying functions. Strong gastric-acid activity has been always found as typical of youthful vigor.

In peptic ulcer a determining factor is *a conflict* between the person's "improvement" drive and the incapacity or resistance of his organism to meet it. In the simplest physiologic terms, an ulcer is caused by excessive gastric-acid and pepsin activity eroding the stomach wall, which remains inert and does not secrete enough of the corresponding, protective mucous substances.

Higher peptic and stomach-acid activity, offering more intense enjoyable vigor, is resorted to in the case of stress, to create additional energy and reactive improvement. But a conflict may result here. Sometimes the organism has to remain generally restrictive functionally. This may also be a reaction to some other or previous over-improvement. Then the stomach wall does not respond to the requirements of the "improvement" through the stomach-acid increase.

Partial necrosis or vascular anoxia of the stomach wall is recognized in stomach ulcers.[19] In experiments, inactivation of the stomach by cooling, tranquilizers, or clamping leads to ulceration if, concurrently, increased acidity is induced, by cortisone or by the requirements of some exertion.[19]

The etiology of peptic ulcer thus appears to be simple. But no logically clear causal correlations are found for it, because all affective reactions are causally paradoxical. Ulcer remains an extremely complex disorder.[19, 20]

The conflict of emotional reactions and their decisive role in ulcer causation have always been recognized.[19, 20] Peace of mind is therefore seen as a desired goal. The direct means for enjoying it, such as drugs, alcohol, or smoking, are often shown to be rather beneficial.[19] But the same means are also found to cause ulcer.[20]

In sum, logical causal explanations of ulcer fail,[19, 20] because the functional responses as well as the negative emotions or stresses work here in seemingly paradoxical ways. Apparent reactive improvements lead to opposite effects, throughout the various reactions and conflicts in the etiology of peptic ulcer.

The conflict between "improvement" and resistance to it, in peptic ulcer, explains some peculiarities about ulcers. For instance, an ulcer may disappear during summer and winter, but may be worse in spring and fall. The reason is that no conflict persists in summer, when the whole organism yields to over-enjoyment, nor in winter, when all over-enjoyment tendencies have subsided.

Also, cancer risk is low while the ulcer continues, because there is no general, unopposed over-enjoyment. For a converse reason, cancer-prone or Type A persons have ulcers rarely, because they yield more generally, unrestrictedly, to functional over-enjoyments.

We may say a word about the main etiologic aspects of the *prevention and treatment* of functional diseases. The cause of chronic diseases is functional exhaustion, at the deepest levels, which results from functional over-improvements. Our most usual functional over-enjoyments, such as smoking and overeating, are the most important clear causes of these diseases.

Smoking is so clearly the cause of heart disease and cancer that legislation now requires a warning about it. Overeating is an equally clear cause of the chronic diseases;[1, 2, 3] this has now been officially established. These two most general over-enjoyments of modern men can serve best as examples etiologically.

Dozens of experiments involving the *underfeeding of animals* have shown that it can lower the risks, by up to 80 percent, of malignancy and chronic diseases. The longevity of the underfed animals almost doubled. Also, the underfed animals were more alert and potentially quite vigorous.

Overweight is found to be a main cause in all chronic diseases.[1, 2]. People know intuitively that they are digging their graves with their teeth.[3]

But overweight cannot be causally understood or effectively controlled without insight into its paradoxical reactive etiology. People overeat to enjoy metabolic stimulation. The foods they seek most are pleasant because they intensify and accelerate metabolism, and therefore intially reduce weight. Scores of popular weight-reducing programs have variously exploited this fact. Such programs can be quite successful at the beginning. But they fail in the end because they increase metabolic exhaustion by over-stimulation. Thus the dieter has to consume even more food, in the end, to derive the necessary, normal metabolic stimulation.

Some individuals accumulate weight even when they eat little. This has puzzled the experts. Naturally, a particular person may suffer from an innate metabolic inefficiency. The stimulation he derives from food is not sufficient to make him exert, move, or work enough to expend the calories consumed.

Such a person particularly should avoid increased, over-stimulating, metabolic improvements, which can only add to his already critical inefficiency. Any functional response decreases after continued increase in stimulation. But experts proceed only by the logic that stimulation brings improvement, which shows in immediate, experimental observation.

The *paradox of stimulation* causality explains why people in more advanced countries suffer so excessively from overweight. They consume the highly pleasant foods that intensify metabolism most. They therefore suffer from the aftereffects of overstimulation. In poorer countries people consume non-stimulating, protein-poor foods that diet experts definitely find to be causes of overweight. But people who have to live on such non-stimulating foods have no overweight problems.

In the confusion, the consumption of *fats* is blamed. But the blubbery kinds of fats, the only ones that could directly, logically increase the similar fats in overweight organisms, are totally excluded from our affluent diet. We thoroughly avoid such fats, because they are unbearably tasteless.

Only poor people—Eskimos, Indians, blacks, or similar groups studied—eat such fats, and they suffer from overweight least. Finally, it has been discovered, through longer-range experiments, that the untasty, non-stimulating, polyunsaturated fats are preferable in weight-reducing diets.[28, 29] Direct, short-range, experimental observations, of course, still show such fats, as all non-stimulating foods, to be less weight-reducing than the rich, stimulating foods.

Typically, *alcohol* is the best means for burning off fats in the body and thus for initial weight loss. Experiments show that the effects of alcohol are equivalent to those of exercise. But the end result is that alcohol induces overweight, very obviously. Experts then blame the clearly insignificant calorie amounts consumed with alcoholic drinks.

Also, the *"junk" foods* are at first stimulating, but then have the opposite effect.[28, 29] They are artificially concentrated, in their stimulation ingredients, to the point of resembling artificial means or drugs.

All told, overweight is the most frequent, grave syndrome of functional exhaustion through our main, nutritional over-enjoyments. But in their direct effects the better nutritional *enjoyments are clearly beneficial.* Even the National Research Council has concluded that "good food should be enjoyed"[3] and that alcohol also can be enjoyed, in moderation.[3, 6]

In fact, most experimental observations show that *alcohol's effects* can be beneficial. This is one of the modern discoveries in "scientific" cardiology.[1, 5, 7] But now a study by the NHLBI, on eight thousand men, shows that alcohol increases the risk of fatal strokes by 300 percent. Of course, many habitual drinkers end up by living only half-awake much of their time. This can have conserving effects. But scientists see mostly the stimulation from alcohol as beneficial.

In a noted study at the Baylor College of Medicine, the beneficial, stimulating effects of alcohol for sedentary men were analyzed in depth. For such men a couple of drinks were found to be as good as jogging.[25] The researchers, though, were reluctant to recommend drinking generally.

Foods that are most stimulating are, of course, *meats, particularly beef*. Such meat is consumed at the highest rates in the United States and in Finland. In both countries cardiac death rates are the highest in the world.[3, 5] A beef diet has also been statistically related to cancer of the colon, which is the second most fatal cancer.

In poor countries where people cannot enjoy exciting, invigorating foods, the incidence of chronic heart disease is correspondingly lower. This has been observed in epidemiologic studies of African tribes or of the people in China, India, South Korea, Yugoslavia, Greece, and in other Southern European countries.[1, 5] Cancer-incidence rates are closely similar to those of heart disease.[1, 2,5] Vegetarian and high-fiber diets are the least enjoyable or stimulating. They correlate with the lowest rates of these diseases.

Food is the principal causal factor in our main functional diseases. Over-enjoyments, as functional over-improvements, are impossible without a corresponding nutrition, by which everything in the body is fueled and built. But because of the causal paradox of nutritional "improvements," *scientists mostly do not find foods to be causally connected with diseases*.[1, 28, 29]

Certainly over-enjoyment of food depends mostly on how much of it is eaten. Simply, enjoyment is the decisive factor here as well, as it is in all functional disorders. But scientists do not deal with such a "non-scientific," commonplace fact as enjoyment, ultimately because of the paradoxical, opposite-causality logic of feelings. The decisive role of foods in the functional diseases is thus missed and misinterpreted.

For instance, the exact daily requirements of the proper foods are stressed, whereas experiments on starvation diets show that even inadequate or deficient, *restricted* food intake is best for health and longevity.[6, 22] In these experiments the life of animals is prolonged particularly clearly when some of the "required" food ingredients is diminished or excluded.

The general result is that no valid, non-controversial science on nutrition exists. Nutritionists complain that no exact policy in the field has been set.[28, 29]

Governmental agencies and scientists can merely rely on common sense about *"good"* foods and *"adequate"* nutrition.[1, 3, 5] But common beliefs about foods can be very misleading, because of the paradox of functional "improvements" providing an initial increased vigor and feelings of well-being. A "good," enjoyable food becomes the primary source of the continuously added vicious-circle over-improvements that cause the functional diseases of which three fourths of us die.

As a result of the admitted causal mystery about our chief functional diseases, scientists rely on general, *seemingly obvious truths about what are good and healthy foods.* These are always the foods that bring the best "improvement" in feelings of well-being. Thus *the very first source of our chief diseases* is instead viewed as desirable in our "scientific" thinking.

Other causal factors of our main, functional diseases can be measured by their *stress syndrome.* These diseases are caused by functional exhaustion or impoverishment, which shows as stress. All chronic diseases are found to be connected with stress.[1, 3, 10, 25] However, it is generally recognized that the decisive factor is not any objectively stressful conditions but the way a person reacts.[1, 3, 24, 25]

We have explained why the people who can avoid stress most efficiently suffer from excessive self-deepening stress. Because of the inexorable organic limitedness, functional impoverishment has to follow over-improvements.

In an extensive experiment in 1974 at the NIMH, a "paradise" for four thousand mice was built, providing in overabundance everything mice could want. The animals gradually lost their natural drives and died out. Conversely, rats exposed to stressful situations developed fewer tumors, in experiments by Dr. Benjamin H. Newberry of the Kent State University. People cannot be experimented with in such ways. But a study at a large New England nursing home by a Yale University team showed that a group of residents provided with the most carefree environment had twice as high a death rate as the other residents.

The clearest functional over-improvements are provided by all kinds of drugs. The "improvement" here is certainly attained in ways that are far more effective than nature can ever provide. Understandably, people in more developed countries such as ours live virtually in a medical-drug culture. In Congressional hearings of June 1983 on medical-drug use, even supporters of drug use testified that drug abuse and overuse have become intolerably extensive.[25] Of course, a drug is "abused" when it becomes ineffective because of its continued, intensified use, which starts bringing opposite reactions.

We are plagued by increasing stress and hypertension, exhaustion and depression.[24, 25] *But we have been using drugs against these same reactions at incredibly high rates.* The best-selling drugs—such as Valium, Tagamet, Inderal, or Tylenol—can serve as examples.[25] We are suffering from exactly those reactions we have been overcoming, with the strongest means provided by our tremendous science and industry.

Prevention and treatment of functional diseases would be *causally simple, though very difficult to carry out.* Almost everybody knows that by stopping the enjoyments of smoking, overeating, drinking, or inactivity he can eliminate risks of chronic diseases. But when it comes to precise causal understanding, the confusion is total. Functional improvement by whatever means, even by the above enjoyments, is experimentally always directly beneficial. It clearly provides organic, reactive responses of ease and well-being.

The feelings of improved health or well-being here become deceptive. They are viewed as signs of health itself by the patient and by his doctor, though the same sense of well-being is derived from smoking, alcohol, or drugs as well as from the enjoyment of the rich foods that we overeat.

Actually, the role of physicians should be to discover and avert the various extensive and unsuspected over-improvements that people so eagerly invent and enjoy. This, of course, would require *a virtual reversal of causal thinking* about the great modern improvements of life. With a new, seemingly paradoxical causal logic, physicians should try to find out, for each patient, what particular over-improvements are enjoyed by him—and are causing his disease.

Such treatments would not be easy. Perhaps the decisive difficulty would be the attitude of patients. A physician who denies relief or prescribes medicines that make one feel sicker would not be popular. People seek and exploit all kinds of "improvements" and use drugs to prodigious extent only for the purpose of direct, reactive improvement.

Furthermore, *the distinction between natural, organic improvement and over-improvement can be difficult,* since both bring feelings of well-being. But such difficulties could be easily solved by our phenomenally efficient science if the paradoxical cause of functional diseases was recognized. We have indicated the awe-inspiring efficiency of modern medicine when it is dealing with causally understood or technically clear problems. Once the paradoxical, admittedly mysterious causality of our functional diseases is understood, physicians will invent hundreds of ingenious ways to discover and deal with disease-causing over-improvements.

For instance, if an arthritic has been taking aspirin, which always "improves" or alleviates arthritic reactions, then aspirin is a cause of his arthritis and should be avoided. Many foods and drugs, as well as other ways and means, may bring such easily discoverable over-improvements and may be found to be enjoyed by given patients having other functional diseases.

Such means may be as varied as are the reactions in functional diseases. But the discovery of the causal connection can be as simple as the natural causes of the etiologically uniform functional diseases. Those causes are, simply, functional over-enjoyments. We easily diagnose our complex hangovers from "sinful" enjoyments that we have learned to recognize as harmful through our cultural tradition.

In our scientific era similar diagnoses could be made scientifically, and as easily. Then the remedy would be simple, though inevitably most painful: discover the "improvement" means used in each case and stop it.

Certainly, the great practical difficulty is to make people abandon their overindulgences. But medicine should at least move in the right direction. It should try to prevent rather than help modern man in his prodigious exploitation of his inevitably limited organic functions, in his pursuit of feelings of well-being or freedom from stress, through his unique improvement skills and means.

Medicine should establish, for the public and doctors, a new, strange understanding that even experimentally clear improvements, in our functional reactions and in our feelings of well-being, are also the causes of our main diseases.

Modern "Improvement" Skills and Medicines, Worse than Bloodletting

Modern medicine is enormously effective, awe-inspiring when it deals with problems that are causally understood. But in the field of our main, functional diseases medicine is presently not even a science. Here it lacks causal understanding, as is now generally admitted; we have seen this for all these diseases.

What is worse, modern medicine proceeds in this field, as we have explained, with a causal logic exactly contrary to the actual causality. Consequently, present medicine, with its extreme efficiency, is more dangerous than were the medical blunders of the past, which also grew because medicine did not have causal understanding.

People of three centuries ago were as intelligent as we are and as eager to be scientific. The richest of them, who could afford it, sought all the exquisite, absurd skills of their physicians. Those "skills," though, were not much worse than mere inefficiencies born of confusion. In contrast, our medical skills are perfected by an immensely proficient and consistent science whose *direct-improvement logic*, however, makes it proceed exactly *contrary to what should be done.*

Consequently our functional fatal diseases are deepened by our scientific skills with tremendous "efficiency." It can be said that the medical treatments, particularly the medicines, that we now seek for our chronic diseases, are worse than were bloodletting and the other highly praised expert methods of the past, perfected without causal understanding.

All our medicines and skills are aimed at providing direct, "scientifically" or experimentally clear improvements, which make the functional diseases worse in the end. If scientists and physicians had the causal understanding of these presently mysterious diseases, they would be appalled by what is happening. They would be outraged, to begin with, about every one of the advertisements of improvement drugs that are now flooding our general and medical information media. All our direct-improvement treatments and drugs for the chronic diseases, costing us hundreds of billions of dollars yearly, would be seen as worse than useless.

The present treatments and drugs providing the improvements are changing the reactively effective functions of the organism, of its organs, cells, and tissues. What is the causal result of it?

If not improved, our natural reactions, of pain or disease, guide the organism in the avoidance of harm and in the attainment of health or normalcy. Evidently, elimination of such pain or "diseased" reactions, by our medical treatments and drugs, *is like blinding a man or getting him drunk* when he has to face a complex, dangerous situation.

It is scientifically decisive to understand the role of organic reactions. We may repeat that man as a conscious, planning being seeks, before everything else, the "improvement" of his reactions. That is why he incurs the functional diseases of which animals are free.

Probably *the greatest of all dangers* to man lies in his increasing *capacity to "improve" or control his reactions*, through their underlying functions. He not only wants to overcome his inexorably limited organic normalcy. He also feels as threats to his health the very reactions, the painful restrictions or stress, by which the organism saves him from disease and from virtual self-destruction.

But modern physicians are, in effect, helping us to increase or enjoy further what we see as improvements and to avoid even more the naturally necessary, negatively felt, "diseased" reactions. Medicine is thus promoting what man already does to excess, and to his gravest danger. Conversely, medicine is suppressing the natural "disease" reactions which save us.

A decisive fact here is that even when physicians are dealing with precise laboratory findings about functional diseases, they are actually dealing only with organic *reactions*. Then, with a logic contrary to the opposite causality of reactions, physicians can only do more harm. Here we have to explain a pivotal misconception.

It is universally assumed that a physician treating a functional disease removes or counteracts its cause. In truth, even when the physician obtains detailed analyses or tests of body products and processes, he only gets data about *reactions* of organs, cells, and tissues.

All organs and tissues are as inexorably limited to their predetermined normalcy as is the whole organism. They preserve this normalcy in the same way as the organism does. If they are functionally "improved," through increased stimulation, they subsequently have to respond by opposite, "diseased" restrictions to restore their normalcy. The whole *paradox of improvement and disease* is the rule here as well.

The physician can never properly use the non-paradoxical, scientific logic here and treat the causes themselves of functional diseases. He could do so only if he could deal with the biochemical factors in their huge multiplicity, causally decisive at every point and instant, and if he understood the principle or causal mechanism of life in the first place. No genius in the world can deal with such a multiplicity, causally interdependent in all its infinite details throughout the organism.

In brief, every physician is dealing *only with reactions* of organs, cells, and tissues, or with their products determined by the reactions, when he treats functional diseases.

A functional "improvement" obtained by stimulation thus seems experimentally or analytically to increase organic well-being, while it deepens the functional disease. And the removal of "diseased" restrictive reactions becomes the medical goal, though these reactions work to restore organic normalcy. Of course, patients, who always identify their feelings of well-being with health, are excited by the medical wonders they enjoy. While enjoying the wondrous improvements, they die, often suddenly, from the *unexplained* modern diseases.

Another general misconception has to be pointed out. It is generally assumed that organic processes can be improved, changed, or added to by advanced medical means.

In truth, *even all our best scientists* working together and using every skill *could not create or purposively change the tiniest organically integrated living tissue.* To do so would be equal to creating life, as an integrated living process. Man can change anything living, tissues or cells, only by destroying something in them or by evoking their reactions, which are governed by the paradoxical logic of reversals.

A prime example of the wonders of modern medicine in changing or "improving" organic functions is the use of *drugs*. Even the most complex drug is ludicrously crude in comparison with biological processes determined by myriad purposive interactions. But drugs can provide wondrous improvement effects. They do so by eliminating functional restrictions or silencing organic demands, through stimulation or tranquilization.

No purposive complexity is necessary in stopping, destroying, or inactivating life or its processes. Knocking out one element in a restrictive organic process can produce a selective stimulating or tranquilizing effect.

Of course, the organism then has to restore its normalcy, by opposite processes. Even if such normalcy may occasionally look deficient, it still is billions of times superior to anything that man-made compounds or artificial intervention could create. Even the lowest living form is ungraspably miraculous in its causal complexity involving endless multiple details.

Every drug has "side" effects.[1, 2] They are actually the *inevitable opposite reactions*, but are not recognized as such because the opposite causality is never thought of; it is too "illogical." The opposite effects can indeed be confusing. As opposites to the enjoyed improvement they may seem the last things to be connected with it, in their every aspect. Also, the opposite reactions may find expression through different organs or parts of body, since all functional enjoyments engage the whole organism. Exciting food enjoyed through the stomach affects the liver, or alcohol taken as a drink causes a headache.

Drugs that provide direct, often spectacular "cures" have been discovered for every functional disorder—weakened heartbeat, hypertension, arterial constriction, diabetes, arthritis, ulcer, or headache.[1, 2] Only, the "side" effects have been worse than the cure. Most of these drugs have been abandoned. This is the usual story, repeated endlessly.

New, improved, more deeply effective drugs are then invented. The drugs now created for functional diseases are aimed mostly at overcoming the inevitable deeper and deeper "side" effects. Such drugs in particular work by the suppression of functional restrictions at their very sources. These drugs are not even intended to rebuild or supply anything in the organism. They act rather through nerves or hormones, in providing complex "improvements" on the deepest levels. *The opposite effects then are equally deep and insidious.*

The reactions here in particular are improved by the inevitably disorganizing and exhaustive drug effects on the underlying functions reached at their basal causal connections with the source of organic life itself. The vicious-circle functional exhaustion and malignancy here are, therefore, bound to be fatal.

However inventive may be the means of reactive, functionally created improvement, they unavoidably have equivalent opposite after-effects. The return by the organism to its normalcy is its never-ceasing purpose. It is ridiculous to expect that man-made chemical or physical means could crete an adaptive improvement in organic normalcy. Even a tiny change would require dealing with billions of organic processes interacting in purposively precise ways at every instant.

Whatever the normalcy maintained by an organism, that normalcy remains miraculously supreme in its own preservation. Even if some adaptive, integrated changes in it were attained, opposite causality would again extend to them, in maintenance of the new normalcy as organic sameness.

But what about *improvements attained by organic ways and means*, instead of man-made, cruder, chemical and physical ways and means? In biofeedback or yoga meditation the organism acts on itself. In treatments by hormones, organically created means are used. Endorphins, produced by the organism itself, can be used to control neural pain reactions.

Methods like *biofeedback* are, again, not intended to change anything in the organism permanently or to supply it with some needed substance. The organism is merely stimulated or tranquilized by internal controls, instead of drugs. This would be also true for the use of means such as hormones or endorphins, acting as mere regulators of reactions.

The aims and results of all such treatments, including biofeedback, are improvements in organic dynamics without permanent change in the underlying normalcy of the organism. Whether such improvements are attained by internal controls or by drugs makes no difference causally. *However the "improvement" in organic dynamics is created*, once it has been enjoyed, the organism returns to the normalcy that it maintains by *opposite processes*. Negative, stressful after-effects from improvements by endorphins and biofeedback are already regularly discovered.[26]

Hormone treatments can be dramatic in their improvement effects. (Then their opposite, crippling effects are equally dramatic, as has become notably evident with the cortisone treatments of arthritis.) But the body itself can always easily produce more hormones than it may ever need.

Hormones are sufficient in extremely minute amounts. The pituitary hormone can evoke physiologic responses even if diluted to one part in a hundred million. Adrenalin can act in a dilution three times as great. Prostaglandins produced by the body in one day weigh one tenth of a milligram, enough to cover a printed dot. Moreover, the dominant hormones consist of steroids, made of elements most plentiful in the body. Also, they are so simple that they can be produced or substituted for synthetically.

Evidently, *hormones are only signaling devices* or triggering switches operated by the whole incredibly complex organic system. It would be sheer folly to start managing the switches in a system of living processes that no genius can causally analyze, create, or direct.

In a word, the organism, conserving its ungraspable, complex normalcy, reacts by opposite processes to the "improvements" by hormones or by any other internal or external means. The organism is too unfathomable in its multiple complexity to be purposively manipulated by man, particularly with the use of a logic contrary to the causality of organic reactions.

Even when drugs are taken supposedly to supply chemicals such as iron or iodine, the desired reaction is attained through stimulation. The biochemical integration of chemical compounds in the organism is too complex to be helped by artificial intervention; all living processes are as intricate as life itself.

When your organism needs some chemical, you will crave for it and will find it through foods in ways that are as uncannily clever and involved as are our responses in tasting our foods. An artificially made chemical cannot help here. It can serve far more readily as a stimulant, by disrupting organic restrictions.

Of course, drugs and chemicals are helpful when they counteract poisons, destroy bacteria, or supply some simple element that body lacks, as in the rare diseases of phenylketonuria or galactosemia. But here the causes are simple and clearly understood. Such diseases are organic and do not belong with the admittedly mysterious functional diseases. The treatment here is more like a correction of a physical deficiency than dealing with the causally unexplained, analytically ungraspable, functional disorders—which are our paramount unsolved problem.

Incidentally, the simple inoculation or vaccination is by far the most successful of all medical treatments. It, revealingly, works by inflicting difficulties on organisms, so that their capacities are expanded. The whole evolution has worked by the imposition of difficulties and restrictions on organisms. Unfortunately, modern man and medicine generally proceed by a contrary logic, aiming at the removal of restrictions and reactive difficulties, particularly through the use of medicines.

Could medicines be used in a differnt, opposite way—namely *for the imposition of restrictions* or the prevention of overimprovements?

Even crude chemical means can easily block living processes. Unfortunately, drugs are now used to stop organic restrictions. But in causally opposite treatments, a blocking of releases could accumulate their reserves as sources of functional capacities. Again, people would find such restrictions unbearable and would feel them as causing diseased stress.

Various kinds of *blockers* are known in modern medicine. Expectedly, they are generally used to stop reactive restrictions. But with the prevailing causal confusion, physicians may start using drugs that have the unintended effects of preventing the over-improvements when such drugs are found, accidentally, to be helpful in the end.

For instance, the beta blocker Inderal reduces the rate of heartbeat and the force of the heart's contractions. Dr. William Friedewald, Director of the HLBI, finds that the use of propranolol blockers has saved thousands of lives in this country.[25] But all the "side" effects of the beta blocker are, admittedly, not yet known.[25] It is difficult to say whether the effect here is only a restriction of "improvements" or also an added tranquilization. Seemingly curative effects would come from such tranquilization, though its "side" effects would worsen the disease.

We may add that even diseases and disorders not belonging to the functional, main modern diseases may be mistreated if the paradox of reactions is not understood.

Any diesease, disturbance, or injury may evoke restrictive, "negative" reactions as the inherently limited organism tries to establish sources for new adjustments. Such "negative" reactions, by organs or cells, then show in tests and analyses as the immediate, seemingly adverse causes of the disease syndrome. Thus life-saving reactions may be treated as ills to be removed, even with all the advanced, experimental, laboratory methods, in nonchronic diseases and traumas as well.

Conversely, organ or cell reactions in these cases may show, under analyses, as particularly helpful if they have stimulative effects and thus provide strong energy releases. Thus, an increase in *such reactions would appear as desirable*, even in nonchronic traumas, *though it would lead to physiologic exhaustion.*

Of course, physicians are too knowledgeable to make mistakes that would be obvious to good common sense. Still, as scientists they accept, in their analyses and conclusions, that the functional processes they are observing have to be improved.[1, 2] Yet physicians are actually observing only *reactions* by cells or tissues; and improvement of reactions leads to disorder or functional exhaustion.

Even providing a clearly more "normal" reaction in the case of an abnormal organic condition, upon exhaustion, is harmful. The exhaustion can be a result of illness, injury, or aging, as well as of functional "improvements" through stimulation.

In the world of reactions, the first causal truths are opposite causality and organic limitedness, from which that causality derives. The paradoxical causal logic of these principles should be constantly kept in mind in every analysis or experiment. Yet it is not even mentioned in medical scientific learning.[1, 2] Nor is it realized that even the best laboratory analyses reveal only reactions by organs, cells, or tissues.[1, 2]

In summing up, we may emphasize the *ominous role of modern medicine* in the field of our main, functional diseases. Particularly is the use of direct-improvement drugs a fatal danger, since it intensifies the vicious-circle of "improvement" and exhaustion with enormous efficiency.

Such drugs, or similar means and skills, can be made tremendously effective by our fabulous science. They can be so exquisite that they cannot be compared with narcotic drugs. They can have incomparably subtler, imperceptible, as well as more extensive and deeper, effects, so that immediate, particular after-effects are not felt. The inevitable opposite processes and the vicious-circle exhaustion then are also equally extensive and insidiously deep. If narcotic drugs can occasionally lead to fatal functional exhaustion, our medical direct-improvement drugs lead to it with incomparably greater, subtle effectiveness.

The same is true of all means and skills that provide us with such efficienct direct reactive improvements, attained through the exploitation of underlying functions. The highly effective improvements here are as convincing as they are deceptive. Even a narcotic drug provides experimentally perfect improvement; when the famous Osler called morphine "God's own medicine," he had clear, experimental proofs for it.

Our chief, chronic diseases are studied only under the "scientific" logic.[1, 2] Physicians learn every day about ways and means of direct organic improvements as well as about the "normal" physiologic processes. *Physicians have never even heard of the central effect of the organic limitedness—the opposite causality of reactions* and their underlying functions. Yet it is only *reactions*, by cells or tissues, that the physician is actually observing and dealing with even in his detailed experimental tests or analyses and in his use of their results.

Furthermore, we have seen how *mere reactions*, in functional diseases, drive modern man to over-improve and thus to exhaust his deepest, corresponding organic functions in a virtually limitless, continuing vicious circle.

But medicine as a scientifically logical discipline cannot recognize that experimentally, analytically clear improvements become sources of disease. Nor is it recognized that *a functional "disease" is the organism's pressure toward normalcy.* Nature would not repeat such pressures if they did not serve an organic purpose. The causal mystery definitely and admittedly deepens; and treatment is hardly possible without causal understanding—still less with a logic contrary to the actual causation.

Even the medical establishment itself recognizes the failure. We may refer here to Franz J. Ingelfinger, the former editor of the *New England Journal of Medicine*, our leading medical publication. He estimated that 80 percent of patients are unaffected by treatment while only 10 percent are clearly helped and 9 percent made sicker by it.[26] Of course, medicine can be fully successful in the treatment of the nonchronic diseases, which now afflict about 10 percent of us.

The clearest recognition of failure by physicians themselves is, of course, their general *admission that the functional diseases are not yet causally understood.* We have seen this for each of the functional diseases.

Physicians know that they cannot treat a disease without understanding its cause. The effort to discover the causes of the chief functional diseases has been immense. But the result has been only mere hopes that the future will bring explanations. Above all, the generally admitted lack of causal understanding reveals that the very direction of thinking in modern medicine is fundamentally wrong.

For otherwise the causes of these diseases would be immediately discovered. They would be found to be self-evidently, primitively simple. Each of these diseases is, as we have seen, *uniform* in the syndrome or effects of its cases. This proves that each functional disease is governed by *one natural, necessarily simple* causal principle. That simple cause, in each case, is man's intense drive to "improve" the inexorably limited, unimprovable organism.

All in all, we have tried to make understandable, for the first time, *how the reactive improvements that medicine wants us to enjoy actually cause the chief functional diseases* of which three-fourths of us die.

Perhaps this is easier to understand by thinking of how reactive improvements do reverse. This is evident from the use of drugs or from any other over-enjoyment; increased avoidance of stress, by drugs, leads to deeper stress. Further, the mere pursuit of feelings, such as those of freedom from stress, make modern man exploit, prodigiously, his deepest functions as the sources of these feelings.

The vicious-circle worsening through improvement explains how that exploitation leads to incredible functional exhaustion. This is as clear here as in all reactively efficient, addictive over-improvements, and is, of course, due to organic limitedness.

Modern medicine cannot recognize organic limitedness in its full and most important, opposite-causality aspect. Medicine would have to choose here, in its insights, between the humanly impossible logic of this causality and the contrary causal logic of our only exact sciences. It has chosen the latter.[1, 2] In all sciences about man still the same choice is made; they have remained "soft" sciences.

The ultimate reason for this choice is the causal prejudice of man, rooted in his inability to recognize the organic limitedness that makes his value pursuits futile. That prejudice is humanly wholesome and inevitable. It enables men to survive.

But recognition of the organic limitedness would be the key to understanding and dealing with organic functions, which are now so recklessly exploited by modern man, with epidemically fatal results.

The gravest, even fatal, functional worsening can result from nothing more than clear and certain added reactive improvements. This is evident from effects of the "divine" morphine as well as of other drugs and improvement means. And any scientific, experimental observation shows such effects to be clear, logically direct improvements.

III

ALCHEMISTIC CAUSAL LOGIC IN PSYCHIATRY AND PSYCHOLOGY

Scientists, when they have to think practically, know that our positive reactions, such as satisfactions or interests, are the sources of our positive motivations and capacities. They also know that such positive reactions are pleasant. Thus our most precious mental resources logically seem to be available to us with perfect ease, with the enjoyment of pleasure. The only requirement would seem to be knowledge of the right procedure or formula. This inherently alchemistic causal thinking is inevitably followed in psychiatry and psychology, as they proceed only according to the usual causal logic, imitated from the exact, physical sciences—the logic of increase of values by addition.

Only the "illogical" but factually true opposite causality of reactions can explain why every positive reaction such as pleasure release has to be "paid" for by exactly equal restrictions which are for man the experiences most difficult to bear. But the opposite causality has no place in the only scientism presently known. Under the logic of this scientism values come from similar, not opposite, causal sources and increase through direct, mathematically logical additions, as is expected in every experiment.

However, as we have seen, a direct increase in positive reactions, in satisfactions, decreases their potential. Mental disorders are caused by a particular exhaustion of that potential. This results from excessive, increased enjoyment of positive reactions as satisfactions or pleasures. Such over-enjoyments are clearly evident as the causes of psychoses and neuroses. Almost every reactive improvement drug enjoyed by regular drug-users has some or most of the effects of psychoses and neuroses.

The reason why psychoses and neuroses generate themselves so intensely and insidiously is that they are caused by the strongest, most general organic force, the drive for pleasure. Mental patients are mentally weak individuals who yield to enjoyments of pleasure or satisfactions excessively, without effective restraints. That is why they incur in equal excess the negative reactions which constitute their disease.

But psychiatry, as a logical science, proceeds only by the logic that the extreme reactive negativity of mental patients should be counteracted directly, by an increase in their positive reactions in various ways. This logic is senseless. Mental patients would do nothing more readily than enjoy more of the pleasant, positive reactions. They have already enjoyed pleasant reactions to extremes.

As to psychology, it proceeds by the same direct, "scientific" logic, which axiomatically governs its experimental methods. Every experiment is conducted and controlled under the usual mathematical logic, of increase of values through addition.

Psychology thus inevitably becomes a virtual modern alchemy. Positive reactions or motivations are assumed to derive from positive causal backgrounds. What could be easier than yielding to the pleasant, positive reactions, or creating such backgrounds by increased inner enjoyments?

This alchemistic fallacy is inevitable under the scientific, mathematically axiomatic, like-from-like causal logic. But also, because this logic does not work in practice, psychology has turned away from the decisive psychologic factors—feelings and their ultimate source, pleasure.

As we have seen, pleasure is the causally, scientifically simple mechanism that makes man tick in all his practical behavior and normal survival. But pleasure is causally paradoxical. Psychologists have far more insight than is needed to see that an increased enjoyment of pleasure lessens motivation. The same is true of all feelings, which derive from the pleasure drive. Consequently, for psychologists as logical scientists, pleasure and feelings are useless as causal factors, though we live every moment by and for pleasure.

Instead, psychologists have accepted the involved, cognitive factors as decisive. This fits in well with the general beliefs of men that they act only according to their reasons. This belief is the main reality discovered by psychologists in the minds of people they are analyzing. Above all, the cognitive world of mind is parallel, as we have seen, to the physical world and therefore agrees with the causal logic of our exact, physical sciences.

Cognitive and ideational factors, such as perceptions, insights, and learning, have indeed become the main factors dealt with in psychology. As we have explained before, such factors can be treated "logically" but are behaviorally ineffective and easy to acquire. Expecting our precious capacities to be created through such easy factors is again alchemistic.

Finally, the assumed unconscious causes in psychology are the most alchemistic of all. Such causes had to be invented to explain how men create for themselves, so ingeniously, their negative reactions, which actually result from simple, mechanistic opposite causality. The assumed unconscious causes are perceptions, reasoning, and planning by the personified unconscious. No organically relevant feelings are possible here anyway, because to feel is to be conscious, in organically integrated ways.

Inevitably Alchemistic Causal Logic in Psychiatry and Psychology

The scientism of our present exact, technical sciences is the only one that scientists accept. The exact, technical sciences deal with our external world. In this world things or forces increase through addition. Logical mathematics become the central discipline for the exact sciences. Actually, all men have derived their "logical," scientifically and mathematically precise truths from observations in this external world.

The whole system here is causally clear, because its logic is humanly acceptable. Physical values derive from value sources of the same nature. This is exactly contrary to the opposite causality of our inner values, which is humanly unacceptable.

Man's internal mental world is diametrically different causally from physical phenomena. It has remained for man scientifically incomprehensible. The reason is, as we have seen, the opposite value causality in our internal organic as well as mental life. Men cannot accept that their inner values, everything they live for, are only results from equal disvalues or from everything they strive to avoid—as satisfactions are results from needs.

Consequently, no exact or true sciences could evolve about man's inner mental world; there can be no science without causal understanding. The human or behavioral sciences have often been called "soft" sciences in contrast to our exact, technical sciences.

Actually, psychiatry and psychology, as well as all fields dealing with man, are presently *not sciences at all.* A science has to explain, predict, and deal with natural phenomena. It therefore has causal laws which as natural principles can be only simple and few, understood by everybody in the same way. This is evident from all exact sciences such as physics. But in psychiatry and psychology no such simple and few causal laws exist. In fact, *every theorist here has his own causal principles that are different from those of others.*[4, 5, 14]

We have repeatedly mentioned that *natural causal laws* are simple and few. Perhaps we should try to indicate the philosophical reason why this is so.

A natural law results, for us, when our thinking, as a form of our existence, coincides with the way nature exists. Thus, our understanding there is as simple as is our existence for us. Think of how our existence includes all experiences for us but is so totally simple that it seems to have no content. Everywhere, the more general a natural causal law is, the simpler, more "meaningless" it is.

Similarly, as in our experience of our existence, whenever we discover a universal causal law, it is simple and one even while it covers endlessly many phenomena. That is why we always have only one simple causal law for any field of phenomena that we causally understand, or only few causal laws for any one of the exact sciences.

Anyway, all exact sciences are built on causal laws that are simple, understood by everybody in the same way, and few, generally only one for any area of science. (The law of opposite-value causality would be sufficient for human sciences.) Indeed a worldwide scientific upheaval would arise upon a discovery of new laws or forces in addition to, say, those of motion and electricity or the law of natural selection.

But in psychology or psychiatry, as in all behavioral sciences, new causal laws and forces are "discovered" every day. There are as many thousands of them as there are new treatises published by noted scientists.

Every psychologist has his own set of causal laws and forces, such as the principles of learning and systems of motivation.[11, 12, 14] Similarly, every psychiatrist has, amidst hundreds of advocated therapies, his own way of treatment based on his own understanding of causal laws and forces.[3, 5, 7]

In short, there is no science in these fields, but only a confusion of endless, controversial, conflicting theories. Scientists themselves recognize that psychiatry or psychology will become scientific only when a unified system is established, under a few and simple generally recognized causal laws or principles. Actually, every noted psychologist or psychiatrist offers a few causal principles that would unify psychology or psychiatry as a science. But the principles offered by him are different from those offered by hundreds of other psychologists.

The imitation of the exact sciences by the "soft," human sciences reveals scientific immaturity in many ways. The old alchemy grew from following the truths of philosophy, which was then the authoritative science. Because such truths were irrelevant for the physical and chemical world, alchemists failed continuously and resorted to endlessly new and more complex formulas.

The reason for the multiplicity and complexity of our human sciences is similar. The causal logic that governs the exact sciences is not true, is irrelevant for the human sciences. Any one of the thousands of human-science theories, arrived at by the imitiation of the exact sciences, is as good or bad as any other. They all are causally untrue and have to fail in practice. The scientists are following here a completely clear scientism from our exact sciences—which, however, does not work. Consequently, efforts are desperately intensified—as they were in the old alchemy also pursuing its own clear certainties.

The *disregard of simple, practical facts* is as typical of our scientific imitation as it was of alchemy. When complexity and multiplicity in a science reach their high levels, anything simple seems hardly worth considering.

Now a simple truth in all mature sciences is that you never get something for nothing. Under the law of equivalence of matter, efforts to create new elements such as gold are futile. But to alchemists such a law would have seemed ridiculously unscientific. It would have offered no inventive or highly "scientifc" possibilities.

A similar disregard of simple truths is typical of modern psychology and psychiatry. The simplest fact of life is that anything of value, in our motivations and capacities, requires effort. The law of opposite causality is comparable to the law of equivalence of matter in chemistry. But ideas about equal "pay" for our inner values—about equal negative value feelings for every positive reaction—have never been considered in modern psychology or psychiatry. The opposite value causality is the most universal fact of organic existence.

The failure to recognize *the simple, universal rule of opposite-value causality* is especially misleading for psychiatry and psychology.

We have seen how the negative reactions incurred through over-enjoyment are as *"ingenious" and intense* as was the over-enjoyment. It seems that the neurotic or psychotic is tormenting himself intensely, with igenious skill, against his own will. The only satisfactory explanation would seem to be that a highly inventive agency, virtually a person inside the person, is acting against him. *The assumed unconscious* has ideas, perceives, judges, calculates, plans, and acts with skillful ingenuity inside the person.[3, 4, 5] This is the world of thought. But man thinks only as a fully integrated organism. (That is why he can think only of one thing at a time.) Therefore, the unconscious would have to be another fully integrated organism inside the organism. Which is incongruous.

In truly unconscious behavior, in dissociative reactions, the person conserves his capacity to think by excluding completely and simply any parallel disturbing thoughts. The unconscious influences or thoughts are here sharply and totally cut off, rather than permitted to play "unconscious" tricks, in the person's thinking. The person thus can proceed with his desired thinking normally, since all thinking has to be fully integrated organically, free of disturbances.

Such a total exclusion of the undesirable thoughts, while it permits normal, organically integrated thinking, often has to be drastic. This is inevitable because the exclusion has to be comprehensive and clear-cut. The excluded thoughts may have been associatively linked together with some organic reactions, which then also have to be kept still.

Consequently, the unconscious, dissociative, or hysteric reactions consist of mere incapacities, paralyses, amnesias, or other forms of inactivity.[1, 2] They have none of the "ingenuity" of all other mental disorders, originating from the inventive perfection of over-enjoyments.

The "ingeniousness" resulting simply from opposite causality can become confusing in other curious ways. *Strange mannerisms* become part of mental disorders.

Psychotics yield to over-enjoyment upon every pretext, even upon a mere thought or fantasy. If the psychotic, in his easy world, derives his enjoyment by merely snapping his fingers or avoiding unlucky numbers, he still suffers full after-effects. Exactly because he derives real enjoyment with such ease, he drives himself into strong negative reactions in this easy way, as if without real, equal cause.

The neurotic or psychotic lives with such trivial mannerisms and preoccupations because greater inner values as satisfactions grow from stronger restrictions, which he cannot bear. Moreover, he cannot abandon the triffling preoccupation, such as the snapping of fingers. For him it is just as real a means of enjoyment as is heroin for addicts. He can only add to it, which he does eagerly. He thus creates a progressively expanding, compulsive system of mannerisms or ideas.

If he has built himself into a Napoleon, he cannot abandon the idea even if it later creates for him only more difficulties. Every step in such buildup brought him real, physiologic pleasure release; that is why he pursued the idea. Consequently, every step down, back to his pre-Napoleon level, would require equally real, physiological deflation or restriction.

In all psychoses and neuroses their causes are organically strong and real pleasure over-enjoyments that bring equally strong, physiologically concrete, negative reactions of exhaustion or impoverishment. But if this *opposite causality*, so decisive for pleasure as the dominant organic drive, is *not recognized*, the negative reactions seem to have no organically real causes.

Then causes are sought in the purely mental or cognitive, endlessly rich and seemingly dominant factors—which, however cannot have any substantial organic effect. Our vast cognitive capacities, such as intelligence, seem very impressive. But they merely serve our value goals or feelings and are organically of little weight; they consist of infinitesimal value reactions.

Since the cognitive world is extremely complex, all kinds of explanations are easily constructed. They are all *alchemistic*, because the weightless and easy cognitive factors here are assumed to create grave reactions. If ideas could change motivations or drives we all would be perfect.

Of course, the wide acceptance of *unconscious causation is even more alchemistic*. According to it, physiologically grave reactions of mental disorders come from something that physiologically has not happened, has not been even felt. For to feel is to experience, consciously, inner organic processes. Psychologists have therefore, properly enough, constructed the unconscious causes not as feelings but as mere perceptions, ideas, or schemes of the unconscious. This, however, has turned the unconscious into a thinking person—into a separately integrated organism inside the organism.

Yet less mysterious, scientifically "logical" explanations are not much better or less alchemistic. In fact, the most logical causal factors are the more purely cognitive ones, for reasons we have explained. As such they are also the least weighty causally for behaivor and motivations.

For instance, *learning* is generally viewed as a central causal factor. Distorted or faulty learning is seen as a cause of various psychotic and neurotic reactions. But learning is behaviorally easy and has practically no causal impact.

One can learn in five minutes that the best reactions for him would be pleasant feelings of satisfaction for whatever he has to do or live through. Nobody in the world would learn how to torment himself. Yet mental disorders are torments brought by a person on himself—through opposite causality.

Whatever the distortions, mistakes, faulty generalizations, or misplacements in learning, they would never be used by the person so that they would increase his negative reactions. It is incomparably more certain that a distortion or generalization would be used by him to increase what is pleasant, emotionally enjoyable. No mistake is possible here because pleasure is the simplest, easiest thing to learn and understand. Yet mental disorders and difficulties are states of intense lack in satisfactions or in pleasures.

The same can be said of such factors as perceptions, thoughts, ideas, reasoning, misconceptions, or mechanisms such as identification or projection.

Everybody would accept the most positive, satisfactory reactions without difficulty, by *any kind of reasoning, perception, or thinking*. And nothing more than satisfaction is necessary, in the way one intends to act or behave, for having perfect, positive motivational capacities and satisfactory mental normalcy.

If a person resorts to *identification or projection* he, again, does so to gain some satisfaction or pleasure. Of course, such easy ways of gaining satisfactions lead to over-enjoyment as a cause of mental disorders or behavioral difficulties. But psychologists see such disorders as originating from cognitive confusions or mistakes, in identifications or projections.

All kinds of intricate combinations of these and similar cognitive causal factors have been invoked to explain the causal mystery of mental disorders.[1, 4, 5] But the simple fact remains that by any cognitive capacity or activity of mind a person can most easily accept the positive, pleasurable reactions, exactly opposite causally to those of mental disorders. *Nothing is easier or simpler than to choose what is pleasant; and our every positive capacity is a pleasure.*

Here we have to mention *conditioning*. Usually it is not a merely cognitive factor. Conditioning is the way in which our "normal" cultural behavior is created. Of course, such conditioning is attained by dealing with our emotional or pleasure drives. Scientists, though, view conditioning in its classical sense of animal conditioning, which actually creates *learning*. But for man learning is easily acquired or changed. It is also ineffective emotionally and behaviorally.

The scientifically "logical" explanations of conditioning are incongruous whether they deal with learning or other ways of acquiring behavioral reactions. It would require no effort whatsoever to condition a person to strive for more and more of the positive, pleasant reactions or positive capacities. Nor is anybody ever conditioned to have useless negative reactions, the disorders—or to torment himself. Again, no miscalculations are possible here, because we instantly perceive or understand pleasures and torments.

Only opposite causality can explain how the strongest organic factor, the drive for pleasure, creates intense, self-generating mental negativity and disorders. But this understanding is presently missing, and "logical" approaches prevail.

Direct reactive improvements or increases in positive reactions are seen as solutions; and explanations for the resulting, inevitable contradictions are sought in the endlessly complex cognitive or ideational world, conscious or unconscious.[3, 4, 5]

The most effective means of direct reactive improvements are drugs. If psychiatrists understood the actual, opposite effects of the direct-improvement drugs, they would see as absurd and dangerous the present cures and would fight with all their scientific zeal against the use of such drugs. The present extremely wide use of such means of easy mental improvement is causally as unreasonable as was alchemy—and is, moreover, a practical danger to mental health.

Positive, pleasant reactions do not come by way of easy, "costless" improvements. Reactive improvements enjoyed freely lead inevitably to equal worsening, to functional mental exhaustion. If the improvements are added continuously, the vicious-circle exhaustion can deepen into a mental disease.

Scientists should have learned these facts by now from the dramatically evident mental devastation resulting from the wide use of drugs by our addicts, as well as from our recent general use of the most popular mind-improving drugs.

We have lived through *periods of popularity of many reactive-improvement drugs*—of Milltown, Librium, and later Valium—now superseded by similar "better" drugs. During one year, prescriptions of Valium reached sixty million with three billion Valium pills consumed.[18] Milltown and Librium have been similarly popular, but then found to be useless or worse.

As a result, the use of Valium and of similar drugs led to an investigation by a U.S. Senate Committee in which their after-effects were exposed as distressful. Users of the drugs as well as doctors testified about the dismaying "side" effects of the drugs, and the Chairman of the Committee, Senator Edward Kennedy, had to warn of the "nightmare of dependence" created by such drugs. Of course, the dependence indicates the strength of the opposite after-effects of such drugs. Still, the direct-improvement drugs come and go in waves of popularity. Each such drug offers marvelous improvements at first, but the negative after-effects follow, deepening the dependence.

A typical instance is the story of LSD. When the exciting initial effects of its use came to general attention, in the Sixties, they were viewed with remarkable enthusiasm. Revolutionary possibilities for dealing with human problems by use of such drugs were predicted by authorities, like R. H. Felix, then Director of the NIMH, or Glenn T. Seaborg, B. F. Skinner, and Julius Axelrod. But the after-effects of LSD become a disorder "clinically inseparable from the paranoid types of schizophrenia."[3]

The initial effects of all "improvement" drugs are similarly exciting. Phenothiazines, such as chlorpromazine, or MAO inhibitors, such as ipronaizid, can make mental disorders "melt away."[13] But the cure they bring becomes worse than the disease. Dozens of similar panacean drugs have been abandoned or restricted.[8, 10] The list of dangerous addictive drugs that is issued by the NIMH has lengthened progressively, as drugs used for their improvement effects are discovered to become addictive, because they lead to a worsening that requires more of the drug.[10]

But our experts are always seeking for new and easy means of mental improvement. Now *biochemicals* produced by the organism itself are viewed as the most promising. There are some 200 known *neurotransmitters*, such as endorphins or enkephalin, that often act as organic painkillers or affective means of improvement. The organism acts by all kinds of releases and restrictions. Endorphins are found to have the same effects as morphine has; their name has been chosen to reflect this resemblance.

A noted study of these biochemicals was made by Solomon Snyder, winner of the Lasker Award. He argues that the organism cannot become addicted to its own products. Research and discussion concerning such assumedly non-addictive organic tranquilizers and stimulants are increasing. The use of these and similar biochemicals has been considered by noted scientists, including Dr. Frederick Goodwin of the NIMH, who has pointed out dramatic improvements even of memory and thought activity from the use of derivatives of the pituitary hormone. But all reactive improvements lead to opposite effects.

The limitedness of the organism to its sameness is the ever-present universal fact. Whatever the organic improvement—best thought of as some increase or acceleration—it only can come from or lead to equal opposite processes, a decrease or slowing down. Stimulation intensifies or accelerates release of organic energy. Restriction as stress then has to follow, to restore the normalcy of organic sameness. Tranquilization may increase the more central releases at the cost of suppressing peripheral functional demands. Then these demands painfully reassert themselves as normalcy is restored.

Evidently, it does not matter causally what means have been used for attaining the "improvement," the functional increase, or acceleration. The organism still has to return to its limited normalcy , by opposite changes. *If over-improvement is attained, the opposite reactions follow inevitably*, even if the stimulant or tranquilizer is an organic product or merely a psychological influence—such as positive thinking, meditation, or biofeedback.

The organism works in myriad ways that no mind can grasp. A tranquilizing agent like enkephalin can, understandably, be sometimes useful to the organism in maintaining its normalcy. But it is pathetic to try to regulate a neurotransmitter or neurochemical, amidst countless other organic controls, when nobody can understand how it is causally inter-related with everything else in the organism.

Yet scientists are ready to take over the controls. If enkephalin is destroyed by an enzyme, as Dr. Snyder found out, then means are sought to block that enzyme. The obviously necessary causal relation of enkephalin with some two hundred other already discovered neurotransmitters is disregarded.

When we look at *cognitive factors as possible remedies* for mental difficulties, we find a similar typically alchemistic confusion. These factors are causally as ineffective as they are easy, though very complex. Work with them continuously fails to produce the effects expected with seemingly logical and scientific certainty. Increasing elaborations are the result, as happened in alchemy.

The large number of *psychotherapies* is typcial of such efforts and elaborations. Psychotherapies aim to analyze and correct, under elaborate, allegedly scientific procedures, the patient's faulty and distorted perceptions, ideas, reasons, or thoughts. New, corrected insights and understanding are to be provided.

In practical reality, *this amounts to mere talk and reasoning*, however complex or technically sounding the theory behind it. We do not need to repeat how easy it is to espouse the most positive attitudes, with perfect insight, in cognitive or ideational terms.

Psychotherapies are, indeed, ineffective in practice, as we shall see later. They are *so many and causally so different that they cannot possibly be scientific.*[5, 6]

Some psychotherapies do concern themselves with treatment of emotions. In which case "logical" improvement becomes the goal. The release of pent-up feelings and conflicts or the liberation of drives and instincts is to be attained.[4, 6] Thus, more pleasure is to be provided, by intricately formulated, allegedly scientific methods. *The alchemy of the easy gain of capacities, through "scientific" formulas, for increase of pleasure, is thus expanded*[5, 6]

Psychotherapies are of course the most extensive, the scientifically most advanced methods intended to provide guidance in behavior and motivations. Other current expert methods for resolving our mental or behavioral problems are, expectedly, founded on similar "scientific" certainties and discoveries.

Indeed, our scientific era is producing a *continuous parade of experts promising enrichment of capacities* through all kinds of easy positive thinking and cognitive insights or through direct increase in our positive pleasant reactions, such as enthusiasm and love. We shall look at this modern "scientism" in more detail in discussing psychology and the behavioral sciences.

This parade is continuing in ways similar to the perennial rise in popularity of various direct-improvement wonder drugs and the subsequent disastrous disappointments they bring. Everywhere the present scientism promises certain and easy reactive enrichment, though it inevitably fails in the end. Calling this scientism alchemistic best expresses what it is.

The Opposite Causality of Reactions in Psychoses and Neuroses

A clear evidence of opposite causation in psychoses and neuroses is the fact that every syndrome of these diseases has been observed to result also from enjoyment of the common narcotic drugs.[8, 10] These drugs bring clear perfect improvement in our emotions. That is why they are so generally and irresistibly attractive. But their effects are an equally clear and intense emotional worsening or impoverishment, which is the proximate cause of mental diseases.

Psychotics have the "capacity," or rather readiness, to yield to intense emotional over-improvements, even without use of drugs. It is generally recognized that psychotics, particularly schizophrenics, have the tendency and habit of living in their inner world as if it were real. Naturally, *in this autistically created reality, the psychotic permits or provides for himself vast and intense enjoyments.*

The psychotic is mentally too weak to restrict such enjoyments. He yields to them continually. The vicious circle thus can deepen the negative aftereffects to an incredible level. The over-enjoyments of the psychotic may ordinarily be weaker than those obtained from drug use. But their after-effects can accumulate through years, in a vicious circle, to extreme intensity and are, naturally, "richer" in mental content. The usual psychosis is, correspondingly, more intricate and extensive than are drug-created psychoses.[1, 3]

The central causal fact in the reactions of a psychotic or neurotic is that he tries to avoid, in the most perfect, excessive ways, the feelings that he is bringing on himself. Thus a *conflict* of behavior here appears to be the most noticed syndrome.[1, 3, 4]

Various cognitive or ideational perceptions and confusions are, naturally, seen as causes of the conflict. In truth the reason behind the "conflict" is opposite-value causality. There would never be any causally decisive, emotional conflict whatever if men could have positive reactions without their opposites. Men always want only the positive pleasant reactions, which make everything easy, free of any conflicts or difficulties.

An excessive *defense* and perfectionism of avoidances are the main traits of behavior of the psychotic or neurotic.[1, 2, 3] His observed, mysterious self-generating entrapment results as he excessively strives to avoid negative, distressing reactions that deepen for him at every turn.

The force behind mental disorders is indeed irresistibly strong. It is the drive for pleasure, the strongest organic drive. Only opposite causality can explain how the excessive pursuit of pleasure, in perfect, most inventive ways, leads to its exhaustion—because of organic limitedness.

The causal mystery thickens because the enjoyed improvments, while they last, provide a very strong positive adjustment and are hardly noticed as they become habitual. This is not very different from what happens in drug use. But under the "scientific" logic, the strong positive adjustment or emotional improvements are never connected with mental negativity or worsening reactions. It therefore may seem, even to a perfect observer, that mental *disorders come without apparent, explainable causes* or are created by some hidden mental agency such as the unconscious.

A good example is the etiology of anxiety, which is the main component in all psychoses and neuroses. Anxiety is the opposite of the feeling of security of survival, which is our most universal value and therefore is not felt as anything in particular. Everything one does is to serve the insurance of his survival. All our values ultimately derive from satisfactions of the security of survival. Consequently all our improvements of life are, in the final analysis, only improvements in the feeling of this security. These improvements are not felt as anything in particular either if they are continual.

But as such improvements accumulate, the opposite reactions finally break out. Evidently, since the over-enjoyments were those of the security of survival, the opposite reaction is anxiety. But neither the universal value of the security nor its all-inclusive, continuous over-enjoyments have been noticed. The anxiety thus breaks out seemingly for nonexisting, unexplainable reasons—through the opposite causation.

Of course experts have sought extensively for logical explanations of anxiety. All kinds of negative, mostly cognitive, mental causes are invoked. Stresses of modern life are blamed, though modern men can enjoy almost everything they want and seek, first of all, the easy, direct avoidance of stress.

Hundreds of explanations have been offered for the phenomenon of our Age of Anxiety. An unprecedented enjoyment of improvements in our age is certainly evident everywhere. But "scientifically" nobody even thinks of connecting it with anxiety. The confusion and multiplicity of explanations will only increase.

Now we may look at *the opposite causality of reactions* in the principal psychoses and neuroses.

SCHIZOPHRENIA. Opposite reactions as results of emotional over-enjoyments are particularly clear in schizophrenia, the gravest and most frequent psychosis. Strong "improvement" drugs,—such as, LSD, phenothiazines, even the simple amphetamines—can evoke reactions that are similar to schizophrenia. Of course, the same drugs can relieve schizophrenia, and have been tried in its treatment.[1, 8, 13]

It is generally recognized that schizophrenics live in a fantasy world of their own making. They are reclusive, self-absorbed, unrealistic, unsociable, secretive, and unable to bear hardships or restrictions. The absence of restrictions shows in the lack of inhibitions or of shame, in unrestrained social behavior, fantasies of grandeur, and loose personal habits or weakness of moral controls.

Evidently, in his self-created, unrestrained world the schizophrenic permits and creates for himself every possible enjoyment. As a result, the schizophrenic suffers from all kinds of negative reactions: anxiety, depression, fear, obsession, phobias, "tics" or mannerisms to a progressively deepening, excessive degree. This is inevitable because he has over-enjoyed all the possible positive reactions continually and in a vicious circle.

This overwhelming negativity of reactions is what leads to bizarre schizophrenic behavior. Even normal people would behave similarly under extreme fear, depression, or the need of avoidances. Schizophrenics do not lose their intellectual capacities. A simple, strong drug that improves emotions or pleasure releases can return a schizophrenic, for a while, to quite normal behavior.[8, 13]

As in all functional disorders, the "diseased," negatively felt, restrictive reactions in schizophrenia constitute a pressure by the organsim back toward normality.

Logically, however, it may seem that schizophrenics should be merely liberated from the restrictions that are making them so negatively minded. Why not just enable them to feel free, to accept enjoyment without irrational, restraining fears. Logically that would make them normal. And would not that be perfectly easy? The strong, tranquilizing phenothiazine indeed does that easily—and makes the disease worse, after initial improvment.[9, 10]

The pressure in schizophrenia back to normality can have bizarre effects. In some cases the excessive release drive may be physiologic, contrary to the psychotic's intentions. To suppress such an excessive over-enjoyment drive, the psychotic may resort to some equally excessive contrary effect, such as that obtained by smearing himself with feces.

Schizophrenic reactions such as stupor or "waxy flexibility" may serve similar purposes. Corresponding, restrictive, inner reactions, like the production of taraxein, are equally part of the "disease" as a pressure toward normality. Or hallucinations may be organically inevitable and necessary after-effects of overstimulated fantasy; one can think here of the inevitable visual after-images.

Sometimes it is recognized, though only indirectly or intuitively, what the organic role of schizophrenia is. Hence the popularity of the writings of Dr. R. D. Laing, who has demonstrated, supposedly from his own experience, that schizophrenia performs an important role for the psychotic and should be left to run its course.

But generally the curative role of schizophrenia is never suspected, though organisms are miraculously purposive and would not repeat the same, causally uniform process if it did not serve a normal purpose. It may be noted that two thirds of mental patients recover by themselves, after periods of organically imposed suffering of the "diseased" reactions, if the organic process is not interfered with.

Modern psychiatry indeed has no causal explanation of schizophrenia, in spite of enormous efforts to understand it.[1, 2, 3, 4] Psychiatrists themselves are puzzled by the increasing mystery. Thus, the most intense physiologically concrete mental disorder seems to arise "without any known physiological basis."[1] No accepted conclusions about the physiological causal factors have been reached. All the biochemical processes have been discovered and endlessly analyzed. But nothing fits in causally.[1, 4, 5] The reason is the opposite causality.

At every step research logically shows as a cause of schizophrenia what is actually an organic reaction toward recovery from it. Or it shows as sources of remedy or improvement the very factors that increase the disorder in the end. This reversed causal logic can lead to endless confusion, particularly because of the infinite complexity and multiplicity of organic processes involved. All the observable processes here are actually governed by opposite causality. We may recall that even strictly physiologic analyses can reveal only the *reactions* by cells or tissues and organs.

Understandably, mystifications about unconscious complexes, hidden agencies, and symbolic causes have flourished. Psychotherapies and psychoanalyses have been advocated for dealing with the mysteries.[1, 3, 6] One can only wonder how such unconscious and symbolic factors—which have not been even felt really, consciously, or physiologically—can cause the gravely emotional, physiologically deep changes.

More sober psychiatrists may seek explanations in learning and conditioning.[1, 2] This implies that somehow schizophrenics learn or are conditioned to torment themselves uselessly. But man is too intelligent to become confused about the direct avoidance of negative, useless reactions in any kind of learning or conditioning.

The same can be said of ideational factors such as wrong associations, false perceptions, or faulty thinking and ideas. They all are emotionally, physiologically insubstantial or easily remedied by brief explanations. Of course, emotional factors are often subsumed under these concepts of ideational causation. That increases the confusion, as causes that are decisive are not distinguished from those that are irrelevant.

Scientifically or experimentally, schizophrenia consists of extreme restrictions, stress, and emotional negativity. It seems that the main task here should be to remove the restrictions and to enable the schizophrenics to enjoy more freely the emotionally positive reactions. This would be "logically" right and easy. But schizophrenics have done that already, to excess.

Drugs can easily provide free, clear enjoyment; and the most efficient affective-improvement drugs have been used in treatment of schizophrenia. But precisely the drugs that provide the most effective free enjoyments also cause schizophrenic withdrawal reactions.[8, 10] The explanation would be simple if the paradoxical opposite causality was understood—if the self-evidently clear organic limitedness of man was recognized.

PARANOIA. In paranoia opposite causation is equally clear. Paranoiacs feel that they are persecuted, exposed to danger, and hated, while they seek to enjoy excessively the sense of their own grandeur or power, of being loved, or of love in various forms—as is generally noted.[1,2]

Naturally, one's own power and love by others are the most enjoyable values, totally insuring survival or security. Their opposites, the feelings of dangerous helplessness or fear and of hateful persecution, are felt with equal intensity by the paranoiac and constitute his disease.

These opposite reactions emerge when further over-enjoyment of the sense of power and of being loved fails due to exhaustion, physiologic setback, illness, after-effects of drugs, psychologic defeat, or age. All of which have been observed to precipitate paranoia.[1, 2]

Of course, the enjoyments of a sense of superiority and love start vanishing as they are added to. They are little felt when they have become usual. They contribute to a very enjoyable, "normal," adjustment while they are continually increased.

The opposite reactions, when they start emerging, are felt very strongly against this continuously augmented enjoyment background. Logically, these feelings of persecution, danger, hate by others, or jealousy then seem to be coming from nowhere, for some mysterious reason, without adequate causes, without any related or particularly noted experiences in the paranoiac's very "normal" and positive past.

A causal explanation of paranoia is, admittedly, missing.[1, 2, 4] Theories about paranoic reactions are numerous and involved.[1, 5] Most frequently they include speculations about unconscious homosexual conflicts, mechanisms of projection, hate turned against oneself, symbolism, or wrong learning and ideas. Homosexuality is easily inferred from the paranoiac's excessive need for general love.

Of course, unconscious, unfelt conflicts and symbolism cannot possibly cause the physiologically deep paranoic reactions. Nor does anybody learn or pursue ideas to torment and scare himself. If the paranoiac does something to himself, as all theories suggest, it is a thousand times more certain that he strives consciously or unconsciously to enjoy the most pleasant feelings, of being secure or superior and loved by others. That is exactly what he has enjoyed to excess.

MANIC-DEPRESSIVE REACTIONS. The very essence of manic-depressive reactions is the change of one mental state into its opposite.[1, 2] It is revealing in practical terms that the remarkable lithium treatment prevents the depressive stage by first supressing the manic stage.[8, 10] Of course, many cases are not so clearly cyclothymic; the moods alternate continuously or at short intervals. Then the lithium compounds can evidently help even if administered continuously.

The alternation of the opposite states would be even clearer if psychiatrists paid more attention to the real causal factor, the pleasure quality of emotions, rather than to external reactions. Externally a person may appear "manic"—excited, overactive, or eccentric—under a severe distress as well as under enjoyment.

Further, the exaggerated positive states are often not noticed, because intense affective positivism may appear as a very normal adjustment. Also, the positive state rarely returns with suddenness, because its causal source, the negative background, is accumulated only very slowly or reluctantly. But the depressive state breaks out with cataclysmic suddenness because enjoyments are pursued tenaciously to the very brink of exhaustion.

Consequently, clinical observation and statistics seem to show, misleadingly, that there is less of the manic states and fewer regular cyclothymic cases—that the opposite reactions are not equivalent.

A mystery is inevitable, in these as in all psychoses, particularly because the biochemicals in the blood of psychotics have ambivalent effects. The same biochemical that brings improvement is the cause of subsequent worsening, and vice versa. This is not causally different from what happens in all over-stimulation. A drug addict has more of the stimulant in his blood but is understimulated. In fact, manic-depressive psychosis is found to resemble the syndrome of morphine effects and after-effects.[1, 8]

The absence of physiologic explanations here is found puzzling.[1, 5] In the causal confusion, numerous theories have been advanced: about self-punishment, ego defenses, unconscious mechanisms, and conflicts as causes.[5, 7] Such assumed ideational causes are incongruous in view of the physiologically deep reactions here.

In general, various experts have expectedly tried, and abandoned all kinds of logically effective remedies offering more positive, enjoyable experiences for the depressive. Actually, an exactly opposite treatment is uniquely effective. Shock therapy can cure depressions definitely and permanently, if applied in causally understood ways, as we shall explain later. Yet shock therapy brings for the patient, physiologically, the most negative reactions possible, resembling those of physiologic annihilation or death.

Other affective psychoses come in less clearly discernible cycles of opposite emotions. This is to be expected. In many cases, the overenjoyment phases remain completely unnoticed, because enjoyments provide very positive, "normal" adjustments. *Involutional melancholia* is a good example. In most cases it is recognized as a "unipolar manic-depressive" reaction.[1, 3]

Whatever the ways and means by which the psychotic attains his over-enjoyment or over-stimulation, they have paradoxical and often unnoticeable effects. If a narcotic drug were administered to a person since his early years and were constantly added to, he would not feel any particular elation. But the negative, depressive after-effect would finally have to break out.

Similarly, in all affective psychoses the depressive reactions may break out while biochemically the psychotic may be in a state of high stimulation—just as in the morphine syndrome.

In turning to *neuroses* we find the opposite causality of reactions in all of them. Neuroses are intense and "ingenious" negative reactions originating from equally intense and ingenious over-enjoyment efforts by the neurotic.

Naturally such over-enjoyments can be varied and confusing. Hypochondria arises from the over-enjoyment of not having something, namely disease. Phobias are opposite effects of an extreme indulgence of avoidances. Not having or avoiding some evil or threat is a pleasure.

ANXIETY REACTIONS. All mental disorders are accompanied by anxiety reactions, because all over-enjoyments are aimed, essentially, at the feeling of pleasure from security of survival. The opposite causes of anxiety are evident from the simplest facts. The use of drugs and intoxication lead, upon discontinuation, to a virtual anxiety neurosis, but are resorted to for the avoidance of anxiety.

The most general proof of opposite causality here is, of course, our Age of Anxiety itself. Never before have people enjoyed more of everything they have wanted—all the values and feelings ultimately aimed at survival security, or freedom from anxiety. But never before have people suffered more from anxiety. As Rollo May points out, anxiety was unknown as a mental problem at the beginning of this century.

The causal confusion about anxiety increases because psychiatrists are mostly studying and analyzing the ideas and ideational contents appearing together with anxiety. Actually, ideas and perceptions in anxiety reactions are purely accidental—as they are in most disorders.

Everybody can see that an irritated or morbid person may blame his irritation or his morbiditiy on the first thing that happens to be in his way. Such a "reason" then can become, through fixation, the ideational center of the person's anxiety reactions. Still, experts on anxiety are invariably analyzing and studying such perceptions and ideas found in the psyche of neurotics. Ideational conflicts and unconscious perceptions, even existential concerns, are seen as causes. They all are emotionally, physiologically of little weight, not even really felt, if they are "unconscious."

But anxiety reactions are as heavy or physiologically concrete as asphyxiation or drug withdrawal. Any depth of negative reactions can be reached through the vicious circle of over-enjoyments; and the feelings of security of survival that are over-enjoyed here are naturally strong physiologically.

OBSESSIVE-COMPULSIVE REACTIONS. The very essence of these reactions is that the neurotic here suffers from feelings and reactions *oppostie* to those he wants to enjoy most.[1, 2] In a typical obsession, the man who indulges in the most loving thoughts about his wife and children is suffering from ideas that he may do horrible things to them. Under the compulsive reaction, a housewife who cultivates the enjoyment of the perfect cleanliness of her home finds it so unclean that she has to dust it twice a day.

All theories about obsessive-complusive reactions are trying to explain observed opposite emotions and reactions.[1, 3] Oversolicitous love or idealistic perfectionism is assumed to be a disguise for aggressive inner wishes or hidden hostility. Mechanisms of reaction-formation, displacement, and symbolism are seen as devices for hiding or abreacting repressed, conflicting opposite drives. The child obsessively avoiding cracks in the pavement supposedly wants rather than fears to "break mother's back."

The real causal explanation is self-evidently simple. Every overdriven mechanism, supporting over-enjoyed emotions, has to reverse in the end. Then all the opposite reactions or feelings follow. As these are overcome by even greater enjoyment of the desired emotions, the vicious circle deepens the negative reactions.

That is why a neurotic loses his obsession or complusion if he can be induced "to do or wish to happen the very things he fears."[1] Victor E. Frankl has used this method in his Logotherapy.[1] A patient suffering from the compulsion to wink or stutter loses it if he deliberately tries to show how excellent a stutter he is. Or an obsession with fears of a plane crash is overcome by a vivid, fearful reliving, in the imagination, of plane crashes.

PHOBIC REACTIONS. The over-enjoyment of avoidances is the cause of phobias. It is only natural that over-enjoyments can consist of enjoying the positive as well as avoiding the negative. The neurotic over-enjoys, in perfectionist ways, the avoidance of what can be feared or loathed.

The decisive factor is not the actual danger from the thing feared but the opportunity to avoid it repeatedly, so that the vicious circle continues to deepen the opposite reactions. The most ordinary things one meets constantly become objects of phobias—closed spaces, streets, outdoors, crowds, insects, germs, cats, cars, trains, or bridges.

It is well known that over-protected children start fearing, unreasonably, the slightest dangers. Similar protective enjoyments are intensified by a neurotic many times over. A female neurotic may start over-enjoying the comfort and safety of her home. As such safety is over-perfected, the unsafety of the street becomes more menacing. If this feeling of unsafety is avoided, repeatedly, by even stronger enjoyments of the home, the vicious circle can deepen the agoraphobia to an incredible degree.

Of course, the opposites of avoidances and their combinations can become very complex. Above all, nobody can accept that he will feel less safe by insuring more safety, though that is what regularly happens with over-protection.

The same unbelievable but self-evidently clear causality applies to all kinds of over-enjoyments creating scores of phobias. Certainly, the vicious circle is what turns mere opposite feelings into an extremely deep fear or aversion.

But scientists try to explain each of the numerous phobias by its own specific causal principles. Thus, agoraphobia has been variously explained as being due to different special causes. Freud held that an unconscious fear of becoming a streetwalker was the cause of agoraphobia. A recent, noted explanation, by Robert Seidenberg and Karen DeCrow, seeks the cause of agoraphobia in the legal tradition which confined women to the home but actually denied them property rights in homes. Such cognitive or symbolic associations of ideas offer endless possibilities for explanations. If a person has a phobia of heights and has memories about respect for his father, the phobia is explained by the fear of the "superiority of Father."

But even the less mystifying explanations, using concepts of learning and conditioning, are not helpful. Nobody learns or is conditioned to acquire needless fears. No "logical" theory can explain the mystery.

To acquire something so tormenting and useless as phobia in

direct, logical ways would be extremely difficult. But phobias grow with self-increasing force, under the neurotic's perfectionist pursuit of exactly opposite reactions, of enjoyments—because of the opposite-value causality.

We may note that the phobic patient is helped by treatments such as Behavior Therapy.[2, 3] The theories of such therapies may be intricate. What matters is that the phobic is forced here to experience strongly all the fears or terrifying reactions he has been continuously avoiding.

This can be very difficult to do. But such therapies have brought complete cures. This is quite unusual for current mental treatments. The seemingly absurd improvement by worsening of reactions is evident here, as it is in shock therapy, which is the practically most effective treatment, when applied properly.

OTHER NEUROTIC REACTIONS. The most frequent modern, emotionally grave reaction is *Depression*.[1, 2, 13] It is a clear opposite of the excitement and stimulation that modern men are certainly enjoying to excess. Opposite swings in mood are observed as a prominent syndrome of depressions.[1, 3]

It is also noted that "depression commonly occurs at the point at which a person has reached the goals toward which he has been striving."[1] A depression lived through fully brings relief, as Dr. Frederick Flach demonstrates in his book *The Secret Strength of Depression.*

Because opposite causation governs depressions, they remain causally unexplained. Unconscious complexes, such as aggression turned against oneself, or hidden conflicts of guilt are claimed to be causes of depression.[5, 7] Here as well, such mere ideas and perceptions could not be sources of the physically deep reactions of depression.[1,4]

Of course, the enjoyment of excitement and stimulation always fades quickly and the progressively deepening depression soon takes over. At that point the persistence of the depressive reactions may seem to confirm the mystifying notion that the neurotic, unconsciously, wants such reactions.

Neurasthenia consists of reactions of tiredness, irritability, and the feeling of pain. They are easily understandable as the deepening opposite effects of excitement, gratification and the avoidance of pain. Such enjoyments have been more richly available in this country; and neurasthenia has been called the "American disease."[1] Theories about unconscious conflicts are used to explain neurasthenia.[3, 5] They are clearly untenable, since the reactions here are physically concrete.

Hypochondria is caused by the over-enjoyment of being free of diseases. Not having diseases can be a source of enjoyment. A neurotic turns it into over-enjoyment. Then as the opposite feeling, the fear of having a disease, arises, it is compensated for by an even stronger enjoyment of freedom from disease. The vicious circle thus deepens, cumulatively, the neurotic's negative feeling of having some disease.

Soon the progressively deepening feeling of disease becomes the dominant emotion, as the corresponding enjoyment potential has become exhausted. Then it may seem that the hypochondriac wants nothing but the symptoms of his imagined diseases. This is a generally accepted view.[1, 2, 4] Karl Meninger has said, "Hell has no fury like the hypochondriac deprived of his symptoms."

The hypochondriac has every reason to be furious about the doctors who believe that he is only imagining his suffering. In fact, he feels tangibly painful reactions and symptoms as strong as were his exaggerated enjoyments of not suffering from diseases and not having their symptoms.

Some other forms of neurotic reactions such as the "*Christmas Blues*" or *Sunday and Vacation Neuroses* are evidently aftereffects of over-enjoyments. Curiously, *Depersonalization Neurosis* has become frequent recently.[1] Its cause is not far to find. Under modern theories and fashions, the discovery of self, of one's own personality or identity, has become a strong, continuous enjoyment for followers of modern psychological movements. Whatever the underlying feelings here, the sense of one's own "identity" can be over-enjoyed. The "mysterious" opposite reactions then can become intense, through the vicious circle.

THE UNCONSCIOUSLY CAUSED NEUROSES. The only unconsciously caused neuroses are the hysteric and dissociative reactions. The other neuroses, as we have seen are caused by consciously pursued and planned over-enjoyments. It is only natural that there be the two differing kinds of neuroses. For there are two different ways in which man pursues pleasures and avoids displeasures. One is by active, conscious striving, the other by passivity, abandonment, or the self-paralyzing "freezing" which is instinctive in animals facing threat.

The theory that all neuroses are unconsciously caused originated with Freud. It has been eagerly accepted because it "explains" with a personalized agency how a person acts so inventively and persistently against himself. We have seen that the simple, mechanistic explanation of this persistent intensity and "inventiveness" is the unrecognized opposite causation.

Freud accepted hysteric reactions as the prototypes for all neuroses. In his first case of psychoanalysis, a girl had suppressed her feelings about traumatic experiences and was cured after she was induced to abreact them by painfully reliving them. It is causally clear that by removing incurred past suppressions normality is restored. The Freudian fallacy lies in not distinguishing between pleasure and displeasure, the black and white in psychology.

Freud assumed that, just as a hysteric or amnesiac suppresses *traumatic* experiences, all neurotics as eagerly suppress their *pleasure* drives, particularly the libidinal desires, in all neuroses.

Universal human drives are pursuits of pleasure, libidinal or general. Freudians recognize this, and claim that our drives suppressed in all neuroses must be released. Repression and the release of libidinal or other pleasure drives are the key concepts in the Freudian etiology and therapies.

The Freudian repression theory is clearly untenable. *Just because tormenting traumatic experiences are suppressed* in the dissociative reactions, *it is assumed that pleasures are suppressed* by neurotics in equally intense ways in all neuroses. Furthermore, this is assumed to happen on the unconscious level, where pleasure drives alone rule.

It can be easily observed how ingenious and forceful men are in pursuing, not suppressing, their universal drives for pleasure—libidinal, aggressive, or general. Neurotics are even more so. They may suppress unpleasant feelings, but never the pleasant, enjoyable ones, such as those of libido or aggression, even if impossible justifications have to be invented for enjoying them. We all know that even our most prohibited pleasures are strongly enjoyed—and are said to be rather preferred—as soon as they can be hidden from public view. And we hardly ever have to disclose our emotions publicly.

Incidentally, the truly suppressed, very unpleasant feelings are not even unconscious. They are intensely, traumatically felt, and to feel is to be conscious. They are suppressed because otherwise they would be strongly felt. What is unconscious is the method of suppression of such feelings.

Hysteric and dissociative reactions are caused by the suppression of tormenting past or present experiences. This is attained by a kind of self-hypnosis which grossly inactivates whole areas of functions.[1, 2] *Hypnosis easily causes such forms* of selective physical or mental incapacities and amnesias or loss of responses.

In *Amnesia* or *Fugue* the person forgets a traumatic experience or problem and wanders away into a different life. Since all mental and physiologic associations with the traumatic experiences have to be suppressed, results can be drastic psychological and even physiological incapacities.

The amnesiac may have to suppress the memory of his whole psychologic past. Or gross suppression of varied physiologic functions becomes necessary if they were associated with the traumatic experience. The results can be a paralysis as wide and accidental as were the associations. It is revealing that such odd, subjectively or superficially controllable paralyses are found to *resemble hypnotically induced* incapacities and sensory distortions.[1, 2, 3]

In *Double Personality* a neurotic suppresses disturbing awareness about his one world while living in another. The two incompatible worlds are developed by him as he lives through excessive mood swings, which are natural in the behavior of a neurotic. As he yields to over-enjoyments during one period, he creates for himself a "loose" personality, Then, as opposite, restrictive reactions set in, he acquires a "stern" personality.

The two personalities can, of course, become traumatically incompatible. Then the neurotic has to suppress one while living with the other. Naturally, all kinds of combinations of over-enjoyments and their periods are possible. More than two personalities may develop if the fluctuations of the opposite reactions affect different functions at different periods.

In any case, the relatively rare unconscious neuroses, caused by "hypnotic" suppression of traumas, are totally *different in their etiology* from the general neuroses, caused by conscious over-enjoyments. The difference is indeed as clear as that between pleasure and displeasure. The unconscious neuroses are caused by the avoidance of what is very unpleasant, and are wanted by the neurotic.[1, 2, 3] In contrast, the other neuroses result from excessive drives for perfectionistic, complete satisfactions and are most undesired.

The unconscious, dissociative reactions are tenaciously maintained by the neurotic even if they may become practically inconvenient for him. Hence his *belle indifference* toward them.[1, 3] The neurotic resists here what can surely cure him—a reliving and abreaction of the suppressed traumatic experiences.

If he is forced, under hypnosis, to relive the suppressed experiences he is cured for good. The treatment and cure here are simple and generally the same. The treatment was widely used, with invariable success, in trench hysteria cases. Naturally, such reliving of the traumatic experiences is very tormenting. That is why they were suppressed in the first place. The neurotic wants to keep them suppressed, and these neuroses are simple blockings or incapacities.[1, 2]

In contrast, the general neuroses are the most unwanted reactions and are extremely complex or "ingenious." The neurotic here would be more than willing to get rid of them by "abreacting" anything, under hypnosis or in any other way.

But these definite and clear, medically simple treatments, involving the use of hypnosis, have long been found to be totally ineffective for general neuroses. In these neuroses normality is regained when the "diseased" restrictions, opposite to the neurotic over-enjoyments, have established normal capacities as pleasure reserves. Two-thirds of neurotics recover by themselves, while treatments often hinder recovery.[5, 6]

The blunder *that human drives for pleasure are as eagerly suppressed as traumas* would have never been committed if the *opposite causality* of reactions was recognized. Under that causality the intense and "ingenious" neurotic suffering is automatically incurred through equally inventive over-enjoyments. The opposite causality of value reactions is as simple and mechanistic as the unconscious agencies of Freud are mystifying. In prescientific systems everything is explained by personified agents.

To sum up, in all psychoses and neuroses the opposite causal background, the over-enjoyment or emotional over-improvement, is almost self-evident. But psychiatrists, in their imitation of the exact sciences, logically cannot recognize opposite causality, though the drug aftereffects which so closely resemble psychoses offer a simple clear proof of opposite reactions.

Psychiatrists proceed by exactly contrary logic. They generally hold that negative reactions derive from negative causal backgrounds. Logically, therefore, direct improvement or increase of positive reactions is accepted as a naturally self-evident remedy. This, of course, implies the alchemistic notion that by the pleasant addition of positively felt reactions our precious positive capacities could be increased or maintained.

Pointless Causal Logic in Psychiatric Treatments

Psychiatrists as scientists proceed only by the experimentally and mathematically direct logic: if a means of improvement brings positive reactions, then continued or consistent use of it will bring more of them. Of course in simpler cases, as in the psychoses resulting from the use of narcotics, psychiatrists know that a reverse is true. But hardly anything is simple in psychiatry. Mental "improvement" means, and after-effects, are as vast and complex as is human inventivenes.

Anyway, a nearly pointless causal thinking about psychiatric treatments becomes inevitable under the "scientific" logic. According to this logic the psychotic is to be helped to do what he actually has done too much already—to be assisted where he needs no assistance at all.

It is true that psychotics suffer only from an extreme lack of positive emotions; psychoses disappear when pleasure-releasing drugs are administered. But the causal paradox of value reactions is inexorable. The mentally weak psychotic, unable to bear restrictions, yields continuously to the enjoyment of his most pleasant, positive inner emotions. And the result is the vicious-circle exhaustion of the pleasure or satisfaction potential. Yet under the direct-improvement logic, psychiatry is trying, in more complex ways, to help the psychotic to increase his enjoyment of positive reactions even more.

We may repeat that the ordinary, functional psychotic and neurotic reactions, as all functional diseases, are the organism's restrictive pressures back toward its functional normalcy. These diseases are natural, uniform reactions. They follow a general causal law or "purpose." Natural organic reactions are always beneficial in miraculously purposive ways that are ungraspable in experimental physical terms. But psychiatric treatments are aimed at counteracting these reactions, by removing the "disease" in direct, scientifically logical ways.

This in effect becomes an effort to increase positive, pleasant reactions directly. And what can be easier than the enjoyment of such pleasant reactions—when they have been made available by painful or "diseased" restrictions.

DRUG THERAPY. A typical psychiatric treatment is drug therapy. It is to provide direct relief from disease by increasing the feelings that are positive and pleasant. Drugs indeed increase such feelings and offer wondrous relief. They do so by removing restrictions, which the organism has to restore afterward.

Every year new wonder drugs are discovered. They provide direct effects that would be sufficient to wipe out all mental disease. But the end result is that mental diseases have increased fourfold since the main "wonder" drugs went to market, in the mid-Fifties, in this country.[17]

By the way, drug-treatment enthusiasts like to refer to the decrease in the number of patients in public mental hospitals, which amounted to a half million in 1955. But this decrease is due to a general new policy against institutional treatments, which have been found to be disastrous.

Certainly, patients in the mental hospitals received to the fullest degree every scientifically logical means of improvement, particularly by way of drugs. The result was failure; and public mental hospitals now are deliberately underused. Other facilities are preferred. In general hospitals alone, mental patients now occupy more than a half million beds.[17]

Every authority recognizes that drugs provide *wondrous relief*, temporarily curing the disorders, but that *no permanent cure* is to be expected from drugs.[8, 9]

The history of drug therapy shows that the more wondrous a drug is, the more dangerous are its "side" effects, [8, 10] which are actually the inevitable aftereffects. Of course, aftereffects often find expression through mechanisms other than those initially involved in the improvements.

The popular meprobamate drugs, providing miraculous relief, had to be listed by the FDA as dangerous.[8, 13] Another virtually miraculous drug, chloropromazine, also has dangerous aftereffects.[10, 13] Iproniazid, compared by Nathan S. Kline to a treasure offering "acres of diamonds," had also to be prohibited by the FDA.[13] Other, various MAO inhibitors have similar spectacular initial effects. But they lead to worse "side" effects and have been discontinued.[10, 13] MAO inhibitors interfere with enzyme action in neurotransmitters—with a natural, necessary organic process as marvelously purposive and ungraspable as are all living processes.

Drug "abuse" is universal and inevitable because of the equally universal after-effects from drugs. Any drug has to lose its effectiveness as the organism establishes countermeasures to maintain its normalcy.

To sustain a drug effect, more of the drug has to be used, which further deepens the after-effects. The patient "abusing" the drug is merely trying to prolong the relief that the drug was offering. His doctor then can blame disregard of instructions.[8, 13] Also, ignorance by patients, and drug complexity are generally blamed in drug abuse.[9, 10] But a typical improvement drug always works wondrously at the beginning, and is "abused" only later, as it starts losing its effectiveness..

In all use of improvement drugs, their seemingly illogical "side" effects are viewed as coming from extraneous toxic residues left by the drugs. Factually this is not true at all. The clearest total improvement, in all functions, is attained from street drugs. And their "side" effects appear exactly to the extent that the body is cleaning itself of the toxic substances.

The decrease or absence, not presence, of toxic chemicals in the blood creates "worsening" with the direct-improvement drugs. Even placebos used for affective improvement have opposite "side" effects, as was shown in experiments by Drs. Jon D. Levine, Howard J. Fields, Newton C. Gordon, and Herbert Benson.[18] Of course, placebos cannot be toxic in any way; yet their aftereffects are negative, opposite reactions.

Many experts claim that drug effects vary according to the circumstances and mental conditions under which the drug is taken.[9, 10] Naturally, if the paradoxical reversals of effects, through all their various stages, are not understood, everything seems to vary unpredictably.

The effects on the complex higher mental processes, in particular, can become confusing. For instance, LSD, affecting such higher mental experiences, brings involved, controversially interpreted after-effects which may result from several reversals, at different stages, of drug effects as well as from organic countermeasures.

Among the hundreds of drugs used in therapies, some may happen to have a *restrictive* overall effect, and therefore can help the organism to restore its normalcy, its pleasure-release reserves. The use of such drugs may be continued upon the incidental discovery of their practical success. The action of a drug of this kind would, however, be hardly understood causally and may be counteracted by other steps in a direct-improvement treatment.

Lithium treatment proves how successful can be the use of a restrictive drug. It is one of the rare treatments that, everybody agrees, is definitely effective. Dr. W. H. Stewart, as the U. S. Surgeon General, reported that "lithium appears to be the best specific agent yet found for the treatment of any mental disease." Lithium is used for the manic-depressive psychoses. By suppressing the manic reactions lithium prevents depression.[1, 10]

Of course, psychiatrists want mostly to counteract depression, directly, and do not fully realize that the suppression of mania prevents depression. Consequently, psychiatrists succeed better with the lithium treatment in the less cyclothymic cases. Here mania and depression alternate continuously. Therefore continuous lithium administration prevents mania even while the drug is here intended only to deal with the depression directly.

If opposite causality were understood, *other drugs could be devised* that could cure other psychoses as definitely as lithium cures depression. Every peculiarity of each psychosis could be met; psychiatry can be perfectly effective when it proceeds with causal understanding.

The main difficulty, of course, would be the suffering to be inflicted on the psychotic by stopping his over-enjoyments. Think of alcoholics or drug-users, forcibly deprived of alcohol or drugs. It would be almost impossible to impose a similar but far more varied, extremely painful, and extensive regimen on the psychotic for counteracting his incomparably vaster over-improvements.

Here a distinction should be made between some psychoses, originating purely physiologically, and most other psychoses, incurred psychologically by the pursuit of enjoyment. The first, such as the manic-depressive psychoses, may result without the person wanting the over-enjoyment, the manic stage. Therefore, he may readily accept the suppression of such a mania.

But in psychologically incurred psychoses the psychotic would resist, in every possible way, the attempt to restrict his over-enjoyments. Moreover, restrictive treatment here would be strongly felt as leading to an intolerable worsening and would never be fully tried. Such obstacles are less strong in the cases of physiologically caused psychoses. Here the method of shock treatment is revealing.

SHOCK THERAPY. The direct-improvement method is reversed in shock therapy. The shock amounts to the infliction of an extremely negative, almost death-like stress, as restriction, on the organism. Schematically, with such a repression of the organism onto a lower level of adjustment, room is gained for new, normal movements up and down. But without insight into the organic limitedness, shock therapy seems like the worst imaginable treatment.

Understandably, shock therapy has been violently opposed, and has even led to street demonstrations. How could the tormented psychotic be helped by exposure to more torment, to the worst physiologic traumas? The shock is contrary to everything believed about mental treatments as ways of relieving the psychotic's stressful reactions or soothingly increasing his more positive, pleasant feelings.

But in spite of its apparent absurdity shock therapy is so successful that it is used far more widely than it properly should be. Its plain, practical effectivness leaves no doubt.[1, 2, 6] It is probably the only therapy that cures definitively, and without "side" effects, the disorders to which it is applicable in its present form.[1, 5, 6] Such a success is unique in psychiatry.

It should be realized that in its present form, as merely a physiologic "stab in the dark,"[3] the shock can be properly used only for treating simple physiologic depressions, which it cures without exception.[5, 7] Because of this unique success, it is then improperly used to treat other, psychologically caused disorders.

The point is that the merely physiologic shock cannot counteract the different, extremely involved disorders caused psychologically by conscious over-enjoyments.

These disorders could be counteracted only by equal, consciously suffered shocks as extreme mental restrictions. It is known that even chronic, "incurable" schizophrenics recover when in danger of death, grave operation, or fatal disease.[2, 4] Naturally, they relapse when the danger is over.

Psychiatry, with its enormous scientific, technical proficiency, could devise means to sustain psychological "shock." This, of course, would be very traumatic for the patients and they would resist it. Similarly, a drug addict resists drug withdrawal, which is a virtual shock for him, though it cures his affliction. Patients do not resist the present electro-convulsive therapy because it does not bring psychologic, conscious suffering.

In a word, sustained psychologic shock would cure the psychologically caused—that is, most—mental disorders as definitely as the purely physiologic ECT now cures the physiologically caused depressions.

Even such an authority as Karl Menninger has pointed out the curative effects of psychologic traumas. He describes unexpected recoveries by patients upon their placement under harder conditions or worse treatment, or upon "most unlikely" events, including intercurrent illness.[2] He concludes that "worse added to worse" often works.[2]

Menninger refers to a classic case to illustrate the point. Two hundred incurable mental patients, in the hospital Charite sur Loire in France, fled from it in 1940 under fear of being killed by the approaching Germans. A special committee found, after the war, that 60 percent of them had established themselves in surrounding communities as fully recovered.[2]

It may be noted that in Behavior Therapy patients are exposed to their phobic traumas, which are felt as shocks by them. This therapy is found to offer the best concrete relief, though it is objected to on theoretical, logical grounds.[1, 5] Some other therapies use similar methods of treatment, under various theories of abreaction, desensitization or "flooding."[1, 5, 7]

PSYCHOTHERAPY. The most widely used but practically the least helpful form of treatment is psychotherapy. Psychotherapists anlayze and deal with conscious or unconscious ideas, perceptions, insights, learning, and reasoning, which have little psychologic effect and are mentally as easy as all ideas and reasons.

Everybody can see that talk and reasoning have no power in changing our practical behavior and merely serve to justify our feelings, our pleasure motives, which determine our behavior. But psychotherapists never deal directly, in their analytic methods and theories, with pleasure, the final root of all feelings. The reason for this is, as we saw, the paradoxical causality of pleasure. Rather, psychotherapists are perpetuating the method of analysis as a cognitive and ideational discussion and reasoning.

Psychotherapists always discover in their analyses that their patients apparently act according to their ideas and reasons, or their faulty reasoning and distorted perceptions. People always invent reasons for what they are doing. In fact, they claim their reasons most forcefully when they are most irrational. But since the proximate cause of behavior, in every case, appears to be some reason, it may seem that behavior could be corrected by straightening out the reasons or providing new insights. Particularly when the real causal source of behavior, pleasure, is left out of view.

For all practical purposes the psychotherapist deals only with such cognitive causes prominently present in minds of his patients. His method of analysis is suited for talk and reasoning, not for emotional, physiologically effectual intervention. He anlayzes the cognitive or ideational causes and tries to correct them in their own cognitive ways, by providing patients with new, deeper understanding.

We may as well repeat that everybody would be perfect if understanding or insights were decisive. Nothing is easier to understand and espouse than the desirability of positive feelings, which effectively relieve every behavioral ill.

No wonder that psychotherapies are often found rather to hinder recovery. Mental patients, in fact, recover better without psychotherapies, by living through their "disease" as a pressure back to normality. Most revealing here is probably the widest study on mental therapies, conducted by H. J. Eysenck, a foremost authority in psychiatry. His study included more than seven thousand cases reported over thirty years.[1, 4, 6]

This study shows that 72 percent of patients recover by themselves regardless of therapy, but that only 64 percent recover with psychotherapy, and a mere 44 percent with psychoanalysis.[6, 7] Similar findings have resulted from numerous other studies, including those by L. A. Gottschalk, J. D. Frank, A. K. Shapiro, N. Q. Brill, E. E. Levitt, and L. Luborksy. Eysenck's conclusions are confirmed by the noted, recent, comprehensive work of B. Zilbergeld on the "myth" of psychotherapies.

But psychotherapies are very popular and numerous, reportedly numbering over 200. Of late more than 60 have flourished.[5, 7] Each one is founded on its own assumed causal basis, fundamental force, or principle. Thus, each one implies a different underlying science, practically contradicting the scientific assumptions of the other psychotherapies. Evidently, a real scientific understanding here is missing.

Yet psychotherapies are applied and recommended for treatment of almost every kind of mental illness or difficulty. Among our more affluent and sophisticated people, it is a sign of a proper way of living to have a personal analyst.

Certainly, psychotherapies can offer immediate relief, actually a delay in the organic restrictions pressing toward normality. The patient enjoys the attention he is getting and the interest his problems are arousing, as well as the direct "improvements" offered through relief from restrictions or "repressions." The delay in the restrictive restoration of normality is extended as much as possible.

That is why transference, the patient's attachment to the therapist or to what he is doing, becomes the main achievement, and admittedly the very core of analytic psychotherapies.[1, 3,4]

When some therapies succeed, they do so for reasons different from the direct-improvement efforts of therapists. For instance, in group therapies, as in the treatment of Alcoholics Anonymous, the participant is forced to accept restrictions through a curious ensnaring effect. As he observes the detestable behavior of others, he loathes it eagerly, with strong emotion. This later compels him to detest and abstain from his own similar behavior.

All in all, modern psychiatry, with its direct-improvement logic and methods, has contributed to the increase of the mental difficulties of modern man. The modern trend of increased enjoyment of "improvements" is here compounded by the inherently alchemistic scientism. The ways and means of direct increase in positive, enjoyable reactions become the logical goals of psychiatry. But the inevitable result of all kinds of added enjoyments is a deepening vicious-circle exhaustion of emotions or, simply, of the pleasure potential.

The number of officially registered mentally ill patients has increased to more than six million in this country.[17] This amounts to a fourfold increase since 1955,[17] when the greatest improvements were started in psychiatry with the expanded marketing of the wonder drugs.

In a study by the NIMH, the widest to date, it has been established that now one out of every five adult Americans suffers from some mental disorder.[18] The rate of one-in-twenty was generally accepted in the Forties, and one-in-ten in the Sixties. This indicates the trend.

The study also shows that of the thirty million adults now suffering from the disorders only one-fifth is seeking professional help, and mostly from general physicians, not from psychiatrists.[18]

Thus, only six million mental patients appear in statistics. Of these, three-fourths are now outpatients, since mental-hospital treatment has been shown to be disastrous. The public mental hospitals have been progressively emptying in the last two decades, as it is finally realized that patients deteriorate under the most fully "scientific", hospital treatment. Even so, the general number of inpatients has also increased since 1955, by 40 percent.[17]

Of all human problems, mental disorders should be the most easily controllable, by using the capacities of the mind itself. Psychiatry should be the most successful area of our unique modern progress. But psychiatry is doing more harm than good. It does so by establishing the general attitudes about mental "improvements." The increasing mental deterioration in this country could not have advanced without "scientific" help in our scientific era.

The scientifically "logical," direct-improvement methods and means in modern psychiatry are not very different from those used by narcotics. Experimentally and logically a narcotic drug, such as morphine, offers a perfect direct improvement. Our psychiatric treatments, however involved, have been pursued under the same experimentally logical way of thinking.

The mental difficulties of modern men thus are bound to be aggravated by our psychiatric science. Revealingly, psychiatrists commit suicide six times more often than other people do; we can refer here to a comprehensive statistical study by Daniel E. DeSole. In underdeveloped countries where people receive little psychiatric professional help, mental disorders are less frequent. Explanations about our higher rate of mental illness blame our industrialization or urbanization.[1, 6, 7]

But our progress and cities provide, to the highest degree, every direct emotional enjoyment or improvement—stimulation, excitement, variety, and ease. We would find underdeveloped or non-urban life really depressing and mentally impoverishing. That is why we have escaped from such a life.

Modern psychiatry and the scientism it expounds are helping us in this escape, in the avoidance of stress or restrictions and having more effective, freer enjoyments of all our experiences. This, precisely, deepens the tendencies of mental over-enjoyment into sources of disease.

It is self-evidently clear that the psychotic should be forced to live through the feelings and reactions he has avoided most. He should be reactively made as "diseased" as are drug addicts when their organisms are purified from drugs during withdrawal. The psychotic should be exposed to properly adapted, continuous psychologic "shock." We have seen how such a shock can cure even chronic psychoses.

Mental "diseases" are natural efforts by organisms to regain their normalcy. That is why two-thirds of all mental patients recover by themselves—more surely than when they are "helped" by psychiatric therapies.

As Dr. S. Kellam of the NIMH has stated, the "major effort in psychiatry today is to reduce the degree to which the physician and mental hospital stand in the way of patient's own capacity to get better."[2] Of course, psychiatry, with its enormous technical proficiency, could do far better than patients are doing by themselves. But then psychiatry would have to recognize the "impossible" opposite causality of functional diseases. (Our mental diseases are almost exclusively functional.)

In the end, the inexorable organic limitedness of man should, again, be emphasized. Because of this limitedness direct, scientifically "logical" addition in positive reactions inevitably leads to opposite effects. Otherwise, everybody would live in an alchemic paradise, by enjoying more and more of positive, pleasant value reactions.

But psychiatry does proceed, in everything it does, by the seemingly axiomatic scientific logic that mental improvements should be increased directly, by calculating their direct positive effects, as the experimental methods mathematically require.

Psychology as a "Scientifically" Inevitable Alchemy

Psychology has adopted without questioning the causal logic and methods of our exact, physical sciences. But, as we have repeatedly explained, the scientism of the physical sciences is alchemistic when applied to value reactions which determine what man does or becomes.

If our positive value reactions increased according to the logic of this scientism, through direct additions, we would have the alchemy of augmenting our most precious capacities with total ease. For these reactions are the sources of our positive capacities while being pleasures in themselves.

We may look at the alchemistic scientism in psychology in its two aspects. First, the very way of thinking in psychology is dominated by the logic that our inner values come from sources of the same, not opposite, nature. Opposite value causality has not been even mentioned, in any form. Only the usual scientific causal logic, from the physical sciences, is applied, in every psychological experiment, observation, or theory.

Secondly, because of the imitation of the physical sciences, psychology has drifted into a kind of general physicalism. The exact physical sciences deal only with external, physically experimental phenomena. Experimental psychology has, correspondingly, abandoned dealing with inner values or value reactions, which are causally paradoxical. Under the behavioristic, presently dominant theories and methods, only external responses and stumuli are to be considered, not the inner mental experiences.

In general, psychologists are mostly studying and analyzing the *cognitive* factors, such as learning perceptions, insights, reasoning, ideas, thoughts, memory, identifications, and the self or identity. This indeed permits the use of the logic and methods of our exact sciences, which deal only with the outside, physical world.

The very function of cognition is to enable man to rule over outside things and events. Correspondingly, our inner cognitive world works as a system parallel to the outside world. In any case, the causal logic of the physical phenomema and the "logical" mathematically structured experiments become applicable to cognitive causal factors.

For instance, you learn about things or objects, and the results of your learning can be, mathematically, measured by the amount of things you learned. You perceive events, and your capacities or ways of perception are reflected in the amount and relations of events perceived. You remember or understand phenomena by association, and constructs of associations in your mind correspond to associations of external phenomena. In short, the abstract cognitive concepts can be generally treated in the same way as the physical world, to which they are parallel and similar.

Also, the cognitive experiences that man particularly notices are satisfactions, which he does not regularly connect with their opposite, causal sources, with his needs to know or to understand. Consequently, the cognitive world indeed does not seem to have any evidence of opposite causality.

Further, association of similar rather than opposite ideas often brings cognitive solutions. But, again, the solutions are satisfactions, determined by needs, which are causally decisive, while ideas are not. The human tendency to notice only satisfactions is misleading in other ways. Thus people often think that they remember, learn, or understand something suddenly or freely, while in reality the needs and "negative" backgrounds for doing so have been accumulated unnoticed for a long time.

In any event, psychologists can deal more logically and effectively with *cognitive factors* than with the paradoxical emotional or inner value reactions. Psychology thus gravitates toward the scientifically logical cognitive world. Also, psychologists easily discover cognitive ideas and reasons behind everything people do or experience.

Of course, psychologists know better than to accept the reasons given by patients. Mostly psychologists try to disentangle or to get at the core of faulty reasoning and perceptions, or to provide new insights and understanding, upon the analysis of the minds of patients. Still, it all amounts to dealing with cognitive factors, which have no decisive behavioral effect.

Here we have to emphasize the universal human fallacy about the role and force of cognitive factors such as ideas and insights or perceptions and learning. As we have seen, the most enriching positive reactions can be fully espoused cognitively with total ease—by reading a couple of pages of explanations or listening to a lecture on positive thinking.

Yet men have perpetuated, for millennia, their beliefs in the power of ideas and reasons. Psychologists have compounded the fallacy about the importance of cognitive factors, as we have just explained. By doing so they are, unawares, making psychology turn even more decisively into an alchemy, into a discipline implying the possibility of mental enrichment through easy, cognitive causality.

Surely, cognitive capacities are our immensely effective instruments for dealing with the outside world. We don't do anything without them. That is why we see them as our all-inclusive powers. Yet these powers are merely our tools. The moving forces are our emotions or values, mostly our conditioned pleasure drives, which alone determine how and where these tools are used. We also misuse and twist our reasons or ideas to fit our feelings and conditioned pleasures or to justify our reactions.

We shall return to the prevalence of cognitive causal concepts in psychology later. But first let us look at the universal acceptance of the *causal logic that positive value reactions come from positive causal sources*. We don't need to explain again that if this logic was true men would enrich themselves mentally with alchemic ease.

Yet every article written or item discussed in psychology asserts or implies that positive reactions derive from positive causal backgrounds. Conversely, negative reactions are blamed on negative experiences. We have here the axiomatic, like-from-like causal logic of all scientism.

Nobody ever thinks of doubting this logic. In fact this has been the causal logic of every theory or "scientific" reasoning in human thinking. That is why the technical sciences could evolve but the human sciences could not, as we have explained before. It should not be forgotten how repulsive to men are ideas about relative or opposite-value causality which alone would be true for human sciences.

Typically, psychologists cannot recognize the opposite-reaction rule even when they discover how general it is. A few psychologists have discovered the "opponent-process" principle that explains the relativity of responses, habituation, various addictions, or even the creativity of restrictions.[18] Still, psychologists cannot believe what they are discovering. The chief exponent and main research analyst of the Opponent-Process Theory, Richard Solomon, says, "I'm suspicious of it myself. I wish someone would come along and prove it untrue."[18]

Now we have to turn again to the most important factor in man's conscious existence—to *pleasure as his only source of causal, mechanistically precise understanding and guidance*, governing his myriad organic and behavioral mechanisms. This time we shall see, in the end, how even experiments in psychology become virtual travesties if the causally all-inclusive but simple, integrated pleasure responses are not considered.

The imitation of the logic and methods of the physical sciences precludes the recognition of pleasure as cause. Physically pleasure does not seem to exist. The like-from-like causal logic does not agree with the causation of pleasure. Nobody can miss noticing that people who enjoy pleasure most, who are eagerly and constantly increasing it, have least of it in the end. Psychologists, with their extensive erudition and insights, certainly know this. Pleasure simply becomes too incongruous to be accepted as a causal factor. Also, pleasure is so commonplace, actually universal, in human existence that it seems simplistic to pay special attention to it.

For all such reasons, pleasure is never discussed as the general causal source in "scientific" psychology. Typically, the more extraordinary, causally less universal feelings such as passions, impulses, or joys are sometimes discussed; so are isolated, separate emotional events. But *the universal causal source of behavior, pleasure*, is never considered as such a source.[11, 12, 14]

This amounts to an unbelievable disregard of the very mechanism that makes man tick. We may as well recall here that pleasure is the single miraculous mechanism by which we can understand what causally happens to us as organisms, and which makes us behave as we do, in even the tiniest detail.

Correspondingly, pleasure can be an equally precise and mechanistic causal—that is, scientific—concept for understanding everything that happens inside men, mentally and physically—if the opposite causality is understood.

Scientifically this is decisive. Think of *experiments or experimental observations* in psychology. They can hardly be taken seriously if the pleasure factor is left out. For only pleasure can account, in precise, mechanistic ways, for every past behavioral adaptation or causal determinant, even from our million-year evolution—for all causally decisive factors everywhere, from the tasting of foods or the making of sexual choices to detailed survival reactions. And every inner value derives from the organic value reactions.

It would be ridiculous to expect that any experiment could account for such countless historical determining causes. But an experiment that leaves out decisive causes is useless.

This is relevant for any reaction and behavior, extensive or detailed. Anxiety causally derives from the survival instinct determined by organic evolution. The taste of an apple is equally determined by your previous, even evolutionary, needs and satisfactions. Through the simple yes-and-no indications of pleasure and displeasure one can make causal conclusions and predictions that account for all the relevant causal details, however involved and irretrievable may be their causally determining history. In contrast, experiments never even intend to deal with the causally decisive past, extending to your needs of yesterday and the determinants evolved during ages of evolution.

Understandably, psychologists have to limit themselves to

short-run, misleading experiments. Added stimulation offered to a subject, in an experiment, increases his performance. But actually opposite reactions will follow afterward. Moreover, the subject's past, his opposite-reaction organic adaptations determined why and how the stimulation works and is bound to have opposite effects.

The point is that pleasure integrates, mechanically, for your causal consideration, whole systems of infinite causal details. Pleasure through inner values or feelings makes it possible for man to understand at once precisely the results of the interactions of myriad mechanisms in all their million-year-old causal meanings. This is totally impossible in the usual "scientific" experiments.

Experimental scientism becomes stilted and misleading; an experiment that leaves out decisive causal factors or their determinantal causal meanings is a travesty.

Causal coherence is presently maintained in experiments by accepting pleasure as cause without recognizing it as causally relevant—by taking it for granted that wishes and drives are behind all behavior.

This is, however, more distorting than to ask for a spade while refusing to call it a spade. Each pleasure reaction has decisive and prescise, peculiar causal meanings and effects, governed by their impossible causal logic. To miss them is to miss causal, scientific understanding; think of how the precise and paradoxical pleasure causality explains the various admittedly mysterious functional diseases.

Now we may look at some particularly significant aspects of this inevitably misleading experimentalism in the main movements of modern psychology.

Behaviorism is the dominant movement and it adheres to the experimental scientism. Typically, it cannot recognize consciousness, which works by innumerable inner-value or pleasure reactions. For less dogmatic scientists consciouness is, of course, the criterion for distinguishing the psychological world from merely physiologic existence. All scientists know that consciousness is a product of biological mechanisms. These are, however, too numerous and involved to fathom.

Only pleasure or feelings integrate totally and precisely all the countless biological mental mechanisms for man's unified simple evaluation and causal understanding. Those feelings constitute consciousness. In contrast, the multiplicity of the mechanisms here cannot be dealt with by "scientifically" experimental methods.

Behaviorists, therefore, had to reject the whole inner mental world. They recognized only external stimuli and responses. They had to claim, confusedly, that thought was movements in the larynx and that emotions were visceral reflexes.

The main field of study in behaviorism is, probably, conditioning. In the "epoch-making" experiment by John B. Watson, he showed that an infant can be conditioned to fear furry objects by being scared with a noise. Watson then proclaimed that children could be brought up by similar conditioning to become anything, scientists and doctors or vagabonds and thieves.

In truth, this kind of conditioning would become a self-defeating mockery. A child growing up—under real, inner-value conditioning—would evolve rather particularly strong adjustments for counteracting such silly interferences as the "frightening" noise. We do become cultural through conditioning. But it is our general inner values, as integrated pleasures, that are to be conditioned.

The later, more advanced behaviorist ideas about conditioning have remained equally misleading. Psychologists still disregard the real emotional or value conditioning. Instead the Pavlovian kind of conditioning remains the model.

Actually, this conditioning is merely a process of learning, organically direct animal learning. Our best authorities on animal conditioning, Howard S. Liddell and Norman R. F. Maier, saw conditioning as learning.[11, 14] The current leading authorities, B. F. Skinner, and H. J. Eysenck, accept the same principles of conditioning, from animal models, without regard for inner-value conditioning.

The decisive fact, however, is that such animal conditioning amounts to learning. When animals learn, say, to avoid a shock, they retain that behavior for good. But for man learning is merely a tool for choosing the most useful or pleasant behavior from countless possibilities. How and when this tool is used is determined by the whole system of pleasures, of inner values, which therefore have to be conditioned.

B. F. Skinner stresses that successful operant conditioning is attained only if satisfactory reinforcements or rewards are used. An incredible amount of such rewards would be required, considering the numerous demands of our cultural and social life we have to meet every day or hour. Also, the more rewards are heaped on, the less effective they become. Where are all the rewards to come from?

We have seen that, in the real, inner-value conditioning, educational restrictions as non-satisfactions of the needs of survival itself create limitless conditioned needs for our vast cultural satisfactions.

But the causally determining world of inner values or pleasure drives does not exist for behaviorists. The operant conditioning of B. F. Skinner remains a mere process of learning. As such, it may indeed not require constant, countless rewards. But for humans learning is behaviorally as ineffective as it is easy. Particularly when it comes to the adoption of positive reactions, the sources of our useful behavior.

Gestalt psychology is probably the second most important movement in psychology. The phenomena that Gestaltists observed are explainable by value relativity and value preferences or value prejudices. But Gestaltists as scientists never considered, in their formal explanations, any value concepts. They thus missed the real causes, from the world of the causally decisive, relative value experiences.

For instance, visual illusions, the main Gestaltist "proofs," are due to value relativity. A line appears shorter when placed together with longer lines, or a circle smaller amidst great circles. Forms or lines drawn on a background that is uniformly slanted in one way appear slanted in the opposite way. Even ideational meanings reverse upon one-sided exaggeration, which reveals them as value processes.

In one example, a drawing that could be seen equally well as a rabbit's head turned left or as a duck's head turned right switches in your perception between the two images in a way you cannot control. Here the "exaggeration" consists of attributing only one meaning at a time to something that has an equally good second meaning or value.

Perceptual illusions, as all value distortions, are countless. They are due to the fact that values appear and disappear depending on the opposites they are compared with. We have seen how size, slanting, shape, color, movement, temperature, and smell acquire their values from the opposite backgrounds they emerge against.

Above all, over-enjoyments of emotions lead to opposite aftereffects; and excessive functional improvements result in an equal "worsening." But Gestaltists were bound to miss such a more important causation, since they avoided value concepts in their "scientific" explanations. Gestaltists thus did not see the universal causality of "illusions" in the fields of the decisive value reactions which determine our behavior and even health.

The Gestalt principles, such as similarity, proximity, "pregnance," or perceptual self-organization, are due to our value preferences or value "prejudices." This can be easily understood if one considers how our sense of values governs and distorts everything we perceive or judge.

Anyway, one simple principle, of value causality, is sufficient to afford a full causal explanation for the Gestalt phenomena. But Gestaltists sought explanations through constructs from the physical sciences, particularly through the concept of isomorphism.

Inevitably, Gestaltists had to formulate laws for each of their more than hundred principles and to endow each of countless Gestalts with its own causal essence. Indeed, each Gestalt is a curiously unique phenomenon irreducible to anything else, unless it is recognized how the simple, though paradoxical, value causation is the unified source of all conscious experiences, including those of cognitive peculiarities and illusions.

The Gestaltist world of multiple causal principles and essences naturally required a miraculous agency or intelligence behind the visible things. The leading Gestaltist, Wolfgang Koehler, has expounded, in his book *The Place of Value in the World of Facts*, a theory of transcendental values and meanings inherent in the physical world. Gestaltists could not accept simple value causation, and therefore had to resort to great philosophical value theories.

Koehler admits that such views go against all the mechanistic thinking in sciences, which therefore "should be turned around." He rightly saw that each Gestalt phenomenon has a peculiar individual meaning or sense—actually determined by the given particular value-background. But he had to attribute these meanings to causes from a transcendental world.

Indeed, all of Gestalt psychology has to remain mystical. The illusions or causal riddles are there, but a natural, necessarily simple cause for them is missing. However, this very mystery has become a source of attraction and of esoteric interpretations. Gestalt therapy becomes an alchemy of trying to gain capacities by mere formulistic and symbolic performances.

The other, *older psychological schools* failed for similar reasons. They too proceeded according to the direct, "scientific," like-from-like causal logic. They formulated theories such as associationism or parallelism by thinking in terms of the "logical," cognitive, but causally ineffective world.

They tried to apply such theories to behavior, to decisive, value reactions, which are actually governed by opposite causality. Expectedly, observations in dozens of fields proved such theories to be wrong; psychologists have always been proving how wrong are theories advanced by other psychologists.

The old schools also missed the most universal causal sources: the limitedness of organisms to their sameness, the ultimate organic needs, the pleasure drive, and the conditioning of all of us. Such causal sources are as universal as atmospheric pressure, and therefore as little noticed. Of course, the universally decisive, opposite value causality was also missed, particularly because it derives from the organic limitedness.

The older schools had to fail, but the imitation of the scientism of physical sciences has generally intensified. The result has been a total elimination of concepts of inner values or, simply, of pleasure, which determines everything psychological and makes men behave or live the way they do, at every moment. The imitated scientism becomes fruitless and irrelevant, disconnected from causal reality.

Revealingly, the enormous research in psychology has not produced a single fundamental causal principle on which psychologists could agree—and which they know cannot be complex or difficult to find. Psychologists are too knowledgeable as scientists to fail to recognize that fundamental causal laws are simple and few, or that psychology as science can be founded only on such simple unifying principles.

Some psychologists have turned to different, less physicalistic approaches.[14] *Humanistic psychology* appears to be the most important and most representative of such movements. It claims as its exponents authorities like Gordon Allport, Abraham Maslow, Henry Murray, or Carl Rogers.

But modern, progressive humantistic attitudes, in particular, favor the belief in logical improvements of inner-value experiences. This can compound harmful fallacies, such as the condemnation of restrictions.

Typically, the most misleading philosophical movements, *phenomenology and existentialism*, have been adopted as guides in the latest psychological theories.[14] Phenomenology stresses the inmost awareness as a direct source of truths, thus promoting direct-value, non-relative convictions in psychological theory. Existentialism represents a typical confusion in modern thought. It stresses extreme negative feelings, of anxiety and despair, without the insight that these reactions come exactly from the over-enjoyment of opposite feelings by modern men.

Generally, psychology has never deviated from the presently dominant scientism, of the physical sciences, and from their causal logic.[11, 12] We do not need to explain again that this scientism and its causal logic, or its experimental methods, are inevitably alchemistic when applied to human sciences.

It is practically as well as scientifically decisive to understand that our positive capacities are satisfactions or pleasure releases—which, however, increase not by "logical," pleasant, alchemically easy additions in them but by the exactly contrary process, of increase of needs or restrictions—by the *opposite-value causation.*

But no experiment has yet been conducted with the logic of this causation, diametrically different from physical-science causal logic. No wonder that our modern, experimental psychology has led to innumerable controversial systems and theories, instead of a few simple scientific laws.

Now let us look at the equally alchemistic acceptance of *cognitive or ideational factors* as decisive causes in psychology. Cognitive factors are as easily manageable as all reasoning and ideas. If they were causally effective, our precious mental capacities would be increased as easily, since we can readily learn that positive reactions are desirable in every way.

Yet psychologists deal mostly with cognitive factors, for reasons we have explained. They can proceed with success or causal coherence only in the cognitive world, which is parallel to the physical, external world of exact sciences. The inner values which actually determine behavior are causally too paradoxical for psychologists as logical scientists.

Let us look at learning. It is the cognitive factor most extensively treated as a decisive causal source. One can admire the skill and erudition of psychologists in their treatment of learning. It has been perfectly analyzed in all its intricate secondary aspects of generalizations, learning cues, signs, verbalizations, symbols, habits, past failures, and associations.[11, 12] It all has been admirably laid out in extensive theories, by such authorities as Ernest

R. Hilgard, Neal E. Miller, O. Hobart Mowrer, and Gardner Murphy.

But whatever the discovered complexities and distortions or past failures, don't people want to learn what is pleasant, first and most of all? And nothing more than simple pleasure or satisfactions are required for perfect behavior. The truth about positive reactions as panacean remedies for all difficulties could be learned and adopted with ease, in all its aspects, in one hour.

Of course, emotions or pleasures distort and determine application of any learning. Emotions, though, are governed by a causality completely different from the logical scientism that psychologists follow in dealing with the phenomena of learning.

What is true here for learning also applies to *other cognitive factors*: perceptions, insights, understanding, reasons, thoughts and ideas. In themselves they could be perfected or straightened out with equal ease. Also, they would overwhelmingly favor adoption of reactions that are positive and pleasant. But they are governed as well as distorted in their application by feelings or the pleasure drive.

It should be noted that psychologists often attribute, indirectly, emotional effects to cognitive factors such as perceptions or ideas. This increases causal confusion. It amounts to mixing up cognitive capacities, which are easy and mere "tools," with emotions, which are difficult to create and are the forces that determine how these tools are used. Thus, what is causally ineffective is not distinguished from what is decisive.

Theories about *attitude* are good examples. As fixational emotions, attitudes can be formidable driving forces. But psychologists regularly equate attitudes with cognitive perceptions. Jean Piaget, the foremost authority here, has shown how children lack logical, cognitive capacities and how this affects their attitudes.

In truth, cognitive mistakes of logic can be as easily corrected as emotional attitudes cannot. Because of such mixups, theories become incredibly complex and research expands desperately, without practical results—in a modern version of the exasperating complexities of alchemy.

But the emphasis on *cognitive psychology is nevertheless increasing*. This is confirmed in a survey by *Psychology Today* on the achievements of psychology in the last two decades.[19] It finds as prevalent an "emphasis on cognitive processes" and an expanding "cognitive revolution." Even in the studies on reactions and stress, the cognitive revolution and an emphasis on "thoughts and knowledge as causal factors" are found to be prevailing. The book *Cognitive Psychology*, by Ulrich Neisser, is found as characterstic of the modern trend in psychology.

Similarly, the survey finds as highly representative the work of Neal Miller, the leading authority on biofeedback as well as learning. Biofeedback in effect amounts to cognitive awareness training, even for control of our gravest reactions such as stress. (We have explained that opposite reactions follow the avoidance of stress, whatever the means used in avoiding it.) Particularly prominent in the most advanced study of learning and cognition has been the work of Ernest Hilgard. He is, appropriately, recognized as an eminent representative of the present trend in psychology.[11, 19]

But even in less general areas, such as existential psychology, the emphasis on cognitive causality dominates. Rollo May, another authority, has stated that our whole culture and society depend on the preservation and relearning of cultural symbols and myths.[19]

Let's look at other assumed causal sources in psychology, such as *self, identity or alienation*. They are inherently cognitive. One's self is to be ideationally discovered, and identity is to be found by deeper insights or thought mechanisms such as idenification. The great achievement is to "know" yourself. Alienation is viewed as the lack of identification or as ideational separation and isolation, which are cognitive reactions.

It is generally held that the discovery of self leads to satisfactory adjustment. Find your identity and it will serve you as a source of positive behavior. Even the best authorities on identity and self do not escape such inherently alchemistic ways of thinking.

The leading authority on identity, Erik H. Erikson, sees his eight "ages" in personality development as states of direct, logical attainment of more positive reactions or attitudes. These include trust, pride, freedom, a sense of adequacy, self-acceptance, enjoyed intimacy, and rejection of despair. There is, of course, no place in Erikson's theory for the requirement of causal backgrounds that are felt to be negative though they necessarily serve as the causal sources of positive reactions.

Another leading authority, Abraham H. Maslow, saw the discovery of the ontological self as an ecstatic experience. He compared it to the intensely pleasant "peak experiences" which he expounded as the sources of most positive, creative adjustments. One can only wonder why haven't we all rushed into discovering our ontological selves. Any such important sources of pleasure inside us could not possibly remain unnoticed.

Similarly typical are theories about *roles and role-playing*, as well as about mechanisms like identification or substitution. The concept of role-playing underlies the widely accepted transactional analysis, popularized by Eric Berne and Thomas A. Harris. People love to see the frequent seemingly whimsical human behavior explained as intriguing games. Erving Goffman wrote widely about most men or women as constant actors and the world as a stage.

In reality, human behavior is causally quite different from a game of playing roles. It requires hard, dead-serious effort. No amount of role-playing or manipulation of identifications, which is easy, can make a real motivational difference. Pretensions and the playing of roles are consequences, not causes, of behavioral mismanagement.

Mechanisms such as *identification, projection, substitution, or dissociation* are frequent in behavior. They are resorted to for the attainment of some pleasure. But psychologists use these concepts in their intricate cognitive aspects to explain various behavior disorders,[11, 14] which are definitely unpleasant, and useless. The direct, "logical," often quite complex and sophisticated explanations here imply that a person creates ways of hurting himself as a result of technical, cognitive confusion.

But men are too intelligent to be confused about the simplest things in their world, about pain and pleasure. Actually, the mechanisms just mentioned become sources of disorders when they are over-enjoyed, when the vicious-circle opposite reactions become inevitable. We shall look at these mechanisms in detail later in discussing the science of behavior, where they are most frequently viewed as causes.

Very popular are the various *consciousness-expansion methods*, from transcendental meditation to the Esalen treatment, bioenergetics, Rolfing, or Est. Hundreds of similar methods have been suggested. The aim of consciousness expansion is to attain precious positive reactions by mere cognitive or ideational manipulations, techniques, mental skills or formulas. True, these methods are not always recognized in formal, scientific psychology. But they correspond to the inherently alchemistic scientism in psychology. If learning and biofeedback are seen as effective causal sources, why not try a more direct and wider use of consciousness?

This agrees with the scientific tradition in psychology since William James. He observed the wondrous effect of intense positive experiences. They seem to be free or costless, since they come easily, as all enjoyments do. James speculated about various ways, including the use of drugs, for tapping these sources.

Finally, the important *Freudian movement* in psychology has to be considered. It is not for nothing that Freud is sometimes viewed as the father of modern, "dynamic" psychology. He made it possible for "logical" psychology to continue. The critical problem, in all behavior, is why and how man acts against himself. The Freudian Unconscious explains that.

Also, Freudian theory confirms that restrictions, as repressions, cause the negative reactions of disorders, and that the release of suppressed pleasure drives brings relief. This agrees with the alchemy of the direct increase or release of positive reactions. Thus scientists can continue viewing restrictions—which serve recovery—as logical evils.

Furthermore, unconscious experiences are not organically relevant feelings; they are affectively without substance. For to feel is to be conscious, to have value reactions through organic changes. As a result Freud, wisely, treated unconscious experiences as merely cognitive conflicts, ideas, perceptions, and schemes. He established the perfect method, analysis, for dealing with such cognitive factors. Analysis became the foundation of the Freudian system and has generally sustained analytic, cognitive psychology in its advance.

Indeed only the inventive, cognitive capacities can render the Unconscious so clever that it can create all the endlessly "ingenious" negative reactions of disorders. The Unconscious becomes a source of limitless explanations.

In each of its various aspects, *the Unconscious is a personified agency* that thinks and schemes as a person does. All prescientific systems require personifications. Some personified agent, a clever spirit, is discovered, which can explain any existing mystery.

There is indeed an enormous amount of psychological mystery presently that has to be explained. Opposite-value causality applies to everything man feels or does. Consequently the whole human world, including our everyday behavior and health, is dominated by the mystery of the most intense and ingenious forces causing us to act against ourselves, contrary to our every intent or reason.

The opposite causality which makes man, universally, act in this way is as simple and mechanistic as are all natural, uniform causal principles. In contrast, Freud chose the most complex and nonmechanistic explanation of all, the Unconscious as a personified agent. Let us look at a typical Freudian explanation.

The Freudian slip is probably the most frequently invoked example of the Unconscious at work; it has become a term commonly listed in dictionaries. Here the Unconscious is seen as an inventive, underhanded demon waiting patiently for the right moment to trip up a person. What better proof for a personifiable agent inside a person?

In an example described by Freud, a student hosting his professor wants to say, "Let us drink to him," in German, "*anzustossen*," but instead says, "*aufzustossen*," which means "throw up on him." Freud could demonstrate with various examples of such slips how clever the Unconscious has to be; the cleverness of the Unconscious was Freud's central proof of his claims.

But the real cause is simple and mechanistic. The student exaggerated his feelings of respect for the professor, in order to be the perfect host. The opposite reaction, a sudden burst from repressed mechanisms, then had to break out. This is true in all cases where a person forces or stimulates himself to feel, behave, or say things in a positive way far above what he really can and does feel.

No scheming demon is needed for the slip to occur. The opposite reaction here is as mechanistic as is the aftereffect of every overenjoyment. An overdriven mechanism has to slip back, at the slightest opportunity, by an opposite process, with all its corresponding reactions and behavioral expressions.

Practically, *Freudianism has become widely known because it offers everything men enjoy wondering about*: mystery, hidden agents inside people, horrible primordial drives, weird secrets of sex, dreams, symbolism, and magic, all in dramatic forms. An idea gains attention and becomes institutionalized by fixation to the extent people talk and think about it. The Freudian theory is perfectly suited to arouse the highest interest of people. Freud saw as important everything that is strange, sensational, dramatic, or unusual—therefore only exceptional and causally the least relevant.

Freud's sensationalism was rather naive. He did not realize

that the assumed horrible drives, such as the Oedipus complex, would be seen as normal if they were really general. If lust for the mother and the wish to kill the father were general, it would be felt as traumatic not to have such desires.

A serious impact of Freudianism is *that it frightens people into thinking that repressions or restrictions can cause behavior disorders and disease.*

We have seen the clear confusion in Freudian theory over repressions as the causes of all neuroses. It amounts to not distinguishing between pleasure and torment. Repression of the strongest, most *pleasant* drives is claimed just because *traumatic* experiences are suppressed in the rare unconscious neuroses. Of course, experimentally or clinically, mental disease is always an extreme restriction—resulting from equal pleasure release during over-enjoyment and serving the restoration of organic normalcy.

It is most significant that in the end *Freud himself rejected the theory of repression*, though it had to and did remain the basis of psychoanalysis. He rejected it in the final revision of his theory, in the book *Problems of Anxiety*. He had become puzzled, noticing that "what was repression appears later as gratification." He then replaced repression as the cause of anxiety with nongratification, or *Unlust*, also termed "object loss."

Freud had the genius to turn the existing confusion in psychology into a dramatic mystery. *He had little of true, practical intuition for psychological causation.* Such intuition is the only useful guide amidst the prevailing theoretical confusion and controversies.

Freud lacked such a practical intuition so completely that he was continuously suffering from anxiety, phobias, mood swings, fatigue, obsessions, hypochondriacal fears, self-torment, and fixed beliefs.[15] He not only used drugs, notably cocaine, but was unaware of their connection with their after-effects and advocated their use to his friends.[6, 15]

But Freudian theory has in practice saved the "logical" scientism in psychology, as we have explained. It has enabled psychology to continue with the inherently alchemistic logic of positive reactions deriving from increased or released, nonrestricted pleasures and satisfactions. Freud is indeed the great genius of our modern alchemy. Freudians expect solutions from mere talk, in analyses, or from analytic dealing with factors such as perceptions and insights that are only cognitive, or with "feelings" that are not even experienced, organically, since they are "unconscious."

In conclusion we have to say that psychology and psychiatry are not yet sciences. Their efforts have been enormous. But they have not yet discovered the few universal causal principles necessary for any exact science. Instead they have hundreds of proposed causal systems and fundamental causal forces. Think, for comparison, of the four forces in physics. We have seen that human sciences too can be built on only a few causal principles.

Practical psychologists proceed merely with good sense and higher intelligence. An industrial or educational psychologist merely looks for what practically works in his field.[16] He never even refers to a psychologically scientific theory.[16] He would not know which one to choose from the hundreds proffered.

It can be said that the present science in psychology or psychiatry will be forgotten, relegated to history, when real science is finally established in these fields. That science will be built as a new, unified, generally accepted system based on one or a few causal principles, as all exact sciences are.

Psychologists and psychiatrists themselves know this; each of them is proposing such a unified system based on some one causal principle or force—different from those proposed by others.

Presently the only generally accepted certainty in these fields is the scientism adopted from the exact, physical sciences. It is governed by the mathematically axiomatic logic, of increase of values through addition. Every experiment or experimental observation is conducted or calculated with this logic.

But the adoption of this logic for value reactions, which determine behavior, amounts to alchemy, to an assumption that positive reactions can be gained or increased through pleasant additions in them. Indeed, everything written or said in psychology is still based on the belief that positive reactions come from positively felt causal backgrounds.

Also, cognitive factors are widely accepted as decisive in psychology because of the adoption of the logic of physical sciences. This logic, unusable for value causality, is easily applicable to cognitive factors because our cognitive world is mostly a parallel reflection of our outside, physical world. But cognitive factors like ideas are easy to create and are causally weightless. No such alchemic ease is possible in the world of decisive, value causation.

In the real, practical world of mental problems and psychology, our positive reactions and behavior are always difficult, and never come without equal "payment" because of opposite-value causality. The ultimate reason here is, of course, the organic limitedness of man which makes that causality inescapable.

Perhaps men can never accept the fact of their organic limitedness as a practically believable truth. But man as scientist will build sciences about himself only when he overcomes this prejudice. We have seen repeatedly how human sciences could be founded on the principle of opposite-value causality, which is as universal as the only "design" of organisms, to conserve their limited sameness.

IV

CAUSAL CONFUSION IN BEHAVIORAL AND SOCIAL SCIENCES

In our practical behavior and motivations a no-free-lunch causal rule is inevitable and not difficult to recognize. Our positive motivations never come free, without equal effort. The reason is the opposite-value causality, which determines all value reactions. But behavioral scientists can never accept this scientifically, experimentally "illogical" causality.

Scientists, of course, well understand that positive value reactions such as interests or enthusiasm are sources of our desired positive behavior. Correspondingly, the theorists and experts in the behavioral sciences have advocated, in various ways, the direct, "scientficially" logical increase in our positive value reactions. Can anything, be easier than such an increase in the pleasant positive reactions?

Yet the like-from-like scientific, mathematically certain causal logic underlies all behavioral theories and their proposed applications to practical problems. Of course, the theories become endlessly varied, controversial, and complex, to the extent that the scientific causal logic of our exact physical sciences is incongruous for value causality and thus for all behavior.

The other general causal delusion, namely the belief that cognitive causes are decisive, is particularly strong in the social sciences. Here everybody believes that ideas and ideologies, or perceptions and reasons, are the determining factors. Of course, cognitive factors are as easy and ineffective as wondrous ideas or perfect intents.

No real science yet exists in the practically important areas of education, crime, or other social concerns. The reason again is the confusion about the causality of value feelings and about the effects of cognitive causal factors.

It is not yet recognized here as well that conditioned nonsatisfactions or restrictions are the sources of desired satisfactions or pleasures, their value opposites. Solutions are sought rather through a direct increase in positive value reactions. Also, cognitive factors such as insights, reasoning, or learning are accepted as decisive. A causally exact science in these fields could make a decisive difference. All true sciences become miraculously effective, after starting with tiny beginnings founded on simple causal discoveries. Problems like those of crime are enormously difficult. But also a real science can be enormously effective and inventive, as can be seen from our technical sciences.

The causal insight that could foster a science here has remained impossible because the present "scientific" efforts have been directed in ways exactly contrary to the actual causation of behavioral problems. The paradoxical creative role of nonsatisfactions and restrictions is not recognized.

The social sciences, in particular, are not even starting as scientific disciplines. As we have indicated already, the social sciences are the most typical "soft" sciences, missing completely the actual, opposite causality of value reactions which determines what man does socially as well. With a causal logic diametrically contrary to what is causally true, the social sciences are moving away from causal, scientific understanding in their fields.

Also, the present persistence of social scientists to study the properly *social* phenomena precludes the social sciences from ever becoming scientific.

Actually, social phenomena should be studied as the products of individual behavior that they concretely always are. This should be done for a wider reason also. A science can be built only on universally valid and uniformly understood causal laws. Such laws are possible for the behavior of individuals, as organisms, reacting in accordance with uniform natural principles; the opposite causality of value reactions is such a principle.

In contrast, proper social phenomena never follow any causal, uniform, or natural laws. Such phenomena are created by men using their endlessly changing and inventive, never limited or uniform, intents and ideas. These are, of course, practically governed by the value reactions or feelings of individuals, ruled by the natural law of value causality.

Certainly, it may be technically difficult to study social behavior as resulting from the behavior of individuals. But the sciences are phenomenally capable of solving technical difficulties. They should, however, start as disciplines having uniform causal laws—which is possible only for individual behavior, never for social phenomena. Cultures and institutions, for example, are as endlessly varied and unpredictable as infinite human wishes or intents and ways of ideational thinking or inventiveness.

Understandably, social scientists write numerous volumes of explanations. But no generally accepted causal principles or uniform understanding are ever established; no real science is being created.

"No Free Lunch" Rule—and Behavioral Theories

Behavioral scientists and experts have, rightly, recognized that positive human motivations and capacities derive from positive, pleasant reactions, such as enthusiasm or interest, love or satisfaction. This causal connection can be seen from any insightful observation or experiment.

Thus it would rationally seem to be the highest duty of science to explain to people how they should intensify such positive reactions—logically, by direct additions, by added enjoyments. According to an often-quoted statement by Bertrand Russell, all that men now have to do is to learn to open their hearts to joy, in order to attain everything they have always wanted.[21]

It is indeed remarkable how every noted author or expert has advocated, in one way or another, a direct increase in some kind of positive, satisfactory reaction—of enthusiasm, interest, enjoyment, optimism, hope, love, enchantment, satisfying attitudes, joys of life, or freedom from restraints and anxieties or from negative feelings.

The theories here have been simple and direct as well as scientifically complex. The "positive thinking" of Normon Vincent Peale is simple and popular. Many well-known authorities have advocated a simple increase in other positive reactions.[1, 2, 5]

But even the complex theories are founded on the same logic of direct increase in some of the positive value reactions. One can think here of such authorities as Erich Fromm, Karl Menninger, Sir Julian Huxley, Lewis Mumford, Herbert Marcuse, René Dubos, Sir Peter Medawar, Jacques Barzun, and Norman Cousins.[1, 2, 21]

Unfortunately, an increased enjoyment of any reaction or feeling can only lead to opposite reactions, as the organism restores normalcy in its dynamics.

Such enjoyments are quantitatively significant organic changes, whether they are induced by drugs or by mental self-stimulation. And any organic change is followed, or has to be preceded, by an equal opposite change so that the limited organic sameness is maintained. A pleasure release is not followed by an equal restriction only if a corresponding restriction was imposed previously and thus created a potential for equal release.

Various popular *advocates of more positive thinking* have perennially attracted enthusiastic followings and written quite a few best-sellers. Their arguments have always been logically convincing, almost self-evident. Wondrous successes are promised and expected. If realized they would transform any person's life into a miracle of mental as well as material enrichment. The promised wonders, though, fail to become realities. People's lives are not transformed. The popularity of any one of the miracle formulas has soon vanished.

But the idea of direct, positive enrichment is seemingly so logical that it constantly reemerges, in a new version. Some new book on the wonders of increased interest, enthusiasm, or love then becomes a best-seller.

In truth men never need encouragement to pursue their positive reactions. Everybody wants to be happy, to have more of the positive feelings. The pursuit of happiness as a universal goal of life is so general that it is guaranteed by our Constitution, which tried to reflect the highest ideals of the rationalistic Enlightenment. Scientific reasoning stands behind the idea of positive enjoyments. It is well known that people who are satisfied or happy are also more successful as well as mentally richer and even healthier.

But people with good common sense also know that the direct, logical pursuit of happiness or positive feelings is self-defeating. Strong natural pleasures would be the richest sources of such feelings. But men have learned what actually happens, and pleasures are condemned as sins.

Pleasant, positive feelings can be enjoyed to higher degrees through many means, not just drugs. But the results are disastrous and paradoxical. Happy people are those who live restrained lives of toil, who do not even strive for happiness. The unhappiest are the over-enjoyers or narcotics and the emotionally unrestrained psychopaths who yield to inner enjoyments most intensely.

Behavioral scientists hold that our irrationality and mistakes prevent us from enjoying positive reactions or satisfactions. Faulty learning or conditioning is blamed. *We are, supposedly, ruled by misleading ideas*. It is argued that through misconceptions and wrong beliefs we have substituted the materialistic or technologic rat race for true, inner satisfactions.

But our intelligence and rationality are supreme. We can understand and build stupendously intricate systems of improvements. Moreover, the acceptance of genuinely felt positive reactions is the easiest thing to learn, understand, find, choose, enjoy, become conditioned to, or be ruled by. Only, the potential for such reactions has to be created first, by restrictions, their difficult opposites.

Certainly, material enjoyments bring reactive impoverishment, because they make possible the most effective and organically true enjoyments, deriving from intensified functional over-improvements. Then "genuine" or "true" inner satisfactions soon become indeed unavailable. *But the reason is not materialism.*

Material and technological progress could be used equally well as the necessary, effective means for building a constructive culture, with vast systems of enriching education, actually through restrictive conditioning. That would create men with rich reserves of potential for inner satisfactions.

A safe existence as the insurance of survival is the source of all our satisfactions or positive reactions. But here as everywhere else *satisfactions become possible only if equal needs as non-satisfactions have been accumulated.* That is why in effective education the security or survival needs are held conditionally unsatisfied, in exquisitively refined ways. Needs that are satisfied immediately and continually bring no sense of satisfaction.

An organism continually satiated with air or water feels no satisfaction of breathing or drinking. Survival continually insured has no felt value, though it reveals itself as the core of all values when its needs are not satisfied, when it is disturbed or threatened.

The same rule applies to all positive reactions: for every satisfaction or pleasure you have to "pay" with equal non-satisfaction as a need, or restriction as displeasure. The organism conserves its limited sameness by meeting every significant change, felt as negative or positive value, with an equivalant opposite change, felt as its value opposite.

Under natural conditions non-satisfactions or restrictions as needs or disturbances arise first and are followed by their opposites, the satisfactions. But man tries to enjoy satisfactions or pleasure releases without regard to the pre-existence of needs as non-satisfaction or restrictions. The necessary equal counter-changes then are imposed by the organism and are felt as diseased restrictions or stress.

We are repeating these simple explanations because the no-free-lunch rule is practically imperative. It may sound old-fashioned and simplistic, but it concretely determines what we can achieve as individuals and as a society. It also explains how we inflict on ourselves our behavioral disorders and difficulties, even our major diseases.

The opposite, negative effects of over-enjoyments are all around us. The simplest, most conspicuous examples are the painful effects of withdrawl from narcotics or alcohol. But similar effects result from smoking, coffee-drinking, stimulating foods and drinks, lazy relaxation, and hundreds of comforts of modern life. All such *habits* bring exactly as much displeasure upon discontinuation as was the pleasure derived from starting them.

It may be interesting to realize that no additional pleasure is felt while a habit is continued. The negative reactions follow continuously and are merely kept at bay by the habit. Every drug addict knows—regretfully only in the end—that he has gained nothing from his drug use. He cannot, though, discontinue the habit because of the withdrawal pain, the "payment" due.

The various *addictive habits* grow because the negative effects of withdrawal are inevitable for every enjoyment that does not derive from previous need or restriction. Such habits can be trivial or grave. People become addicted to narcotics or to reading detective stories, because of the negative, opposite reactions that would follow upon withdrawal or discontinuance.

All behavioral stresses or difficulties grow by the opposite-value causation, not by a lack of skillful management of behavior. The decisive fact is that the negative, opposite effects are always inevitable, whatever the "unearned " enjoyment may be. Normal organic satisfactions or pleasures can come only from equally strong needs or restrictions; and all human values are merely elaborations of organic satisfactions or pleasures.

The no-free-lunch rule is evident from all our habits of enjoyments—living comforts or coffee-drinking as well as the use of drugs, nicotine, or alcohol. In each of them the inevitable negative reactions upon withdrawal are the reason why the habit cannot be abandoned.

But the etiology here is generally not understood, because it is governed by opposite causality. Scientists prove that even cocaine and alcohol are not formally addictive.[19, 20] Yet alcoholism or a cocaine habit becomes as compulsive and grave as any drug addiction.

Many habits and addictions are formally treated as nonaddictive, as being caused by what scientists call mere psychological addiction. But practically, as well as scientifically or causally, the addiction here is real and clear, however confusing it may be to specialists. After all, psychologic feelings reflect organic changes in the same way as do physiological reactions, which are the only things observable even in laboratory analyses of the myriad physiologic processes.

Practically, even the coffee drinkers cannot abandon their habit because of the inevitable, opposite, withdrawal effects. Yet the opposite causality that governs such after-effects, physiologic and psychological, is not recognized by scientists.

Thus, even a clearly addictive over-enjoyment means such as marijuana becomes a subject of endless, controversial confusion and disagreements between experts. Is not it significant that doctors themselves become addicts thirty times more often than other people, as we shall see later?

Of course *the simple, general, no-free-lunch rule can have involved effects* under more complex conditions. We may look at a few such conditions. The key factor here as well is the maintenance by the organism of its normalcy, through equal value opposites. And man, understandably, has to maintain the normality of his organic inner values, of his needs and satisfactions, in strict correspondence with realistic outside values.

Your inner value feelings for a personal achievement or a business goal must correspond to its realistic value. That is how we order our priorities, in a sane, normal management of our motivations. Real needs as the potential sources of values or pleasure have to be accumulated behind each motivation so that it can have the corresponding required, real force.

For similar reasons, when you have valued an aspired achievement or goal highly, you cannot later dismiss it easily as unimportant when it has to be abandoned. Your need to attain that specific value must be satisfied, particularly if you have already enjoyed by anticipation that attainment.

Also, because the inner values must be realistic, an over-enjoyed, exaggerated evaluation of one's own achievements causes difficulties. You may enjoy your ability or success beyond its realistic value. But the return to reality, to its lower value, becomes inevitable sooner or later in normal adjustment. And such a return to the lower, realistic value brings negative, opposite value feelings. Only psychotics or emotionally unbalanced people try to enjoy what is not real, without weighing, intuitively, the requirement for a return to reality.

It may be difficult to grasp how our inner-value experiences can be so precisely related to objective external values. But the scores of billions of synapses in your nervous system can amply serve as a switchboard for relating every detail of your value world to your inner values.

Anyway, a person's inner-value system is maintained *normal by a realistic correlation of values with facts*. A deviation from this normality in some way leads to opposite reactions during the return to that necessary normality.

Under the no-free-lunch rule, a strong accumulation of needs is necessary to have satisfactions as motivations. *When you worry* about work to be done tomorrow you are realistically meeting a factual "disturbance" and are accumulating physiologic "resources" to cope with it. Similarly, the organism suffers stress, and pumps adrenaline, when danger is encountered.

A painfully accumulated need thus provides motivations as satisfaction. In the classic experiments by Kurt Lewin, subjects were eager to return to their uncompleted tasks. They had accumulated the needs, as satisfaction sources, for completing the tasks. In any event, normal behavior requires a strict, often painful correlation between outside objectives and inner values which derive from equivalent accumulation of needs. *Nothing is given free, and no easy reasoning helps.*

When a person merely reasons how much he intends to work more, he is not building up effective emotional motivation. Everywhere, reasoning or cognitive truths are ineffective against values or satisfactions, made possible through *painful* acceptance of needs, in *realistic*, restrictive preparations, during *evaluations of factual conditions*.

For instance, you may rationally reason that you do not have to fret about the speech you are to give. But your value reactions will make you feel otherwise. They will reveal how much you risk in prestige or in the feelings about your own excellence enjoyed for a long time; or how much you have to lower various values or satisfactions about yourself indulged in during the past.

Behavior experts advise us to dispel our worries rationally or to "shelve" them. Everybody would enjoy doing so, and could perfectly justify it by clear reasoning.

Yet normally adjusted people still worry, in spite of rational wishes not to have the seemingly counterproductive feeling of worry. They could invent excellent reasons for shelving the worries, as good as those suggested by experts. But they have to meet reality, which requires hard preparation, as the creation of needs, for future motivation as a goal of satisfaction.

What matters in all value reactions are *not reasons but feelings* and the length or intensity of their experience. A person may carry a lucky charm merely for comfort, without rationally believing in it. But if he loses it suddenly, he will experience as much distress as the total of the reassuring feelings he derived from it during the length of time he carried it.

Generally, the opposite reactions during a return to reality as mental normality are exactly equal to the exaggerated, unrealistic past enjoyment as a deviation from reality. Of course, opposite causality is always paradoxical.

A person enjoying a love affair lives through many pleasures. And people like very much to remember pleasant experiences. But when the love in the affair turns out to be untrue or unsustainable, the lover *"pays" in suffering* precisely for all the pleasures he had. Then he hates to remember them.

Conversely, a person *gets a "repayment"* if he has under-enjoyed a situation or was feeling scared but later sees the reality to have been less terrible. Everybody hates to remember unpleasant experiences. But people like to tell how they were feeling bad or terrified under conditions which turned out to be less negative or, in fact, valuable.

Any value experience, great or small, is governed by the same rule. Whether the experience was overvalued or undervalued, the opposite reaction follows. If you try to falsify a memory, to attribute emotionally to your past a greater value, the opposite feeling will soon emerge.

Many disorders in feelings and behavior grow from exaggerations or falsifications incurred by a person in his value system, which requires a strict, difficult compliance with actual values. *Social complexes* are typical disorders resulting from exaggerated, unrealistic enjoyments in one's value system. An inferiority complex derives from exaggerated feelings of superiority. Irrational guilt or shame results from a person's over-enjoyed feelings that he is praiseworthy or graceful. The complexes are causally mysterious and paradoxical because they come by the way of opposite-value causality.

The *inferiority complex* is a frequent behavioral affliction of modern man. The person suffering from it has, most likely, superior qualities.[21] He may know very well that he is superior and still suffer from the complex.[21] In truth, the person who strongly enjoys his superiority is the one most afflicted.

This is confirmed by the best-known work on the inferiority complex, by Alfred Adler. He observed, as his case studies show, that his patients suffered from inferiority feelings or from a sense of failure and incapacities exactly when they had lived with, or enjoyed by expectation, particularly strong feelings of superiority and success.[21]

Typically, Adler turned to the concepts of unconscious causes, which can easily explain any mystery. He assumed that some individuals unconsciously want to fail in what they wished to enjoy most, because of conflicts in their unconscious past. The paradox was there, as Adler perceptively realized, and only the world of the Unconscious as a personified, endlessly clever agency could offer explanations.

In our modern life the inferiority complex is frequent, because the over-enjoyment of superiority has become almost a necessity. In the competition for prestige or position among modern urban "strangers," success depends on how superior one can make himself appear to be. The way to do this best is to feel genuinely and aggressively one's own superiority. Such an exaggeration in feelings is inevitably followed by equally strong, unwanted, totally dissimilar, and therefore causally unrecognized opposite feelings.

A *guilt complex* can become a disturbing, unproductive reaction, though guilt is usually a creative feeling. A normal sense of guilt as conditioned non-satisfaction is the source of useful motivations as satisfactions from the avoidance of guilt by worthy behavior. An irrational, incapacitating feeling of guilt grows from an exaggerated, unwarranted enjoyment of pride or merit.

A neurotic may be depressed by a sense of guilt for everything that happens to him, though his misfortunes may be due to bad luck. He may well know this. But if he has over-enjoyed the sense of pride about his own achievements even where his successes were due only to good luck, he cannot reason away his feelings of guilt even if a failure is due to bad luck. You cannot cherish or be proud of something for a long time and then rationally forget about it when it is discovered to be unreal or less valuable.

Opposite feelings, of guilt and merit, or shame and pride, are causaly interdependent. Students experience guilt and shame to the extent that they cherish and enjoy feelings of merit and ability. Those students who do not indulge in such higher feelings of merit and pride do not suffer from a sense of guilt and shame. This is so obvious that it hardly needs explanation. But it clearly reveals the causal dependence of negative reactions on their value opposites.

Excessive shyness is another good example of opposite-value causation. Usually, the person suffering from it has the least reason to feel shy. He is the one who aspires most to have, and has to a high degree, the qualities of social grace or refinement that should prevent one from feeling shy. Moreover, shy persons are individuals living in a rich inner world where they naturally enjoy at will the feelings of these qualities.

But the accumulated enjoyment of any feeling makes opposite reactions inevitable. A person living in his easy inner world and enjoying his own perfection finds the real world so much more difficult and himself imperfect.

A boy secretly loving a girl dreams about her and enjoys being suave or intelligent in imagined situations with her. Then, upon approaching her in reality, he feels much like a man who, having lived in warmth, feels cold when he is exposed to the outside air.

We all live with *countless complexes* as difficulties or compulsive peculiarities of behavior. Our complexes are as many as the values that we over-enjoy. To that extent we are all irrational and confused though only the more conspicuous complexes, such as that of inferiority, are identified.

Complexes are causally too confusing to be easily recognized. They are particularly mysterious causally because their causal source is the person's exaggerated inner world, as universal or customary for him as an atmosphere that is not noticed exactly because of its universality.

Scientists, of course, want to help us in logical ways. A person suffering from an inferiority complex should, supposedly, be strengthened in his feelings of superiority. Which can only deepen his complex. This is similarly true for all complexes—and for all opposite-value reactions. One may as well try to cure drug-addiction difficulties with more drugs.

Finally, we have to explain some *seeming exceptions* to the general opposite-value causality. Sometimes it seems that enjoyments lead to more positive reactions.

People who have enjoyed leisure during a vacation often return to work with heightened motivation. Children permitted a break of free play may resume their studies more eagerly, in some cases. Actually, opposite causality is the reason here as well.

Every person lives with a definite "normalcy" of conditioned values. While he vacations or plays he cannot help accumulating the feeling of continued deviation from this normalcy. He therefore returns to it with accumulated zeal. The boy who has spent an afternoon on forbidden street enjoyments returns home with a greater sense of conscience, for the same reason.

This does not mean that the sense of what is right is increased by doing wrong. Nor do people become more diligent by cultivating idleness. The conditioned, moral "normalcy" is easily effaced by transgressions, unlike the innate, organic normalcy.

Still, a person living through a very happy period may be able for some time to be positive-minded. This is so because the necessary restrictions are more easily accepted by the person while he enjoys an abundance of pleasure releases—which have to be "paid" for later.

All kinds of similar *compensations* and shifts within the motivational pleasure economy are to be expected. Value experiences in practical situations are always complex, though governed by simple value causality.

For instance, a soldier returning from war, or an inmate from a concentration camp, may in some cases still suffer from negative reactions. Here the causal reason can be excessive anticipated enjoyments. While suffering during the war the soldier may compensate for the misery by enjoying anticipated post-war pleasures. Future pleasures can be truly enjoyed and a true enjoyment, however obtained, counts organically.

Also, under unusual circumstances, as during a war, a person may lose his usual, conditioned restraints. People like to get rid of such restraints (as can be seen also in various kinds of bacchanalia orgies). Once freed of restrictions and a sense of reality, a person may readily resort to unrealistic inner enjoyments. One form of such enjoyment is the *avoidance* to suffer through in full a difficult or horrifying reality. This can be seen in dissociative neuroses. The reality, though, has to be relived later, with all its trauma, to regain mental normality—much as in the painful abreactions during treatment of hysteric neuroses.

In sum, even while living through difficult conditions a person may "overspend" in his emotional economy. He then has to "repay" for the feelings enjoyed beyond reality: he has to suffer equal restrictions or stress. All kinds of stresses after difficulties are similarly explainable

A grave, general problem of behavior is a frequent *prevalence of irrational hate*, particularly in our social relations. The cause here is exaggerated attempts to enjoy feelings of love, which is a most desirable and useful reaction. But love, as satisfaction, can come only from equal, conditioned needs as non-satisfactions; the needs of survival itself are conditioned to create love, by education and culture.

If, however, feelings of love are created and enjoyed by mere enthusiasm, without the previous difficult conditioning of needs, then reactions opposite to love become inevitable. Such opposite reactions are, analytically, irrational hates.

Because of organic limitedness, every value reaction, as a physiologic change, requires an equal opposite change, an opposite-value reaction. The love fired up by mere enthusiasm is excitement and satisfaction. The reaction that follows is depression and nonsatisfaction. In terms of behavior, the enthusiastic love is induced as a feeling of compassion or obedient submission to fellow men. The opposite reaction that follows is one of cruelty and aggressive self-assertion against others—against all kinds of "strangers" who can be hated.

Excessive, unjustified hate becomes a wide problem not only individually but also nationally and internationally. Our spiritual and political leaders, as well as scientists and experts, understand how productive are the feelings of love or of pride and other satisfactions. Everybody is urged to feel more love for "his" nation or "his" fellow men.

The resulting, equally widespread, opposite feelings then lead to hate of "others" and of foreign nations. Similarly, exaggerated feelings of pride, induced without a realistic basis, create opposite reactions, a sense of humiliation by others. This is a frequent problem between social groups, stimulated to enjoy more pride of themselves.

If pleasant and productive reactions such as the feeling of love came without an equal emotional "payment," everybody would enjoy them limitlessly and there would be no negative feelings in the world.

Cognitive, Weightless Factors Seen as Decisive

Particularly in the social sciences cognitive and ideational factors are accepted as being decisive. Social scientists deal mostly with social ideas, ideologies, perceptions, reasons, learning, movements of thought, traditional views, socially conditioned knowledge, doctrines, and social philosophies.[2, 6, 7, 21]

Also, the "logical" effects of factual conditions, supposedly evaluated by reasoning, are seen as important. In general psychology it is at least sometimes understood that reasons or ideas are not decisive and that the best factual conditions can lead to negative reactions. Such unusual insights are missing in the social sciences.

No scientific, simple and few universal causal laws exist in the "soft," behavioral and social sciences. In social and political thought men formulate and interpret social behavior in accordance with their beliefs. Men have always deluded themselves that they are motivated by *reason and ideas*.

Men see the tremendous powers of intellect, without reflecting much that the intellectual capacities are only tools in human action. With these tools men have built their immense civilization, their vast institutions, the whole material and ideational civilized world. Man wants intensely to be guided by this superb, precise intellect, and soon believes that he acts only according to intelligent reason and ideas. Otherwise he would feel insecure and inferior.

The forces that determine how the intellectual powers are used are the value feelings of the individuals constituting the society. These feelings, however, are too multiple and complex, as well as scientifically and commonly confusing, actually paradoxical, to be considered. Consequently, according to the general belief that ideas and reasons are causally decisive, everybody attributes various social problems to wrong reasoning by others; he mostly feels that he alone has the right reasons.

To take a common example of the belief in ideas as causes, we may look at the general view that *ideologies*, of democracy or communism, are politically decisive. In truth, the real political, forces are the regimes and societies, established under the pressures of the feelings of the masses. The ideologies invoked by the masses are mostly merely sloganized ideas, confusedly selected from some theory and miscarried in practice.

The leading ideological theories have been constructed by great thinkers. Such theories are understood least by the more aggressive masses which enforce and dictate how a regime, of democracy or communism is established.

The determining causal sources in the creation of a regime are the physically forceful, mostly confused interactions by such masses motivated by their raw emotions. Political leaders then maintain such regimes by pretending to follow but actually by controlling the feelings of the masses.

Even if a leader may understand an ideology, when he puts it into practice the realities of human behavior determine what form or direction the society takes. Generally, the ideology becomes distorted or its goals turn into a parody as restrictions have to be imposed in disregard of slogans about freedoms. In practice, the real forces of behavior, the feelings of individuals, determine what works and what does not, in spite of ideologies or reasons.

Certainly, ideologies may be continuously pronounced as the express bases for some social or political action. In reality, the reasons are emotional. After a people is identified or named as communist or democratic, its concrete, selfish interests become synonymous with the name. Similarly, Christians would be ready even to die for the sign of the cross, though it would be their inveterate emotional ways of life and interests they would be defending.

The belief in ideas and reason as causes has always been a dominant human delusion, perpetuated in noble philosophies or serving as truth in murderous outbreaks of political passions. One meets constantly with lofty statements about ideas being the strongest forces in the world. The reality shows how fatuous this is for the practical life of simple mortals. We all can see that men do not act in reasonable ways which would be most useful for them as well as simple. Then everybody tends to think that people have wrong reasons or ideas—that he alone has the right ones.

Yet in the social sciences the fallacy about cognitive and ideational factors as decisive causes rules supreme. Typical themes or subjects in these fields are social and political ideologies, social perceptions and ways of thinking, historical views, currents of thought, teachings, cultural patterns, institutions embodying social ideas, socially determined knowledge and learning, social and political understanding or lack of it, and conscious or unconscious social intents.[2, 21]

Let us look at *intents*. In everyday life one would be silly to believe that our behavior is the product of our intents. We all have really excellent intents. If carried out they would make our behavior perfect and just. However, we are not perfect and just, whether we act individually or as a society.

Intents are certainly important factors in the world of cognition, the world of the prodigious tools of man. For instance, we build our tremendous institutions throughout our civilization the way we intend them to be; and they are among the main subjects of social studies. But social institutions and intents are behaviorally ineffective in their cognitive aspects, under which they are viewed. Such institutions have been declaring as their goals the most reasonable attitudes, which could bring instant utopia or paradise on earth. Yet nothing much changes. As a result we may blame others as being unreasonable or believing in erroneous ideas and facts.

In every country, peace and understanding have been the intended purposes of cultural, social, and political institutions or parties, even of the establishment itself. But the results have been rationally unintended and unexplainable, objectively unjustified hates generating social strife and wars, which have brought so much misery and destruction and millions of deaths.

Yet social scientists and philosophers have viewed social phenomena, particularly social movements and progress, as results of human reasons and ideas, or of man's intellect and his imaginative intents—those immensely effective tools of human action.

Even mere *ideas and teachings* have been viewed as decisive. The ideas of democracy, teachings of Christianity, or movements of modern thought such as the Enlightenment have supposedly shaped the Western civilization. Similarly, Confucian or Buddhist teachings and currents of Oriental thought are viewed as causal sources of achievements or failures in Eastern societies.

Is this much different from beliefs in the divine wisdom and power of the words of scriptures? The old missionaries believed that the truths of the Bible, revealed to primitive aborigines, could transform them into worthy Christians, just as the right words of baptism were to transform their souls.

Surely, the civilized people believing in the truths of the Bible or of the Confucian teachings have achieved much. But the great, simple truths of such scriptures are carried out in practice only through the force of motivations, of inner values. The most useful, perfect, and simple truths can be found in every general opinion held by anybody. If only they could be brought about!

Our *inner values* as the conditioned forms of pleasure are the forces that determine everything in our life and behavior. They determine where and how the intellectual skills are used or reason and truths followed. This execution of intents requires hard effort, and only the organic force of pleasure provides the power for carrying it out. Behind every social phenomenon, however extensive or complex, at whatever stage, that simple organic force determines what will and does happen.

We don't need to repeat the explanation of how the best intellectual ideas and reasons are weightless and easy, while only our inner values, our pleasure drives, provide effective motivations. Because of this causal role of pleasure drives, the behavioral and social sciences cannot be scientific as long as the *opposite-value causality* is not understood.

Without such causal, scientific understanding the social sciences will permit the *miraculous intellect* to continue bringing us *more harm* than good, intended or not. Intellect as a splendid instrument has made possible the prodigious modern overimprovements. These become the causes of our major functional diseases as well as of our other, reactively determined, indivudal and social difficulties. This happens as the intellect serves to compound the "scientism" that encourages increased enjoyments of the modern improvements, under the experimental logic imitated from our exact physical sciences.

Before we conclude, we have to consider in a little more detail the most widely accepted cognitive causal sources, such as self, identity and alienation, or identification, projection and substitution.

Self and identity are viewed as products of cognitive experiences. They are "discovered," sought for, and "lost," or regained through understanding, new insights, and the removal of conflicts between inner perceptions or ideas. Solutions through the formula "know thyself" are recommended by modern theorists as they were by the Delphi oracle.[2, 21] *Alientation* is seen as the negative outcome in the search for self or identity.[2,21]

In reality, the sophisticated search for self or identity is merely an attempt to obtain more pleasure releases, which are indeed ultimately found inside oneself.

Impoverishment in these releases then seems like alienation, particularly because the person here does avoid his self, his organic preservation of identity. He actually is avoiding the restrictions necessary to reestablish the "identity" as organic sameness or normalcy after over-enjoyments. But behavioral scientsits are not considering this paradoxical, emotional, value causation. They deal only with the logical and "scientific" cognitive aspects of the self or alienation.[2, 21]

The difficult problem in "scientifically" logical theories about the self or alienation is how and why a person brings on himself unwanted, negative reactions with such a persistent intensity as well as seeming inventiveness. Some hidden, perverse intents then remain the only explanation.

Clearly, the causes of such assumed, unconscious intents can be only *cognitive or ideational*, never emotional. For emotionally the result here is painful. Such a self-torturing action would logically lie outside one's emotional management. Even unconsciously man would hardly torture himself by merely misdirecting his feelings.

Self-punishment through the intents and schemes of the always-conflict-ridden Unconscious is one of widely accepted explanations in behavioral theories. The Freudian death instinct is part of the theories. Evidently, anything negative in a person's behavior can be explained under the assumption that he wants to punish or destroy himself. That is why we hear so often about self-punishment and the death wish.

In a classical work, *Man Against Himself*, by Karl Menninger, every disorder and failure, even disease, is shown to be explainable as a form of unconsciously intended and cleverly brought about suicide.

Of course, if the intention of suicide really existed, anybody could kill himself without delay, by crossing a street or using the chemicals and machines around us. All the people with unconscious problems would have committed suicides already.

By the way, *suicides* generally have remained mysteries causally.[21] They are clearly not logical. They are committed by rich professionals and celebrities more often than by miserable wretches. Suicides by teenagers from the best families are becoming epidemic; this is the group better cared for than anybody else. Suicides remain causally unexplained and conroversial[2, 21] though suicide statistics have been collected in various countries for a century. Why not merely correlate the statistics with historically known conditions of life in each country?

The reason for the unexplainable mystery is opposite causality. We have seen how those people who can avoid stress most perfectly suffer from excessive stress. Here we may recall that the rate of suicides by psychiatrists is six times higher, and by physicians three times higher, than the average.

Anyway, self-punishment, as an unconsciously intended action, can explain virtually every negative behavioral effect or failure. Self-punishment is a popular explanation also because it appears very dramatic. It does so by actually being the least common, and therefore least true, for human nature.

Yet even criminals are assumed to leave clues deliberately, so that they can be caught. Theodor Reik has been a noted authority on the theory of self-punishment. According to him punishment of crime may become the main incentive for people to commit crimes.

Very widely accepted are the concepts of *cognitive mechanisms* such as identification, projection, or substitution.[2, 7, 21] Here as well, complex cognitive or ideational factors become the only possible logical explanations for the effects of these mechanisms. It seems too obvious that such effects could not be incurred by way of emotional management, since they bring painful, negative feelings.

Identification with persons or things can explain any imaginable problem. Negative behavior can be easily attributed to identification with negative social models or events. The manic-depressive supposedly identifies himself with a dead relative or the paranoiac with a persecuted group.

Projection is another mechanism often referred to and very convenient for explaining negative behavior. It is assumed that a person projects onto others his negative traits of aggression, thus starts seeing them as hostile and logically fears aggression from them. In reality people ingeniously use and twist logic to have pleasant feelings, not to create fears for themselves.

All kinds of projections are frequent and may lead to fears, but not for cognitive, logical reasons. The person who eagerly resorts to projection over-enjoys his own superiority and sense of power over others. He is therefore bound to suffer from just as excessive opposite feelings, including a fear of the power of others over him.

Substitution and displacement are particularly convenient for explaining any conceivable causal mystery of behavior. For supposedly the very gist of these mechanisms is that anything can be substituted for by anything else, even its opposite, often in deliberately disguised or distorted ways.

Equally convenient cognitive or ideational causal explanations are offered by the concepts of a dozen other conscious or unconscious mechanisms: dissociations, symbolization, negation, compensation, introjection, regression, isolation, or reaction formation.[1, 6, 7] Concepts of such mechanisms are widely used, even by highly perceptive behavioral and social scientists. The reason is obvious.

Various mechanisms, mostly distortions of reality, are regularly resorted to by people for obtaining some mental enjoyment or pleasure. This amounts to emotional exaggerations or over-enjoyments. The inevitable results are negative reactions and disorders. Thus, scientists are right in observing a connection between *such frequent mechanisms and mental disorders*.

But the scientists cannot recognize here the real cause, the paradoxical emergence of opposite feelings from improved enjoyments. They accept instead a logically direct causality for these mechanisms in their cognitive aspects. Scientists explain that these mechanisms bring negative feelings or tormenting disorders because the person confusedly or mistakenly makes cognitive and ideational connections or arrangements so wrongly that they finally hurt him. Such explanations are widely accepted for these and similar behavior mechanisms.[4, 6, 7] They are unbelievably incongruous.

Human intelligence is supreme, and pleasantness is the easiest thing to understand, consciously or unconsciously. Also, nothing more than pleasure or satisfactions is necessary for perfect behavior.

Clearly the person seeks some *pleasure through these mechanisms. But the scientists hold that he incurs the unpleasant* disorders through them, by various mistakes or confusions. It is thus assumed that people here torment themselves with suffering and mental disorders by wrong cognitive arrangements or procedures. This amounts to accepting that the person does not know when he is hurting himself, since everything here is otherwise as clear and simple as pleasure and pain.

The incongruity of the explanations here is only a more general instance of what results from acceptance of the extremely impressive and complex but causally ineffectual cognitive factors as causes of behavior.

The explanations from complex cognitive factors are always rendered "scientifically" logical. Thus, they are exactly contrary to the actual, opposite causation of feelings or inner values, which are the practical determinants of our behavior and reactions. Man does act against himself. But he is too intelligent to do so because of some cognitive confusion. The real explanation is the opposite-value causality.

Still No Science for Problems of Education, Crime, or Drug Addiction

Science, in any field, becomes possible as soon as causal understanding of its phenomena is established. And sciences have the unique effect of transforming their fields into virtual miracles, as has happened in the technical sciences. A science starts with novel discoveries through simple but causally true insights which were not recognized before.

In the present, "soft" behavioral sciences such as education or criminology, the efforts have been remarkable. And the results? They probably would be disastrous if it were not for the restrictive cultural and moral wisdom that still persists, to help us to cope with the rising problems in these fields.

We may as well repeat here the key facts about human behavior. Satisfactions, as positive reactions, make everything positive attainable. But no satisfaction is possible without an equal need as non-satisfactions. Thus, the imposition of difficult, conditioned non-satisfactions or restrictions is the solution. This is embodied in the wisdoms of our restrictive cultural tradition, evolved through ages.

But our scientific experts proceed only by the experimentally scientific causal logic which shows that increase, not restriction, of satisfactions should be the positive goal. Therefore non-satisfactions and restrictions are treated as hindrances and evils, under various sophisticated theories, in progressive education and in other fields subject to our modern scientism. This indeed has to appear as the only right policy if the paradox of opposite causality is not understood.

EDUCATION. The needs of survival itself, which dominate all motivations, have to be conditioned into desired behavioral needs through education. Schematically, the child is conditioned to feel a threat to survival if he does not behave in the ways his parents or educators want him to behave.

In practice this conditioning is attained through simple love between parent and child. They feel, instinctively, to be part of each other. As parents feel threatened if they or their child does something wrong, the child feels the same. Thus, the moral conditioning of parents is being automatically inculcated in the child, every minute of his life.

That is why only strong love between the child and parents or their substitutes can insure good education, and why the same moral or motivational standards persist in families through generations. Good parents must be persons conditioned to feel moral threats and moral pleasures strongly. And the closeness of feelings, the love, between parent and child has to be instinctively deep.

Of course, this conditioning, like an atmosphere, is so omnipresent around the child that he does not notice it as anything in particular. For the same reason, the survival needs that are conditioned are not noticed.

Thus, generally, neither the most universal needs nor their conditioning, in education, are noticed as important.[8, 9, 10] Educators, rather, write about the conditioning of isolated habits of children, about how they are cuddled, fed, played with, or stimulated.[8, 12, 12] But these are only minor incidents within the constant conditioning of the enormously strong needs of survival itself.

It is the all-inclusive survival needs that are transformed by their conditional non-satisfactions into vast and tense moral and cultural needs, as sources of equally extensive satisfactions. Then, as the universal needs and their conditioning are overlooked, it may seem that education merely fosters deeper, better satisfactions. The difficult, negatively felt needs, the sources and value opposites of satisfactions are then viewed as odious obstacles to the wondrously creative satisfactions. The universal human prejudice against recognizing the causal, negative sources of values dominates here as well.

According to a generally accepted theory, promoted by such authorities as Abraham Maslow and Carl Rogers, the higher satisfactions of self-realization or of knowledge arise after the lower needs have been satisfied.[8, 21] Thus, only satisfactions, never any needs or non-satisfactions, are to be cultivated.

We agree that needs for food, shelter, or physical well-being have to be satisfied first. As natural drives that are not conditioned they would overrule any conditioned, refined, and therefore weaker needs. But whatever higher natural needs and satisfactions may exist, it is not satisfaction that should be promoted to enrich them.

Needs that are satisfied cease to be operative. And all natural satisfactions in their unconditioned forms are useless. They have to be transformed by the conditioning of operative, still unsatisfied needs.

As to the assumed higher or intellectual satisfactions and interests, they do not exist preformed in the organism. They have to be created by the restrictive conditioning of the crudely simple and selfish organic survival needs. Confusions arise about all kinds of higher satisfactions because the continuous conditioning of the most universal survival needs is not seen. Without educational conditioning children remain brute animals.

The central fallacy, in education as in all human sciences, is the failure to recognize that satisfactions are causally impossible without their value opposites, the needs as non-satisfactions or restrictions. We have to repeat this because it is crucial. If there were the slightest possibility of creating satisfactions without their difficult opposites, it would be turned immediately into a most intensely expanding enterprise, for our easy enrichment with our precious positive capacities, as pleasurable satisfactions.

Any such trick would be automatically grasped and exploited by everybody. Men are uncannily smart in finding what is satisfactory or pleasant. Educators as well as their pupils would like nothing better than to enjoy free satisfactions as interests. Education would turn into an orgy of enjoyments.

In reality education has been always hard. Also it is, necessarily, deceitful. Men are motivated only by the pursuit of pleasure. The imposition of the conditioned non-satisfactions has to be *effected through inducements of pleasure* or rewards.

In fact, the most effective and subtle mechanism in educational conditioning results from the striving by the child and his parents or educators to attain perfect pleasures.

In a refined educational conditioning the child starts suffering anxieties if he happens to deviate from the conditioned requirements. The loving educators want to help him, and provide more effective, refined ways of compliance. It all becomes a "neurotic" perfectionism in over-enjoyment of educational merits. This "neurosis" is beneficial. It deepens, through its vicious-circle worsening, the educational conditioning as greater and greater compliance enjoyments are pursued.

Thus, in a closely sheltered and refined education, the highest success is attained not by threat or punishment but by perfected, conditioned enjoyments of love. Punishment here would destroy the "neurotic" refinement. The precondition for such a success is a tightly closeted confinement of the child within the conditioning sphere of love and of the refined educational satisfactions.

That is why a tragic parody results from scientifically logical attempts to use such seemingly gratifying and wonderful methods on street-smart juveniles. If there is no threat for such juveniles, they just continue doing what they know is immediately pleasant. Then there is no chance even to start their conditioning or any refinement in it.

Such juveniles view a well-conditioned child as a sissy and softy, or a neurotic jerk who does not know what is good for him. He indeed is neurotically fearful to make a move away from the closeted imprisonment of conditioning through the needs of love. That is why the street is so devastating in education. Even ethically well-oriented movements, like the Moonies, can draw children away from families, which are indeed enslaving them in logical terms.

Smothering parental love and the double bind have been often pointed out as sources of negative reactions and conflict.[8, 21] But wise and loving parents cannot do differently. They have to deal with the child as with a part of themselves. They have to enslave him while they are making him happy in the restricted, conditioned ways that they are imposing on themselves as the only sources of happiness.

An important result of the *educational "deceit"* is the belief that the child should always follow only what he himself really wants. This is a necessary part of the perfectionism in educational satisfactions. The child has to believe that he himself attains the praiseworthy achievements.

Of course after the sources of satisfactions are created—through conditioned non-satisfactions—it does seem that the child himself deeply wants the right behavior. The logical radical or free educator, as well as the naive idealist, then may cry for a natural fulfillment of each individual's deepest freedoms and interests or individual identity.

All education has to appear contradictory if it is not understood how satisfactions derive from their causal opposites. Everybody can see that some satisfaction was always the motivation in his successes.

Educators know that positive responses come through happiness, contentment, joy, pleasure, hopes, feelings of success, enjoyment of rewards, or other satisfactions.[8, 10, 11] Negative reactions are seen as coming from non-satisfactions, worry, frustrations, anxiety, stress, fear, or concern.[8, 10, 11]

It is not realized that satisfactions cannot exist without operative, not-yet-satisfied needs, which derive from conditioned non-satisfactions practically felt as frustrations and anxieties. Success, praise, or reward has only as much value as previous worry, fear, or concern. Any pleasure or relief in education derives from conditioned restrictions or stress.

Even if there were ready-made higher needs, their unrestricted, unconditioned satisfaction would extinguish their effectiveness, as in all satiation. They would become inoperative before they could be turned, by conditioning, into useful, cultural needs. A satisfaction potential is only as great as previously accumulated stressful non-satisfactions, the corresponding needs.

Education, as all existence, provides value experiences through disturbances or stress. We read novels to enjoy happy endings, but without stressful troubles lived through by the heroes, novels would make no sense. Education can be similarly made adventurous and exciting—in ways quite different from the logically direct enjoyments of satisfactions.

The spoilt child is the one who receives the fullest satisfactions lavished on him by way of the most direct, logically complete, unconditioned love. But he has the least satisfaction potential or feeling of love, which too is a satisfaction deriving from equal non-satisfactions as needs. To explain the paradox, modern theorists argue that the logically and naturally fullest love here is a hidden hate.[8, 21] This is a most frequently invoked explanation of our parent-child relationship problems.[10, 21] It enables theorists to proceed with their logical theories, by arguing that the satisfactions of direct, natural love here are not what they most fully in fact are.

Practical education, rooted in tradition, imposes as much as it can of the necessary, conditioned non-satisfactions, restrictions, and stresses—the sources of satisfactions and positive reactions. But if the causal paradox here is not understood, *it may seem that indeed our traditional education is perpetuating wrong approaches*. This has been regretted by reformers old and new, from Rousseau or Pestalozzi to our modern critics, including John Dewey, Bertrand Russell, Ashley Montague, or Charles Silberman.

Particularly do the "progressive" educators find it easy to condemn all traditional education. They have only to describe our present education to prove how shockingly education suppresses all the pleasures, freedoms, and values that any enlightened person accepts as goals of education.

Every aspect of our education has been thus found to be outrageous by our leading progressive educators—A. S. Neil, Reston Wilcox, Ronald and Beatrice Gross, Sylvia Ashton Warner, Edgar Z. Friedenberg, Jonathan Kozol, Herbert Kohl, and Kenneth Clark.[21]

All of human education and culture could not possibly be so totally wrong. But the progressive educators can found their theories on experimental observations of the direct effects of satisfactions. Children always perform better when more satisfactions are offered; and everybody can testify that his motivations have come through finding satisfaction in what he was doing.

A *permissive educator*, offering more pleasures, is easily more liked and better followed. He can therefore show greater success. Actually he depletes the sources of motivations. To sustain his success he has to go down to offering more and more permissive pleasures. Anything less than the primitive, strong, natural pleasures then becomes uninteresting for the pupil.

That is why "free" educators can have great initial success but fail quickly. One national survey showed that two thousand "free" schools were successfully started in a period of five years in this country, but each lasted, on the average, only eighteen months.[21]

In a further disregard of the no-free-lunch rule, educators believe in the inherently easy, *cognitive or ideational* causal sources in education. Most educators view ideas, insights, reason, and understanding as causally decisive. Pupils as well as future educators should, supposedly, study and learn to appreciate extensively our treasures of thought and ideas.

A good example is *the great-book method* promoted by many authorities, notably Robert Hutchins and Mortimer Adler. The famous studies by Jean Piaget would support the view that cognitive development determines attitudes or motivations.

The exalted dictum "knowledge will make you free" is as frequently cited as it is fatuous. A rationalist asserting his freedoms in the name of reason or knowledge can become a morally dangerous pest. Socrates is the classic genius of rational education. Probably he was rightly condemned for the corruption of youth, by the Athenians, who were generally tolerant in matters of ideas; he did not, though, deserve the death penalty for merely wrong teachings.

It is also alchemistic to expect that by *enjoyments of our treasures* of art or literature we can become better people. Such enjoyments can serve as excellent lures in cultural conditioning, in the restrictive refinement of our natural drives. But educators tend to favor a deepening of such enjoyments. This would be more obnoxious than helpful. Artists and people who enjoy art most deeply lead rather dissolute lives. Art in itself does not improve people; Nazi leaders enjoyed great art and music.

Neither our great ideas and treasures of thought nor our esthetic enjoyments are educationally important in themselves. They could be forgotten today and it would make little difference. Completely different, contrary wisdoms and treasures are taught and enjoyed in different cultures, and the educational result is the same. Treasures of ideas and art, though, have helped as attractive enticements in educational and moral conditioning, in most cultures.

A general, practical problem at schools is how to teach students efficient reading or mathematics and other *abstract subjects*. The great modern "discovery" has been that students are more interested if tasks are adapted to their natural interests, as in learning-by-doing or by use of games, pictures, toys, and gadgets, serving more natural or immediate curiosity and gratifications.

Surely, motivations are increased when more natural pleasures are aroused. One can only agree here with noted educational reformers like Pestalozzi, Montessori, or Dewey. But the pleasant, natural interests should be used only as stepping-stones for children if they are incapable of abstract thinking. Such interests should be avoided as soon as possible.

The very essence of abstract interests is that they are completely different from natural interests, which are enjoyments through countless sensory mechanisms. Such endlessly multiple sensations can be only disruptive for abstract thinking, aiming at the reduction of experiences to generalized "ones." Mathematics, the queen of sciences, is a good example. In any abstract thinking or intense scientific work the best condition is isolation from sensory distractions.

Learning is difficult because the very gist of it is the conditional restriction or non-satisfaction of natural interests. Satisfactions of survival needs, of security, superiority, growth, or self-realization, are held suppressed here until the desired knowledge or understanding that has to be learned is acquired. In a word, not enjoyment or release but difficult conditioned restriction or non-satisfaction of natural interests is the key to success in abstract learning as well.

Once the abstract ways of thinking are established, a whole world of understanding and knowledge opens, becomes accessible to the person. Surely natural, organic interests are the beginning of all interests, and turning back to them can provide immediate great success. But that would amount to regression in the teaching process.

All education, imbued with the wisdom of ages, shows that knowledge is acquired by hard work, not by increased enjoyment. The required *satisfactions as motivations are made possible by the creation of needs* as non-satisfactions, through "deceitful" conditioning.

To conclude, all education, continuing under the old, persisting wisdoms, is prevented from becoming a science by a universal human failure of causal understanding. Satisfactions or pleasures are indeed the direct sources of our positive educational motivations and interests. Then, logically, why not increase them directly, permit them to flourish? The paradox of opposite-value causality is not recognized, particularly in the experimentally logical scientism in education.

Actually, if satisfactions came without their laboriously painful opposites, no education would be needed. Who needs help in finding or experiencing the pleasures of satisfactions? But the causal source of every satisfaction is a need as non-satisfaction.

A causal logic *contrary* to the actual causality here has made *impossible even the beginnings* of a science. Yet only a science could help us in this difficult, presently confusing field. A true science can become virtually miraculous in devising new, unexpected solutions even for the most complex difficulties.

PROBLEMS OF CRIME. In the field of crime the problems and the lack of causal understanding are similar to those in education. Criminals are persons who have not developed positive capacities and motivations, mostly for accepting restrictions or for delaying present enjoyments in favor of long-range, future gains. Crime is the pursuit of immediate satisfactions with total freedom.

Solutions for crime would be similar to those for education. Restrictive conditioning would provide the person with motivations or capacities for success, and with the ability to delay immediate enjoyments while working for such success, as well as with self-restrictive attitudes limiting willful freedoms.

Expectedly, causal understanding is missing here as it is in education. The positive role of restrictions is not recognized, because they are definitely felt as negative and experimentally always have a negative direct effect. In fact, the various theories on crime are based on the usual *scientifically "logical" thinking that negative reactions originate from negative causal backgrounds.*

Even while theorists recognize that prosperity and freedoms bring crime, they look for non-satisfactions and limitations or frustrations as causes of crime. A leading criminologist, Norval Morris, finds that rapid economic and social progress brings crime. But he still views frustrations or non-satisfactions as possible direct causes of crime.[13, 21] Another noted criminologist, Marvin Wolfgang, recognizes that crimes come together with increased social freedoms; but he does not see increasing enjoyment of freedoms as their cause.[13,21]

Let us look at the main theories on crime. Theoretical understanding is important here because only a true, causally understood science can offer final solutions for such humanly difficult problems as those of crime.

Various *deprivation theories* are, expectedly, dominating the field.[17] The best-known theorists here, Robert Merton and Seymour Lipset, have argued that hopeless deprivation is felt strongly by poorer groups when they observe the success of others.[16] This would seem to explain why crime rates have soared together with the great modern surge of general prosperity. Bitterness and hopelessness can certainly contribute to crime. But their source is not straight deprivation.

Before our modern, liberal era, poverty was viewed as an undesirable scarcity of means. That created more intense motivations to work hard out of it. The greatest men and most capable groups, in every nation, have been formed by such poverty. Even lack of opportunities is no cause for bitterness or negativity to restrictively conditioned people. They always have a rich satisfaction potential. They can enjoy it equally well without the challenging, disturbing opportunities.

But the modern poor feel bitter hate and behavioral impoverishment because they have been encouraged merely to look for satisfactions in their expectations. They are not taught to accept hard effort or stressful preparations. Instead, they are lured by progressive leaders to enjoy their pride or "identity" and to expect that equality and freedom will bring them full satisfactions. A sense of deprivation then has to follow, whatever the degree of real opportunity.

Relative over-enjoyment rather than restriction is evident from the typical aspects of the modern poverty that breeds crime. In contrast to the old poverty, the present main problems are: use of enormously expensive drugs instead of anxious thriftiness; truancy from free, well-financed schools; avoidance of hard work; the lowest moral discipline; dissolute family life; and splashy spending at the first opportunity. The demands of gratification and freedom are such that restrictions are felt as violations of human rights.[13, 21]

An important fact should be explained here. *Relative*, not absolute, changes or improvements are decisive.

For instance our blacks may still be poor. But *relatively* their existence has improved *enormously*. They have progressed from threats of starvation and inhuman subjugation to conditions of welfare care for everybody in need and official protection against any kind of discrimination.

Psychologically, such a total change has to result in a feeling that there is not a worry in the world, no limits to the freedom of enjoyments. Correspondingly, our blacks have little of the "neurotic" attitudes of the conservative middle class. Rather their criteria of values and attitudes *derive from their traditional value standards*, which change only very slowly.

Indeed the relatively enormous improvements for the blacks, enjoyed under the criteria of their different traditions, are the actual explanations for the steep increase in their crime rate. There is no such thing as a racial or genetic criminality. But according to FBI statistics the rate of crime among our blacks has increased so that 45 percent of the criminals in prisons now are blacks. Considering that blacks constitute only 12 percent of our population, this would indicate that the blacks commit crime six times more often than whites.

This disparity has appeared together with the *relatively* huge improvements for blacks. The cause here is the same as in the general, conspicuous increase in criminality together with the equally unique increase of prosperity in our modern times, which is quite different from deprivation or discrimination.

For comparison, think of the Jewish people. They have suffered from discrimination and deprivations more than any other people, in Europe and even in this country after their arrival here as poor and distinctively strange immigrants. Their very traditions are those of deprived people, living under intense restrictions, reflected in their moral and family customs. But they have the least problems when it comes to crime or education.

The highest modern increase in the rate of crime has been in *juvenile delinquency*. Juveniles now commit 50 percent of the crimes in this country. The juvenile delinquency rate increased during our most prosperous twenty-five years, before 1973, more than sixfold by some estimates.[12, 21]

Juveniles, of course, have enjoyed more than adults the improved conditions of ease. Probably the most noted social phenomenon of our times has been our extreme, spoiling solicitude for our children as well as the unique enjoyments of freedoms by our youth. Wherever conditions have permitted it, these enjoyments have reached excessive levels, with a corresponding increase in juvenile crime.

Juvenile deliquency is high also because youth assimilates the modern spirit of freedoms totally, while older people become steeped with years in the still-persisting, restrictive tradition and in the wisdom about over-enjoyments.

All crime rates go up together with *unusual economic improvements*. This has been confirmed by crime waves during periods of increased prosperity in the middle and late 19th century.[13, 21] The increase of crime together with the unique expansion of prosperity of recent modern times is a generally recognized fact.[13, 14] It is so universal and clear that criminologists accept it without even arguing about it.[12, 14, 15]

Yet logically scientific theorists, as all our learned people, have always tended to connect crime with economic stress. Only the more careful recent studies have shown that this is not true at all; and theories about economic difficulties as causes of crime have been abandoned.[14, 15, 16, 17]

Typically, during the prosperous, pre-recession decade crime increased alarmingly. From 1961 to 1974 the rate of robberies increased 255 percent, aggravated assault 153 percent, forcible rape 143 percent, and murder 106 percent.[12] During the subsequent years of recession and inflation the increases declined.

Revealingly, crime rates are higher for the second generations of immigrants.[12] Here the obvious, sudden relative change between the generations is the improvement in the conditions of life and the assimilation of increased freedoms.

In short, deprivation theories about crime explain as little as all "logical" theories of behavior do. Everything that is now considered essential for *satisfactory adjustment is enjoyed by young delinquents more* than by other youth. Delinquents are more sociable, spend more time in play, are physically stronger and suffer less from fears, inferiority, insecurity, conflicts, or turmoil.[21]

The most interesting study here is probably the one by that great prophet of the counterculture the late Paul Goodman. Using the best research findings, like those of Sheldon and Eleonor Glueck, he concluded that juvenile delinquents were more "vivacious, extrovert, less-controlled, more manly inclined, more aggressive, less fearful of failure and defeat, more independent, more intiating, less submissive."[21]

Such qualities can, certainly, insure more satisfactions and freedoms. Goodman praised these qualities, and blamed what he saw as the universal absurdities of education.

The theories of *delinquent subcultures* may rank next in importance.[15] It is argued that juveniles unable to find satisfactions in usual ways seek excitement, adventure, fun, and other enjoyments in their own special peer groups. Recognized as representative of these theories have been the studies by Richard Cloward, Lloyd Ohlin, Clifford Shaw, Henry McKay, Albert Cohen, and Walter Miller.[2, 17]

From all the involved explanations in the theories, one thing is clear and generally accepted: delinquents find in the subcultures easier gratifications and more freedoms. The explanations become complex and controversial because according to present scientific, liberal views satisfactions and freedoms are positive causal values.

The *differential association* theory also is often referred to.[2, 17] Its main representatives have been Edwin Sutherland and Donald Cressey. Adherents to this theory hold that criminal behavior is learned. A person becomes criminal when he lives with criminals. But this only proves that the value atmosphere we live in, day by day, is decisive.

In contrast, learning is a causally ineffective, cognitive factor. One can easily learn the most useful, excellent ideas. But the simple values of the people he lives with constantly will dominate him in spite of the wisest ideas. The effect can also be indirect. A person living among people who steal or lie every day feels virtuous if he steals or lies only once a month.

Various *psychological*, psychosomatic, and psychiatric theories on crime have been advanced. But as we have seen, the inevitably alchemistic, "logical" scientism in psychology or psychiatry would rather show as desirable the direct enjoyments and freedoms which dominate in criminal behavior.

Not surprisingly, several studies have indicated that the work and theories of psychological experts have contributed to confusion and failure in dealing practically with crime.[21] A well-known, classical experiment, the Cambridge-Somerville Youth Study, showed that psychological counseling can do more harm than good. In this study of 650 boys, those who had received expert counseling committed more offenses than those who had not.

The variety of controversial theories concerning crime has increased because no generally accepted causal explanations about crime have been reached.[15, 16, 17] However complex or varied the theories on crime may be, they all are founded on the same experimental scientism imitated from our exact sciences. This scientism inevitably perpetuates the like-from-like causal logic which is inherently alchemistic for human sciences and exactly contrary to the causality of value reactions on which criminality depends. The theories on crime are becoming more "scientific" and less relevant practically.

Typically, *the labeling and social-interaction* theories finally have abandoned dealing with inner motivations of criminals—with the actual, inherent causes of crime.[17, 21] Instead, mere external data about crime are used. This excludes the confusing value concepts. In a purely formal objectivism, the studies here turn to mere correlation of social interactions and to records or registration of crime.

Practically this has amounted to attributing crime to the methods of our social and legal systems that "label" criminals. Unfortunately, the causes of crime are the criminal's inner motivations, his value feelings or lack of them. But the concept of labeling is "scientifically" less confusing than that of value feelings. And external facts, instead of the criminal's inner accountability, can be treated as causes more easily by experimental scientists. The experimental "scientism" is thus conserved, while the real causes, the confusing value reactions, are left out.

The value *reactions of criminals* are indeed as confusing as the paradox of value causation. The observed feelings of criminals show strong non-satisfaction and a sense of restriction to an unusual degree. Logically, then, the causes of crime seem to be deprivations and frustrations or repressions.

Actually these extreme negative feelings can come only from over-enjoyment of satisfactions and freedoms. The opposite-value causality is as true here as it is for all mental negativity. Criminals suffer from such negativity and even from overt psychoses.

Plain common-sense observation reveals the prevalence of over-indulgence by criminals in easy enjoyments and freedoms. Starting with their early years, criminals avoid disciplining and restrictions. They are truants, avoiding hard work that others do. They find special freedom and the most direct natural gratifications in their street gangs or "subcultures."

Drug use becomes for delinquents as necessary as it is for burnt-out celebrities. Overindulgence, in various forms, is the way of life of delinquents. Typically, to have more of it they extend their days into late nights. Of course, one's material, financial status is always relative, as everybody can remember from his childhood.

But true to experimentally "logical" scientism, researchers record the immediate, direct feelings and reactions found in the minds and behavior of criminals. What the criminal says and what clearly shows how he feels are recorded as evidence. The life-long, *opposite causal background remains unnoticed* by the criminal and unreported by the researcher. To a criminal the atmosphere of overindulgences he lives in is as little noticeable as is the universal, restrictive conditioning to a well-educated child.

Also, it can be experimentally demonstrated that by providing more improvements delinquency can be avoided. This is not very different from curing, temporarily, psychoses with stimulating drugs. Prison reformers particularly have recurrently demonstrated miraculous successes from increased improvements. The miracles, though, have not lasted long.

We agree that harsh punishments are not the solution. Logical conservative views can help as little as the logical scientism. People can be influenced only by inducements of satisfactions. All conditioning uses pleasures, while obtaining restrictive results in the end.

By the way, restrictions are more easily imposed by inducements of self-determination. The interaction by juveniles in self-regulating groups, devised by good common sense, has been found successful.

The key to solutions of problems of crime would be causal, scientific understanding. These problems are as difficult as is all creation of positive reactions, by painful restrictions through inherently "deceitful" conditioning. Tradition has generally helped with moralistic, inevitably contradictory prescriptions. Which become difficult to sustain in our scientific, logically liberal era.

Science with its potentially miraculous powers would be the solution. Criminologists admit that presently not much can be done because of the lack of scientific understanding of crime.[15,17]

But is an exact science here really possible? True, the present scientism has created only an enormous amount of controversial theories. The reason is that this scientism is contrary to the causality of values or behavior—and to the wisdom embodied in traditions.

A real science could start here, as elsewhere, with a very simple causal insight. Yet its final results could be as unexpectedly miraculous as have been those of technical sciences. We admit that the imposition of restrictions is practically the most difficult thing to do or accept. Moreover, how can the "deceit" necessary in conditioning be effective if it is openly, scientifically disclosed? But science, with its stunning, unpredictable inventiveness, could solve even that. Particularly since the restrictions and "deceit" bring success and pleasure at the end of each effort.

The main obstacle will be the entrenchment in the human sciences of the present "scientism," with its wrong causal logic. To correct this, the very direction of "logical," scientific thinking here, adopted from our exact sciences, would have to be reversed.

Practically this would amount to *a reversal of every "scientific," seemingly progressive, liberal attitude of our scientific era.* It is needless to explain how enormously difficult that would be. Understandably, we still do not have even beginnings of a true science in areas such as crime.

DRUG ADDICTION. Drugs provide a perfect, immediate remedy against the agonizing aftereffects of over-enjoyments flourishing in our rich and liberal era. Delinquents in particular seek this remedy because their enjoyment pursuits are the most liberal of all. Over-enjoyment's aftereffects are insufferable boredom and stress. Men are extremely clever in finding pleasant remedies. Particularly do persons used to various unrestricted enjoyments understand or rather feel, intuitively, how effective the remedy by drugs can be.

The increase in the use of drugs is probably one of the main indicators of how much we are becoming entrapped in the scientifically liberated enjoyment habits of our era. Most affected are persons who have overcome or have not absorbed the restrictive, mainly middle-class traditions. Contributing factors have been our less-restricted and scientific attitudes; the decline in moral and religious restrictive customs; a scientifically liberal education; and the enormous improvements of life, in relative or absolute terms.

Our sciences have helped us prodigiously in the attainment of such enjoyments and freedoms. But science has been unable to offer much understanding or help with drug problems. The reason is its *general confusion about the effects of enjoyments*, including those from drugs. Science has weakened, instead of strengthened, the remaining restrictive attitudes in our culture.

And in our scientific era, science has the decisive influence on behavior trends.

The present scientific confusion about addiction is vast.[18, 19, 20, 21] There is no reason why it should be so. Addiction, as we saw, is *a universal phenomenon, uniform in its causal syndrome.* Evidently it is governed by one causal law, which as a natural principle *can never be complex.*

This law derives from the fact that an excess increase in pleasure releases is followed by equally excessive, unpleasant restrictions. To avoid such negative reactions more pleasure release is usually sought, through the same or stronger means of enjoyment. This makes abandonment of the enjoyment more and more difficult, in a vicious circle.

But this simple causal law of addiction *requires the recognition of opposite-value causality*, which is not thinkable for "logical" scientists. Quite revealingly, doctors become addicts at excessively high rates, by an admitted lack of previous realization how addictions can become so viciously compulsive. Reportedly every tenth doctor becomes addicted to drugs or alcohol. This amounts to an addiction rate thirty-five times higher than that for the general population.

Of course, the physiologic processes governed by the simple law of addiction can be ungraspably mutliple and complex. For instance, the drug-withdrawal effect may seem irregular. It is excessive at the beginning, because the organism has built up strong, restrictive countermechanisms during the stimulation by a drug. These mechanisms then cannot be dismantled at once when the drug is discontinued.

The present incredible confusion about addictions is reflected well in the numerous theories on drug addiction.[18, 19, 20] Everybody can see that drug addiction is a problem of organic pleasures and displeasures. But the leading scientists have used any other concept except that of pleasure in their explanations.[18, 19, 21] This, of course, is done to remain within the scientific framework of concepts like learning or conditioning, which are not causally paradoxical.

Theories of *conditioning and learning* dominate present explanations.[19, 20, 21] Leading authorities here have been Alfred Lindesmith, Lawrence Kolb, and Abraham Wikler.[2, 21] These theories view conditioning in its usual terms, of learning by animals. We do not need to repeat that for man learning, as any cognitive factor, is easy and behaviorally without effect.

The incongruity of these theories is apparent, however complex the theorization may be. The addict could learn in five minutes that the use of drugs is not good for him. No imaginable condition could prevent such learning. But the learning is powerless against pleasure drives.

Yet pleasure is too paradoxical to be understood as a cause. Theorists argue that pleasure or euphoria could not be the goal of the drug user because he suffers from the drug use. Consequently, it is argued, he could abandon the drug without emotional loss but does not do so because of faulty learning experiences or wrong conditioning.

Certainly, conditioned animals can behave very compulsively and uselessly. When an animal learns, through conditioning, a way of behavior, it repeats it forever, inflexibly. But man varies his learned ways endlessly. He can always change his learning easily, in avoiding what is useless or unpleasant.

It is feelings that cannot be changed easily and that become compulsive. But the theorists themselves would not find any evidence of emotional conditioning here. Nobody is ever conditioned to seek useless and disturbing reactions, as are those from drug addiction according to the theorists themselves.

The *deviance theories* may be next in importance. The main authorities accepting deviance and anomie concepts have been Theodore D. Graves, Robert C. Hanson, Richard Jessor, David P. Ausubel, and Robert Merton.[2, 21] Here again, the decisive factors are seen to be cognitive intents, learning, perception, identification, role selection, and goal-setting. They are to explain why the addict chooses, cognitively, the group culture of deviance and anomie.

These cognitive factors are involved enough to make possible various logical explanations. But by cognitive insight everybody would condemn addiction and would abandon it after a short, reasoned evaluation—if it were not for the compulsive pleasure drives. Yet the real cause, pleasure enjoyment, is too paradoxical and technically nonscientific for the modern theorists guided by experimental scientism.

Unconscious motives are stressed where learning and conditioning or intents and perceptions as causes become too untenable. Conflicts from an unconscious past have been widely discussed as the cause of drug addiction, notably by Sidney Cohen, of the NIMH, and by Anthony F. Philip. But unconscious causes would be particularly incongruous here. They would be merely ideational or mental and never really felt, whereas drug addiction is physiologically grave and dependent on strong physiologic—therefore conscious—past feelings of pleasure.

Similarly misleading are other *psychological or psychosomatic* explanations. The causes and effects of addiction are not directly psychologic. They are physiological as is the pleasure release or enjoyment, and are causally as paradoxical.

A practically important reason of confusion about drug addiction has been the experimentally clear *observations that drugs can be quite beneficial*, in their direct, logical effects. Drugs relieve our anxieties, conflicts, self-criticism, irritability, sexuality, aggressiveness, or hostility. They enable us to feel more at ease and thus to function in the way we intend to. Louis C. Lasagna, Lawrence Kolb, and Robert W. Rasor have described how people using drugs regularly have led normal, productive lives.[2, 21]

Even our drug-rehabilitation programs have proceeded with the realization that drugs can improve or normalize behavior. The presently most common, methadone treatment is here typical. According to its leading theorists, Vincent P. Dole and Marie Nyswander, methadone is used to make the addict feel more normal.[21]

In practice methadone is as addictive as heroin. But logically, what more can you want than restoration of normal reactions? Such programs may work if, with good common sense, the "normalization" by drugs is used as a temporary means of imposing more restrictions in the end.

Perhaps the endless, heated *arguments about marijuana* illustrate best the lack of understanding of the simple cause of addiction. The arguments show how vast the confusion is. No acceptable conclusions have been reached after fifteen years of official investigations and studies, recorded in four big volumes, and after countless discussions by best authorities.[18, 19, 20, 21] The beneficial effects of marijuana have been clearly, experimentally demonstrated.[19, 20] As clearly, various findings have revealed its debilitating and exhaustive after-effects, which lead to wider addiction.[18, 20, 21]

Further, it is argued that, since smoking and alcohol are also addictive but legal, marijuana should equally be made legal. The popularity of this argument indicates how widely marijuana is being used.

All improvements from addictive substances are directly attractive and seem beneficial. Smoking or alcohol have such effects, and therefore have been generally accepted as tolerable. But they cause at least a third of the deaths from cancer and heart disease. Their undoubtedly similar effects on other functional diseases or disorders have not yet been fully assessed.

Far greater damage would result from general, legalized use of drugs or substances like marijuana. Drugs are far more effective than smoking and alcohol. According to NIMH statistics narcotic drugs can shorten lives by fifteen to twenty years. Starting to legalize the use of drugs would amount to opting for a society increasingly plagued by premature deaths and malignant diseases, with most people turning into wretched addicts. The legalization of narcotic drugs for treatment would be a step in that direction.

Only a true, causally understood science could offer solutions here, as elsewhere, by its potentially unlimited powers and skills of invention.

Of course, mere explanations that addiction has bad effects would not help. Knowledge alone has no motivational force. Drug addicts soon learn that drug use is self-defeating. But they arrive at feeling this way when they are too deeply addicted to extricate themselves.

What is needed is a general, complete change of attitudes. Presently youth does not believe older people or their explanations and warnings. But youth would accept as true a scientifically, universally established fact. This is where *science could affect general attitudes*. But first science itself would have to reverse its "logical" ways of thinking.

Science would have to establish as an axiomatic truth the fact that equal opposite, negative effects follow all enjoyments and that this makes the enjoyments from drugs always totally self-defeating, as they merely create withdrawal pain. Of course, science here would have to turn against universal, human value beliefs. But scientific recognition that the earth is round was also contrary to universal beliefs.

Now, think of a society where anybody still believing in a pleasure gain through drug use would be viewed as a total fool comparable to a believer in a flat earth. Also think of the aura of modernism or fashion that such a scientifically new way of thinking would acquire.

Our youth, eagerly absorbing new, modern trends and learning scientific axioms, then would certainly view a drug-user as stupid or unable to control himself. Thus emotional, causally determining attitudes would universally change. Peer pressure, a most decisive influence, would reverse as drug use became ridiculous. How exactly all this could be accomplished would, again, lie within the unlimited skills of a true science.

In our scientific era only science can change our beliefs and general attitudes. A confused scientism, turning against restrictions, has created the modern trend toward permissiveness and greater emotional improvements or enjoyments. This has made inevitable the use of drugs as the only perfect remedy against over-enjoyment aftereffects. Now science has to reverse the trend. Of course, it is easier to promote tendencies of enjoyments than of restrictions. But science can be miraculously effective and inventive when it proceeds with causal insight.

Social Sciences without Scientific, Causal Understanding

As we have indicated, the fallacies of the "scientism" perpetuated in the human sciences have been accepted in the social sciences totally, without even the occasional doubts or exceptions found in general psychology. The social sciences are thoroughly dominated by the beliefs that cognitive or ideational factors are decisive as well as by the "scientific," causal logic contrary to the actual, opposite causality of value reactions.[2, 21]

These fallacies, inevitably, prevent the social sciences from understanding causally—that is, scientifically—social phenomena, which are determined by human value reactions, as is everything that men do.

First, however, we may emphasize that the method of the social sciences, to deal only with properly *social* phenomena, automatically precludes them from ever becoming exact sciences.

Any exact science starts and proceeds by discovering or recognizing causal laws that are understood in exactly the same way by everybody. Such laws derive, ultimately, from causally simple, natural principles that are always clear and uniform to man and mind. We have seen that such principles also govern the value reactions of man as an organism created by nature.

But for properly social phenomena it is never possible to have uniform, simple causal laws or principles. These phenomena are products of the human mind, of human inventiveness and imagination, which are endlessly varied and change all the time, and which also are different for each single social event, institution, interaction, project, idea, or intent. Variety and constant change here are as extensive as ingenious human thoughts and variations of human wishes or plans.

Only the behavior of *individuals* follows causal laws. We have been explaining the simple law of value causation that governs all individual behavior. But social scientists persist in studying only the *social* events distinct from individual behavior.

Social phenomena could be studied scientifically, in compliance with causal laws, if they were treated as results of the behavior of individuals. But that is not what the present social sciences have ever intended to do.[2, 21]

Some social scientists have theories about treating societies or social institutions as inherently predetermined or self-regulating entities resembling organisms.[2, 21] This seems to offer possibilities of discovering unified causal laws; scientists generally recognize that organisms are governed by natural, uniform causal principles. But again, the social units or institutions are products of the limitlessly varied and constantly changing human inventiveness or imagination. Uniform, simple causal laws here are out of the question.

Social scientists, studying only the properly "social" phenomena, like to think in terms of societies and cultures. The theory that a *society or culture is the causal unit* has, supposedly, been the starting point in the social sciences since the work of Emile Durkheim.[2]

Social philosophy has always stressed the essence or "spirit" of societies and cultures. The most noted authorities here probably are Plato, Hegel, Spencer, Comte, Weber, Marx, Spengler, and Toynbee.[2] The concept of the superorganic, used by Sorokin, Kroeber, and Ogburn, is the modern equivalent of the idea of the spiritual essence of societies.[2, 21]

But societies or cultures are causally unreal and confusing for a simple reason. Only individuals can have a will or perform human action, individually or socially. Moreover, the individuals are governed by their own pleasure drives. These drives are so dear and overpowering for the individual that he would never permit some society or culture to interfere with them. If he does what society or culture requires, he does so, again, by following his conditioned pleasures.

Thus, in causal, scientific terms *only the individuals, motivated by their inner values, determine* what happens in all human activity, social or individual.

Of course, the effects of simple value causation can be complex. Moreover, they are seemingly paradoxical. Individuals, by themselves or in society, often do what they never intended to, because of opposite-value reactions.

Thus, it may often seem that something above individuals is compelling them. Society or culture, viewed as a causal determinant, then offers convenient explanations that can become endlessly varied. In truth, opposite-value causality explains such seemingly paradoxical behavior of man, who is the only real and concrete agent in society, not a mere metaphysical construct like Culture.

Indeed it can be said that *opposite-value causality* governs all social phenomena. They are determined by human value reactions which follow this causality. In particular, the major practical social problems, the unwanted negative reactions by people, are explainable only by the opposite causality; motivations that are wanted never create problems. But social scientists do not even suspect the paradoxical opposite-value causality.

Perhaps the best examples of the opposite causality at work socially are the most frequent *social disorders of political strife and wars*. They result from excessive, irrational social hates or other negative reactions that nobody wants and that grow mainly from overenjoyments of opposite, positively felt feelings.

Social cooperation, necessary for survival, requires individual sacrifices and the renouncement of individual feelings. This is achieved by increasing the love or positive feelings toward "our" society. Thus, love of self becomes also love of one's social group, along with various important interests and feelings. Such social selfishness, over-enjoyed as a source of social motivations or love, breeds hate of "other" societies or groups. For evidently, love of a glorious, worthy "us" is emotionally justified only if there are despicable, unworthy "others."

A typical example of negative social reactions growing from opposite over-enjoyments was the events in the Nazi Germany. People there enjoyed to an ecstatic degree national love, trust, hope, a sense of belonging, identity, pride, and a feeling of security. The result was excessive hates and fears, or feelings of humiliation and insult, that caused the persecutions and war turned against other races and peoples.

In similar ways, all intense nationalism creates international conflicts, as well as internal strife. Particularly in the developing countries patriotic love as a readiness to bear sacrifice for the nation has to be intensified far beyond what the people can really feel. Then opposite reactions, negative feelings of hate, become inevitable.

As Gunnar Myrdal explains "these strivings in the individual countries, in themselves good and rational, result in international disintegration."[21] He logically argues that the highly positive nationalistic emotions are turned into hate by a "masochistic and perverse" tendency of the people to "revolt against their own innermost ideals."[21] Opposite causality is always "perverse."

Even quite unaggressive, gentle people can become similarly perverted. In India social cooperation has had to evolve as integration within castes and religious groups, rather than within different territories. The separate religions and castes cultivate exemplary love and peace.

But the result is equally exemplary negative reactions against the "others," against other castes or religions. These reactions can be unspeakably cruel, in caste discrimination, or in outbreaks of religious strife, in which thousands are killed; more than a half million people were killed during the partition of India.

In the no-free-lunch world of value causality, such negative reactions, unwanted and irrational, are inevitable wherever increased positive feelings have to be created. Learned social critics want to unite people, to create greater federations and *a world government*.[2, 21] But enormous amounts of love or positive feelings would have to be created to induce remote groups to bear sacrifices for each other.

The feelings here would have to be exaggerated beyond all reality. It is the exaggeration of positive emotions that always brings unwanted negative reactions. This has to be understood in thinking about nationalism and internationalism.

People in advanced nations do not suffer much from irrational hates turned against "others" because such people do not have to exaggerate their nationalism. They have developed, through long, difficult conditioning, real love or the readiness to bear sacrifice for various groups or "strangers" in their country.

This kind of nationalism, growing by virtue of an effortful, more general love, can even help internationalism. But logical international critics all blame nationalism. They want to create a world government by a logically rational joining together of peoples who have never even thought of the practically difficult sacrifices necessary for cooperation with each other.

Rationally it seems that pronounced national defensive or separatist policies grow from misunderstanding. Evidently, it is always more productive to cooperate with all countries. Also, misunderstandings can be corrected by mere explanations or a change of outlook. Arnold Toynbee argued that the "fashionable Western liking for political disunity and dislike for political unity" could be changed as easily as all customs can.[21]

True, customs can be changed. They are changed with disastrous ease when the change offers more satisfactions or freedoms. The modern changes toward liberalism and license show this. But no reasoning or mere "liking" can create positive feelings or prevent negative reactions.

Highly learned political critics, following views such as those of Toynbee or Nobelist Norman Angell, are explaining every day how shortsighted or unimaginitive our politicians are.[2, 21] *Actually our politicians have a better, instinctive insight* about what we and foreign peoples can and do feel as nations. To be efficient as a nation we have to cultivate feelings about "us," which inevitably leads to opposite feelings about the "others." Such feelings, not reasons, are decisive.

The opposite-causality rule is further illustrated by *the paradox of improvements and hardships* affecting societies.

Satisfactions are hailed by a people as sources of its successes, though they lead to immobility or motivational impoverishment. Hardships, "challenges," or difficulties create motivations and capacities, but are deplored by people as obstacles.

Scientists here are as "logical" as the people are in blaming non-satisfactions or restrictions. Particularly, the now-fashionable emphasis on studying the spirit of each era leads scientists to accept as true such views of peoples. Even the various theories of "challenge" hold that satisfactory solutions through a challenge are preconditions for it to work effectively. But only dire needs make the difficult benefits from a challenge appear worthwhile. Otherwise, we would be engaging in new challenges every day, since they are potentially all around us.

It is generally known that *peoples from harsher environments are more capable.* Nordic conquerors, in two continents, are examples. But it has also been pointed out that great cultures arose in southern, fertile valleys.

Evidently, peoples have to be forcibly driven, by events, into harsher regions, the bleak North or the Arabian desert, if they are to evolve stronger motivations. There they acquire motivational capacities and power to conquer and to develop more intense cultures when they come upon fertile regions. Europeans coming to America exploited exuberantly its richness of land and resources by virtue of capacities and motivations evolved under the conditions of scarcity of land and resources in Europe.

Peoples do not evolve capacities if they are not exposed to disturbing changes. When isolated, in the tropics, in mountains, or the cold North, peoples have not evolved high cultures. Anything that is constant becomes normal for man and evokes no special response.

The climate of the "temperate" zone actually imposes the most disturbing changes, with its deadly winters after extremely favorable summers. The demands, and opportunities, brought about by such harsh changes have made us build and accumulate protective means and reserves—to create the sources of our civilization.

The *cyclic theories of history* are providing interesting facts about how societies decline upon the attainment of highest satisfactions. These theories offer, more comprehensively than others, a general law of history. The expounders of these theories, from Vico or Hegel to Spengler and Toynbee, have demonstrated that doom follows the highest flourish of civilizations.

Explanations here would be simple if opposite-value causality were recognized. Societies organize and fight hard to attain sorely needed material or political security. Such attitudes disappear when people attain what they need and can enjoy their riches or security.

But the cyclic theories have offered lofty, intricate explanations. Spengler and Toynbee have postulated purposive, humanly interesting, meaningfully involved principles.[2, 21] This is metaphysics. In the real, natural world, universal causal principles can be only completely simple.

Social or political movements also can be better understood, historically and practically, if the *paradox of restrictions* is recognized. Political movements arise from the pursuit of freedoms. But the movements become restrictive when they have to face practical problems and responsibilities. They soon become conservative, instead of being revolutionary. The parties of liberals, democrats, socialists, and communists have done so.

Such reversals in social movements lead to various confusions.

A movement may be treated as liberal if it retains its revolutionary doctrines or slogans, though actually it may have become conservative. Or a movement may be assumed to have been historically as conservative as it is now, even though it may have originated as a revolution.

A good example is the constantly repeated confusion about the early Christians. They are viewed as unselfish, spiritually minded, submissive, and refined moral idealists. Here the present qualities of Christians are imputed to their revolutionary predecessors. It is indeed naive to assume that the poorest Roman masses were so morally idealistic and materially unconcerned or refined and gentle, in what evidently was their social revolution. As the classical work of Edward Gibbon shows, they were, in fact, hatefully aggressive and selfish revolutionaries. Their methods, though, were necesarily different from those of the physically destructive freedom-fighters of today. Religion and beliefs then comprised most of politics.

By the way, religion should be more comprehensively recognized as the central force of political organization of many ancient cultures. This explains, for example, why great cities, like those of the Maya, were often mysteriously abandoned. Gods could be changed by a clever priest or magician. Then the city built for previous gods would lose its function or be avoided as religiously contaminated.

In our times it would be practically relevant to understand better the *paradoxical effects of satisfactions and freedoms in our own democracy.* We should cease emphasizing our once revolutionary and seemingly logical ideals of liberty, individualism, and the pursuit of happiness.

We constantly read how disruptive can be democratic freedoms. Government with strong authority is evidently the best, in practice. Democratic governments acted dictatorially during the two world wars and accomplished awesome feats.

We should realize that, similarly, a strenuous effort is now required to work for the virtually miraculous future awaiting us. We should permit our democratic governments to act dictatorially, in their various programs and policies. Yet because of our liberal and hedonistic tendencies we are diluting the power of our governments and thus depriving ourselves of the enormous benefits that accelerated progress would bring.

However, a contradictory fact about our progress should be mentioned. The freedoms and enjoyments that people pursue create endless difficulties and disruptions, as well as still-higher demands. To meet such troubles, we have to find new ways, to be more successful, more productive, as individuals or as employers and officials. Thus, the very difficulties that people create lead to desperately intense, though misunderstood and confused, progress. Causally understood and planned progress would probably be greater, free of frictions and counterproductive confusion.

Another extensive source of causal confusion is *social attitudes* and general value feelings. They are causally as *paradoxical* as individual value reactions. The best, most enjoyable conditions or causal backgrounds lead to feelings of dissatisfaction and to emotional negativity. In fact, every causal background creates opposite value perceptions and reactions.

The best examples are the reactions in our own society. It is dominated by feelings of non-satisfaction or stress and insecurity. Accordingly, social scientists have logically blamed factual conditions of non-satisfaction or stress in our society. In truth, the cause of our reactions of emotional negativity and stress are our excessive enjoyments of pampering and security, surrounding us in our uniquely advanced era.

Similarly in all social or cultural eras, the most acutely felt, best-recorded reactions come from strong, opposite causal backgrounds that are not recognized as causes and are least noticed when they are universal—therefore being causally most important. Any condition that is really universal is hardly noticed, still less recognized as the causal, opposite-value factor.

We may also mention *fixation* as a source of extensive confusion in the social sciences. We have explained how any accidental value can become incredibly strong or "true" and endlessly elaborate or rich through the vicious circle of fixations. Avoidances of some danger also can create a strong fixation, because they too can be repetitively enjoyed. Thus, customs and taboos can become, through the vicious circle of fixations, extremely compulsive for no apparent or rationally explainable reason.

Particularly in social behavior, fixations grow without limits. In natural, individual behavior, organic needs do not permit endless fixations. Experiments show that animals do fixate on some one food, but after a while change foods because of natural requirements. Such controls are absent in social fixations.

Socially people enjoy most easily what is customary, which becomes even more customary by being enjoyed. The result is like that of ants circling on a track with a scent which becomes stronger as they circle on it. Social scientists have sought for causally logical explanations of the endlessly rich and strong customs and taboos.

The functional theories, supposedly best expounded by Bronislaw Malinowski and Alfred Radcliffe-Brown, hold that customs serve useful purposes.[2, 21] Actually, the most pronounced and richest customs or cultural patterns are fixational—and thus rather misunderstood causally. They are as useless as behavioral disorders, growing by a vicious circle and having no logical or useful function.

However, theories ascribing various logical or useful functions to customs have been offered by the best anthropologists—Frazer, Boas, Benedict, Levi-Strauss, or Mead. It is accepted as axiomatic that the culturally richest phenomena must have important causal reasons.

Scientists have attributed to customs various seemingly logical, all-important causal meanings and functions: revelation of the very genius of a people, mythical or spiritual cultural forces governing societies, cultural conscious and unconscious predetermination, or inherent universal patterns of social etiology.

In reality the richest customs are fixational and causally as meaningless as psychotic mannerisms. Their extraordinary richness and strength grow endlessly through the "neurotically" senseless, vicious-circle automatism of fixation.

Of course, the very confusion or mystery and the meaningless richness of customs permit scientists to construct whatever explanations suit their convictions. Levi-Strauss could build, on observations of customs, expansive theories about hidden archetypal or metaphysically symbolic causes. When "scientific" sexual liberalism started, Margaret Mead used research on cultural customs to prove that sexual freedoms lead to healthier human development. Not surprisingly, it was easy for her to discover what she wanted to prove.

In a noted book on Mead's work in Samoa, Derek Freeman shows how easy her research was. She did it from a city office in Samoa, in nine months, by calling in two dozen young girls for what to them was gossip. They naturally told her what they thought was interesting, and therefore unusual. Universal, restrictive customs are too commonplace and dull to be particularly "noticed" or dwelt on. Actually, the Samoans are very restrictive about sex and have a remarkably high rate of rape and violent crime, as Freeman demonstrates. He points out that this would have been evident to Mead from local newspapers, if she had read them.

Customs of peoples and groups are incredibly multiple and elaborate in their affective meanings, mostly in direct proportion to their fixational, causally accidental, meaningless nature. The more remarkable or sacredly rich a custom is, the more likely it is a result of endlessly self-increasing fixations growing from causally non-serious, meaningless repetitive enjoyments.

The really decisive customs, such as the traditional restrictive attitudes, are so general and hard to follow that they are not noticed as anything particular and are never exuberantly enriched.

In sum, fixations make customs so rich and strong that they appear as the most sacred treasures and deepest truths of a culture. But fixations grow from causally unimportant, gratuitously easy, repetitive enjoyments, by way of mere vicious-circle automatism. They are *as meaningless as endless neurotic elaborations*. Yet scientists view them *as embodiments of highest social and cultural truths or wisdoms*.

Another widely misleading view on social behavior is that offered by *sociobiology*, which apparently is gaining increased recognition. Sociobiology is misleading for a simple reason. It claims that nonconscious, genetic causes determine our behavior. In reality, our conscious, most thoroughly planned pursuit of pleasure or satisfactions is the one and only determinant of our motivations and behavior.

Sociobiology is based on the ethological ideas that inborn, genetic patterns of behavior are important causes. A Nobel prize was awarded to Konrad Lorenz for his ethological studies on animals. Ethology, extended to human behavior, has been notedly expounded by Robert Ardrey, Robin Fox, Desmond Morris, Anthony Storr, and Lionel Tiger. We are told, for instance, that the territorial imperative or aggression, which governs animals, determines human behavior. The best-known sociobiologists are probably Edward Wilson and Robert Trivers.

Sociobiologists claim that patterns of behavior encoded in our genes are decisive for human behavior. Thus, something we are never aware of supposedly determines what we do. This is mysteriously interesting, which has attracted attention. In reality we do only what pleases or satisfies us; and nothing in the world is more consciously experienced or planned than our pleasure experiences.

The point is that *only conscious pleasures determine what man does* and that he has evolved *consciously planned, overwhelming systems*, built by his supreme intellect, for attaining all his conscious pleasures, direct or conditioned, present or future.

Certainly, all human drives, including pleasure, are organic or genetically determined. But what man has done with these drives, especially with the all-inclusive pleasure drive, is as unique as man's consciousness and intellect.

Man has intensely and perfectly sought and discovered every drive that is pleasant and has incorporated it in his conscious value system, which supremely governs everything he does. Any value, purely organic or conditioned, in such a value system is behaviorally decisive to the extent it is consciously felt as pleasant. If it is outside this system it has no effect on behavior.

Consider even a case where a person may have territorial or aggressive instincts not yet entirely taken over into his conscious value system. He may want to occupy an undisturbed "territory" around his desk or to kick his neighbors when he is angry. Compare with this the "territorial imperative" within our value system of individual and national acquisitions, conquests and explorations of lands and territories. Or think of our drive of aggression and superiority systemized within our competition for fame or political power. All our human pursuits, cultural or physical, are similarly integrated in our non-instinctive value systems.

How ridiculous, amidst such value systems, would be the guarding of territory around one's desk or kicking one's neighbor! *People simply do not behave according to ethological patterns.*

The systems of our conscious drives or values, embodying every one of our decisive pleasures, are so gigantic that some still lingering, innate patterns of behavior are preposterously meaningless for human behavior. These systems are consciously managed most effectively, even exploitatively, through our stupendous intellect. Against these systems any genetic, non-conscious behavior patterns are as powerless as would be a beaver dam against the Tennessee Valley Authority.

Man often mismanages or over-exploits his enjoyments of the conscious pleasures, exactly because he is not limited by natural, genetic patterns. He thus incurs negative, beastly reactions. Then it may seem that indeed man is still a slave to his animal instincts.

All in all, sociobiology has no practical meaning for human behavior, which is determined only by *consciously* felt pleasure drives that are totally, superbly managed as well as exploited by our fully *conscious* pursuits, implemented by our *prodigious intellect*. Even our functional physical and mental diseases are caused by such pursuits.

Misleading causal theories, like sociobiology, can only deepen the confusion over grave everyday problems.

Finally, we may say a few words about *economics*. Practically, the central problem of economy is its recessions. If an economy could grow in a continuous boom we would soon have an economic utopia. Actually, recessions alternate with booms because of opposite psychologic reactions that are economically precipitated: a stimulation by increased consumption leads to an exhaustion of resources of production and precipitates effects opposite to stimulation.

Nobel laureate Paul Samuelson says that business cycles would be explainable if we could view them as alternating psychotic reactions, "each stage leading as inevitably to the next as the manic stage of disturbed people leads to depressive stage."[21] We can indeed view them in this way.

Stimulation is the cause of depression in economic behavior as it is in all our excessive negative reactions. People want to stimulate the economy, because a boom brings benefits to all. Particularly under the influence of Keynesian theories, economic stimulation has been perfected.

The ensuing opposite reactions from economic over-stimulation are psychologic or behavioral, but arise because of economic exhaustion. True, an economy is not inherently limited, as an organism is. Therefore, opposite-value causality does not govern an economy. But opposite psychological reactions are inevitably precipitated by economic exhaustion if increase in consumption is used as the stimulant of an economy, in accordance with "logical" or mathematical economics.

Consumption is indeed the motivation in every economy. Logically or mathematically, therefore, consumer confidence, or increased buying, appears to be the very source of economic expansion, as it indeed is in its immediate effects. But the final effects of an increase in consumption are paradoxical, much the way the after-effects of all stimulation are.

Increased consumption is tantamount to a decrease in available capital as means of production. The result is higher interest rates, atop of inflation self-increasing as more of it is expected and worsening because of a lag in productivity due to the deepening scarcity of capital.

Costs of materials and production rise with inflation and the scarcity of capital. Even labor costs increase because of higher wages during inflation. Also, in the atmosphere of inflation interest rates rise still further.

High interest rates were the central, single obstacle to recovery in the last recession. A drop in interest rates translated, with elementary certainty, into a recovery for all business, particularly for central industries such as housing. In Japan and Switzerland, where people saved three times more than we did, the recession was negligent, even during the decline in world trade, so important to their economies. Savings increase capital as certainly as consumption decreases it.

If consumption or buying were the source of expansion, an economic boom would never stop. Nothing is easier than consumption. People would buy like crazy, if they were sure of employment. But even as the Keynesian "multiplier" theory shows, it is capital that creates employment.[2, 21] And capital accumulation is practically never anything else than a decrease in consumption—a proportional decrease ensuing from the elevation of incomes, according to Keynes.[2, 21]

However, the pivotal *cause of economic slumps is psychological.* Keynes called it the "opposite error of optimism." A feeling of pessimism or depression becomes inevitable after the overstimulated enjoyment of optimism. Economically, such overstimulation is that of a boom built on an exaggerated basis, not on the real availability of capital.

The economic community starts realizing that such an artificial uplift can easily break down. Everybody can see how expansion becomes more difficult under "overheated," continuous consumption. Prices increase and interest rates rise. Correspondingly, materials, capital, and even labor become more costly. Everything is against further expansion, and recession appears possible. Exaggerated optimism inexorably leads to opposite feelings.

Then the concern, by any group of businessmen, about recession and about others feeling the same way can spread and precipitate a panic. The economic *interdependence of all businesses* is the decisive, understandable contributory cause here. If you expand your business while others contract the businesses which you are supplying or on which you depend in many other ways, you will ruin yourself. In short, as concern about recession spreads, through imputation of equal fears to others, everybody starts retracting before others do so and ruin him. The result can be a stampede.

Reactions during a slump are clearly abnormal, as irrational as is the behavior of psychotics. People are paralyzed and refuse to save themselves. All they would have to do would be to reject irrational fear.

Evidently the cause is psychological. It is an exaggerated general reaction opposite to the equally exaggerated previous stimulation of optimism. This reaction cannot be helped, because its cause lies in the past. It has to be lived through, as mental disorders have to before they disappear. The classic experts on business cycles, W. C. Mitchell and J. A. Schumpeter, found that a depression must be let to "run its course" or to "digest the maladjustment."[2, 21]

Neither the positive exaggeration nor its equal opposite would result if the economy grew with a corresponding increase in capital. When capital is plentiful, the economy expands without exaggerated, artificial stimulation. Then no causal reason exists for a subsequent, exaggerated apprehension to arise, or to become projected onto others. *The role of capital is all-important and paradoxical.*

Man's technical, material progress grows through the accumulation of capital, best thought of as machines. Our present progress has resulted from a thousandfold increase in machines. In the ideal future all work will be done by machines. That future will be attained by making machines that make more machines.

This seems nonsensical in logical economics, based on the belief in consumption as motivation. But causally capital accumulation can be compared to the paradoxical restriction of organic driving forces that increases the potential or reserves of such forces. Particularly since economy becomes a physical extension of man, of his capacities. Ideally, capital as the means of production, as machines and the accumulation of power, can do all work under the direction of man.

But in "logical" economics, consumption rather than capital is the source of progress. Typical here is the book of Marx *Das Kapital*, which has been the bible on capital for socialists. The role of capital as an extension of man and as his servant is disregarded. Instead Marx sympathized with the condemnation by Luther of interest on capital. Consumption is stressed instead.

Marx argued that capitalism will collapse as underpaid workers are unable to buy what capitalists produce. Similar "logical" arguments and theories have been numerous and elaborate.[2, 21]

But capitalism has increased the numbers and wages of workers enormously. It has done so by accumulating capital through "exploitation" of workers and consumers. This is still mostly condemned. But capital has to be created from profits if people do not save. Workers have to be underpaid and consumers "cheated."

Practically, our seemingly logical, experimentally scientific economics is inherently misleading. Consumption does fuel economy, *but as consumption increases it exhausts the power that drives the economy*. Optimism or stimulation does create expansion. But it leads to opposite reactions and depression unless the expansion is founded on reality, is sustained by capital accumulation, by the restriction of consumption. Unreality or an exaggeration of optimism is what creates the exaggerated pessimism of all depressions.

Psychological causes are decisive in economic behavior. This is very important. The central economic causal laws, and theories about their effects, are always founded by economists on psychological assumptions, particularly about motivations, profit incentives, expectations, preferences, value perceptions, marginal evaluations, economic optimism, or stimulation.[2, 21]

But the psychological causes here as well are governed by opposite-value causality, which is diametrically different from the logical or mathematical thinking of economists. The same "scientifically" axiomatic logic rules in modern psychology.

No wonder that economics has remained the "dismal science." Economists rarely agree in their predictions or explanations, except on what seems clearly logical and is mostly reversed in practice. For, in reality, the economy continuously follows the rule of opposite causality in the all-important recessions and expansions as well as in all its decisive movements, determined by psychological value reactions—the bases of economic laws.

Predictions by economists have been constantly confusing for those who have to use them,[13] and not taken seriously by others, as you can read every day. The predictions have been less often right than wrong[13] on the main, paradoxically reversing economic trends. Even our best economists, including the Nobelists Frederick von Hayek, Milton Friedman, and Wassily Leontieff, have recognized the unreliability and irrelevance of predictions by economists.[13] Ninety percent of economic theories have been discarded as wrong;[2, 21] and no scientifically unifying breakthroughs have yet been reached in economic theory.

In conclusion, we may emphasize that our future progress will require gigantic capital accumulation, since machines will have to do all routine work. Yet economists still hold to their experimentally or mathematically "logical" theories about the promotion of increased consumption and stimulation through it.

Progressively disastrous recessions await us if due to increased consumption the disparity widens between capital availability and our enormous future aspirations requiring equally enormous capital. Even presently, the peculiar persistence of high interest rates reveals that our inventions are greater than the availability of capital.

Future inventiveness will be even vaster, as sciences advance. The aspirations of expansion will increase progressively. Then crippling depressions, as paralyzing as psychoses, will follow each such aspired expansion if the booms are stimulated by increased consumption, which decreases capital.

All behavioral crises, leading to economic depressions as well as to psychoses, grow from disparity between over-stimulated aspiration and normalcy as reality. The availability of adequate capital for corresponding expansion is the reality that can insure a progressive normalcy in our economic *behavior*, determined *psychologically*.

The greatest of all economic achievements would be the control of economic expansions and recessions. This opportunity is missed, even counteracted, by our economists. Their very logic of thinking and mathematics is contrary to opposite-value causality, which actually governs the psychologic, and thus the decisive, economic behavior, particularly in recessions and expansions.

Economists themselves recognize that *psychological* assumptions are the bases for establishing economic laws and for understanding how they work.[2, 21] Those assumptions are bound to come out diametrically different from the facts as long as opposite-value causality is not recognized.

V

OUR HUMANISTIC THOUGHT A CAUSAL OBSTACLE TO PROGRESS

Human value beliefs are contradictory, as is all human existence. Insight into the actual, relative-value causality would be contrary to normal, wholesome human attitudes. But in their practical lives men have to comply with what is causally right, with the relative, opposite-value causality. They have to impose on themselves restrictions or conditioned non-satisfactions to have pleasures and satisfactions as the desired motivations.

That is why our morals and culture, evolved through traditional wisdom, are restrictive and illogical. But the present, scientifically progressive, humanistic thought wants to make them logical. Why suppress satisfactions or freedoms when they are the very sources of our positive motivations?

The result is cultural trends toward more freedoms and permissiveness in pursuit of satisfactions or pleasures. Since such progressive truths are contrary to what is causally, factually true, our progressive, humanistic thought has fostered misleading, degenerative modern cultural trends. This follows from the strongest humanistic causal tenets, about the enjoyment of our inner values, which are always satisfactions or pleasures in their final terms.

Less importantly for practical life, the causal confusion in modern humanistic thought has generated and permitted causal fallacies in our literature, esthetics, and philosophical beliefs.

Modern literature passionately defends the belief that freedoms and deeper emotional satisfactions bring us self-fulfillment. Our best authors have continuously exposed as intolerable the seemingly senseless, necessarily contradictory, traditional restrictions.

In esthetics the lack of causal understanding about fixations and about effects of contrast has resulted in absurdities. Through value fixations esthetic admiration has often deepened into superstitious cultism. Contrast enhances value experience, but because of causal confusion it has become in modern art merely a gross opposition or absurd distortion of normal esthetic values. A fixation on such sensational "originality" grows easily. This causes mere absurdities to become revered as creations of genius. Certainly, these fixational feelings can be genuinely, sacredly deep—as have often been the most distorting cultural fixations.

In philosophy, the modern humanistic thought has permitted perpetuation of causal confusion about knowledge and values.

All knowledge results, at bottom, from value differentiations. It is therefore goverened by the relative or opposite-value causality. But this is unacceptable in philosophy, which seeks for absolute, final truths about reality in itself. The second most important expressed or underlying concern in philosophy is values. But the actual causal sources of our desired values are their abhorrent value opposites. The overall result is a total failure of philosophical efforts. Philosophy has produced unbelievably vast, controversial complexity and no coherent answers.

A further source of confusion in humanistic thought are value fixations, which are nonsensical but can turn our meaningless customs into sacred treasures and institutions. We become enslaved to such customs and fashions. We waste on them our surpluses, which are the main means of progress.

Our whole culture becomes a self-deepening enslavement into our nonsensical fixational customs and value beliefs. This is true for our fashions and sports as well as for our inalienable rights and freedoms. In practice such inalienable rights are our inveterate customs, deepened into sacred values by fixation. But they dominate the very direction in which we are culturally moving. Fixational stagnation, contrary to the demands of progress, is the result.

Our progressive, humanistic thought compounds fixations. It attributes particular significance to our deepest or richest values; and no values are deeper or richer than the fixational ones.

Generally the progress of man is bound to be hindered by our "progressive," humanistic thought, which moves contrary to causal truths. Progress will come through science, built on causal understanding. Man's future will be unimaginably miraculous, as are the results of all true sciences. It will also be totally different from humanistic beliefs.

Humanists always see progress as being characterized by enrichment or deepening of value experiences. Indeed, it makes no sense humanly to have progress without an enrichment of inner values. But any pursuit of inner enjoyments is a futile effort, comparable to chasing one's own shadow. Moreover, if it is deepened it brings, not progress, but rather affective disorders, through the vicious circle of "improvements" and exhaustion.

Of course, progress without the humanistic, presently cherished values will be abhorrently strange, in present terms. We can even imagine human monsters, adapted to live in space. But the very justification of the progress of man is that it might become so inconceivably differently superior as to bring sense, in the end, to the otherwise nonsensical human existence.

Humanistic Value Beliefs—Contrary to Causal Facts

Men have to believe in value gain, in value experiences not dependent on equal value opposites. In practical life this belief has been always counteracted by the restrictive moral tradition and learned teachings. But now a more consistent logic of value beliefs dominates our more scientific, humanistic thinking. Particularly because this logic agrees with the scientism imitated from our exact, technical sciences.

However, this causal logic is totally wrong for value causality and thus for everything that man is or does. Consequently, our progressive, scientifically oriented modern thought has become a source of confusions. Its logic, contrary to the opposite-value causality, permits the easily self-sustaining growth of degenerative trends of enjoyment and permissiveness in our affluent modern age.

Perhaps most revealing is the causal confusion about value itself, about what values are. It is certainly recognized that values are all-important in human behavior and thought. Discussions about the importance of various values are endless.

But it is now generally recognized, even in the best philosophies, that *value is causally unexplainable*, irreducible to anything else or ontologically self-defining, much as "yellow" is just yellow.[9, 10] In short, modern thought, admittedly, does not understand values causally or how they arise and work.

When values will finally become causally understood, the causality of values will be the first thing everybody will learn about in studying the human world, determined by value reactions. As it is, neither the actual opposite-causality rule nor any other, necessarily simple causal law of values has yet been established or applied in modern thinking or science. This is revealing.

For value is ontologically and semantically, as well as in organic and behavioral terms, a uniform principle, as is pleasure, its ultimate causal source. And all natural, uniform principles or laws are elementarily simple causally. Evidently, human thinking is inherently averse to the causal understanding of values.

In practical terms, because of its totally wrong causal logic, our humanistic thought becomes confused and misleading concerning our morals and culture, which are sustained by tradition. That is why centers of higher learning become nests of culturally and morally disturbing, degenerative or violent movements. In all times, students at universities have been the leading revolutionaries rising against the traditional, inevitably illogical and "deceitful" restrictions or morals. Of course, such revolutionaries become conservatives as they grow older and learn, practically or intuitively, how it all really works.

Probably one of the most often-discussed educational problems is *the teaching of our values* to our children or to those who do not yet "understand" the values.

It is generally believed that values are to be taught by way of providing understanding and insights, through reasons or ideas. Parents and educators are to explain, or to discuss and make clear, what the values are and how precious they are. The delusion about cognitive insights or reasoning and ideas as decisive causes is general here as well. The emotional conditioning by which cultural values are imposed on us is not noticed, because it is like the atmosphere we live in. Moreover, it seems impossible to man because it works by creating values or satisfactions through their opposites.

Thus, even when values are seen as deriving from feelings, the other delusion, about the sources of values, reigns supreme. It is never recognized that our values as satisfactions come through a conditioning that imposes non-satisfactions, needs, as the sources of our cultural satisfactions.

The universal human prejudice about value causation prevents man from ever accepting that his lovely inner values derive from their harrowing causal opposites. Rather the inherently alchemistic logic is accepted that our values, as satisfactions, come from causal sources or backgrounds of similar values, of satisfactions. This is the emotional, causally effective belief behind the modern spirit of hedonism and permissiveness. Humanistic philosophy has always expounded that our positive values emanate from some higher positive source, but merely philosophical ideas have no practical effect.

Now let us look at our chief values, in order to explain their "impossible" causality, particularly their origin from their ugly opposites. This is practically important because our inner values determine how we live or even conserve our normalcy and health.

Freedom is, probably, the highest value for modern men. You can hear every day how valuable freedom is. It is claimed by the bright teenager as his right and necessity, or is invoked by the President as the goal of our nation. It certainly has been proclaimed as the fundamental principle of human existence in most modern social theories and political declarations.

But freedom derives its value from pre-existing restrictions. Total freedom, enjoyed by a man on some island, would have no value meaning. People are led, in revolutions and wars of liberation, by the pursuit of freedom because of pre-existing restrictions felt as intolerable.

Restrictions are, however, necessary in all political or social integration. As such integration has intensified in modern times, restrictions on individuals have increased. Consequently, freedom has become the most meaningful value.

Of course people living under constant restrictions do not particularly notice or resent them, especially since such restrictions bring benefits for all. Rather, the rare freedoms enjoyed or proclaimed by such people are strongly felt or seen as the dominant principles.

Then it may look as if the more advanced nations have progressed through the enjoyment of greater freedoms. This is what learned humanistic thought extols or implies. Idealistic leaders, or revolutionaries, in developing nations accept these erudite ideas as guiding truths, though the people of such nations need restrictions more than anything else.

In our individual lives, we all live for freedoms or, simply, for more effective pleasure releases. Of course, within organic limitedness, release is possible only to the extent of previous restrictions. But whatever we do or achieve, the driving force for it comes from such releases, from attainment of freedoms. The most important freedom here is the relief from complex inner restrictions, such as guilt or the weight of conscience.

Anyway, men always perceive that only freedom—actually a release from restrictions—is a moving force. We are, correspondingly, reassured by experts that we should only pursue our own freedom, a free self-fulfillment. Of course, the restrictions are always there, imposed by conditioning to serve as the sources of the release, of the enjoyment of freedom, for desired goals.

In one's individual development such restrictions are not noticed to the extent that the conditioning is constant and universal. Rather, ideals and promises of freedom are prominently noticed and emphasized, in good education, as it actually sustains the restrictions without which freedoms would have no meaning.

Then come the learned or liberated youth with rational, liberal ideas, to discover how in truth freedoms are suppressed all around them. The outrage may break out in student riots or in radical progressive movements, widening the generation gap. Parents or former teachers are seen as hypocrites and liars who talk of freedoms but impose restrictions. Moreover, the parents seem to be merely cruel and ignorant, since logically restrictions clearly appear as obstacles to motivations, which are satisfactions.

On higher theoretical levels, the idealization of freedom has led to the glorification of individualism. For our humanistic social critics and leaders nothing is more abhorrent than the "ant-hill society." But social progress has proceeded and will do so by way of closer social integration.

The most desirable practical goal would be social cooperation so close that individual interests would disappear and the common good would become the main concern. Needless to say that such a cooperation would bring benefits for everybody to an extent we presently can only dream of.

And if people are conditioned to derive satisfaction from such "ant-hill" cooperation, then the ideal of love for others becomes a reality, genuine and deeply satisfactory as well as practically most successful.

Here we come to the other specter in humanistic thought: human conditioning, "brainwashing." The cultured humanists do not realize how totally conditioned they are themselves. To the extent that we are cultural our instincts have been completely changed by conditioning. Our only natural drive is selfishness. It has to be turned totally around, by conditioning, which is not noticed because it always surrounds us like atmospheric pressure.

Thus conditioning creates our moral and cultural motivations, our conditioned satisfactions. When we have such satisfactions we can attain what we rationally, reasonably intend: then we can be truly "human" or rational. Here we may emphasize that we all have perfect intentions concerning the most positive, pleasant, and loving behavior. We become negativistic and hateful or mentally and behaviorally impoverished exactly when we have not been conditioned.

Only conditioning, abhorred as brainwashing, can create in man the potential for positive "human" or cultural reactions. It is true, though, that *scientifically logical* conditioning becomes a crippling distortion, useless and cruel in the end. The really effective, practically creative conditioning has to come through ingrown moral traditions.

Love is a value, in our behavior and beliefs, as important as freedom. Causal confusion about it is similar to that about freedom, and adds to the feeling of outrage of radical, learned youth. The generation gap has become a perennial problem.

Love has been hailed as the greatest value on earth, in various theories, by Empedocles and Plato, or Buber and Tillich. It is shown to be a deep satisfaction and fulfillment, now sometimes compared to genuine, natural sexual enjoyments. One can refer here to the greatest authorities—from ancient teachers and saints to modernists like Sorokin, Unamuno, or Sir Julian Huxley.[1, 14]

Love is virtually a panacea for all human ills. The behavioral experts, stressing positive reactions, see love as a main source of positive motivations. In a collection of essays, *Love Today*, the powers of love are expounded as solutions for nearly every human problem.

Even our physical as well as mental health can be helped by love. We can refer here to such a scientific authority as Karl Menninger, particularly to his book *Love against Hate*. At the other end of the spectrum, best-sellers like that by Leo Buscaglia on the miracles of love are as convincing, and causally confused, as our scientific works on love.

Certainly love can help us everywhere, because it is the general source of pleasure releases. This is clear even from the universal human expressions about love in any language. We "love" our most selfish and hateful enjoyments as we "love" virtues and God. Love is satisfaction deriving from equal need as non-satisfaction. This is evident from the clearest example of love, our sexual love. Or from any other kind of love.

We have seen how the love we have for our parents or their substitutes grows from conditioned non-satisfactions of the need of security or survival. Here the warm, heavenly love comes causally from the most infernal of all emotions, the apprehension about threats to our survival. All love, highest or lowest, derives from its unrecognized, ugly value opposites.

People love some god to the extent that they suffer threats and needs. Disasters and afflictions, more than anything else, make people turn to their "loving" gods, with feelings of love and gratitude. Peoples have gods where they have wants, dangers, fears, or values growing from needs. The love of gods here is deeply genuine because the needs are distressingly real. For more advanced people God is the source of love and morals, as well as of wisdom or intelligence, because these qualities are needed most.

In the simplest kind of love, trained animals really love their master. But this love is created by conditioning the animals' fears, deprivations, and needs. If the trainer proceeded with real love, satisfying the animals with what they really want, they would remain wild beasts.

Human love is a similarly conditioned feeling. Only a thorough conditioning of man's similar, instinctive survival needs can transform the overwhelmingly selfish instincts of man, as an organism, into their own denial, selfless love. That is why creation of love is so difficult. Otherwise everybody would increase, without end, this deeply gratifying feeling that is so clearly beneficial in every way.

But in humanistic theory, love is a value enjoyment far removed from ruthless conditioning through non-satisfactions or infernal fears of survival. Love is seen as a feeling given and received in an absolutely generous, nonconditional, unrestrictive spirit of "pleasure and delight," in the words of Rollo May.

In his erudite book *Love and Will* May reviews the humanistic beliefs about love and finds that obstacles to the enjoyment of love have been merely ideational—lack of "intentionality," or the failure to understand the nature of love and to expand consciousness, as well as misunderstandings about the "daimonic principle."

In any case, for our learned, rationalizing youth love is to be a freely, generously given satisfaction, a feeling to be enjoyed without conditions or restrictions. This is what has been generally always taught. But such youth see how restrictive and "deceitful" is the love they receive from their parents or parental authorities.

The *pursuit of happines* is expressly or implicitly accepted in humanistic thought as a chief human value. All men live for greater happiness. The enjoyment of values, often viewed in their loftiest aspects, is seen by humanists as the fulfillment of all conscious existence. Without such enjoyments nothing seems to make sense. Here we have a central fallacy of humanistic thought.

The enjoyment of values, actually of satisfactions, is hailed as a logical goal of life and progress, whereas our capacities and progress, even our values themselves, can be only impoverished by enjoyments. Whatever their forms, enjoyments are as easy as the creation of positive values is difficult—because satisfactions can derive only from needs as non-satisfactions.

Happiness, as all satisfactions or pleasure, is a source of positive reactions but is governed by the paradoxical opposite-value causality. The surest way to lose the feeling of happiness is to over-enjoy it, to increase it directly. Happiness comes from a preceding experience of hardships and labor.

Those who have written about happiness have found it paradoxical and confusing.[14] The writers most enthusiastic about happiness often fail, in their stories, to connect it with the opposite causal backgrounds that they themselves are describing. Usually, a moment of bliss is described as occurring after or during a period of great stress, which is mentioned only incidentally or as a curious coincidence.[14]

The inducement of feelings of bliss through painful torment or exhaustion has been always practically known. It has been practiced by shamans, flagellants, penitents, ascetics, yogis, practitioners of Zen, or savages performing exhaustive dance rituals.

But the causal paradox of happiness has not been understood. Humanistic thought has deepened the misunderstanding and turned it into a critical cultural confusion. Our culture is sliding, pleasantly and degeneratively, into hedonistic trends. Particularly have youth espoused the new spirit. This was best evident in the youth movements of the Sixties and Seventies. The attitudes have curiously changed in the Eighties. But then, young people mostly react in opposition to their previous generation, to their parents, whom they perceive as hypocritical and confusedly insensitive.

Perhaps the best survey of the hedonistic youth movements was the noted book of Kenneth Keniston, *The Uncommitted, Alienated Youth*. The opinions and attitudes of young people showed that they wanted an increased "awareness, passion, pleasure, immediacy of feelings...zest and exuberance," which would give life spontaneity, wholeness, and fulfillment.

It is a clear, logical proposition to have enriching positive emotions or capacities directly and fully, without the seemingly unnecessary restrictions, the logical obstacles to satisfactions or inner values. This corresponds to what humanistic experts have always expounded. More intense, genuinely real or direct value enjoyments, free of negative limitations, have been extolled as solutions and ultimate goals by our most authoritative cultural critics—Bertrand Russell, Sir Julian Huxley, Erich Fromm, Lewis Mumford, Herbert Marcuse, Jacques Ellul, and René Dubos.[1, 11, 14]

Such critics, rightly, blame our modern ills on the increasingly negative, stressful reactions of modern man. It is not realized, though, that these reactions come from too intense enjoyments that are most genuine and naturally or functionally direct.

Instead, the critics blame technology and materialism, which merely help men to attain more perfectly the deep and genuine direct enjoyments they pursue. Various complex theories are advanced, explaining how modern men have brought on themselves this affective negativity through a materialistic and technologic rat race.

This amounts to a strange assumption that men would not notice how they are depriving themselves of real pleasures. Men are too intelligent ever to miss what is deeply, genuinely satisfactory, in their uncanny pursuit of it, however varied the trade-offs. The most genuine, true, positive feelings are totally easy to understand, and each person knows perfectly what to do to enjoy them. The trade-offs merely serve to make such clear efforts more effective. The only reason why men fail here is that opposite reactions follow the enjoyments, even the satisfactions from the loftiest feelings.

But the belief in a *deepened enjoyment of inner values as the goal* of human fulfillment and progress is the dominant axiom in humanistic thought.[1, 2, 4, 5] Humanistic theorists have taken seriously even such social critics as Paul Goodman, Norman O. Brown, and Charles Reich, who have condemned all restrictions, particularly the restrictive sexual and traditional moral norms, as causes of evil.

When the counterculture youth movements first appeared they were seen as bringing a welcome change. The "flower children" or hippies were compared to the early Christians. Even sober humanists like Jacques Barzun, Abraham Maslow, or Arthur Koestler hailed the new spirit.

Of course the liberal enjoyments led to mental exhaustion, disorders, drugs, and the need for stronger experiences, as in the murders by the followers of Charles Manson. (Murder here became a reactively sought "refreshing" change after excessive enjoyments of orgiastic love.)

The emphasis on enjoyment of inner values has strengthened the present general trend in our culture toward deeper, more genuine or natural enjoyments. This has led to deepening opposite effects—increased emotional impoverishment, anxiety, and mental disorders.

The "pursuit of happiness" was guaranteed in our Constitution, in the spirit of the rationalistic Enlightenment. But as Howard M. Jones writes in his book *The Pursuit of Happiness*, that guarantee was accepted then as a mere "glittering generality." It was different from the later, powerful ideas initiated by writers and theorists such as Emerson and William James.

The pursuit of happiness has since become a strenous endeavor, exploited by countless experts, institutions, vast enterprises, and the mass media. As Jones describes in the book, the experts have expounded the promotion of all kinds of enjoyable feelings: more positive attitudes, optimism, less restrictions and more freedoms, self-satisfaction, enthusiasm, interest, peace of mind, relaxation, and avoidance of "conflicts," which practically means avoidance of stressful restrictions.

Recent experts and authors of best-sellers have found the final, logical solution—the enjoyment of oneself as the most direct, strongest natural gratification.[14] We are advised to enjoy our own selfish pleasures and freedoms, in disregard of others or of the moral rules of self-restriction.[14] Certainly, the enjoyment of oneself in unrestricted natural ways is the very essence of feeling good. It is the shortest way to ultimate satisfaction. The now-used term "The Me Generation" expresses the trend well.

Of course, the leading theorists in humanistic thought are too cultured to approve of more direct, selfish, or crudely natural enjoyments. They have in mind the more general enjoyments of inner values, often associated with esthetic or "spiritual" pursuits and creations. Esthetic enjoyments can indeed serve as necessary enticements in cultural conditioning, to attain restrictive refinements in our natural drives.

But for the humanistic theorists the goal is still a deepened value enjoyment, not the restrictive conditioning, imposing nonsatisfactions, which for them is a "brainwashing" that they can only abhor.

Actually, enjoyment in any form exhausts rather than enriches our motivational satisfaction potential. The alchemy of gaining that potential while having enjoyment is as impossible here as elsewhere. All enjoyments are organic at their bases, and therefore follow the opposite-value causality.

The "spiritual" enjoyments that humanists extol may not have directly noticeable effects of impoverishment. Such enjoyments derive from very general organic inner values, such as the sense of secured eternal survival or of a life force and self-fulfillment through growth. Therefore, an equally general, undefinable sense of restriction or anxiety has to arise as an after-effect. To overcome such general negative feelings the person may, sooner or later, resort to more concrete means of enjoyment, including drugs.

These later, compensatory enjoyments then create concrete problems. The more deeply involved "spiritual" or esthetic enthusiasts indeed frequently turn to use of drugs. This became apparent from the expanded use of cocaine through the imitation of higher, more cultivated social groups. Drugs certainly can offer inner enjoyments more exalted or "spiritual" than any artistic or cultural experience can provide.

Enjoyment of beauty is one of the highest human ideals. Whenever humanists speak of ultimate progress in the ideal future of man, they expect him to attain the highest enjoyments of beauty and a sense of harmony. Beauty is the very prototype of sublime, spiritual value, extolled in philosophy and literature.

Beauty is even viewed as a source of knowledge and understanding. The saying "Truth is beauty, beauty is truth" has been a frequently quoted dictum. It reflects a major humanistic belief.[1, 4, 11] Jacob Bronowski, a typical exponent of humanistic thought, claims that "Eddington or Einstein arrived at the truths in the same way as did Shakespeare or Rembrandt."[4]

The actual causal facts about beauty are very different. They woud appear under humanistic value beliefs to be repugnant and illogical. The causal sources of a divine feeling of beauty are its hellishly unpleasant value opposites. Beauty as a feeling is a satisfaction growing from ugly, vexatious non-satisfactions or disturbances.

There is hardly a difference between esthetic pleasures and the enjoyments of spring weather, sexual contemplation, soothing rest, drinking pure water after thirst, or enjoying a meal after hunger. But such satisfactions, including those involving weather and sex, come from tense needs as harrowing non-satisfactions. The greater the harrassment or threat, the deeper the sense of beauty. Think of the beauty of the world, sublime beyond words, felt by the man doomed to death but permitted to live.

Any feeling of beauty could be created experimentally by first imposing deprivations or threats. Such experiments would be too cruel to be tried. But "experiments" in which the positive opposite is induced first and the negative follows next are being performed by thousands of drug-users around us.

The feelings created by drugs can be as sublime and genial as the most spiritual experiences. This has been confirmed by scientists, philosophers, and writers—by William James, Henri Bergson, Aldous Huxley, or Somerset Maugham. The evidence of opposite causality here is striking.

A highly effective drug such as LSD creates an experience of supreme beauty or religious exaltation. But the after-effects are a virtual inferno. They are so horrifying or impoverishing that the person may commit suicide or kill somebody in bestial rage, as ecstatic love turns into unquenchable hate, however complex such feelings may be. A cruelty here may become as necessary as is a bitter food after the over-enjoyment of sweets.

Feelings of beauty are mysteriously confusing also because, in conventional terms, beauty includes all the generally integrated reactive values that go beyond separate satisfactions such as those of eating. These generally integrated feelings may include all kinds of endlessly involved satisfactions, of survival, security, sex, functional fulfillment, or comfort. But they all have an organic origin, and therefore are subject to opposite-value causality.

The ideal, deepened enjoyments of beauty seen as the highest goals by humanists thus can only lead to exhaustive, opposite after-effects. Surely the feelings of beauty can even appear to reveal the existence of God. But so can the initial effects of drugs, or an ecstasy after torments such as those lived through by flagellants or Zen practitioners.

Humanistic causal convictions are equally contrary to facts in regard to other values. For instance, *harmony and order* are believed to emanate from a higher source of harmony. Actually the exalted human sense of order or harmony in the universe grows from men's desperate need to find order amidst the chaos that governs the universe.

As men painstakingly work for and constantly center on the rare and desperately sought order, they value it above everything else, however little of it they can find. They finally see it as the very essence of their world.

Conversely, harmony is not noticed as value where it is complete in fact. The most extensive and continuous harmony governs your breathing or similar functions of life. But this harmony is not seen to be of value as long as it is not disturbed.

The same paradox is true for values like benevolence or goodness in the universe, felt by men as revealing a *providence* in it. People discover these values only to the extent that they live with strong corresponding needs as non-satisfactions and disturbances. No satisfaction or value is possible without equal needs or value opposites.

People do not have providential gods for air, light, gravity, or the solidity of ground, though these are the things that are most "providentially" there. Instead, people have providential gods for disasters, drought, pestilence, and death, or for any conditions of grave needs that are the sources of their important satisfactions.

In more advanced thinking men extol some universal *purpose* or sense of its existence, actually to the extent that they desperately seek for the ever-missing ultimate purpose of their lives. We do not think much about purposes that are always perfectly there. Our everyday pursuits are such purposes, always present and meaningfully complete. But they are not seen as relevant in value terms, because they are never wanting.

Man similarly evolves elaborate ideas and beliefs about higher reason, intelligence, or truths in the world, exactly as his search for these values deepens because they are universally missing. Even *morality* is for men a primary value because it is badly lacking. Natural appetites such as sex are as important as morals for normal life. But they are not valued, because generally they are not lacking.

In conclusion we may emphasize once again the decisive humanistic causal delusions about such values as interests or positive attitudes which constitute our daily capacities or motivations. The very essence of value reactions such as interests is satisfaction or pleasure. But men have to create the potential for such satisfactions, as capacities, by the accumulation of corresponding conditioned non-satisfactions as needs.

Consequently, beliefs about cultural and moral values have to become contradictory or deceitful. Educators have to extol and promise satisfactions and freedoms while actually imposing non-satisfactions and restrictions. For organically satisfaction or pleasure is the only driving force.

This leads to practically important conflicts when humanistic thought becomes more scientifically rational and precise. Traditional education then has to appear as a system of deceit and hypocrisy. Moreover, it seems to impose the non-satisfactions for useless, cruel reasons, since satisfactions are clearly the sources of all positive value reactions. Our whole cultural establishment thus seems to be steeped in such cruel hypocrisies.

Our "enlightened," learned people, particularly the young students, then naturally, revolt in outrage against the old generation or the establishment as a perpetuator of hypocritical lies and useless restrictions, in denial of satisfactions.

By exposing the negative, opposite causal sources of values we are not rejecting values. On the contrary, we are providing causal, scientific understanding of them so that they can be promoted or sustained scientifically, in our scientific era.

We are making clear the decisive creative role of restrictions or conditioned non-satisfactions. This is not very different from the traditional wisdom by which men have progressed.

But the causality of values as satisfactions or pleasures deriving from their harrowing, restrictive opposites would appear repugnant and illogical in modern humanistic thought. Instead our "scientifically" progressive and liberal thought hails the ideal of direct, logical enjoyment and the deepening of our inner values, which always are organic satisfactions. A practically important causal fallacy is thus compounded, since organic, deepened enjoyments can only lead to functional exhaustion and disorder. We have explained before that even spiritual enjoyments are ultimately *organic, therefore governed by the opposite causality.*

Causal Confusion in Literature, Esthetics and Philosophy

The humanistic blindness about the actual, "negative" causal sources of cultural values is best evident in literature and art. Here the humanistic attitude about value enjoyments and the results of the causal confusion about values can be seen in their most expressive forms.

Further, in philosophy, values are its main underlying concern. Inevitably, the causal fallacies about values are expanded. Also, the relativity of knowledge makes inevitable a universal failure of philosophy, of its efforts to attain absolute, non-relative, final truths. Such efforts have to fail because knowledge comes through relative value differentiations, however refined and complex.

In truth, if value relativity is real, philosophy has to fail. It has indeed failed, as is generally recognized in modern philosophy itself [9, 10] Philosophy seeks for the most universal truths. Such truths should be the simplest and clearest. But the only results of philosophy have been increasing, unbelievable complexity and controversial confusion, without any clear answers at all. No modern thinker seriously expects coherent solutions from philosophy.

LITERATURE. Evidently literature is very important culturally. The level of culture could probably be measured by the number of books read. Unfortunately, modern *fictional* literature would teach us the opposite of what is causally true about practical life. It perpetuates in emotionally expressive ways the "logical," liberated humanistic views about values.

Writers are generally the sensitive enjoyers of values and believers in deep feelings. They are naturally embittered by the seemingly needless restrictions or illogical, restrictive, necessarily superstitious traditions, as well as by the inevitable "hypocrisies" and contradictions of our practical world. This passionate sense of the truth of values and of the denial of their enjoyment by the establishment is what makes writers create their most vocal, widely recognized works, however involved or sophisticated their rendition.

Since the real value causation is exactly contrary to such a sense of values, fictional literature is never true to life causally.

Causal understanding would be the first thing a fiction writer would need. He creates his own characters and their behavior. Evidently, with a causal understanding contrary to what is causally true, he is bound to create a virtual freak world, with his characters behaving in ways that are inherently, causally impossible for them.

It is true that all men, similarly, lack causal understanding. But in practical life the constant contradictory, "illogical," selectively evolved cultural ways lead men to the right behavior. The fiction writer creates his world without such seemingly illogical contradictions.

Indeed, every causal fallacy of humanistic thought or psychology is compounded in literary fiction. We find everywhere in literature the belief in positive reactions from pleasant experiences and in negative effects from restrictions or frustrations, as well as the alchemy of weighty value reactions arising from ideas, insights, thoughts, perceptual coincidences, or unconscious causes. In a typical, impressive work, by Sartre or Beckett, the characters may be suffering from never-ceasing anguish and despair, whereas in reality a background of such experiences would create reactions of joy and optimism.

The clearest evidence of helpless confusion about causal reality in literature is the disordered lives of the great writers themselves. Writers, as a rule, clearly lack the healthy intuitions and attitudes by which other people remain normal. The typical, most impassioned authors have led disordered lives. Writers are over-enjoyers destroying themselves through causally confused attitudes. In fact, the most genuinely motivated author writes in order to resolve the contradictions and problems that afflict him so much because he lacks the "illogical" adaptations of normal behavior.

Leslie Fiedler says that great writers need a "charismic weakness," a psychological flaw, which drives them to alcoholism, drugs, or psychic disturbances. Our greatest masters—Fitzgerald, Lewis, O'Neill, Hemingway, Faulkner, Steinbeck, or Tennessee Williams—would fit this description, as would most of the famous writers of "genius" of the world.[14] According to Gore Vidal, "it is difficult to think of a single contemporary American writer of any note who is not either an alcoholic or on the way to becoming one."

However, under humanistic learning we are to value the creations of such helplessly confused authors as treasures of truths, or even to see the authors themselves as examples of great humanness. Of course, such authors are only expounding more passionately what all men ideally believe, however different may be such beliefs from practical human adjustments. Writers are superb in expressing what most people feel or want to experience.

But to expect useful causal insights from our writers is like asking business advice from bankrupt spendthrifts. Isn't it typical that Hemingway, the greatest literary expert on the resourcefulness of men, drove himself into total mental impoverishment leading to suicide?

Another source of confusion about the value of literary works is our general blindness in discerning our fixations.

Our value feelings about literature are often fixational, particularly in our appreciation of classical works—of Homer, Cervantes, or Shakespeare. Actually *The Odyssey* is a kind of ancient, exaggerated, miracle Western, without authentic, psychologically true characters or genuine, real-life interests. *Don Quixote* was intended as a hilarious story, but is a series of jokes so sad that it now serves as a great example of how to render the tragic sense of life.

Even Shakespeare is for us a genius mostly because of our value fixations. Anybody presently starting to write as Shakespeare did could not expect many readers, or any serious response. Such a work would be found artificial, contrived, exaggerated, lacking in subtle characterization, imputing childishly stupid thinking to characters, relying on blood or miracles for drama, and not rising above impossible plots or unnatural, artificially contorted language.

But the work and style of Shakespeare have become for us,

through long fixation, as sacred as are similarly contorted passages from the Scriptures.

The classics are significant as literary monuments. But they are clearly works of poor talent: they fail to render what is real and true to life, to be convincing and concretely interesting. Arguments that interests were different in past times are not true. People in all times have the same, sensible interests for what is real or true. But the old masters did not deign to go below highly learned or unusually remarkable and extraordinary matters; or to abandon the traditional, fixationally valued forms of authorship.

ART AND ESTHETICS. In our culture, art has become a fixational cult as sacred and superstitious as a religion. Such cults are general, to be found in all cultures. We are not different, since we too have not yet understood how bizarre are the effects of fixation on us. We are not yet aware of how we become helplessly enslaved by fixational, meaningless cults accidentally created by ourselves.

In fact the humanistic emphasis on the verity of values makes our fixations particularly insidious. For no values are richer or felt more deeply to be true than the fixational values. Our fixational cult of esthetics has become truly sacred for us—accepted without questioning and causal understanding, as are all superstitions.

Of course, in our cults we avoid superstitions that are scientifically untenable. But substantially we are not less superstitious in our esthetic cult than are savages about their rituals and customs. Our beliefs in the exalted verity of our esthetic values are deeper than the more casual beliefs of savages.

We attribute the highest meanings to our esthetic values without causal understanding. This amounts to a metaphysical superstition. We impute here deep, transcendental significance to values that we neither understand nor ever question causally. Nobody knows what art is or does, in causal and value terms. Even the best theorists in esthetics can offer only controversial discussions.[6], [7], [8] Yet no culturally self-respecting modern person would reject art or its mysteriously exalted, esthetic value.

The superstition in art is particularly evident from the requirement that we should admire only authentic objects of art—much like the true bones of saints or the real hair of the Prophet.

Objectively, a reproduction that improves an original work would be at least equal in value to it. The very styles of painters have been imitated to perfection and improved. Skillful imitators, such as Tom Keating, Hans van Meegeren, David Stein, or Elmer de Hory, have recreated styles of painters in all their most significant peculiarities.

It can be said that such imitators have often expertly deepened or purified the styles they have imitated, so that the imitation can not be detected. These forgers have painted generally undetectable imitations of old masters as well as of the most original modern painters—Picasso, Matisse, Modigliani, Braque, Klee, Miro, or Chagall. Such imitations can be distinguished from the originals only by application of involved techniques, by experts specializing on each given master.

In any event, all masters, old or new, can be improved in every respect, even by making more distinct the stylistic and contemporary peculiarities of their work. It is thus clear that everything in art could be improved by reproduction—including the particularly essential characteristics of styles.

Therefore, objectively, reproductions can serve better than originals for every art lover, except for rare experts using laboratory techniques and equipment. Museums could just as well be enriched by imitations. *Such an idea is a sacrilege because modern esthetics is a religion.*

We admit that a given inventor of a style deserves special merit. But his work is not better than a perfect imitation, and is worse if a reproduction renders the style more exactly. This happens with other style inventions, say in clothing fashions, every day.

Fixation offers a full explanation of why and how art enjoyment has become for us a cult as sacred as a religion. Art objects yield enough pleasure and a wealth of value details for an enrichment of experience which then serves as background for increased appreciation. This deepens the vicious circle of fixation with automatic inevitability. Also, art objects are continuously present in our culture and have been with us for hundreds of years, so that the fixations can reach any degree.

In addition, art is associated with higher culture, with richer, more civilized classes of people. Such conditions foster fixational appreciation. For instance, Christianity was associated with the higher, Roman civilization; and during its time of expansion people did not dare to reject Christianity for fear of being viewed as uncouth barbarians. Anyway, our long, continuous artistic fixations can deepen our feelings for the values of art to an incredible extent.

Art enjoyment is mysterious, almost supernatural, because its causal sources are not evident. First, the feeling of beauty derives, as we have seen, from general, nonspecific needs served by myriad organic mechanisms. We experience beauty as if with every cell in the body. Mind cannot grasp such a multiplicity.

Secondly and most importantly, the causal sources of a feeling of beauty are its never-suspected value opposites, vexatious needs as non-satisfactions or disturbances. These value opposites are, in human thinking, further away from beauty than anything is, though a satisfaction is always as sublime as the need, its source, is tormenting.

Here we have probably the most *crucial fact about esthetics*. We may as well emphasize that our esthetic experiences reveal, causally, not any transcendental, noble reality but the impact of our ugly, prosaic, organic disturbances or non-satisfactions. If this were understood, the whole, vast sophistication about the *lofty, metaphysical nature of art would collapse.*

That sophistication has indeed been endless.[6, 7, 8] Art has been viewed as a revelation of God, a manifestation of sacred laws of nature, an expression of inner transcendental knowledge, and so on.[6, 7, 8] Support for such views is found in the works of our greatest authorities—Plato, Kant, Schelling, Hegel, Goethe, Coleridge, Nietzsche, Croce, Dewey and Heidegger among many others.[6, 8]

Esthetics can be useful in cultural conditioning, as many cults can and have been. It is only to be regretted that our modern art has created incredible absurdities—perhaps more so than other cults—as we shall see in a moment.

Art could be used as an effective conditioning medium because of its richness of attraction. Generally, the impact of esthetics can be *as limitless as human ingenuity.* Think of how in music its standard value, of human voice, can be reproduced amplified or refined a hundredfold by instruments and orchestra. In painting, various colors and forms can be similarly amplified, contrasted, purified, refined, exaggerated, and enriched in ways as unlimited as the inventiveness of artists.

Of course, increased sophistication brings methods of artistic enrichment far different from simple amplifications. Striking effects are attained by a contrast created through underemphasis or a background of imperfection. Such use of contrasts to contrasts, on several levels, increases with sophistication, as do the endlessly varied, inventive combinations of other ways of value enhancement.

Now we may look at the *cultic absurdities of modern art.* The worst of them result from the failure to guard against fixations and from misinterpretations about contrast as originality in art.

Contrast, in its sophisticated forms of originality, is the primary means of enrichment of artistic enjoyment. After all, an opposite is the causal source of any value. Artistic styles emerge as contrasts, through "impossible" opposition to previous styles. The prototype of modern artistic styles, impressionism, was viewed as most unartistic when it first appeared. Its very name "was given by a journalist in a spirit of derision."[14]

Artists have learned much since, and contrast in styles or art values has reached its totality in modern art. Beauty has been replaced by ugliness and artistic refinement by abstract smears. This has come about mostly in absurd ways because of a lack of causal understanding.

Surely a sophisticated artist or art lover may genuinely derive greater enjoyment from a contrast that may amount to a rejection of previous values—to non-artistic primitivism or ugliness. Such contrast is relevant. It serves a purpose. It deepens esthetic experience through opposition to previous artistic values. But this is generally not understood by art critics and their followers. They start accepting as a significant artistic change in style any gross ugliness or merely atrocious smears after they have confusedly seen what sophisticated artists have done.

Above all, *this confusion intensifies because of fixation.* The more absurd an artist is, the more attention he can attract. Then, as his work is more frequently evaluated because of the attraction, it gains more value through fixation. A vicious circle is started that can deepen the value feelings about the artist's work to any degree.

The result is competition in absurdity. Everybody, and particularly artists, know that merely being noticed makes the difference between becoming a recognized genius and remaining an obscure failure. The artist who gains attention first, by some absurdity, can win increasing fame through the limitless power of fixation. As he is noticed, his style is more frequently evaluated and fixationally enjoyed, which in its turn makes him more noticed and famous.

Picasso became a recognized genius by starting a new total absurdity, a style of unprecedented body distortions, disjointed noses and limbs, or eyes in the stomach. We do not doubt that admirers of Picasso derive genuinely a deep value experience from his style. All fixational values become sacredly rich.

Still, such modern esthetic fixations come mostly through the competition in absurdity. Everybody knows about the absurdities of originality in modern art. They are accepted as the very essence of it—the result of a further general fixation.

Think of abstract art, pop art, sop art, plop-plop art, or other constantly added, very "original" styles of art. A bed mattress streaked with paint has been a noted work of art. So has been a six-by-six-by-six-foot cube that the artist ordered by phone. Brillo boxes are made to look exactly like Brillo boxes. The "portrait of Marcia Tucker" is a four-inch square piece of unpainted wood on empty canvas.

Paint smears on canvas made by apes, or by a donkey's wagging tail, can be foisted on art critics as works of art if enough effort is made to conceal the deception. Prizes have been awarded in exhibitions by unsuspecting critics for such "paintings," notedly for those made by two gorillas.[14]

The art of Paul Klee or Joan Miró is earnestly compared to "paintings" by four-year-olds. Many artists, including Picasso, have been viewed as genial continuators of primitive art.[7, 8] Actually, primitive artifacts are queer or distorted because of lack of skill, and particularly because of the intent to make them extraordinarily strange for greater impact in rituals. They certainly resemble modern art, which opposes previous artistic skill and strives for mysterious sensationalism.

It is not very important to point out the absurdities of modern art, which is news to no one. What cultic customs or values people prefer does not matter much. But men may as well understand how they become enslaved into a cult of sacredly deep feelings which is, objectively, nonsensical.

With such causal insight intelligent people would at least stop adoring as revelations of transcendental mystery mere smears of paint, inflated plastic hamburgers, or welded heaps of broken car parts. Then art lovers could also learn to distinguish and *appreciate real talent*. Contrast as originality enriches artistic experience. But the deepest contrast of, say, a beautiful face is not a broken piece of stone. No, it is a face almost as beautiful but morbid in its multiple details and tone of expression, like those of a decaying corpse. To render such a real originality requires great talent; and we should start demanding that it replace the present competition for mere outrageousness.

Also, perhaps we should avoid the exalted—in fact causally *silly—mystification* about the nature of esthetic values, whose causes actually are prosaic, harrassing, organic non-satisfactions.

The enjoyment of art or music does not make anybody better ethically or otherwise. In fact, cruel despots—including the Nazis—have been great lovers of art. The persons most deeply absorbed in art suffer from affective difficulties leading to alcoholism or drug use. Such sobering facts have to be weighed against the advantages that art offers as a medium in cultural conditioning.

PHILOSOPHY. For millennia philosophy has been a highly esteemed and enjoyed endeavor. It is an effort to attain pure, complete satisfactions on the cognitive level.

This is inherently impossible, because cognition is, in the last analysis, a value process consisting of value differentiations. Therefore, pure, complete knowledge in itself is as impossible as an experience of values without their opposites.

It can be said that causally philosophy is on the cognitive level what neurosis is on the emotional level. Both are efforts to attain final satisfactions in themselves, without their negative value opposites. Which is self-defeating. A pure satisfaction may seem simply, directly attainable, just at the reach of the hand. But as it is attained it disappears, because satisfaction acquires or regains its value or meaning only through its opposites, which are lost through satisfaction.

Actually the cognitive "neurosis" in philosophy is culturally beneficial. It deepens our intellectual preoccupations. Every failure here leads to a search for more extensive, elaborate satisfactions cognitively, much in the way this happens in neuroses emotionally. Such cognitive search creates more knowledge, though it never leads to final satisfaction, to definite philosophical knowledge.

Philosophy is indeed recognized as a failure by modern men, who are too realistic to continue with practically delusory efforts. No modern man expects solutions or even coherent answers from philosophy.

Philosophers themselves would now consider as naive and anachronistic an attempt to build philosophical systems on universal, necessarily simple, final truths.[9, 10] This, however, is exactly what a philosophy should normally do. Instead, modern philosophers limit themselves to explaining how such philosophical efforts have had to cease or why and how the various philosophical approaches have to fail, for controversially interpreted reasons.[9, 10, 14]

A successful philosophy, as a system of universal truths, should be absolutely simple and clear. Universal truths can be only simple. This is evident from everything that has been discovered about universal truths or causal laws. The more universal a causal principle is, the simpler it is.

But the only concrete achievement of philosophy has been its staggering, unbelievable complexity. Understandably this complexity expands as still more explanations are added with the same impossible, "neurotic," philosophical method.[9, 10]

The pivotal universal fact is that *philosophy has to fail* in its proper efforts *if knowledge is relative.* The relative-causality insight becomes here as well a totally new, though humanly repugnant, general outlook. This, of course, changes the very way of thinking about philosophy.

To begin with, it evidently becomes unnecessary as well as useless for us to refute in detail the various known philosophical systems. When you reach a totally new, say, mechanistic view in a field of knowledge, you do not have to refute various preexistent, metaphysical theories in it.

And the relativity of knowledge is a fact. It is sufficient to look at the general common goals of philosophies and their incongruity to see why philosophy is a futile endeavor because of that relativity.

The main philosophical goal has been the attainment of knowledge of everything in its ultimate essence, in its final, unadulterated reality. This is impossible because knowing something requires inclusion of its value opposites, through which it is known. The very sense of *knowing requires not-knowing.* If something is known fully, as is existence or being, it gives no sense of knowing. In practical or scientific knowledge we merely find answers to something we did *not* know. We do not seek there for final truths, for knowledge of anything in itself, in its final essence.

In contrast philosophers have tried to explain the whole world in itself, to reduce it to *one essence,* like substance, or to units like monads that are parts or expressions of one essence. This is true of systems ancient and modern, with the Being of the Eleatics, the one God of Medieval philosophers, the Idea of Hegel, the Space-Time of Alexander, or the Monads of Leibniz.

Of course, such explanations can never attain what they intend to because of the relativity, the infiniteness of knowing. Every step in knowing is a satisfaction which is lost as it is reached. Then a further step is required to have cognitive satisfaction, which ends in the same way.

If everything is explained by, say, Idea, then knowing stops, gives no satisfaction, unless the Idea is explained. If it is explained by, say, Spirit, then this has to be explained in its turn. Nothing can be known in itself or provide final, philosophical knowledge as satisfaction.

But *finality of knowledge* is required under the philosophical goal of a definite cognitive satisfaction. There is no satisfaction if you have to go on differentiating endlessly. Yet this is how knowledge or understanding works, by further and further relating. This is clearest if the way we know something is made clearer. For instance, the concept of space makes it clearer that we know things by relating them spatially. Or time similarly becomes the relationship of changes. Consequently, we can see that space and time are endless.

But any phenomenon, in any of its aspects, becomes endless if you try to know it philosophically, with finality. If you want to know what an apple really, finally is, you will have to analyze, not only the infinite constellations of molecules in it, but also its endless aspects of shape, color, taste, and so on.

Philosophers have recognized the endlessness of remarkable phenomena, such as movement, extension, creation, or causality. They have found this endlessness paradoxical, as can be seen from the paradoxes of Zeno, the antinomies of Kant, or the arguments of the illusion of causality of Hume. But endlessness is true of everything, even of the tiniest and dullest thing or event.

Think of the infinity of a simple atom, necessarily having infinitesimal differences or phenomena inside it at some point—its own galaxies and atoms; scientists have mentioned the possibility. If philosophers were true, objective thinkers they would recognize that a speck of rubbish is as endless as the starry world of heavens and as remarkable as a story of Creation. What is small or humanly unworthy is not less real than what is great and noble.

Here we come to the preoccupation with *values in philosophy*. After the problems of knowledge, the world of values is the widest source of philosophical thinking, and of confusion, because of the relativity of value causality.

Values have been the main underlying concern in all philosophies. This cannot be different in philosophy, as a pursuit of noble satisfactions. Indeed, value satisfactions are always found in philosophies; and each philosopher has managed to defend or find acceptable the general value tenets of his time, including those about slavery, social inequality, or cultural prejudices.

Our present nonconformity is only another, contemporary value tenet, of men deliberately pursuing individual, rebellious freedoms. Also, our value beliefs have become more sophisticated. It would be too naive today to accept that virtues are equivalents of happiness or that the golden mean of virtues—of the Athenians, of course—was to be a value absolute, as Plato and Aristotle taught.

But the increasing sophistication has strengthened the belief in values as sources of philosophical truths. The more knowledgeable and down-to-earth modern philosophers have been turning to *value experiences as the primary sources of final truths.* This has come with the increasing realization that reason cannot supply such truths. Existentialism can be viewd as the final, extreme, and perverse development in this modern movement.

The turning point was probably the monumental work of Kant. He proved that philosophical truths cannot be obtained by reason. He then accepted practical reason, actually the world of moral values, as the source of ultimate insights. After Kant pure reason is no longer viewed as the only, exclusive capacity to discover philosophical truths.

However, is not it self-evident that any true philosophy can be pursued only by reason or abstract thought? To find reason as insufficient in philosophy amounts to admitting that philosophy is inherently impossible. It is clear to everybody that value feelings are most misleading, most subjective, and prejudiced in discovering what is rationally, philosophically true.

In any case, value experiences have been accepted as sources of truth superior to reason by the greatest modern philosophers after Kant. In fact, the most directly emotional capacities have been accepted by modern philosophers as guides. Think of the "intuition" extolled by Bergson, the "immediacy of feeling" postulated by Bradley, the "loyalty," by Royce, and even the "animal faith", by Santayana.

The leading post-Kantian philosophers, Fichte and Schelling, saw the ultimate truths in the feeling of the ethical self and the sense of beauty. The rising romanticism was nurtured by the philosophical trend toward emotional value beliefs. Even the greatest later philosophers have continued the same trend. Schopenhauer's Will, Nietzsche's Will to Power, Bergson's Elan Vital, and Croce's Spirit are emotionally or intuitively discovered realities.

Practically, philosophy has rendered the worst possible service to the human sciences by its value outlook. Positive values derive exactly from their negative opposites. As we have seen, man's whole "positive" universe is a world of values whose causal sources are opposite, negative values. But under any value outlook, the actual, opposite causes of a value are never even suspected as its causal sources.

By perpetuating the direct, humanistic view of values, philosophy has hardly helped science to discover the *actual, "negative" causes* of man's world in fields from medicine to economics—and even in physics. Of course, to understand anything scientifically is to understand it causally.

The philosophically most relevant confusion is probably the failure to recognize the "negative," evolutionary causes of man's *world of mind* itself. In philosophy our mental world is seen as emanating from a higher sphere and revealing the universal Mind as its source, accepted as the supreme reality. But actually, the world of mind or intelligence has become miraculously rich because of man's endless efforts to cope with difficulties of his existence, with the *mindlessness* of creation, in human terms.

Imagine intelligent beings on a faraway planet so clever that they have evolved a perfect existence without any difficulties—perhaps by being able to act in the myriad miraculous ways of living nature while governing them with intelligence. Such beings would not need technology, science, mathematics, abstract concepts, language, or any disciplined system of thought. (Even if they were communicating with us right now, it would not be in our mental terms of mathematics, science, or any kind of disciplined thinking that could make sense to us.)

Anyway, our world of mind is divinely rich and disciplined precisely to the extent that diabolically chaotic difficulties have forced men to invent intricate ways of dealing with them. But such "negative" causality is generally incompatible with the ideas of humanistic philosophy. Thus, even modern philosophies have remained at a stage of understanding comparable to that of the natural sciences before Darwin.

The enormously complex and rich world of mind is viewed as emanating from a higher Mind. The human mind thus becomes a superior essence contrasted with the material and "negative" causes that have actually created it. Occasionally, in the more modern philosophies, attempts have been made to attribute some mental qualities to the lowly material world. A good example is the philosophy of Bergson, who elevated the instinctive forces of nature to the status of highest creative sources.

Perhaps the most interesting modern philosophies are those inferring a mental nature for the lower, material world from the simple fact that man understands the material world. This fact meant nothing to the old philosophers looking for more exalted explanations. But it can become a subtle proof. If the mind understands the material world, they both must have a unifying principle or be of the same nature.

Such more sophisticated inferences about Mind in the world are the main ideas behind the Neo-Idealism of Green, Bradley, or Royce as well as the theories of other noted modern philosophers such as Santayana, Russell, and Whitehead.[9, 10] The old idealists, from Plato to Hegel, assumed the ideas of mind to be the higher, ultimate realities.

Indeed an idea or concept of a thing seems to be more spiritual or mysterious, more valuable than the thing itself. This is part of the delusion which shows as valuable or divinely revealing that which has actually required more effort to be dealt with because of its senseless disorder.

Here we may recall that the simple laws and principles of matter are the most "divine", because they have created and continuously control man and mind. These principles are simple to the mind, since they govern in the same way the existence of both nature and man, including his mind as one expression of his existence. Indeed anything that is all-inclusive, most meaningful, appears as totally simple or even as having no meaning. Being includes everything and has no knowable, perceptible meaning—much as gravity or the general force is not "perceived" because it governs, causally determines everything.

Generally, the belief in *mind* as a higher essence *different from matter* is the most essential part of all philosophies. The ultimate reason for this belief is *man's incapacity to understand the myriad processes of mind* as a living system. For man his mind is as ghost-like as the life inside animals that moves them. It is not yet understood how immensely superior to man's mind as intellect is living nature in its myriad, purposive multiplicity—since the mind as our intellect can deal with only one thing at a time.

In any event, without the belief in mind as being diffent from matter there would be hardly any philosophy. For to explain man's world without considering mind as a different reality, nobody would need anything more than the sciences of physiology or of behavior.

A most obvious reason for philosophizing is the possibility that reality might be different or more than the material world around us. Philosophy, in contrast to the sciences, implies the presence of a non-mechanisitc, spiritual reality, of a separate, immaterial essence, which mind is assumed to be.

The material world then may be viewed as consisting of mere appearances of mere phenomena created by mind. Such phenomenalism may range from nonsensical solipsism to theories of idealists, phenomenalists, and other quite varied philosophers, including Berkely, Kant, Fichte, Schopenhauer, and Mill.[9, 10]

It is indeed easy to speculate that the world we see may not be real. But if nothing is real, then everything is equally real, since this is the only world we have. Moreover, if some higher spiritual reality or Mind is determining everything, that mind would be awfully busy fabricating a multiplicity of ingenious appearances just to deceive us. For, everywhere, the material, mechanistic world continues performing for us consistently, through immense multiplicity, without ever revealing any interruptions or outside intervention in its physical causation.

The general philosophical assumption of a nonmaterial mind leads to a clearly untenable position. It inevitably implies the impossible parallelism of our mental experiences being constantly arranged so that they coincide with physical events. The mental feelings of pain in your injured finger then would come not from the physical injury but from parallel immaterial, mental arrangements emanating in your mind from the world of higher mind.

It is impossible, "improper" for the immaterial mind to act materially or physically; mental and material essences remain eternally separate causally. This general philosophical tenet stems from the *universal, truly imperative human belief that mental experiences are nonphysical.* The source of this belief is the unfathomable multiplicity of the living processes of the mind that remain forever ungraspable to the mind as intellect.

But the assumed parallelism between mind and the physical world implies, more concretely, the absurdity of our Creator going to such trouble just to delude us that physical events create our sensations.

Still, it is inevitable for man to believe that mind is completely different from matter. It seems that Lincoln's hand signing the Emancipation Proclamation was indeed moved by something totally different from what moves a stone.

The mystery disappears, however, if it is understood that mere *matter, in living nature, can be immensely superior to mind* when it comes to creation. Even an insect seems to be moved by an immaterial, spirit-like life. We shall explain later how living nature works purposively with a myriad of elements at every point and instant. In contrast, the mind can deal only with one thing at a time. It is this incredible limitedness of the mind that makes mysteriously unexplainable all living processes, including those of the mind.

Now, it is not difficult to accept that our living, *value reactions* are only organic or material—but unfathomably mysterious because of their colossal mutiplicity. They are clearly expressions of the organic drives that are best understood as pleasures. And nobody would doubt that such drives are organic or physical.

Thus, our value experiences, which can be "spiritual," even religiously ecstatic by being merely deeper organically, are as real—or unreal—as the organic or physical world we know. And it is easy to understand that even our cognitive processes of mind are merely products of such countless physiologic *value reactions*.

It is truly unbelievable that philosophy, the discipline dealing with knowledge, has not "discovered" the first, causally most important thing about knowledge, namely the fact that *man is not able to think of more than one thing at a time*. This limitedness of the mind makes it ridiculously clumsy and powerless in comparison with the capacities of living nature.

If philosophers had "discovered" this first truth about knowledge, they would have understood how living nature and living reactions, including our thought processes, have to remain unfathomable to man's pitiably limited mind. But exactly because this limitedness of mind is so universal, it has not been recognized. The most universal, and therefore most important, facts are often not "noticed", even by great thinkers.

Of course, individual philosophers, by dint of their deeper insights, have recognized how superior to the abstract mind are our value feelings, the living processes within us. Hence the emphasis on value experiences such as intuition or esthetic sense.

But it is incongruous to try to apply value feelings in the philosophical search for truths, unless philosophy is *totally turned around* toward the recognition of opposite-value causality. (We have seen throughout this book how that causality offers universal explanations.)

As it is, philosophy has remained a pursuit of abstract understanding and knowledge, by its very definition. To abandon abstract thinking here is to abandon philosophy itself. And feelings are the worst hindrance to abstract thinking. Everybody knows that emotions distort thinking. Philosophers more than anybody have to remain indifferent to feelings, as is expected in all rational, normal philosophy.

In short, to accept that value reactions, such as intuition or "practical reason," should be sources of philosophical truths is *equal to admitting the complete failure of philosophy* as it has been always known and practiced.[9, 10] Indeed, philosophy has in effect recognized its own inherent failure by realizing that abstract speculation cannot reveal philosophical, final truths.

The thinking of modern men, including philosophers, is too precise and advanced scientifically to continue with the futile, properly philosophical, cognitively speculative pursuit of truths. The philosophical, cognitive answers are as confusing as they are complex and varied, to a fantastic extent.

The result is a widening incongruity. The most modern philosophical movements have virtually abandoned the only true philosophical method. They have turned to such noncognitive sources of truths as pragmatic success, intuition, emotion, instinct, common sense, literature, esthetics, or any experience.[9, 10] We can refer here to pragmatism, empiricism, phenomenology, or existentialism, and to the eclectic systems of philosophers such as Dewey, Santayana, Russell, Whitehead, or Hocking.[9, 10]

The search for universal truths of pure reason has been abandoned, but *the new direction is even worse.* Nothing is more misleading than intuition and emotional value experiences *if their opposite-value causality is not understood.* The real source of a value reaction is its exact value opposite. The actual, deeper, causal reality revealed by experience of satisfaction or beauty is non-satisfaction or harassing ugliness.

Opposite causality is true of all value experiences—the Kantian practical reason as well as the subsequently postulated esthetic, intuitive, pragmatic, phenomenal, or common-sense sources of truths, all deriving from value convictions.

The more advanced modern minds are, understandably, starting to realize how superior to abstract thought can be emotional or value experiences. We have shown repeatedly how pleasure or value experiences can "explain" what thought cannot fathom and how they can reveal all the *causal*, "negative" sources of the human universe. But these discoveries would require the application of the opposite-causality insight. This causality is , however, still the last thing that even the modern men would be ready to recognize.

The result is that modern thought is rejecting traditional, abstract philosophy and its cognitively speculative methods, yet is sinking into even deeper confusion by looking into the rich but actually paradoxical, emotional or intuitive sources of truths.

The two dominating modern philosophical approaches, positivism and existentialism, are typical here. Positivism in particular exposes the futility of the old philosophical methods of seeking for universal truths of reason. Existentialism accepts only emotions as sources of insights, in total departure from the traditional philosophy of reason; and the result is a striking confusion.

The way *positivism* would have it, there "would be no books written in philosophy, but all books would be philosophically written."[14] Instead of great universal truths, positivism stresses the limitation of knowledge to empirically verifiable facts and to tautological statements or conventional fictions.[9, 10]

Existentialism is generally recognized as the most advanced movement in modern thought and philosophy. In existentialism, the pursuit of universal insights is totally dominated by emotional convictions. The final sources of truths in existentialism are the deepest negative feelings: anxiety, dread, despair, isolation, futility, and senselessness.

Such an excessively negative sense of the world cannot arise without equally excessive opposite emotional causal backgrounds or expectations. Existentialism, grows from the reactions of the uniquely pampered modern man. The existential philosophy is thus more a result of causally confused, mentally disordered attitudes than a way of attaining ultimate insights.

Perhaps it is only proper that this utter confusion has become the final achievement in philosophy. It confirms how totally misleading is the *value outlook* which governs all philosophical thinking. The resulting confusion is best evident from the unbelievable complexity of philosophy. Nothing that man has created is more complex and controversial than philosophy, though the universal truths that it seeks should be absolutely simple.

Our Cultural Self-Enslavement into Senseless Fixations

The causally confused humanistic value beliefs contribute to the deepening of our self-enslavement into senseless and costly cultural fixations. *The vicious-circle automatism of fixations is still not understood.* Actually, in humanistic thinking a higher, often transcendental, significance is attributed to our sense of deep values, which are strongest, almost sacred, when they are fixational.

It may be recalled here that fixation makes even meaningless incidental recurring values irrationally strong and "true." Through the vicious-circle of fixation values deepen endlessly: a value experience expands the background for its enjoyment, which leads to increased pursuit of the experience.

We may recognize the fixational, senseless nature of the irrational customs of primitive peoples who may spend all their surplus means and efforts on elaborate, often disfiguring fashions or endless rituals. Yet *our own unrecognized value fixations are worse.* We are as unaware as primitive men about the way we become slaves to our fixations. But our beliefs in our "sacred" values have a far more extensive cultural and social as well as economic impact.

For instance, because of our fixations about freedoms or individualism we do not permit our democratic governments to act "dictatorially" enough to move toward the potentially immense progress awaiting us. Also, our great material wealth and ease make our senseless material value fixations enormously extensive and wasteful. Which exhausts the means necessary for our progress, to a huge, decisive extent.

The important fact here is that people expand their fixations when they have surpluses, in means or in free time, and that *surpluses are the decisive sources of progress.* If people have means barely sufficient to survive they cannot progress. It is always some available surplus that makes material or technical progress possible. But surplus conditions also permit people to yield to expensive fixations. If the means of enjoyments are limited or merely sufficient for the satisfaction of natural needs, fixations do not evolve.

We have mentioned how the organic tendencies of animals toward nutritional fixations are interrupted by natural needs. Generally fixations do not evolve around natural, normally restrictive satisfactions. But in times of increasing wealth, above-normal satisfactions become available and tempting. Then restrictions are needed.

All fixations grow from over-enjoyment tendencies, from yielding to easy enjoyments, which are easiest when they are fixational. Restrictions can break habits of fixation. When restrictive non-satisfactions as new needs are imposed, the potential for new, different satisfactions is created.

But our humanistic thought perpetuates *beliefs about the verity of our deepest values*; and the fixational values are preeminently that. This expands and deepens our fixations, which can be so easily cultivated in our affluent and unrestricted culture. In our wealthy society we see all around us fixations for which we waste our surpluses.

We spend our surplus resources and efforts on what fashions and customs say is "in," right, beautiful, enjoyable, or new, though it may be less beautiful, less worthwhile, and even less enjoyable than what we have already. The proverbial "competition with the Joneses" consists of such wasteful fixational pursuits, and that competition is so universal that it remains mostly unnoticed as anything particular.

Generally, *fashions and social conformity* become subtle and extensive, through fixations, in more advanced cultures. Primitive customs are simple, fixational repetitions of what has been done before. In our culture fixations expand, are compounded, as we become fixationally minded about our value fixations themselves.

We know, or rather fixationally feel, how strong our fixations and general opinions become, even when they change. The imitation of customs and opinions becomes a fixational value. The pursuit of fashions becomes an eager, fixational occupation, however irrational or silly. Similarly, social conformity becomes fixationally compulsive.

Compliance with fashions or conformity with what others are doing thus dictates our lives. For instance, we obsessively have to wear what is fashionable or what the others are wearing. We thus waste money on the fashionable attraction, frills, or "beauty", though we could have simple, useful, and therefore really beautiful clothes without such a waste. The fashions of one time look ridiculous and ugly at another.

The same is true for fashions in cars, furniture, or hundreds of other social "musts." The costly things on which we spend our surplus means are thrown out when the fashion changes. Hundreds of billions of dollars thus have been wasted on cars alone—enough to bring decisive progress to the developing countries of the world.

The extensive use of the car, in general, is mostly due to a value fixation that grows from the natural pleasure of riding. In all times carriages or coaches have been fashionable in similar wasteful ways. The "car culture" is not rational in terms of economy or transportation.[14] Our proverbial love affair with the car is a fixation run wild because of the enormous mass participation made possible by our affluence.

Most wasteful are the fixational fashions cultivated by people in their competition for status and prestige. The whole life of a person may be wasted in such competition, in pursuit of what is "in" or fashionable. Our noblemen wasted so much in this way that progress was delayed for centuries. Their fixations were different only in forms of enactment from the fashions of savages disfiguring themselves with neck bands or nose plugs.

The latest modern fixations on social musts and status are particularly costly because of mass participation. Now most everybody wastes as the noblemen did in the past. The resources spent on primary necessities have proportionally decreased. The rest is wasted on fixational status competition and customs.

The competition with the Joneses has been constantly increasing. Almost every self-respecting citizen now tries to excel in his compliance with expanding social or seasonal customs and fashions—from expensive yearly vacations to lavish weddings. The Christmas season alone determines the course of commerce and a great part of industry for months, while hundreds of billions of dollars are wasted.

Merely because we "must" have something or a fashion is "in," we waste on appearances, fashionable living, social observances, "cultural" interests of the moment, conspicuous consumption, or pursuit of habits set by our prodigal celebrities. Our whole material culture consists of such efforts. Marxists and radicals can easily prove how every one of our cultural values amounts to a useless "bourgeois" aberration, though they themselves evolve even stronger fixational cults.

Of course, people do not see the irrationality of a fixation precisely to the extent it has become general. Games like baseball or football can hold in their grip a whole nation of fans. But people from another culture would find our games hardly interesting at all. They would rather see our often hysteric and violent enthusiasm about our games as ridiculous for adult, rational people.

But from within our culture it is foolish even to question the value of our games, though objectively their influence is appalling. Such sports make our young people, even those capable of direct intellectual interests, imitate as their heroes men excelling merely through the animal qualities of superior muscles and quick reflexes.

Even more serious than our fashions and everyday customs are our *cultural* value fixations. Our sacred principles of freedoms, individualism, human nature, basic rights, or constitutionality are actually fixations about *our ways of life.*

Any one of these principles can mean, and has meant, different things at different times with their fixational ways and "truths." Under the same Constitution our blacks were unequal and now are equal; abortion was a murder and now is a right of women. A series of similar principles have been constitutional and unconstitutional under the same Constitution, as our customs have changed.

Our concrete, cultural, "inalienable" rights and "universal" freedoms become even more easily mere embodiments of our *inveterate, fixational customs* and "certainties."

But such social and cultural principles or values, in all their glory of "truths," are *invoked as sacred, unquestionable verities.* They become the greatest obstacles to progress, which always requires impossible new changes and rationally planned effort.

We have already mentioned that progress comes through closer social integration or that all culture is a product of conditioning, though humanists are horrified by what they see as an ant-hill society and brainwashing. Eugenic planning could prevent inhuman, shameful degradation and suffering for hundreds of millions of people, but a mere mention of such planning would seem scandalous. Value fixations are strongest about our most important ways of life, which have always been with us.

Also, our higher *culture, of learning and thought,* stagnates in cultic superstitions and conformity because of fixations. We have seen how this happens in art and literature as fixational cults. We serve various value cults; and all cults become superstitious, because fixational values seem unquestionably true. Cultural and social uniformity becomes compulsive through the automatism of meaningless fixations under which mere frequency of experiencing a value increases its strength.

The very notions of what are culture, learning, and the treasures of civilization are determined by fixational tradition. Here fixation is the decisive factor. In different societies the treasures of culture and thought are so different that ours may appear contemptible according to their customs.

The subject-matter of our learning, particularly in the humanities, self-expands through fixational value appreciations, leading to constantly added elaborations. We have seen how fixational, as well as causally confused and therefore practically misleading, are our literature, arts, and philosophy. Our treasures of culture and learning are important as enticing, "deceitful" means of conditioning. But this is not understood and they grow mostly through fixation, in confused, compulsively distorting ways.

Here we may indicate how fixations *can serve moral and creatively cultural conditioning* if confusions are avoided. Moral traditions become compulsive through fixations. Consequently, they serve better as means of restrictive, creative conditioning. Also, the cultic deepening of esthetic or cultural enjoyments can make them more effective in helping the sublimation of cruder natural drives into more refined and more easily controllable cultural pleasures.

But success here remains uncontrolled and depends only on the general capacities of people as long as the humanistic attitudes favor rather than oppose the enjoyment pursuits in fixations.

A more restrictive and capable people may not let their fixational enjoyments grow beyond control. But a people with a looser mentality may drift into more and more permissive customs under self-expanding fixational enjoyments and "truths." Even their religion may lose itself in freer, more pleasant habits—such as rituals of sacred orgies—through fixational elaborations of enjoyments.

Thus, fixations can be helpful in a culture that generally is able to remain restrictive. Otherwise they bring moral and cultural degeneration or distortions. The unsuspected fixations expand readily into richer, more enjoyable elaborations; and the moral customs lose their restrictive effect. That is why some of the richest, most elaborate morals often lack real, creative morality.

In particular *our progressive, humanistic attitudes contribute to such moral degeneration.* The followers of modern thought hail not the restrictive but rather the enjoyable aspects of fixations. They extol the sacredly rich, positively felt, gratifying, beautiful, or enjoyble cults and customary values. Sexual license during cultic rites then may seem almost admirable.

In any case, even superstitious and senseless moral fixations are serious matters. They should not always be condemned, considering the inherently contradictory and "deceitful" nature of cultural conditioning. Pleasures have to be used in any, restrictive conditioning; and they tend to become fixational. If wisely used, fixational, conditioned pleasures can serve as effective means for deepening the conditioning.

Also, it can be harmful to interfere even with obviously primitive fixations. Taboos or rituals observed by a people may be very irrational, even culturally destructive. But if a taboo is discredited or abandoned as clearly ridiculous, the people lose the moral discipline conditioned by the taboo.

Similarly, our religious and moral traditions should often be conserved even if they are totally inconsistent with our scientific thinking or knowledge.

In conclusion we may mention, first, the fixational waste of surpluses. Most of what is left after the satisfaction of our primary needs is now wasted on virtually senseless fixations. Yet it is surpluses that make progress possible, if they are turned into saved-up capital instead of being wasted. And the progress awaiting us is potentially miraculous, against our standards. We may indeed be compared here to savages who spend all their resources on ridiculous costumes and rituals, unaware of very different possibilities beyond their fixations.

Even more importantly, our culturally decisive beliefs and "truths" easily become fixational. It is generally still not understood that mere fixations can enslave us and render absolutely "true" our often senseless customs. Our lives are controlled by such customs.

Particularly, the "truths" rooted in habits of the ages prevent sensible solutions in the most important matters of human progress. Think of the sanctity of the births of predictably abnormal, undesirable, or mentally defective infants, or of the sacred individualism and our "inalienable" rights that mostly consecrate our customary, fixational ways of life.

Fixations perpetuate stagnation, while progress requires extraordinary changes.

The Future beyond Present Beliefs or Imagination

Heightened, perfect enjoyment of lofty value experiences is generally viewed as the goal of man's ideal future under our progressive, humanistic thought.[1, 2, 11, 12]

This is clear from the work of our best authorities in varied fields of humanistic thought, philosophy, the human sciences, psychology, history, religion, or social criticism and predictions. We can refer to a series of such authorities—Bertrand Russell, Sir Julian Huxley, Erich Fromm, Lewis Mumford, Karl Jaspers, Paul Tillich, Arnold Toynbee, Herbert Marcuse, Sir Peter Medawar, Herbert J. Muller, Glenn Seaborg, René Dubos, or Herman Kahn.[1, 11, 12, 14]

A Nobel memorial collection of essays on the role of values in our world shows that the belief in *value enjoyment as the goal of progress is general.*[2] It is inevitable that men see in the ideal human future the attainment of what they have always strived for—the enjoyment of inner values.

Unfortunately any enjoyment, as an organic "improvement," is more likely to bring disorder or exhaustion than progress. Of course, in the learned and noble humanistic thought the values to be enjoyed are general, lofty feelings such as those of beauty and harmony. Still the emphasis is on enjoyment—which can be only organic, therefore subject to the opposite-reaction rule. That emphasis is inevitable, *since enjoyment is the ultimate criterion of any value.*

Quite importantly, even for our practically decisive value reactions, such as interests or love, our humanists see only the positive, logically enjoyable feelings as the goal. They can never recognize the actual requirement of distressful, hideously tormenting, conditioned non-satisfactions as needs that are the causal sources of our positive reactions or satisfactions.

In practical reality the enjoyment of any value leads to or derives from equivalent opposite, "negative" value experiences. We have indicated how even highly cultural enjoyments are bound to lead to opposite feelings. If the enjoyments are deepened, the resulting exhaustion can further lead to seeking relief through stronger "improvements" such as drug use.

All human enjoyments derive, at their basis, from organic satisfactions or pleasures, therefore are governed by the opposite-value causality. Thus, every value experience has to be "paid" for by equivalent opposite value experiences, before or afterward. The rule of no alchemy, of no "free lunch," is inexorable.

If we really attained what the noble theorists see as the ideal, deeply enjoyed future, *we would sink into affective and behavioral impoverishment or mental disorders*. Unquestionably sublime, even religiously spiritual, value experiences are provided by use of drugs. The end result, however, is emotional exhaustion and psychosis. Naturally the lofty experiences viewed as future goals would have to be organic. Therefore, their effects would not be causally different from drug after-effects. Organically opposite changes have to counteract any "improving" change, in whatever way it was induced.

Our progressive, humanistic thinkers, however, cannot accept opposite-value causality in any form. Particularly since they aspire to greater scientism. They would not hold tenets that are "scientifically" impossible. They readily espouse the scientific, like-form-like, causal logic, which nicely fits in with the classic humanistic creed about the noble ultimate sources of our positive inner values.

We may as well look at some practical examples of the application of the causal logic accepted by scientists and humanists in regard to the creation of value reactions.

Probably most typical recently have been ideas about the wondrous affective improvements attainable by the organism itself, particularly through *neurotransmitters or endorphins* such as enkephalin. The management of such improvements has been widely discussed and sometimes viewed as offering important possibilities for man's capacities and progress. Endorphins can provide reactions of relief or pleasure, and thus of direct mental enrichment.

Scientific arguments here are interesting. Scientists recognize that similar reactions can be obtained by the administration of drugs, particularly of morphine. Endorphins, however, are viewed as being causally different. Drugs are known to bring "side" effects, actually after-effects. But endorphins are expected to be free of them. Similarly, no negative after-effects are expected from improvements attained by other organic means, say, through biofeedback. It is argued that natural organic products such as endorphins could not have toxic, negative effects.

The research here is too recent to show the inevitability of exactly equal after-effects. Similar discoveries in the past have been hailed as miraculously promising, yet have ended in disappointments or in disasters, as in the case of cortisone treatments.

The organism may sometimes need pain relief to maintain its normalcy or sameness. But this very maintenance by the organism of its sameness makes inevitable the subsequent opposite effects from any reactive improvement, even from direct neurological relief by neurotransmitters. Whatever the organic change, it requires an equivalent opposite change. This is the inevitable law under which every organism survives.

Still the *experimentally clear, direct-"improvement" logic* is never doubted. There seems to be no reason why our intelligence could not be improved "after we succeed in stimulating the working of the brain just as we have done with other less exalted vital parts," according to Jean Rostand, an internationally known biologist.[14]

Similar views about mental improvement have been held by various scientists, notably by the psychobiologist James L. McGaugh, the biochemist Floyd E. Bloom, and the psychiatrist Nathan S. Kline. In psychology various drugs or other reactive-improvement means have often been hailed as miraculous discoveries, by authorities as varied as Freud and Skinner.

Humanists and scientists looking into the future have, generally, viewed *drugs as important means* of mental improvement and control. Aldous Huxley saw the use of his fictional soma as an essential part in the lives of future men. Herman Kahn predicted that by the year 2000 men will be wearing pleasure consoles and using drugs for political control as well as mental improvement.[14] The control of behavior by electrodes or electric fields has been often discussed, and is particularly well known from the experiments by R. Heath and W. Ross.

In his well-documented book *Future Shock*, Alvin Toffler predicts that the psychological environment of people will be changed with precipitous speed by the extremely efficient means of science and technology.

According to the synergistic views of R. Buckminster Fuller, the future progress brought about technologically will be completely different, qualitatively superior to the means used in promoting it. Assumptions of mental improvement through *emotionally easy, technical means* underlie various modern theories, particularly those about cybernetics and system analyses.

But whatever the direct, seemingly logical, experimental improvements attained by the affectively easy drugs or technical means, they can only lead to equivalent opposite effects. Organic limitedness is inexorable. Only by first imposing greater, conditioned non-satisfactions as needs or restrictions can we expand our potential of satisfactions or pleasure, the source of our capacities.

This simple, paradoxical, and difficult creation of man's capacities is the only possible practical source of human progress. But most of the humanistic thought about man's progress consists of ideological or philosophical "discoveries." *Ideas of purported world-shaking importance* are expounded every day. So are contrary ideas. The belief in the power of ideas rules supreme in humanistic thought. It has been perpetuated for millennia. How different is the reality!

Ideas are easy and behaviorally weightless. In contrast, the simplest availability of satisfaction or pleasure for what men intend to do determines everything. That is why restriction, the simplest but most difficult thing for man, is the source of all human creativity and advance—while even the greatest discoveries of ideas are as ineffective practically as is empty talk.

We may as well make a general note about *restriction* as the closest thing to what could be called a panacea for human enrichment and progress.

Restrictions, of course, are evils according to progressive humanistic and scientific beliefs about human improvements. The restriction of satisfactions, of the clear sources of our positive capacities, is logically seen as an obstacle to their increase. The paradox of value causality is not understood.

This is the fallacy that underlies the present, admitted, causal confusion in all fields dealing with man, as we have seen for each of these fields. The modern fallacy about the role of restrictions has to be pointed out again and again.

Anyway, in man's individual behavior, restrictions are the sources of his capacities as well as of his physical and mental normalcy or health. In his social and cultural progress man's capacities are similarly increased through restrictions.

Morals are the basis of our cultural and social cooperation and progress. The very notion of morals is that of the restrictive control of our pleasure reactions. Morals embody the wisdom that our capacities come through restrictions. Moral norms oppose our natural pleasures and selfishness, which are the fundamental organic forces in us. We may recall here the paradox that restriction or "damming" up of the natural life-flow provides the potential for its use as we culturally or practically desire it.

Inevitably, the cultural or moral restrictions and the corresponding *human sins* against them are causally paradoxical. Humanistic moralists, logically, have to demonstrate that sins are ugly. This is a joke for modern scientific man. Sins are pleasant, invigorating, satisfactory, liberating, and felt as positive in every way, in their direct effects.

Conversely, the restrictive, traditional morals seem to be humanly detrimental. Enlightened liberals and rational radicals have repeatedly exposed the backwardness of our traditional morals. They do not realize how—"ridiculously" enough—they can indeed ruin themselves through sins, as over-enjoyments, much in the way some silly moralist predicts.

Sins as over-enjoyments bring us our various diseases and calamities, from heart attacks to the economic disasters of recessions. But because *sins are not causally understood*, moralists do not recognize the decisively important, real sins of modern man. In the confusion, many harmless sins are still condemned, while the real sins, the over-enjoyments or reactive "improvements" are not recognized as sins.

Modern moralists are becoming liberal, by adopting what seems scientifically logical. A direct increase in satisfactions is approved and restrictive non-satisfactions are viewd as undesirable. Our moralists are trying to liberate us even from our already acquired restrictive moral feelings such as guilt and shame. Such feelings are now seen as unhealthy.

The greatest achievements in human culture and progress have come through *social cooperation*, brought by a new, additional system of *restrictions*.

Without social cooperation men would still be primitive savages having only what a small family group can build or create. That is how men lived through all prehistory. Paleolithic man, like Neanderthal or Cro-Magnon man, had nearly as large a brain as we have. But he made no progress through hundreds of thousands of years. Then human progress grew explosively during the last ten thousand years.

What had so explosively changed? Nothing, except that the human population increased at exponential, explosive rates. This happens with any species to the extent it is successful, and man is extremely successful because of his brain. Progress, however, comes from difficulties that require new, necessarily painful or restrictive adaptations. Men, using their brains, had no critical difficulties until they encountered deadly threats from other equally intelligent men.

In their natural state family tribes only kill or enslave strangers—or eat them, which rare species do. Thus, when the human population explosion brought men into contact, they had to organize into larger and larger groups. Survival required this. A group of a dozen families working together can destroy hundreds of isolated families.

Obviously, social groups had to become more and more integrated, in a competitive vicious cycle. The final result was the nation state. Its emergence illustrates the process. As Europeans continued integrating and threatening each other, a point was reached when everybody had to accept a total, national integration. Thus, nationalism emerged throughout Europe at the same time. To justify the sacrifices required, ideologies of nationalism grew as rationalizations—to be viewed later as the sources of national movements. Philosophers and social scientists often speak of the *social nature of man*. This is another example of causal confusion about values.

Of course, social values are as remarkable as is our dire concentration on them, because it is so difficult to create them, by conditioning. What is really *natural* to men, and therefore easy and universal, like pleasure or the natural appetites, is never seen as anything remarkable, worthy of philosophical notice.

However, the very first tenets of humanistic theory reveal *how unnatural to man is social integration*. Nothing is more odious to humanists than restrictions on our individualism or on our "inalienable" rights, of individual freedoms. The most popular works on social horrors are the satires by George Orwell and Aldous Huxley. They, as many other authors, have observed the increase in social integration—necessary for human progress—and have depicted it as repugnant.

We can only repeat that men "brainwashed" to bear sacrifice for their fully integrated "ant-hill" society would live in a most complete love for each other. They would also reap benefits for everybody to an extent we presently can only fantasize about.

Of course, social integration has to be conditioned through our ingrown, deeply felt, moral traditions. An ideological, rationally direct imposition of social integration can indeed turn it into a cruel parody. Ideas do not really move people. Therefore, regimental enforcement becomes necessary in any system of rational conditioning. The Pavlovian methods of conditioning are ineffective. We have seen that such conditioning deals with animal learning; and for humans learning is not motivationally decisive.

The general fact is that social culture comes by way of *opposition to or restriction of* our natural, individual drives, through conditioning. Love of neighbor is the ideal. It has usually become a universal tenet together with the emergence of great civilizations requiring closer integration; Toynbee's theory of universal religions confirms this. In any event, the love of neighbor comes through the opposition of our central and only natural drive, egotism. And such love can make attainable virtually everything we want.

Any scientist can invent a society in which benefits for all would be enormous if only people could suspend their selfish drives. All proposed utopias can be explained as clearly feasible if human selfishness is discounted. But to make men progress by changing them for their own good, this *central natural drive* in men, their selfishness, has to be *opposed*, conditionally restricted.

It can be said that *opposition or restriction is the source of all progress*, in human existence as well as in nature. Opposition between living matter and the Field is, as we shall see, the principle that governs the living process and makes it so "inventive" as well as subject to countless laws that become purposive through selection. Darwin's theory shows that evolution works by destructive opposition. Also, the apparently highest achievement of evolution, *human consciousness*, has come together with an increased brain and is a product of added restriction. The brain is a typical organ of restriction. That is why inactivation of brain, by alcohol or drugs, provides a great release of pleasure.

Consciousness can be best understood as a life above the animal life, inside human organisms. It permits man to relive, to remember, or "replay" the experiences of that other life. Of course, additional, subsequent experiencing is possible only if the lower experiences are not fully lived through, if they are restricted. Such continuous reliving of past experiences remains possible as they are continuously kept restricted.

All higher living capacities or actions by organisms are possible only because there are reserves of living energy behind them. Such reserves can be created and maintained, in the limited organism, only by restrictions accumulating that energy. In short, consciousness is a new, added living capacity, created by additional restrictions, for reliving past experiences that have not been totally lived through because of restrictions imposed and continuously maintained on them.

Then the reliving or "rehearsing" of past experiences makes

possible human memory and the projection from it of the future, of consequences of events. This projection is the beginning of reasoning and planning, the most powerful tools of survival. The additional life that consciousness creates has, correspondingly, become a new, vast world in human minds.

The further step in the progress of men, as conscious beings, has been the imposition of *restrictions through moral and cultural norms*. This has come again by way of selection working through destructive opposition. Only those societies or cultures could survive which evolved restrictive methods for the increase of capacities, individual as well as social.

The final step in human progress will follow the same trend, of advance through restriction, but on a potentially extraordinary scale. Up to now, a blind, fumbling, and inevitably slow social and cultural selection has imposed the creative restrictions. How incomparably more effectively this could be done by planned engineering!

Of course, the imposition of restrictions is possible only through "deceitful" conditioning. The question arises, how can men deceive themselves knowingly, by a plan? We have to leave the solution to the potentially miraculous and unpredictably inventive future sciences of man. Once scientists reach a causal understanding of value reactions, and particularly of the creative role of restrictions, the human sciences will gradually become as limitlessly inventive and efficient as are all exact sciences.

Probably the first goal of scientific human progress will be an *increase in the longevity* of man. Here as well, the key to the solution seems to be restriction.

It is naturally to be expected that the length of life would increase with the slowing down of the rate of living. The widest, best studies on longevity, by Raymond Pearl, Max Rubner, and T. K. Van Voit, have established as axiomatic the principle of an increase of the length of life through a slower rate of living.[14] Women live longer because after menopause their biological life slows down to an eventless existence.

Experimentally, the life of animals has been extended, more than doubled, through underfeeding and the retardation of maturity. This can be seen in various studies, notably by C. M. McCay, C. A. Hochwelt, B. N. Berg, J. H. Northrop, H. S. Sims, R. Weindruch, and R. Walford. Similar results have been obtained by other restrictions: feeding antioxidants, freezing, hibernation, or enforced inactivity. In experiments by Paul Segall and Paola

Timiras, rats deprived of tryptophan, the amino acid essential for growth, lived twice as long as usual and remained vigorous.

The extension of life by restriction can be more clearly observed in less complex, primitive organisms. Insects prevented from maturing, as when their wings are clipped, live many times longer than usual. Plants that would mature and die in months, such as spinach or sissal, live for years and years when they are kept cut.

The most advanced sciences of man would certainly be able to impose on man far-reaching restrictions on the deepest organic levels, with even more extensive effects. And restrictions increase human capacities, as the evolution of the brain and consciousness shows. Life could be prolonged as much as it could be slowed down by restrictions.

But presently the creative effects of restriction are not recognized, because they are paradoxical. Instead, stimulating and directly invigorationg means are seen as beneficial.[14] They work, precisely, by an acceleration of the normal rate of living. Inevitably they reverse in their effects, as all stimulation does. Various seemingly wondrous, stimulating means of rejuvenation have been tried, to be abandoned as they eventually became disappointing.[14]

Even science-fiction writers may presently have better ideas than our experts on longevity. We can refer here to *2001: A Space Odyssey* by Arthur C. Clarke, who has remarkably predicted important scientific developments. In this story men are put to a sleep, a kind of deep hibernation, during which they nearly cease living and do not age. Similar ideas are frequent in science fiction. It is natural that with such a total sleep people could live for thousands of years, while continuing to awake and work for short periods.

The belief in life after death has to be mentioned here. Even an atheist must have some kind of such belief. Nobody could continue living with a real, emotional conviction that he will end in nothing. Yet our general beliefs in life after death are as crazy as they are compelling.

This, however, should not apply to beliefs about a soul. As a perfect essence the soul would have nothing to do with human value experiences, which derive from ugly value opposites. Still, for man his value experiences are the only thing that is real.

It is preposterous to think that such experiences could continue after death. Even a small, biochemical, organic change can distort our value experiences completely. How could such experiences continue when everything in the organism is destroyed?

Humanistic theorists may argue that, even if life after death is impossible, we should continue believing in it, by a kind of Kierkegaardian, existential denial of reason. Unfortunately, the enjoyment of something that is not true, and thus is "exaggerated," brings opposite reactions, whatever the enjoyed value may be. Enjoying the belief in life hereafter, though this belief has to collapse at the time of death, amounts to increasing, by accumulation, the horrors of death for the last moments of life.

When science will enable men to engineer their feelings, they will plan to experience as much of the fear of inevitability of death as possible and will leave little of that fear for the last moment. Then death will not be very much more distressing than falling asleep. But if the enjoyments of belief in afterlife are cultivated, they can only deepen into neurotic mood swings. Even the strongest believer in the hereafter clearly fears death as much as everybody does. The belief in life after death can never be felt as real. Trying to sustain the enjoyment of such a belief amounts to emotional exaggeration leading to opposite feelings and neurotic reactions.

It is clear that our beliefs in a life hereafter come from our strongest drive, the avoidance of the threat of death. Suicides, not fearing death, never think of life after death, never mention it, though logically they would be the first ones to expect a better hereafter. In a word, the *prevention of the fear of death* is the goal of our beliefs in a life after death. Yet that fear is the source of all our values. Every human value is, fundamentally, a value of survival. And survival derives its value from our fears of death.

Thus we are asking for *mountains without valleys* when we want the removal of the fear of death while also wanting to have feelings of values. Even God could not give us what we want here.

This is true also in purely organic terms. Organically death amounts to the inevitable equalization of organic values with equal disvalues. Death is understandable as the final annihilation of one's organic growth. Every achievement in this growth is an organic value; and all inner values derive from organic values. Thus, death, is a reduction back to zero of all our values.

What has not grown cannot be destroyed, but what has is. Nothing can change this. We know it instinctively. A person who is about to die should logically enjoy life to extremes while it lasts. He does the opposite. He tries to reduce the organic growth, as value, so that less is left for destruction.

We want other inherently impossible things from God. Wanting creation to be good without being bad also amounts to asking for mountains without valleys. The usual philosophies here are too convoluted to convince. A God-is-dead attitude is a result. Actually, we should see something of God from the way the world is working and advancing. It is progressing or evolving through opposition, hardships, and restriction. This should be closest to what the humanly graspable workings by God might be.

Here the *humble, traditional believers are nearest to God.* They see God's world as one of restrictions; and they bow in awe of a strange and incomprehensible, even seemingly cruel, will of God.

As the Ultimate of everything God is simply unknowable, beyond man's limited, relative knowledge. The vast endeavor of learned theologians to explain the wonders of God perpetuates a futile confusion—and is an awful waste of intellectual effort. Also, the more humanistically enlightened the explanations are, the further away they are from any insights about God in the world progressing through an opposition or restrictive hardship which is merciless in human value terms.

Man's self-contradicting values cannot be relevant to the "purposes" of God, which may follow a timeless logic, deriving their meaning now from the future, from the final, inconceivably miraculous future reality. No merciless cruelty is ever inflicted on man anyway. Everybody always receives as much pain as joy. Man and his values are just too irrelevant here.

A chief absurdity is the view of God as Intelligence. In comparison with the way a living mechanism works—by myriad performances at every instant—the intelligence is ridiculously clumsy, since it can never deal with more than one thing at a time.

Generally, the learned philosophical ideas about the universe and man's destiny are as lofty as they are credulous. Something *spiritual* is always implied as the higher reality, superior to the merely material world. In truth, *anything that can ever have meaning or be real for man is material* or physical.

It is revealing that no man, not even the greatest philosopher, has ever had a single thought other than in terms of matter. This is particularly evident from the most astounding, truly "transcendental" fact that all languages everywhere have the same classes of words—nouns, verbs, adjective or adverbs.

Language can be made to express thought quite closely. But nobody, however intelligent or skillful, has ever used new, different word classes, other than those used by all men, primitive or advanced. *This proves that men can think only in terms of matter* in space and time.

To give a short explanation, nouns derive from relations of matter, of things, in space. To every man, as a permanent organism, the stable things are the primary reality, so perfectly common to all men that its terms serve as the first categories of universal communication between men. But since there is also change, men have to add verbs, to express relations of matter in time, which is always only the relationship of changes.

Adjectives express merely relations of matter to matter, neither in space nor time. Adverbs derive from such relations of matter to matter in time. Gerunds, as verbal nouns, derive from relations of matter in time related in space. Other such combinations of relations are expressed by other classes of words.

But absolutely never has anybody used or invented word classes that would go beyond expressing the relations of matter in space and time. This is probably the most "supernatural" fact about human thinking.

Different peoples, never even suspecting each other's existence, obey here the same rules of thought without deviating even once. If any people had ever used a different, new word class, it would be totally incomprehensible, untranslatable for us or anybody else. But all languages can be understood by us and can be translated, however peculiar their usage of the classes of words. (I should know at least something here practically, since I have made translations from fourteen languages in my work.)

This virtually miraculous law of uniform classes of words is not particularly noted, because it is so universal or commonplace and simple. Theoreticians of linguistics have discussed, endlessly, other more involved, mystifying, even supposedly metaphysical "laws" of language.

Here again we meet the general fallacy rooted in value outlook: failure to recognize that *the simplest universal law is richest, most extensive in governing countless phenomena*. The principle of motion or force is so simple that it seems meaningless; but it governs endlessly many, miraculously creative, secondary uniformities.

In the same way the simple law of the classes of words, seen as unworthy of notice, is the source of countless secondary, involved "laws" of language, which are really incidental consequences of that simple, universal law. No wonder that linguistic theories have become so confused and controversially complex. New, detailed "laws" of languages are continuously discovered and appear mysterious, even supernatural, because their simple, universal basis is not "noticed."

Here we have to recall the explanation about causal laws. All such laws are simple and material or mechanistic, like those of matter or movement. They are simplest to man because man and his mind are also created and governed by them. He exists in their terms.

The simplest causal, material laws thus are causally most meaningful and all-inclusive. As we have seen, they are most "divine" because they regulate as well as create everything, including the mind and the mental world. Ideas about some spiritual reality superior to the material world are due to a confusion of insights.

It is naive to miss the simplest universal principles while noting the unusual, "remarkable" phenomena which are least universal therefore least decisive causally. The postulated, elaborate, spiritual, world of mind is indeed particularly unusual, different in form from the universal, physical principles.

Our spiritual world is therefore the least true when compared to what the universal, divine reality might be. We have explained how man's mental, spiritual creations become so involved and valuable precisely because of the difficulties our inherently feeble mind has in coping with the humanly senseless, mindless world.

The philosophical focusing on "spiritual" truths is contradictory and distortingly narrow. Speculations about spiritual or transcendental reality are inherent contradictions: they are expressed in human thought, reflected in language, which never extends beyond the terms of matter.

Moreover, this spiritual focusing precludes ideas about the really mind-boggling potential miracles around us. There can be countless universes in dimensions or terms different from ours surrounding you in the room you are sitting in. Such new insights can become relevant when man expands his view toward wider, usually not perceived, realities like the Field, which we shall discuss later. Also, unfathomable "miracles" of living nature become explainable after the extreme limitedness of the mind is recognized.

Most confused are the *humanistic ideas about an ideal, spiritually enjoyed future of man.* The final destiny of man is envisioned as some state of beatific enjoyment of values, of beauty and harmony. One can think here of the World Soul of Goethe, the Oversoul of Emerson, the Noogenesis of Teilhard de Chardin, or the Transfiguration of Toynbee.[14]

It is not realized that a heavenly value can derive only from its infernal opposite, in any value experience whatever. This rule is inevitable as long as men remain organisms, limited to their sameness; and men cannot survive or continue living otherwise than by remaining such organisms. Of course, organic existence is the source of all, even the highest, "spiritual" experiences, which have meaning only to the extent they have human, organic value.

Miracles greater than any spiritual visions of humanists are conceivably possible within the limits of man's *material* existence. A living organism works by operating, purposively, every molecule within itself. Imagine what you could do if you could guide, within yourself, each of the purposefully manageable molecules by planned designs, under your powers of consciousness. Let us note here that consciousness also has evolved mechanistically, as we have explained.

By dealing with every molecule consciously, along organically integrated ways, you would understand even the tiniest mechanism within yourself and diagnose or repair any defect in it. You could, similarly, create any new form, organ, or limb imaginable organically within yourself, or create new living forms, new animals, as easily as you now build some mechanical device.

You could even reconstruct the past history or predetermine the future of your organism as simply as you can now reconstruct mechanisms in a machine or predetermine their future action.

We could similarly resurrect the past or determine the future of the whole world if we could govern its processes by the two mechanistic, material capacities: consciousness and the ability of living nature to deal with myriads of elements at every point and instant. This would be equal to divine creation and omniscience.

Of course, these two mechanistic capacities cannot be combined in man's way of thinking or acting; they cannot even be thought of for the non-living processes in the world. We can only conjecture about such possibilities by thinking of how miraculously the pleasure mechanism governs every cell and molecule in the organism and "knows" their every evolutionary purpose developed through millions of years.

But the point is that *merely material, mechanistic capacities offer possibilities greater than philosophers dare to imagine* in their visions of a spiritual future. The purely material living nature is immensely superior to the mind. Thus the mind as a living process is so incomprehensible to the mind as intellect that endless mysteries and delusions about our mental, spiritual world remain overwhelming.

Finally, we have to consider the inevitable *"monstrosities" that future progress will bring.* Man will create progress, scientifically, after his escape from the present delusory beliefs about values and from his value fixations, as well as from the fixational view that man in his present form is ideal.

Man's evident biological enslavement to values such as beauty or virility will be overcome. Even simple reflection shows that our sense of these values merely drives us to perform biological functions such as reproduction. Aren't we here indeed only blind slaves of nature?

Future men free of such enslavement will view as mentally retarded persons still preoccupied with values such as human physical perfection or with beauty in general; all beauty as value derives from our biological, enslaving needs. Such persons will, in fact, be mentally less capable than other future men free of such blind, merely biological compulsions.

Men will transform themselves into "monsters" so that they will be able to live naturally in oceans, which cover three-fourths of our earth, or on other planets and in space, which men will conquer. Man will not necessarily have to grow gills or wings. We cannot predict what surprises the usually astounding scientific ingenuity will bring here. New physiologic capacities combined with mechanic adaptations will certainly enable men to do more than sea animals can do, or to meet the strange conditions of space.

The pivotal fact is that a relatively small physiologic change can save immensely in efforts and expenses for necessary support systems. It is fantastically unreal to think of spaceships sufficient to support man, in his present organic form, in thousand-year travels. Causally understood, exact future sciences of man, using exponentially progressing genetic engineering, will certainly be able to change man's physiology so that he will work and travel in space without being helplessly, totally dependent on machines.

Presently scientists are thinking only of technical possibilities, fixationally, without considering how man also could be changed. If not changed, man is doomed to stay within our solar system. It has been calculated that a speceship capable of bringing man—as he is now—to a star and back will never be feasible practically.

It would require immense amounts of provisions and fuel, therefore would be so heavy and unwieldy that it could never be launched or built. For inevitably such voyages would have to last thousands of years, away from the sun and earth, on which man, in his present form, depends in every detail for growing or building anything. To build or maintain even one engine a factory is necessary, which depends on a series of other factories for materials and parts made available on earth.

Similarly fantastic are speculations about huge space habitats. Even a tiny space capsule or laboratory costs billions of dollars, built to be operated for mere days or months, in total dependence on countless factories and organizations on earth. Of course, the difficulties increase geometrically with the size, or length of operation of such systems.

A totally different world of possibilities has to be opened if man is to travel to another star system or begin living on a different planet, as he inevitably will.

Life continues merely by the use of energy, and its forms can be endlessly varied. The billions of kinds of genes on earth can certainly provide every imaginable combination of traits to be adapted for the cells in the human organism. Thus a new, "monstrous" man could well be developed, able to subsist in space by the mere use of radiation and atoms rich in energy, which are usually available in space, while he creates his own few machines, during his self-supporting existence away from earth.

It is never useful to try to predict in detail what the surprisingly miraculous real sciences can bring. But it is clear that the human body will be transformed when man becomes a self-creator, when the true sciences of man evolve. Yet in our present thinking nothing could be more repulsive than such ideas about turning men into monsters.

This kind of thinking will, however, change as men will become citizens of a wider universe, companions of intelligent monsters from other star systems. Isn't it rather pompously conceited of us to hail the present forms of our bodies as eternal ideals to be maintained by future men capable of experiences of a galactic scope?

Almost as monstrous must seem the solutions that could help *more immediate human progress*. We already mentioned some pivotal, presently still primitive, possiblities of radical human improvement such as artificial insemination and the eugenic selection of future individuals with higher capacities. Such or similar possibilities could be turned into virtual miracles by the exact human sciences.

In principle, men can have their really human, mental identities perpetuated in their children best when artificial insemination in some form provides them with children of higher capacities. Our spiritual, cultural tradition could easily permit such a new orientation. We could see even now as selfishly stupid a man insisting that only his sperm can give meaning to the future of his child.

The selection of more capable future individuals would be a most compassionate as well as uniquely important achievement for human advance. We all want to be more capable, more fully human. But the present views here preclude sensible ideas.

If you or I were not born, it would not matter to anybody, including you and me. The same would be true if we were aborted because of a risk of low mental capacities. In fact, I would find that inhuman cruelty had been committed if I were born mentally deficient and had been permitted to live, to acquire consciousness—which starts evolving, slowly, not sooner than months after birth. Could anybody, sensibly, feel otherwise about a similar problem?

Thus, rationally, the selection of individuals with higher capacities would be the *most humane* thing to do, even if extended to the humanly "atrocious" possibility of putting to permanent sleep early infants—who do not yet really, consciously feel or know anything. They do not know or consciously feel even their own existence; they are nonexistent for themselves.

We admit that such ideas cannot be rationally thought of or discussed. Instinctively we have to feel such thoughts to be horrible. The human race could not survive without these feelings. We have here again biological compulsions governing us. But if we could be non-biological and humanly compassionate for a moment, we would realize how much suffering could be saved by early eugenic selection.

The decisive fact is that such early infants do not feel consciously but only respond instinctively as animals and fish do. You and I know this from our own experience. Months pass before an infant starts realizing or consciously feeling anything. It would not have mattered to me at all if I had been put to sleep forever before that.

Moreover, such atrocious ideas will probably not have to be considered. As prenatal examinations become perfected they will soon enable doctors to learn much about the fundamental capacities of a future individual. If only men could start realizing how humane it is to select individuals with higher capacities or how cruel it is not to do so.

Of course, after an infant, however defective, starts acquiring consciousness he has to be cared for, sacredly and unreservedly, so that he can grow and live a full life without suffering. *To prevent and not to create suffering is the only law of humane morals.*

The selection of more capable individuals would finally bring to all men the most meaningful treasure, the capacities now enjoyed by a rare few. Everything else in the human world depends on the capacities of men. It may be noted, though, that early, prenatal prediction of capacities will require new insights.

For instance, scientists will have to understand the paradox of restrictions, which have a direct, "negative" effect but are sources of our capacities. The aptness to bear restrictions could become a simple and most important criterion in the selection of higher capacities through prenatal examinations.

Once science gains such simple, causal insights it will find the necessary ways for enriching, through eugenic selection, our future generations with the humanly most precious gift, the capacities of higher minds. This will entail no suffering whatever. And the highest, most humane moral principle will be fulfilled. Men will endow other men with the most cherished treasures they want for themselves.

It is a pity that *our ideas would be offensive to the best, most valuable people in our culture.* These are the morally strong, practically creative people, who deserve the highest esteem and appreciation. They live by wise moral traditions, which, however, are too narrow to permit wider rational insights.

As it is, any ideas about the eugenic selection of men would presently be found outrageous. Instead, a most appalling crime against humanity is permitted to flourish. *The human race is being degraded* as the intellectually least capable individuals reproduce at highest rates. The more intelligent persons, of any race, have few children, and the less intelligent many. A couple of near morons may have a half-dozen children, uneducable, unemployable, potential criminals, to be cared for by welfare, who will produce more of the same.

But presently it would be considered scandalous even to conjecture about the possibilities of limiting any reproduction freedoms. The limitation of reproduction here could, however, be attained without hurting anybody.

Less intelligent individuals have more children not because they want to care for them or love them. They have them because they are thoughtlessly irresponsible in their uncontrolled sexual habits. Also, welfare mothers know that more children bring more income. If such parents were paid for not having children, and were provided with easy forms of birth control, they would be glad not to have the children. We would have a new, less expensive welfare system, with less-gifted individuals living better than others in exchange for having childless lives, which they may find even happier.

Thinking of a more remote, exponentially increasing future progress, we can expect that most of human existence will become monstrous if judged by our present standards. Value enjoyments will be understood as futile. Merely intellectual activity, through the brain, will take over. Science-fiction writers may not be too unrealistic in depicting future men as having enormous brains.

The brain of man is already an excessive addition to his organism. It has increased disproportionally in the short evolution of man. Its further radical increase would, probably, not be organically difficult. Our brain is already unusually independent from the organism. It can be cut without causing pain. The most highly evolved parts of it can be partially separated from the rest of it, in lobotomy.

Thus, the brain seems like an externally oriented, excess outgrowth ready for a further, organically abnormal increase. But though organically external and "abnormal," as if superimposed and superficial, the brain is evidently a miracle phenomenon of evolution and progress. The paradox of enrichment in evolution through an increase in restrictions is confirmed here; the brain is a restrictive, abnormal organ imposed on the organism. In any case, man will transform himself and the whole universe around him by the use of his seemingly superfluous and humanly extraneous brain.

Man's future existence, dominated by the brain alone, will be *"monstrous"* in many ways. Man will probably live a constantly controlled and restricted, and therefore enormously prolonged, life in a laboratory-like environment. Soon he won't even have to move from his "laboratory." We are already advancing toward doing office work while staying home. We see and hear what happens in the world while we sit in our living rooms.

Radar can offer new possibilities. Science will certainly improve it immensely. Man will be able to perform better than bats or dolphins. He will be able to see, or even "touch" and analyze, objects on a faraway planet, from his "laboratory" on earth.

The next unique advance will be discovery of other cosmic media, other "Fields" different from the Field, which limits transmissions to the speed of light. Not much can be done even with a highly improved radar when signals sent to a star return only after years.

The universe is limitless in everything. Only our science is still primitive. When it advances toward dealing with realities such as the Field, men will discover and teletravel new "oceans," much as men sailed strange new seas while discovering the New World.

By the way, it can be speculated that we presently do not hear from intelligent beings on other star systems because our communication methods are so primitive. What good is it to try to send a signal to us, in our medium, when that would take a hundred years? In that time we would be discovering new, faster media, as such highly intelligent beings would be able to predict.

Most of our revolutionary future progress will be brought by the human sciences as they become truly scientific, through a totally new causal understanding. But even in the physical and life sciences, the removal of the universal human prejudice will bring radical changes.

The causal, "negative" source of the "positive" physical universe, as man knows it, will be discovered. The results will, necessarily, be surprising. They will amount to a discovery of the presently unsuspected, real, physical causes and mechanisms which create and govern all physical phenomena, including the living processes and thus the mind itself.

For instance, the causal mechanism of life reveals itself as a fire opposite to ordinary fire. The Field and matter, as opposites, inevitably have opposite chain reactions against each other. Life as "negative fire," acting contrary to ordinary fire, accumulates energy. We all know that energy is accumulated by life.

But *if the "fire" of life is understood causally*, its chain-reaction power can be scientifically augmented, much like acetylenic fire can be intensified to make metal burn. Look what electricity is doing for us now, after we have learned to accumulate this force that seemed so feeble when it was first perceived.

When the power mechanism of life is understood, then new, very intense kinds of living processes could be grown using any natural elements, even without water. Or they could be engineered to accumulate energy under very low energy levels, anywhere above the minus 459 degrees of zero energy. Thus the chain reaction of living process could be turned into a source of power more effective than the chain reactions of nuclear burning, in reactors, or of fire.

All sciences increase at exponential rates, though they start with small gains, after discovering their necessary, mostly simple, but "impossible" causal insights. An understanding of the real, paradoxical organic laws as keys to the human sciences will turn man into a *self-creator* advancing himself at similar, accelerating, finally explosive rates.

Think of how *immense* such *exponential advances* can become through centuries! The future would be too blindingly strange for us if we were to visualize it.

We have mentioned that our very inability to imagine our final, unfathomably immense, and different human progress may harbor the hope, the only hope, that our existence may somehow have meaning or be redeemed in the end. That is why progress deserves the highest human interest.

Certainly, up to now progress has mostly brought us misery and diseases, as well as violence and the deaths of millions. But that is so because this progress has moved us away from understanding the paradoxical causes of human value reactions, the sources of man's capacities.

Progressive humanistic thought is a main obstacle to creative, causally understood progress. Its ideal is enjoyments of noble inner values—actually of deep, organic pleasure releases. Our humanists can only reject restrictions, which are clearly contrary to what values as satisfactions are. Restrictions are always negative, in affective, value terms, under the "scientifically" enlightened views of progressive, humanistic thought.

But as we have explained, restriction is the source of all progress everywhere, from the evolution of life and consciousness to enrichment of our individual as well as social and cultural capacities.

The humanists, however, want mountains without valleys. They want enjoyment of values without their value opposites. This is perpetuated in the deepest humanistic convictions, including those about man's exalted, forever enjoyable, ideal future, even about sustaining the belief in the hereafter.

If our humanists had it all their way, we would inevitably sink into mental impoverishment, in spite of lofty intents, in pursuing our inner value enjoyments. Even the most "spiritual" experiences, like the religiously ecstatic feelings induced by drugs, lead to psychotic mental exhaustion. And organically it does not matter in what way the enjoyment, as affective "improvement," is caused. If it has occurred, the opposite process has to follow.

Conversely, the sources of satisfaction or pleasure releases are equal needs as non-satisfactions or restrictions. Therefore our important positive capacities, such as interests or love, which are satisfactions and pleasures, have to be created, through conditioning, by the imposition of harrassing, ugly non-satisfactions and restrictions—which our humanists can only abhor.

VI

ADMITTED CAUSAL MYSTERIES EVEN IN THEORETICAL PHYSICS

Physics deals with the material reality of man's universe. The universal human prejudice consists of man's inability to see the causal, negative sources of his positive values. This prejudice extends to the physical reality because the act of knowing is a value process; and the material reality exists for us in the way we know it. All knowledge derives from differentiation of values, from the relating of value opposites. As we have seen, we would not know matter—it would not exist for us—without nothingness as its opposite, as its causal source.

Let us state the most important point here, even if it may become clearer only later. *Force determines everything in the universe but is a nothingness to man*; nobody has ever perceived force in itself.

Why is the causal source of practically everything in the cosmos a nothingness to us? The reason is that the universal force is the opposite of matter, of man's physical reality, and therefore is unreality itself for him.

The universal force and matter are opposites in everything, statically and dynamically or causally. Every form and effect in matter is created by the universal force as nothingness. Conversely, all properties of the universal force can be inferred from what matter as its opposite is or does. We shall explain this causality through opposites for all physical phenomena in detail later.

But even now we may point out the most significant fact that force without opposition has no humanly perceivable existence. Newton's insight about force reveals that force, perceived by man only as its effects of action, always *requires equal counteraction* to be so perceived.

Further, we may recall that matter is dynamically similar to force, as the equation of matter and energy indicates. In that equation energy is merely the effects of force. Man always perceives only such effects, not the force itself. But the equation reveals matter as dynamically equal to force—as an opposite force. Therefore, matter too requires opposition to have concrete forms; otherwise it would dissolve, as force, into formless dissipation.

In short, matter as well as the universal force *derive their reality through opposition* between them. And the matter-energy equation confirms that the amount of matter determines the possible amount of the effects of force.

But man, existing by virtue of matter as his reality, sees the opposite of matter as unreality, as nothingness. Thus the "negative," causal source that determines what matter is or does throughout man's "positive" universe is a nothingness for him—force as nothingness.

It may be added that the human prejudice against the actual, "negative" cause of matter has, of course, no effect on physical phenomena objectively. These phenomena are outside us and have nothing to do with our inner-value world or its prejudices. Therefore physics, dealing objectively with these phenomena, could evolve into a superb exact science. Physics deals perfectly with the universal force, though that force is still a nothingness for physicists as human beings.

Only in the higher *theoretical physics* does this human prejudice have its effect of precluding insight into the real, "negative" causal sources of the physical universe. For, evidently, theoretical physics has to cope with man's ultimate knowledge or understanding of reality; and knowledge is a value differentiation. Man's world as it is known to him derives from its opposite, but he cannot recognize that opposite.

This prejudice of man is, understandably, his strongest *primordial conviction*. Nothing has more cognitive value for man than physical matter. For he himself is matter and exists with the help of matter in everything. Consequently, the causal opposite of matter has equal unreality for him; it is a total nothingness to man.

Even in other than purely cognitive terms, matter has for man values only in the way he is deriving them from differentiation against equal disvalues. Matter is for man mainly a reality of persistence and force, which have no meaning without their value opposites, without potential annihilation of that persistence, by opposition, and without counterforce.

Actually whatever reality values we may attribute to matter, they derive from their equal value opposites, from equal "non-reality" values. Thus, in all terms of humanly meaningful value experiences, the real, *causal source* of man's "positive" universe is its impossible, unrecognizable, "negative" opposite, nothingness, as universal force.

To obviate philosophical difficulties, we can say that we know material things by differentiating them against nothingness much as we know mountains by viewing them against valleys. Now think of somebody seeing or valuing only the mountains and disregarding the valleys. That is what man does in his understanding of physical reality. For him the "nothingness," *the causal source of his reality, is a total unreality*.

This human prejudice is so fundamental that even physicists, as human beings, do not overcome it. To them also, the "nothingness" is unreality or emptiness, though every physical event is clearly determined by force, which is always the invisible "nothing."

More precisely, it is the universal field of force as the "nothingness" that causally governs everything. Even physicists themselves recognize that, for instance, the electromagnetic and gravitation phenomena are caused by something in the "empty" space. But generally physicists have chosen not to be absurd where common sense would show them to be so most emphatically—where the strongest human prejudice denies reality to the universal force as "nothingness," to the opposite and *causal source* of matter as man knows it.

Consequently, theoretical physics struggles with unbelievable complexity and admitted mystery, whereas its final, fundamental principles should be simplest and clearest. The universe is now viewed as having no final causes, even no understandable reality.

Uncertainty and the absence of observable causality are recognized now as the first principles of the higher modern theory of physics. The most common theme becomes the explanation of why human understanding inherently does not agree with physical reality—the theme of the "quantum weirdness" of physical phenomena, revealed by the most advanced physics.[3, 5, 12]

Self-Evident yet "Impossible" Unified Causal Field

Physicists know, as we all do, that force is a nothingness for man, while it determines everything in the universe. Physicists also know that matter consists of atoms, as systems of matter or energy, *compressed and operated by invisible force*. which has to be around them to effect the compression. The "particles" constituting atoms are similarly held together by a compressing force. Moreover, these "particles" are now found to be waves, which cannot exist without a medium or field.

This compression of atoms and the wave nature of their constituent particles have remained mysteries causally. The self-evident explanation of the mystery would be the universal field of force as "nothingness" opposed to matter. Opposing force surrounding matter inevitably has the effect of compressing it.

Physicists further know that all *transmissions* of energy—which is equivalent to matter—are carried out by *waves* in "empty" space. Clearly a wave is nonsensical without a medium. As Einstein said, waves must be *in* something. Of course, the universal force is as "dense" as matter, since force clearly operates matter, which it could not do without being at least equal to matter in what we call density. (We shall explain later why the dense field of force inevitably remains imperceptible, because of its causal universality.)

Also, *quantum and wave mechanics* reveal that everything in the physical universe consists of *waves* or acts as waves. This too has remained mysterious causally and is the main reason for the often-discussed, inherent strangeness of physical phenomena, as they are revealed by modern, quantum physics to be vibrations of nothing as emptiness.

Here again the universal field of force as "nothingness" offers the self-evident and only possible causal explanation. Such a field is a perfect medium for the creation of universally present waves, which are impossible without a medium.

We may also consider here that matter is dynamically equal to force. As such it is a fluid medium, interacting with its opposite, the universal field of force, which is also a fluid medium. Waves are the only way the two fluid media can interact.

We should emphasize that any force inherently requires its opposite in order to become a perceivable reality. This applies both to matter and "nothingness" as two universal media of force or energy. We already indicated that, according to Newton's Law, force is real, perceivable through its action, only to the extent that it meets opposition as equal conteraction. Even in common-sense observation, unopposed force becomes a formless, meaningless effusion.

In a word, the universal field of force has to remain imperceptible everywhere except where it interacts with its opposite, with matter as opposite force or energy. Conversely, matter becomes a perceivable reality where it meets its opposite, the "nothingness" as the field of the universal force.

In every way this field of force determines what matter is or does. Force as the universal determinant is known to physicists and to everybody. In sum, *the universal field of force is the self-evident, yet missing, unperceivable unified causal field* that physicists have always sought for.[3, 5]

This is also clear when we look at the *generally known physical forces* such as electricity and gravitation. Here we should keep in mind that such forces are only the effects of the universal force acting on matter, and that man sees only these effects, not the universal force itself.

Physicists recognize four universal forces—gravitation, electric force, the strong force, and the weak force. Incidentally, physicists do not formally recognize the kinetic force, which effects all movement. Is this force, as well as movement, too commonplace to be "noticed"? It is certainly most universal. Even the four recognized forces could be causally reduced to the kinetic force, since they result from movements in and around matter. In fact, the kinetic force is the most direct effect of the universal field of force. All physical phenomena result from the movement of matter by the universal force, as will become clear later.

In any case, even the formally recognized forces are explainable causally as effects of the universal field of force which remains a nothingness to man.

This is clear for the *electromagnetic forces*. Every physicist, even a thinking electrician, realizes that electric current and electromagnetic effects are created by some force around the wire or magnet. Electric and magnetic fields are the causal sources here, and they consist of forms of force as nothingness in space.

Further, it has been established that the *strong force* and the *weak force* can be causally unified with the electric force. Evidently, they derive causally in the same way as the electric force does. Here we have the most universal principles at work. As such they can be only simple, though the mathematical explanations here become complex, as they do even for simple events.

The strong force holds together, actually compresses atoms. The weak force disintegrates them; compression becomes disruption under unbalanced conditions. Naturally, both these forms of compression are created by a surrounding universal field of force, by "nothingness." In any event these two forces, being causally unifiable with electricity, are created by the "empty" space, as electricity clearly is.

It may be noted here that physicists prefer to offer their explanations in the long-established mathematical terms of particles, such as the W and Z particles, which can be "real," while force is unperceivable. Surely, by complex mathematics physicists can easily derive all force relationships from effects in particles, since these effects are results of the same universal field of force that operates both particles and forces.

We may also note that physicists often assume, directly or implicitly, some force in their explanations without realizing that they would have to establish why and how this force is there. Thus, they may speak about the explosion of the Big Bang or about the clinging together of quarks, without reflecting that this requires forces which would have to be explained first as to their reason and terms of existence.

The same is true of movements or actions by any "particle" or quantum—by an electron, proton, neutron, any of the newly discovered two hundred particles, or a photon. All such actions require a force. Its existence and causality have to be established if the actions are to be causally, scientifically explained. The universal field of force can, of course, be the causal source of all such phenomena, since force determines everything while remaining a nothingness.

The fourth principal force, that of *gravitation* derives even more clearly from conditions in the "empty" space. It is now generally accepted that the cause of gravitation is the curvature of space explained by Einstein. He was one of the first physicists to recognize that the "empty" space is not a mere nothingness.[1, 3] However, the curvature is not a full explanation. Curvature is a concept of condition, not of force, which gravitation is; bodies can slide on a curvature only when force acts on them.

Anyway, what happens in gravitation is recognizedly determined by the "empty" space, actually by the universal field of force, which is always as imperceptible as emptiness. We shall see later how gravitation results automatically from shielding off, by bodies of matter, of the pressures of the universal field of force.

All in all, the *"nothingness" in space* is clearly evident as the *universal force* that creates and operates our generally known forces as well as particles of matter and other forms of energy—all consisting of waves. Particles are now generally found to consist of quanta waves, which can be only in a medium,[5, 6] that the "dense" field of force is.

Explanations of physical causes that are now admittedly mysterious or hidden to man become automatic and simple if it is considered that the universal force is always a nothingness while it clearly moves, creates and determines everything in the cosmos.

A full explanation here, of course, requires the recognition of the "nothingness" as the opposite causal source of matter. It may be difficlt for man, proceeding according to normal prejudiced common sense, to recognize nothingness as reality; man never recognizes the causal "negative" sources of his values.

But physicists would need, practically, only to consider a universal force, which is always a nothingness, as the opposite of matter: such a force indeed governs all phenomena, uniformly, throughout the universe. And as we shall see in detail later, the presently admitted mysteries in physics do become explainable by the concept of a universal field of force, as nothingness opposite to matter. The nothingness is of course the opposite of matter in every sense, for man.

At the same time physicists have desperately sought for a unified causal source, such as the Unified Field that Einstein set out to discover.[1, 3] Physicists could have found in the universal field of force every causal property required, since force can cause anything.

Above all, the explanation could be based merely on what is clear already: the universal field of force as imperceptible in itself as all force, and therefore the nothingness everywhere around us. *No new principles or discoveries thus would be required for this Unified Field.*

Why did not physicists turn to thinking in terms of these self-evident ideas? Because the human prejudice here is too strong. Nothingness as reality is too unthinkable. The emptiness of space is too convincing, in every way, under an imperative common sense, even though scientifically or objectively space is clearly not empty.

We simply have here an instance of the most deeply ingrained human prejudice, against recognizing the "negative" causal source of "positive" values, which are in this case the most primordial cognitive, and even affective, reality values for man.

We may as well explain the final, full *mechanics of the inexorable relativity of knowledge* here as a value process of the differentiation of reality values of the physical world. Differentiation of course amounts, in final terms, to the relation of opposites.

A universe consisting throughout of matter alone, without nothingness, would have no cognitive or other meaning, no perceivable existence for man. We cannot know anything unless we can differentiate it against something else, ultimately against its opposites, which determine what it is for us.

If an apple remained the same but everything in the world doubled in size, the apple would become half its size and nothing else would have changed, Every reality value, everything we know or experience as real, similarly derives from its opposites.

Whatever matter is for us, however it exists, it does so as the opposite of nothingness. The "nothingness" and matter are two equal causal opposites. Where the one is or moves in, the other is not or moves out. From this universal causal interdependence matter and the "nothingness" derive their every form and quality or property.

Let us look at the properties of the two opposites, using the name Field for the "nothingness" as the causal opposite of matter.

If an atom is round, the Field surrounding it has the opposite form. Where the Field thrusts in, the matter yields, and vice versa. Forms and movements of matter create the endless phenomena of our world, but opposite forms and movements of the Field are their determinants. Indeed, the Field is better viewed as the dominant causal opposite. It is dominant because it is vaster, of more extensive strength, as it surrounds matter everywhere.

Anyway, the Field-matter interaction creates our world, with its varied qualities of substance, color, sound, forms, and dynamics, all of which derive from configurations and movements in matter determined by the Field. Of course, our subjective values of, say, color or moving forms come from our differentiations of the values within our world of matter. No direct reference to the Field is necessary there.

The properties of the Field can be inferred as opposites of the properties of matter, its causal opposite. The Field is a force as strong as the resistance to it by matter, which is dynamically similar to force. The Field is as dense as is matter, opposing it. Otherwise the Field could not have the concrete, compact effects on matter that it as force clearly has. The Field is universal and homogeneous, just as matter is everywhere the same substance of its forms. Of course, matter has various forms, just as the Field has various, corresponding opposite forms—or rather, areas surrounding matter.

Both the Field and matter are fluid or elastic media in their final essence of force or energy. Since the one opposes the other and the Field surrounds matter, the Field acts as a pressure around matter, pressing into it and compressing its "particles," which are actually wave systems or waves.

These properties of the Field as a strong or dense, compressing, elastic, homogeneous, universal medium make causally understandable all physical phenomena, as we shall see in explaining them separately later.

Practically, the most important property of the Field is its total universality, as extensive as the "nothingness." The Field is universal and homogeneous simply because it is a force. It is inherent in any force to expand without limit and to equalize any pressure difference within itself. The Field thus fills space totally and uniformly. This has a very important effect.

Because of its total homogeneous universality the Field cannot be perceived or "known" in itself, since perceiving is impossible without differentiation.

Think, for comparison, of atmospheric pressure. It is far less universal than the Field. Yet it is still not generally perceived or "known." It was not discovered even by early scientists using all kinds of machines and instruments, under various methods. Einstein said that fish cannot know the water in which they live. Of course, the Field can be perfectly known through matter as its opposite everywhere around us.

This universality of the homogeneous Field compounds the human prejudice, because it makes the Field unperceivable in its every aspect. The Field becomes for man a true nothingness, not only statically but also dynamically or causally.

It is not difficult to understand that a totally universal, homogeneous medium would be unperceivable in its static aspects. A fish that never moved would indeed never know water around it. But even in its dynamic or causal effects the Field automatically remains unperceivable, unregistrable in itself.

Here it should be realized that all *physical phenomena result from the Field moving matter.* The Field is the vaster causal opposite of more extensive strength. Therefore it moves matter, or permits it to move, by yielding to it. Thus, all causation in the universe is that of matter being moved by the field as the dominant causal opposite. The result is that there can be no hindrance, drag, or any other differentiable, knowable effect from the Field itself.

For comparison, think of a *uniform stream of water moving your boat.* There is no hindrance or drag from the water because it is the water itself that effects the movement of the boat. It can be said that *the boat experiences nothing at all of the water* which totally, uniformly carries or dominates it.

Similarly, the Field cannot be experienced in any direct way by us, as beings of matter, because the Field itself creates all effects in matter by moving it. There can never be any hindrance by the Field to anything material moving, even though the Field is as dense as any substance can ever be. Molecules in your arm are moved by the Field; therefore, the arm can move through the dense Field without hindrance.

Furthermore, *no instrument or method can ever discover the Field* as exerting hindrance to movement or as becoming perceivable in any way—except by differentiation against matter.

In simple, practical terms, the Field as the universal force and the dominant causal opposite creates all physical phenomena by moving matter, through direct movements or pressures and yields. The example of the boat moved by the water, therefore, can illustrate what happens with all physical phenomena. There is no hindrance, friction, or any other differentiable, knowable effect from the Field for any material phenomena *because it is the Field itself that causes the movements or pressures which create the phenomena.*

Now, any instrument, in any kind of experiment, exists or operates as matter and works on matter. Therefore, whatever the instrument or experiment may be, every action or observation here is a result of matter being moved by the Field, which in itself thus again remains unperceivable.

Physicists themselves recognize that a totally universal causal medium would be undiscoverable by any instrument. Here we can refer to a proper authority, the founder of operationalism, P. W. Bridgman, a Nobel laureate in physics. According to him, "an instrument can never discover whether the medium exists, because the instrument itself is part of the conditions affected by the medium."[7] Of course, the Field as the causal opposite of matter is evident from what matter is or does everywhere.

Here we have to note the *difference between the Field and the old ether* or similar concepts, such as fields or the curvature in space. They were conceived as kinds of matter or as something similar to matter[6] rather than opposite to it; the opposite-value causality reflected in the physical world has never been suspected or mentioned.

The result was incongruity. Ether or the fields, as causal media of light or electricity, would have to be enormously strong or dense. But nothing of the kind, similar to matter, could be discovered in space.

In contrast, *the Field is an opposite of matter*—"nothingness," as a universal force remaining imperceptible or unregistrable, as all force does. This is clear from everything we have said about the Field and matter. But the discovery of the Field requires the recognition that the "positive" universe as man knows it derives from its "negative" sources, in his knowledge. Such a recognition was and still is impossible in the "logical" physics.

Confusion in physics increased because of the incongruous concepts of ether or the fields viewed as being similar instead of opposite to matter.[1, 6] Physicists saw the necessity of a universal causal medium, but perfect experiments, by the best physicists, did not reveal any medium or ether.

The leading physicists who have offered important causal

explanations have done so by recognizing a medium: ether, forces in space, fields, or the curvature of space. This is true of the work and theories of Boyle, Huygens, Newton, Faraday, Maxwell, Fresnel, Kelvin, Lorentz, Hertz, Lodge and Einstein.[1, 6, 7]

The Unified Field introduced by Einstein is to be a universal, physical causal source—expectedly discoverable or calculable in the way matter is and, necessarily, having to be quite strong or dense. The opposite causal nature of the Unified Field in relation to matter has never been mentioned; just as ether and the other fields were never thought of as opposites of matter.[6] *The requirement of an opposite for all human reality has never been considered in physics.*

As could be expected, even the most thorough experiments, by many great physicists, failed to reveal any medium in the "empty" space. Of course, the medium looked for here was to be a kind of matter, not its opposite. Experiments on ether interference or drag were performed by Fizeau, Fresnel, Hertz, Stokes, Lodge, Miller, Kennedy, and Michelson and Morley.[6, 7]

Certainly, the experiments showed that there was no interference or drag of any kind in space. It was therefore concluded that no medium—thought of in terms of matter—was there.

All in all, physicists were ready to recognize a universal causal medium, but did not consider that a totally universal causal medium would automatically be unregistrable, equal to nothingness. Physicists thus avoided insulting the good common sense under which nothingness can never be something.

However, the usually reliable *common sense is here wrong*. For man space is empty because he, apparently, can see and move freely through it. Actually, seeing is receiving light waves that only a very dense medium can transmit. And nothing moves unless it is moved by force, which is a nothingness for man but is, necessarily, stronger and denser than matter since it controls and changes matter.

There can be no interference to movement in a medium if it is the medium itself that effects the movement. But even Newton and Einstein argued that a causal medium, like ether, would interfere with movement of bodies.[1, 6]

Of course, physicists are too knowledgeable about physical phenomena to ignore *the necessity of a universal causal medium* or a unified field in physical causation. Particularly were the great founders of modern physics certain about such a medium.[1, 6] The more recent theory is so sophisticated, in its emphasis on uncertainty and merely mathematical concepts, that it does not bother about physically concrete certainties. The early physicists were less defeatist.

We can refer here to the practical founders of modern physics, particularly of its most important field, electromagnetism. Michael Faraday established very concrete "lines," "wheels," and "tubes" of force in space as "states of stress in an elastic body."[6] James Maxwell provided mathematical equations for the concrete constructs of Faraday.[6]

Einstein used these equations in his theories. He stressed that "we have two realities: matter and field."[1] However, he admitted that "we have not yet succeeded in formulating a pure field physics." According to Einstein the "field is, for the modern physicist, as real as the chair on which he sits."[1]

Other founders of physics—Lord Kelvin, Sir Oliver Lodge, Sir George Stokes, and Sir Edmund Whittaker—had in their theories ether models as concrete as were those of Faraday and Maxwell.[6] Sir Oliver Lodge even used the argument that a dense ether can exist without being noticed, much as water cannot be noticed by fish.[6]

Revealingly, Newton wrote, in his private correspondence, that attraction between bodies without anything between them "is to me so great an absurdity...that no man can fall into it."[6] He speculated about particles of ether being finer in the vicinity of bodies;[6] but he finally found the cause of gravitation mysterious and attributed its existence to God.

It is indeed "an absurdity" not to recognize a universal medium when happenings on one star can have effects on another. Only such an omnipresent medium can explain why physical phenomena everywhere in the cosmos are causally connected as well as uniform.

Actually only the "nothingness" is everywhere. As the Field it creates the same causal effects at every point in the universe. But physicists have chosen to avoid the humanly unthinkable fact that nothingness could be a reality—that the negative can be the cause of the positive.

Understandably, physicists are mystified. As Bridgman wrote, "it is in any event a bit shocking, I think, to realize that the concept of empty space, which appears unavoidable and a necessity of thought, can have no guarantee that it is anything more than an artifact of our thinking."[7] Henry Margenau, while recognizing that everything falls in line with the theory of fields of

Faraday and Maxwell, notes "the jolt one receives from the idea that the universe is filled with invisible solid matter."[9]

A physicist has to be rather independently original in his thinking to recognize the immense causal forces in the "nothingness." Here should be noted an explanation by a leading authority in the theory of physics, John A. Wheeler. He has explained that all of space is filled with infinitesimal electromagnetic fluctuations of "stupendous energy." Such a cosmic energy would certainly constitute the universal force (which we named the Field).

But, as a rule, modern theoretical physics has accepted a general unreality of physical phenomena as inevitable, even as the essential aspect of it.[5, 10, 11] The present rules in this theory are uncertainty and causal indeterminacy or mere probability, even the principle of complementarity, which permits a yes-and-no answer to the same question.

Causal uniformity, observed in the universal, constant occurence of the same effects all the time everywhere, certainly proves one causal source. Naturally, one cause can have varied effects under different conditions. But the modern theorists, not seeing the cause, hold to the rule of merely statistical, aggregate probability. Physical reality is reduced to mere "probability waves of emptiness."[5, 12]

The universal, most fundamental causal principles should be simple, evident everywhere as concrete, elementary physical realities. In contrast, modern theoretical physics finds no such princples, because the real, physical cause is not seen. *Explanations become merely symbolic or mathematical*—complex and confusedly metaphysical.

According to Sir James Jeans, reality is "mathematical, and since mathematics are formulas of symbols, the world is also only symbolic...the universe begins to look more like a great thought."[6] The prominent physicist Sir Arthur Eddington found that "reality, the unknown something which underlies the world both of sense and science, is spiritual in nature."[6] Another great authority, Erwin Schroedinger, found that "the ether in which all events of the universe take place could reduce to a mathematical abstraction."[8]

The uncertainty principle, formulated by Heisenberg, is generally accepted as the most noted rule in modern physics.[9, 10] So is causal indeterminacy; it is often referred to also because it permits metaphysical speculations, such as those about the freedom of will.

The principle of complementarity, explained by Niels Bohr, is the next most important rule in modern physics. It permits double truths to such an extent that even love or justice could have two contrary, "complementary" meanings, according to Bridgman.[7]

Confusion shows in the fact that the two most prominent modern physicists, Albert Einstein and Max Planck, could not agree with the uncertainty principle and the rejection of definite causality.[11] As is frequently referred to, Einstein stated that God could not be playing dice with the universe. This problem, reportedly, was the main point of dispute between Einstein and Bohr, who is quoted as saying, "Albert, stop telling God what to do."

Presently, under modern theoretical physics, all mechanistic definite *causality, and even the reality of the physical world, have vanished.* According to the theory of quantum physics, "nature does not present us with a single instance...of a causal connection" and "it is impossible to demonstrate the existence of the real world by purely rational methods."[2]

Finally, modern physicists have acquiesced and now, conveniently, rest unbothered by the "quantum weirdness," which is noted as a mere curiosity.[5, 12] They only repeat the accepted dogmas of uncertainty and acausality. They view the usual thinking about causality as a misleading habit of thought, a backward attitude from the old physics.

We simple mortals, though, would think that no science is valid without causal understanding, without knowledge of what comes from what, or why anything happens. Is any coherent system of thought possible without such understanding?

Of course, physicists know what they are doing, or rather what they can do. Their uncertainty and acausality dogma is therefore particularly significant. It reveals that the physical reality as man knows it is causally incongruous, that the very method of human causal thinking here is wrong. The reason is the prejudice against recognizing the "negative," real causal source of the "positive" universe.

The actual causal source, the "nothingness," remains unrecognized. As a result it seems that physical phenomena are mere waves or fluctuations of emptiness.[5, 11, 12]

Without the real, "negative," universal causal source—the causally unifying Field of force as nothingness—modern theoretical physics can only describe, in abstract, mathematical, or merely "statistical-probability" terms the effects of that source. Of course, effects of any cause vary under various conditions. Such effects become causally irreducible, specific phenomena if their one cause is not seen.

Thus *more than two hundred different kinds of particles*, with an equal number of antiparticles, have been discovered. Each of them would, logically, require its own kind of causal principle. But nature does not know or invent multiple, complex causal principles. One causal source clearly governs all physical phenomena, since they are causally uniform and connected throughout the immense universe. This one causal source would not possibly consist of various, fundamental, different, and complex causal principles for the various kinds of particles and phenomena.

Only the Field, the universal "nothingness," can provide the explanations, since it creates and operates the particles and everything else in all their observed details, with automatic simplicity, as will become clear later.

Of course, physicists have sought for fundamental, simple constituents of particles and forces. Curiously, they persist in using the concept of particles even for explaining forces. For instance, gravitation supposedly derives from gravitons, magnetism from monopoles, and the strong and weak forces from vector bosons. In terms of concrete reality, particles can never be conceived as forces, or as mere "probability waves of emptiness." Particles are matter, which in physics is steady and immutable, exactly contrary to forces, which are immaterial and evasively transient.

The use of mathematics, therefore, remains the only way to proceed. It permits one to relate all physical phenomena, forces and particles, since they all are effects of one universal cause, the impossible Field, which then can remain unidentified. It is often said that, mathematically, physicists do not have to know the reality they are dealing with.

Anyway, particles remain the only reality for physicists, since forces are expressions of the Field, which is not recognized as real. But particles become confusing, because they are created and operated by the Field interacting with matter. That interaction, between two fluid energy media, naturally results in waves. In fact, it is now clear that the "particles" do not exist as particles, and are actually wave systems, revealed and explained by quantum and wave mechanics.[6, 8]

The assumed fundamental particles—quarks, bosons, gravitons, and monopoles—are indeed mere mathematical constructs. For otherwise, as constituents or bearers of the general phenomena and forces, these particles should be present everywhere, seen as absolutely clear and simple in every observation. In truth, they have never been observed directly and have been only inferred from extremely rare observations under extraordinary conditions.

Moreover, all the "primary" particles appear to be not elemental at all. They exhibit causal variations; and this requires still further elemental causal constituents, still more particles, to account for the variations.

This confusion is inevitable as long as the unifying cause is not seen. The one causal source, the Field, can create various particles as well as make them perform in different ways, under various conditions, as we indicated. But for the modern physicist each different performance again requires a separate particle.

For instance, quarks now are supposed to have their own elemental constituents: prequarks, maons, quinks, or rishons; so far there are ten kinds of them.[12] They are supposed to account for the increasing number of "flavors" and "colors" of quarks. Further, quarks have properties of "charm," "truth," and "beauty" to be similarly accounted for. Equally varied are the "up" and "down" quarks, and even the "strange" quarks and "naked bottom" quarks.[12]

More kinds of quark effects are discovered continuously, requiring various other elementary constituents as particles. Also, each kind of quark or element has its negative quark or element as a negative particle.

In fact, any one of the assumed two hundred fundamental particles would require still further, more detailed, elemental constituents, further particles, in the same way. If the one simple causal source is not recognized, then any one of its naturally varied effects becomes, in its mathematical formulation, a causally irreducible phenomenon. Hence the constantly increasing number of kinds of elemental particles.

Also, physical phenomena become *causally unpredictable or indeterminate* if their cause is not recognized. Their causation certainly becomes imperceptible or unreal, because their cause, the Field, a continuum of force, is as imperceptible as all force. This is typically illustrated by quanta, which are constituents of everything else according to modern physics.[5, 11]

Quanta are found to be only mathematical constructs of *waves of mere probability*, *"vibrations of nothingness,"* which consist of nothing and are dealt with as merely theoretical concepts.[11] The "quantum weirdness" is constantly reaffirmed;[5, 12] quanta have no more reality than mental symbols.

This is inevitable because the quanta are waves that result from interaction between the Field and matter as fluid media. The Field is a nothingness as force, and matter is dynamically similar to it. They both acquire their reality only by virtue of the opposition or counteraction between them; this should be clear also from the Newtonian law about force and counterforce, as was indicated before.

We shall see later why all "particles"—and most clearly the electrons—consisting of quanta are waves or wave systems while they are in a normal state of action or in transition, but become particles when they are isolated and in a static state. Thus the static, "real" particles disappear when they perform normally. This has led to the theory of uncertainty, which is probably the most typical, most often invoked tenet of modern physics.[8, 10]

The ghostlike unreality, or uncertainty and indeterminacy, in theoretical physics *could not possibly be due to some inherent mystery of the physical reality.*

Man exists as a physical being. There is total sameness between this existence of man and that of the physical world. Human understanding or thinking is a process of man's ultimately physical existence; in fact, men can think only in terms of matter, as we have seen from the astounding uniformity of the laws of languages.

Indeed, the general, basal, simplest forms of thinking, reflected in logic and mathematics, are perfectly, directly congruous with the terms of existence of physical phenomena.

Almost everything in physics can be dealt with mathematically. This means that the most fundamental, universal terms of human thinking, and thus of the existence of man, are sufficient here. Mathematics are the same for every man because they derive from the most basal, common ways in which all men exist as natural, physical beings.

In the end, we may repeat that recognition of the Field requires no assumption of new hypotheses or of new anything. It requires only the abandonment of man's already clear prejudice against recognizing the "negative," causal sources of his positive values.

Without this prejudice the Field becomes evident from phenomena of matter as easily as a dark blackboard becomes evident from white marks on it, or the sand of the beach from footprints in it, which reveal also its properties.

It is clear that force determines everything in the universe. But force is a nothingness to man because the universal force, the Field, is the causal, "negative" source, the opposite, of man's "positive," exclusive world of matter, the world of his every primordial value.

The very universality of the homogeneous Field, as the universally expanding and self-equalizing force, makes it totally undifferentiable, unknowable to man—much more so than is atmospheric pressure. Also, moving bodies cannot experience any hindrance, drag, or any other differentiable, knowable effect from the Field because it is the Field itself that moves them.

Similary, no differentiable, knowable effect of the Field can be revealed directly by any material phenomena, because it is the Field itself that creates all physical phenomena by moving matter, in various ways, even in instruments during experiments.

Also, the total "negativity" of the Field in universal causation makes it unreality itself to man. The more intense a value is to man, the more impossible is to him its causal, "negative" source, which actually creates the value. And no cognitive value is more intense for man than that of the reality of matter. The cognitive value here is decisive because the problem here is one of knowledge—of perceiving the universe as man knows it.

But even man's sense of other values about matter reveals the existence of the Field, if opposite-value causality is understood.

Man feels matter, in and around him, as expressing firmness, stability, permanence, or strength. None of these values, as properties, would be possible without a causal background of opposite properties. Matter as "energy" would dissipate itself into a loose, ever-changing, and powerless diffusion without the opposite properties of the Field—without counterpressure, equal persistence by a permanent opposition or counterforce.

If we find in matter values such as affirmation of freedom or self-realizing existence, they require opposite-value backgrounds of restriction and of potential non-existence as a "threat" of annihilation by opposition. Freedom without restriction is nonsensical. So is existence without nonexistence. (It is said that man became aware of his own existence when he realized the possibility of his annihilation or death.)

In a word, whatever values, cognitive or affective, we have about matter as our "positive" reality, they derive from their value opposites inherent in the "negative" Field. Of course, it is impossible for man ever to accept a universe governed by such opposition and negativity, by oppression and the potential of annihilation, which are the properties of the Field as the dominant causal opposite.

Automatic Causal Explanation of the Particle-Wave Dilemma

The practical proofs of the reality of the Field lie in the causal explanations that follow from it, for the fundamental physical phenomena which have remained admitted mysteries in the modern theory of physics. We may start with the *particle-wave dilemma*. It is probably the most discussed mystery in physics.

As particles are discoverd to be waves, scientists are faced with the mystery of nothing being something. For under the present views, these waves are in and of nothingness as empty space. In the simplest case, the photon is a mere wave of emptiness but also a quantum of matter.

Thus the particle-wave duality implies that something is there and is not here at the same time—that the "box is full and empty."[9] Einstein wondered how a "corpuscle [can] have anything to do with a wave"; he viewed even photons as particles.[1, 13]

The explanation is simple and automatic if the Field-matter opposition is recognized. *A wave in any medium is a propagation of a discontinuity or emptiness in it. But "emptiness" in the Field is automatically a quantum of matter as the opposite of the Field.* (Emptiness in anything is an opposite of it, in terms of being.)

A discontinuity or "emptiness" in the Field results where the Field extends itself while thrusting into matter to absorb matter enrichment that has resulted from excess expansion of matter, of its "particles." This is most cleary evident from the way light and radiation work.

When the Field thrusts into matter, it creates a loosening or "emptiness" behind. This then is the beginning of the wave in the Field as a medium. The "emptiness" is propagated further and further by the wave, *as in any medium.*

Of course the two persisting opposites, the Field and matter, can merely move or shift each other, continuously, each winning at one point exactly as much as it loses at another. They cannot annihilate each other; if they could they would not have remained as the two ultimate, permanent opposites through endless time.

The opposite shifts and movements, between two equal, opposite, fluid media, create all kinds of oscillations or waves. In fact, all matter "particles" exist and work as waves or wave systems, according to modern quantum and wave physics. Matter in any form is the opposite of the Field—an emptiness in it. And the two equal, fluid opposites can interact only by way of uniform oscillations or waves.

Any fundamental unit of matter—atom, nucleon, electron, or photon—has been discovered to be a wave system or a wave.[8, 9] Quantum mechanics explains all effects and forms of matter in terms of waves. Schroedinger and de Broglie offered explanations of all "particles" as wave systems.[8, 9] Heisenberg and Bohr worked out equations for dealing with these systems both as particles and waves.[9, 10] Here we have to explain *how atoms are created and how they work.*

The Field, surrounding matter everywhere and acting as its opposite force, evidently compresses it. The compression of atoms is a universal fact and one of the main, admitted mysteries in physics.

Atoms are created as the Field surrounds and presses into masses of matter. If the mass is large it breaks up, is divided by the Field. The division goes on to the point where the resulting spheres can resist further breaking up.

The smaller a sphere of the fluid matter, the greater is its relative resistance to the Field, because its surface, as the area of resistance, increases, in relation to its mass, as it becomes smaller. For similar reasons smaller spheres, grains, or bubbles of any mass break up less easily.

The resulting spheres of matter, the primordial, hydrogen atoms, are all uniform because the Field pressure is the same everywhere.

Conversely, if quanta of matter are smaller than the hydrogen atom they join together, under reciprocal gravitational attraction, to the limit of the hydrogen atom. Within that limit the Field cannot break them up. Thus photons and other bits of matter in space create new hydrogen atoms, which are known to be in space everywhere. (The causally mysterious, recently discovered, universal "Dark Matter"[12] is explainable as a world of particles that have not yet accumulated into completed, primordial, hydrogen atoms capable of emitting light or radiation.)

Hydrogen constitutes 90 percent of all normal matter in the universe and is far more prevalent in the space between stars. Such new atoms are not regularly created on earth, where the generally impoverished, "burnt-out" matter absorbs all loose quanta such as photons or electrons.

The larger, "burnt-out" atoms are created under specific conditions during the creation of stars and planets, when violent, opposite chain reactions create implosive pressures by the Field stronger than its usual pressures. Then the Field compresses the hydrogen and other small atoms into larger ones to gain from them the well-known "packing loss" or "packing fraction."

Each atom, consisting of fluid, elastic mass, has a margin of compression, the electron, by which it exerts its normal, balancing counterpressure against the Field. When two such atoms are compressed into one, they can be managed, kept in balanced compression by the Field, with one margin of compression, while the other is taken away by the Field. The new balance established between the Field and atom is then maintained by the always dominant, surrounding Field.

The new, multi-unit atoms can be further compressed by the Field in the same way. *Heavier and heavier atoms are thus created.* Explanations here, as elsewhere, become simple if the fundamental, equally simple, causal force is visualized. (We have explained that the reality behind mathematical, complex equations can be only simple.)

Each newly created multi-unit atom becomes a sphere as the Field compresses it from all sides uniformly. The compressed units, the nucleons inside the atom, then take the form of spherical layers in it. This is their simplest, inevitable form under the spherical pressures.

The mass of each nucleon remains the same as it is in the primordial hydrogen atoms. For inside the atom as well the strength or effectiveness of the Field against matter remains the same. Each nucleon, as spherical layer, can still maintain mass to the universal limit at which it can resist further breaking up by the Field.

In fact, the spherical layers here can exert such resistance rather more effectively than the sphere of the hydrogen atom can. Their surface of resistance has proportionally increased. And just as smaller spheres or grains break up less easily, all forms of fluid mass are stabler if they have more surface in relation to their mass.

Even if, conceivably, the Field may momentarily break up the system of spherical layers, the same process would repeat itself. The mass of the layers would tend to revert to basic spherical units, but these would again be compressed by the Field to form the layers as the simplest, spherical forms in the spherical atom. This result is inexorable because the same pressures and masses are always there to act in exactly the same way as before.

In short, the nucleons always remain spherical layers, each maintaining the same unit mass that the primordial hydrogen atoms have, minus the packing loss—that is, an electron for each compression, as will be explained later.

Moreover, each nucleon, as a spherical layer, has *the same thickness or depth.* For, to the same extent that a more external layer becomes wider, its mass becomes freer, more able to expand and to occupy more room. The reason for this is the concentric pressures by the Field around the spherical atom. As the lines of these pressures, converging toward the center, become denser, more crowded near the center, the matter there becomes more compressed, more compact, and occupies less room.

The total effect is that the nucleons, while they are inside the atom, act as *spherical stationary waves* of the same mass and of the same length corresponding to the same thickness of the spherical layers.

However, the radiation waves that the nucleons yield have varied wave lengths, because the more external nucleons, as spherical layers, are larger in volume, and therefore render longer radiation waves. We will explain this in a moment.

Nucleons act as waves because the Field and matter are fluid media continuously opposing each other. Nucleons are *stationary*, or *standing* waves, since they form themselves within the fixed limits of the atom. Stationary waves, in any set, are always of the same wave length. Here in the atom they become invariable because their length, determined by the same thickness or depth of the layers, does not vary. They are also *spherical* waves, spherical layers in the atom.

The stationary wave nature of nucleons makes explainable their effects revealed in quantum physics. Quantum mechanics show all effects of nucleons, or of nuclear "particles," to be those of spherical stationary waves, of "standing waves, represented mathematically by the surface harmonics of a hypersphere."[5]

Einstein praised de Broglie's explanation of "particles" as systems of standing waves which measure only in integral numbers and can change only by jumps, as quantum theory requires. But Einstein pointed out that such a system cannot exist without a medium.[1] Atoms as spheres consisting of "vortex rings in a perfect fluid" have been explained already by Lord Kelvin.[6]

Indeed, quanta phenomena, particularly those revealed by light spectra, can be explained as effects of *systems of spherical stationary waves*.[6, 8] Only stationary wave systems can have effects always measurable, relatable in integral numbers. Also, radiation energy is released as discontinuous quanta, because waves, in any medium, have the effect of distinct oscillation impacts and of separate "spillovers."

The typical radiation measurements in squared numbers are due to the *spherical* form of the nucleons inside atoms. The nucleons are spherical waves, as layers. They produce radiation by shedding excess energy in the forms of subwaves, which have the same properties of stationary, spherical waves.

A more external subwave as a layer, when it is absorbed by the Field, requires longer time to be taken away because it is so much more extensive when it is more external. This creates a longer radiation wave. The ratios of the lengths of such waves are, again, those of squared quantities. The result is radiation waves, in the Field, of varied lengths measurable in squared ratios.

But the radiation waves, of varied lengths, still carry the same energy quanta. For, as we saw, the total mass of each more external layer, as wave or subwave, is the same as that of a more internal layer. This explains the mystery of the *precisely inverse relationships between the lengths of waves and their energy levels*: each of the different waves still carries the same quantum of energy or matter.

The usual explanations of atoms as consisting of nucleons in the form of particles do not correspond to reality, according to the founder of modern quantum physics, Max Planck.[2, 6] "The particle as imagined in the classic picture does not exist," in the words of Sir Edmund Whittaker.[6]

Significantly, the Nobel Prize for work on the structure of atom has been awarded to E. P. Wigner, J. H. Jensen, and M. G. Mayer, who have established its "shell model," which has its protons and neutrons arranged like onion shells, with nothing in the center.

A most important mystery in physics results from the fact that nucleons and electrons are wave systems operated by the Field.

When isolated outside the atom and not in transition, the electron is a spherical particle. The Field compresses it from all sides equally. But when inside the atom or in transition, the electrons are waves, operated by the Field as a medium of force.

Thus, the electron is a particle and is not a particle, is there and is not there. It disappears as particle when it is in action or movement. This is true of all nuclear "particles," though it has most clearly been observed for the electron as the only really active "particle" in atoms. Thus, it may seem that matter itself disappears, since matter is still identified with particles.

Such disappearance of nuclear particles in action has led to a wide mystery in physics, expressed in the general *Uncertainty Principle*. Physicists see the electron as being real, as a particle, only in its abnormal, isolated state, outside the atom. They cannot perceive it as real, as a particle when it is in its normal, wave state: then they cannot observe anything coherent of it because they are looking for a particle.

Therefore, it is argued that the very act of observing the electron in action disturbs it. This and similar arguments are hardly tenable, particularly since all "particles" inside atoms have become equally uncertain.

The same mystery applies to all nuclear "particles."[9] In the formulation by Louis de Broglie, an electron or any subatomic "particle can not be observed as long as it forms part of the system and the system is impaired once the particle has been identified."[10]

Identification here, of course, amounts to isolation of the subatomic particle outside the atom. Generally, this has led to the conclusion that "perhaps all the particles are generated in the disintegration process rather than existing preformed in the nucleus of the atom."[8]

The uncertainty observations are focused mostly on the electron, which is the only changing, active, subatomic "particle" offering practical effects, whereas the protons and neutrons are too stable to do so. According to the often-quoted statement by Sir James Jeans, "while a hard sphere takes up a very definite amount of room...it is as meaningless to discuss how much room an electron takes up as it is to discuss how much room a fear, an anxiety, or an uncertainty takes up."

The electron has been observed and measured as a particle in various experiments, notably by Sir Joseph Thomson and Robert A. Millikan. But conclusive experiments, beginning with those of Clinton J. Davisson, have shown electrons to be waves. The electron even passes through two pinholes simultaneously, as only a wave could do; and electrons form typical wave patterns, shown in electron-interference experiments.

Comprehensive theories, particularly by de Broglie, Schroedinger, and Heisenberg, have established the dual nature of the subatomic "particles."[8, 10] The yes-and-no theory of complementarity was formulated by Bohr to account for the dual effects of the subatomic particles, particularly the electrons.[7]

If electrons were particles inside the atom they would, naturally, be all uniform and behave in the same way. But as has been established, under the exclusion principle of Pauli, there cannot be in an atom two electrons having the same set of quantum numbers or the same behavior status.

This is what has to happen with spherical waves or layers in the atom, since there can be only one of them at each distance.

The mystery of the ghost-like nature of the electrons disappears when we consider what electrons are. When the Field compresses two lighter atoms, to create one heavier atom, it takes away one margin of expansion, as the packing loss, and leaves one, by which the new atom can still be managed or kept under balance by the Field. These margins are the electrons.

When two primordial units are compressed they can be viewed as one proton and one neutron, with one electron left, and the proton tending to regain the lost electron therefore being positively charged.

The electron that is left can also be taken away, as the Field further compresses lighter atoms into still heavier ones, each time gaining another packing loss. This is reflected in the atomic weights of elements. The packing loss is a well-known rule for explaining the atomic weights with their mass deficits of "packing fractions."

Throughout these compressions by the Field, the process is that of doubling up two smaller atoms at each compression, which takes away an electron. This doubling up determines the order of elements in the periodic table, characterized by patterns of even, doubled, and redoubled numbers of electrons or of atomic numbers.

If the compressed units do not double up easily, evenly, then more electrons remain in the atom and it is more active. For electrons are the only active subatomic particles. This degree of activeness of each element then determines its place in the periodic table.

When atoms are flooded with energy, the lost electrons as

potential margins of expansion can be regained, though they are lost again to the Field instantly. Thus all the electrons, as potentials, can temporarily appear, during radiation. But under normal conditions, *atoms have only the few electrons left in them* by the compressions during their creation.

In the varied cases of the creation of elements, the units that the Field compresses may not double up evenly, as when there are three of them instead of two or four. Then complete compression is not achieved. One extra electron is still left in the atom. This extra electron then makes the element more active, as the Field tends to take away this electron by compressing two atoms that have such electrons into a molecule. The process here is similar in principle to that of the creation of elements. The result is *chemical bonds.*

This process makes *causally* explainable, in many aspects, the periodic table of elements, which is dominated by double-number patterns of atomic numbers. Each period in the table ends with a number consisting of additions of two, eight, and sixteen atomic numbers. An element is more inert to the extent that the nucleons in it, or their doublings, showing as atomic numbers, double up evenly. If the doubling up is total, the element has no extra electron to be shared, no potential to form molecular, chemical bonds readily.

That is why an element theoretically having 18 or 54 electrons is as inactive as one having only two electrons. Otherwise, if the many electrons were actually present in the atom, they would make it exceedingly active, capable of sharing electrons in as many ways as there are electrons.

Elements are more inert to the extent that their atomic numbers can combine into the sets of 8 or 16—plus the basic set of two.[9] These sets, evidently, represent a simple doubling and redoubling of atomic numbers, at several stages. Atomic numbers, of course, indicate the number of primary compressions of the nucleons, as each proton results from one compression.

In any event, the properties of elements, determined by their electrons, depend on the simple patterns of progressive redoubling of compressions of the nucleons, as spherical waves, by the Field.

But if this simple process is not perceived, then it remains a mystery why these atomic number sets govern the inertness patterns of elements. Physicists have constructed the *electron shells* to explain these patterns. The shells are, admittedly, *mere fictions*. Nobody thinks that they actually, physically exist. Their existence would require a metaphysical, quite complex and intelligent predetermination.

The pivotal fact is that almost all *electrons in the atom are only potentially, not actually there.* They are merely potential margins of expansion of nucleons held together by the doubled and redoubled compressions by the Field.

That is why electrons in atoms have as little physical presence as "anxiety or uncertainty," though their potential to appear and act is real. It shows when an atom is enriched with excess energy. Then the atom regains, for short instants, the lost electrons, to lose them again to the compressing Field, which thus creates radiation.

In this process physicists observe the presence of electrons, but then are mystified why, generally, the electrons "take up no room" and do not act in any way. The fictitious shells are to explain the mystery. They supposedly keep the electrons bound or inactive in definite, intricate, predetermined ways.

Thus, we find a convenient description of a causation worthy of intelligent, metaphysical intervention, instead of a *simple causal* explanation of fundamental principles. The causal—that is, scientific—facts here are decisive. They explain the properties of elements, which determine what happens in chemistry and physics.

We indicated the *causal* reasons of these properties, of the inertness and activeness of elements, particularly of the sharing of electrons in the chemical bonds. Chemists and physicists have a tremendous practical knowledge of these properties. But the theoretical explanations offered are the admittedly fictitious, virtually metaphysical shells. In contrast, the concept of the Field provides a simple causal insight.

The central fiction in physics is the assumption that protons and neutrons, as "*particles*," are *physical spheres*, with electrons as smaller spheres orbiting around them. Bohr's theory is a main, last support for the concept of such orbiting electrons, though he had to admit that they also are waves in his yes-and-no theory of complementarity.[7]

Bohr speculated that electrons—by virtue of some naturally unexplainable system—are held in orbits having only the precise radiuses of squared whole numbers: 1, 4, 9, 16, 25, and so on; and that radiation is a product of electron jumps from one orbit to another.

The assumed process "is indeed a miracle, for when the jump

occurs, another entity is born or dies."[9] There is no explainable reason or physically imaginable cause inside the atom to account for such strictly, mathematically precise, and necessarily physical, predetermined orbits.

Also, the squared-number magnitudes of the orbits would hardly be conceivable if we tried to accept them as realities. Think of electron numbers in atoms approaching a hundred and each electron supposedly having its own squared-number orbit. Would not the orbits and thus the atoms reach sizes measuring in thousands of multiples of the basic orbit? Atoms do not have such proportionally immense size differences.

At the same time, emissions by spherical stationary-wave systems create exactly the relationships of the squared whole numbers. We shall see later how the nucleons as spherical waves can account in full for such relationships as well as for the other peculiarities of the radiation of quanta and their wave lengths.

The complex, specially invented complementarity theory of Bohr was unnecessary: the "electron wave picture fits all facts."[9] There is "no real existence for either Bohr's or Rutherford's atom model," wrote Schroedinger.[8]

In the famous *experiments by Rutherford* or by Compton, particles were assumed as the interacting units. Consistent agreement about particle interactions were discovered. But equal agreements would have been found if waves had been assumed as the interacting units.

Quantum physics shows that all movement is an effect of waves anyway. Moreover, Compton found that photons and X-rays as well interact in the same "particle" pattern. But they are clearly waves. Einstein also found similar complete agreements in actions by photons, which he viewed as particles though they are waves.

In the Rutherford's experiments, a stream of alpha particles passed through metal foil but some rare particles—about one in a hundred thousand—"shot" back, at narrow angles. Rutherford said the effect was like that of shooting bullets through a tissue paper and then seeing some of the bullets shoot back.[9] Moreover, the "shooting" back occurred with long delays, sometimes ten billion times longer than the mere collisions of particles would permit. In similar experiments, performed notably by Joliot-Curie, alpha particles could be observed radiating out of the foil half an hour after the experiment.

The absorption and re-emission of "particles" as wave systems is the explanation here as in most phenomena of moving matter quanta. The mere passage of hard spheres through the "tissue paper" could not explain the shooting back of the "particles."

A beam of rapidly moving nuclei, as well as of electrons, behaves in the same way as a light beam of photons,[8, 10] which are waves that are transmitted by the "empty" space or are absorbed and re-emitted by particles as wave systems.

It is incongruous to assume that a photon has traveled as a particle all the way from the sun. Or that electrons run all through the long wires, though the amount of electrons supplied at one end of a wire does appear at the other.

Evidently, matter quanta are transmitted, by the Field, as waves, or run by way of local absorptions and re-emissions by particles as wave systems. Even in the Wilson chamber, particles passing as mere physical, infinitesimal spheres could never create the tracks. A process similar to ionization, to absorption and re-emission, produces straight tracks in the uniform bubble chamber, much like ionization creates the path of lightning in nature.

The persisting concepts about subatomic particles as spheres or balls of mass have stranded us with explanations of matter that are as specious and convoluted as were the Ptolemaic inventions.

Thus, interpretations of Rutherford's experiments have led to accepting the *atom as an emptiness* with its electrons as small as bees in a football field, or nucleons as small as softballs in it.

The argument that the electrons circle so fast as to form a shield does not help. The electrons of other atoms would be moving equally fast, and therefore would penetrate the shield and enmesh the atoms instantly. In the confusion electrons are often viewed as being similar to clouds.[9]

The modern, quantum theory and wave mechanics have forced physicists to recognize that all "particles"—atoms, nucleons, electrons, or photons—are wave systems or waves. Atoms and the "particles" in them become explainable as formations of compressed wave systems. But physicists can offer only mathematical, admittedly mysterious, causally unexplainable descriptions. The reason is that atoms as such compressed wave systems and their actions are utterly inconceivable as realities if the Field as the compressing medium is not recognized.

Causal Explanation of Gravitation, Electromagnetism and the Mechanics of Light

The reality of the Field becomes particularly clear and concretely meaningful when we look at the admitted causal mysteries of the main physical phenomena of gravitation, electromagnetism, or light.

These phenomena are determined by something in the "empty" space. Every physicist recognizes this, directly or implicitly. But nobody ever perceives this something in the space, though it must be very strong or dense to create effects such as the force of electricity or the speed of light. Recognition of the Field here becomes compelling.

As we explained, the Field could be a thousand times stronger and denser than any substance, yet still would remain a total nothingness, even under investigation by any imaginable instrument or experiment. For it is the Field itself that causes all physical phenomena or effects by variously moving the matter everywhere, even within instruments; and anything moved by a uniform medium can have no experience of the medium regarding the movement.

GRAVITATION. Physicists recognize that the greatest directly evident mystery in physics is gravitation. Objects here are moved and connected by something around them which is not there in man's view. A physics professor, supposedly, started his course by showing his students a falling sphere and telling them that this was the greatest miracle.

Even Newton himself remained mystified by the fact that objects can attract each other without anything between them. Accordingly, he stated that the force of gravitation is a result of creation by God—of supernatural intervention.

The causal explanation of gravitation is clear and automatic as soon as the Field is recognized. Think of the pressures of the Field coming toward a planet from all over the space, If you are close to or on the planet, the pressures coming from the space behind the planet do not reach you or act on you, directly and fully. Thus, there is slightly less of the Field pressures coming from the side where the planet is.

Since matter and radiation are compressed and driven by the Field pressures, they gravitate or incline toward the planet, from the side of which there is slightly less of the Field pressures.

The force of gravitation is weak, in comparison with forces that compress atoms and create electricity or light waves. This is so because the Field pressures are all around a planet and everywhere in it as they surround atoms in it. Thus there is only a slight shadow of one-sideness of the Field pressures around the planet.

Also, understandably, the force of gravitation decreases quickly as you move away from the planet. The decrease is proportional to the generally established square of distance from the planet. This is exactly what should be expected from the shielding effect.

Physicists have calculated that the evidently similar shielding of assumed gravity rays or gravitation particles would make the force of gravitation decrease at the same ratio of the square of distance.[9] Sir Edmund Whittaker refers to calculations by Le Sage.[6] According to the theory of Le Sage, gravitation results from shielding off, by matter, of impacts of "ultramundane" particles that move from all sides with enormous velocity.[6]

Evidently, this would have the same effect as the shielding against the Field pressures. And the calculations by Le Sage showed that the shielding effects would decrease with distance at the same above ratio as the force of gravitation does.[6] But the assumed particles, or rays and waves of gravitation, have remained mere fictions.

The curvature of space is the cause of gravitation according to Einstein's theory. He stated that this curvature is as concrete as are depressions on a bowling green. Then what is curved in the space must be equally concrete.

Nothing like that can be found in space, unless the curvature is that of the Field, as a universal, unperceivable, yet strong or dense field of force. We shall see in a moment that the gravitational-pressure gradations in the Field are identical with the curvature. We have indicated that force must always be the decisive factor in gravitation. Even with the assumption of the curvature of space, there has to be a force to move matter along the curvature.

In his theory of General Relativity, Einstein assimilated gravitation to inertia. From his descriptions, illustrated by accelerating elevators, one can only conclude that we or gravitating objects must be accelerating away from earth. This is hardly conceivable for gravitation on earth or on any other body.

Maxwell, whose equations are generally accepted in the Relativity Theory, constructed the gravitational attraction from forces in the space around matter. He found that this space or medium possesses "an enormous positive intrinsic energy, and that the presence of dense bodies influences the medium so as to diminish this energy."[6] He abandoned the explanation because he was "unable to understand in what way a medium can possess such properties"[6]—clearly inherent in the Field.

Gravitational, "shielded" areas, with their one-sided, weaker Field pressures, affect all physical phenomena, governed by the Field. Radiation, resulting from thrusts by the Field into atoms and carried by it, becomes weaker and one-sided here, however slightly. A result is the red-spectrum shift in radiation coming from massive stars.

Of course, radiation, propagated by the Field's pressures, inclines toward such stars when it passes them close by, because from their side there is slightly less of the Field's pressures. All movements, as results of Field pressures, are similarly affected. Thus centripetal attraction becomes explainable without thinking of "strings" of attraction.

The main effect of gravitation is, of course, the straight movement of matter by the gravitational "pull." Actually, there is no pulling or attraction, just as there are no "strings." Matter particles being compressed by the Field from all sides simply slide toward that side from which the Field pressures are less strong. Denser matter slides gravitationally with more force, more weight, because such matter is exposed to more of the Field pressures on its more numerous or more massive particles.

The difference between the general and the *gravitational acceleration* is a curious problem. It was raised by Einstein in his theory of General Relativity, in which he tried to assimilate acceleration and gravitation. Whereas a big or heavy body requires a greater or longer-applied force in order to be accelerated, all bodies big or small, heavy or light, fall with the same, instant acceleration.

Evidently, the force that makes bodies fall is already inside them, around their particles, constantly, and therefore does not need to be added or accumulated from the outside as in general acceleration. Consequently, gravitation is hardly explainable by concepts of any *outside*, matter-like forces or conditions, such as gravitational waves and gravitons or the necessary forces moving objects along the curvature.

The Field around bodies such as stars has gravitational pressure gradations in itself which surround the bodies. This is a natural result of the shielding off, by the stars, of the Field pressures around them: the shielding effect there gradually decreases with distance from the shielding body. These *gradations* can be viewed as constituting a space structure *identical with the curvature* of space.

By using the concept of the curvature of space Einstein could explain phenomena like the abnormal revolutions of the perihelion of Mercury. The concept of Field pressure gradations, identical with the curvature, could be sufficient for the same kind of explanations.

There is no need to attribute, as physicists sometimes do, any mystifying properties to the curvature of space. Spherical curvature of the whole universe has been a main mystification.

It is speculated that a cosmic voyager traveling long enough in the universe in a straight line would return to his starting point. But there are perfect spherical curvatures of space around our planet or sun. Still we can travel, within these complete curvatures, in a straight line without any indications of the assumed, inevitable return to the starting point. Thus there is no physical proof that travel in a straight line in the assumedly curved universe would be impossible.

And it is pointless to claim that a new, different geometry would apply to a curved universe. If everything around us became universally curved or twisted in any one way, we would not notice any change and our logic of mathematics or geometry would not change. In a world that universally became larger in some way or aspect, all relationships would be changed in the same way and nothing would be changed. The geometric logic that straight lines are always different from curved lines would still hold even in a supposedly curved universe. Geometrically, a voyage straight out of such a curvature would still be possible.

In sum, gravitation is clearly a product of forces in the "empty" space that are as concretely strong or dense as gradations on a bowling green, in Einstein's comparison. At the same time, these structures of curvature must be as imperceptible or undiscoverable as is nothingness.

Only the Field as the universal medium of force can have such concrete yet unperceivable structural gradations in itself as "nothingness." Force of any strength or form is a nothingness to man, though it determines everything in and around matter, and therefore must be as strong or "dense" as matter.

Above all, the causal explanation of gravitation is automatically simple, as we have seen, if one recognizes how the Field's pressures coming from all over space are, necessarily, shielded off by bodies of matter.

ELECTRICITY AND MAGNETISM. Physicists know that "the energy of electric charges and currents is not situated in the conductors with which they are most obviously associated but is diffused throughout the surrounding medium."[6] This "energy" and its source must be very strong considering that electric currents can be increased to high voltages.

But physicists do not find anything of that kind in the space surrounding the conductors. Thus electricity remains causally a mystery: its concrete, physical cause is not recognized.

A self-evidently simple causal explanation of electricity would come from insight into the Field. Electricity, evidently, works by discharging or equalizing differences in electron charges. Of course these charges, as all effects in matter, are determined by the pressures of the Field. And since the charges are, clearly, equalized by the "surrounding medium," the equalization must be that of the pressures in the Field.

Indeed, equalization by the Field of its own pressure differences is automatic for it as a medium of fluid force. Any fluid medium equalizes pressures within itself. Further, we should keep in mind that electrons are the only source of regularly inducible changes in matter. Electricity is, therefore, the only regular phenomenon of the Field's pressure equalization.

In short, *electricity is the effects of automatic equalization by the Field of differences of its pressures* that correspond to the differences of the charge or enrichment of matter with electrons.

When matter is enriched, by the addition of electrons, it is more compressible. The Field presses in, thus forcing the electrons along the conductor until the pressures, and matter enrichment, are equalized throughout the Field, inside and around the conductor. The result is electric current as well as fields and movements in the Field around the conductor.

Converse inequality is created by matter losing electrons, in which case the process is merely reversed. Thus the polarity of electricity, as a source of opposite electric effects, results either from surplus or from lack of electrons in conductors.

As the Field presses into conductor it leaves instantaneous loosenings behind, which create fields and waves. Naturally, if other matter is passed through or exposed to such fields or waves, its atoms "expand," acquire electrons for short instants, because of the loosenings. It thus becomes enriched, therefore compressible by the Field, which then creates secondary electric effects. This makes explainable the various phenomena of electromagnetic fields and transmissions by such fields, as well as the electric inductance.

Naturally, material objects situated close to electric currents are moved, slightly, by the different pressure changes in the Field and by the loosenings in it. The result is various kinetic and "gravitation" effects within the fields around electric currents.

It should be emphasized that the Field works toward the equalization or equilibrium with unlimitedly "skillful" success, as if by a clever maneuvering of all possibilities. The Field can do so because it operates and interconnects everything everywhere. Think, for comparison, of how "cleverly" water equalizes its level in connected channels or vessels. The connections within the Field are incomparably more extensive.

Objects with *charges of the same pole are moved apart* by the Field because this leads toward equalization, through dissipation, of the pressure inequality accumulated where such objects are together. In any compressing fluid medium its pressures tend to dissipate clustered masses that differ from its equalized-pressure conditions.

Conversely, two objects with *opposite charges are moved closer together* because this lessens pressure inequality overall; a balance in one confined area is created from imbalance at two locations.

The automatic "skillfulness" shows here as the Field works to connect the opposite charges, to discharge them, to eliminate them as inequalities. The Field can do this because as a universally connecting medium it makes the charges work almost as if they were already in contact, except that the actual discharge is not yet effected.

It is interesting to note that such electric phenomena can be shown to resemble those of dynamics in fluids. Bodies with cavities through which liquid flows, and bodies pulsating in unison in a liquid, exert mutual forces on each other similar to those of electric attraction and repulsion.[6]

Expectedly, if the Field cannot connect bodies to attain equalization in charges, it dislocates, at least, the charges within the bodies. One effect is that a neutral body acquires, in its parts facing the charged body, a charge that is opposite to that of the charged body.

Here the Field balances or compensates for the pressure

inequality that the charge constitutes: the inequality is matched by an equal opposite inequality, within the parts of the body that are closest to the charge. Then, as one side of the neutral body contains all the positive charges, the other side is left negatively charged, or vice versa. This makes causally explainable the various phenomena of electric induction.

Interesting is the fact that no electric effects arise in hollow spaces inside conductors. Scientists, though, know that space, not conductors, creates electric effects.

Evidently, it is the immense Field pressures accumulating through vast space that determine, overwhelmingly, all effects. The Field pressures from the smaller space inside the conductor cannot prevail in any way against those immense outside pressures.

MAGNETS. If the Field pressures, while creating a current, have to pass through a metal, they dislocate its particles, make "pathways" in it. This turns the metal into a magnet. Physicists know that magnets result from the deformation of metal by current, on a scale of submicroscopic domains.

Naturally, these "pathways" are directional: they make the passage of the Field pressures easier in that direction in which the original pressures were moving when they created the "pathways." One can think here of a river stream smoothing down, by slanting or bending, the obstacles in it in the direction in which the stream flows. Indeed, the magnetic deformations even exhibit herring-bone patterns under the microscopic iron-powder method of inspection; a herring-bone formation facilitates movement in one direction.

Anyway, magnets are metals deformed by electric flow, actually by the *directional* Field pressures that create the electric flow. Some metals retain the deformations even after the electric flow has stopped. They become permanent magnets. The directional deformations in a magnet constitute directionally unbalanced or *asymmetric* abnormalities in matter.

Naturally, the Field, operating all matter and establishing balanced normality in it everywhere, tends to align together *opposite directional* imbalances, to attain a more balanced, normal operation of matter in the metal. This explains the *magnetic attraction*—even at a distance, since the Field interconnects everything.

Nonmagnetized ferromagnetic matter is attracted because it offers at least a half equalization of the asymmetry. This makes it act as a magnet of the opposite pole, after each asymmetry close to the magnet becomes automatically impressed further and further on.

Natural magnets are created by the perennial Field pressures that equalize differences in the enrichment of matter on earth. Matter is richer in electrons in the warmer zones than in the cold polar regions. The result is electric flows between a pole and warmer regions. Such flows show in the Northern and Southern auroras, and are effected by the Field pressures, which create the magnetic "pathways" in lodestone.

The same Field pressures that subsequently pass through such "pathways" then make magnetic needles point to the poles. Of course, the magnetic "pathways" are, in the main, perpendicular to the electric flow. That is why magnetic needles around a conductor arrange themselves crosswise to it—which gives the wrong impression, as if they were moved by forces circling the conductor.

Also, if you slice a magnet perpendicularly to its polar direction, each thin slice exhibits the full force of the magnet because it embodies full lengths of the perpendicular "pathways." Further, compass needles are made elongated so that they have more layers upon layers of such "pathways" and therefore point more steadily to the pole.

We should keep in mind that currents are created by the excesive presence as well as absence of the electrons, by enrichment as well as impoverishment of matter. Now, due to climatic changes the impoverishment of matter at the earth poles can become more impressive than is the enrichment of matter in the zones away from the poles. If that happens the electric polar currents reverse. It then may seem that the "magnetic poles" of the earth have reversed. Discoveries about such reversals in the past have remained mysteries causally.

A practically important effect of electromagnetism is the automatic tendency of the Field to align magnets, or rather their "pathways," in more convenient ways when the Field pressures again have to pass through them while creating current.

It is easier for these Field pressures to move through a magnet when they can move along its "pathways" in the direction in which the "pathways" were directionally formed. Conversely, it is hard for such Field pressures to move through magnets in opposite ways or crosswise to the "pathways." The Field then tends, "skillfully" as always, to make the most convenient alignments.

These tendencies or forces in the Field can be exploited to operate *electric motors*. The mechanical problems then are how best to arrange positions and movements of magnets and current so that this tendency of the Field to align or move the magnets is heightened and accumulated more effectively.

Of course, similar results of movement are attained also by the conductor moving along with changing magnets, with the changing magnetization of metal by current. The decisive fact is that the Field, governing and interconnecting everything, creates movements while it "skillfully" effects arrangements for the best flow of its pressures through the magnetic "pathways."

In all cases, the position of the magnets or the direction of the magnetizing currents has to be continuously changed or reversed. At each moment the Field arranges the most favorable ways for its pressures. The Field would tend to maintain each such arrangement. This would create immobility.

The changes or reversals are needed to disrupt, again and again, each such arrangement so that the Field has to renew it continuously and thus keep the electric motor running.

Converse effects are used in *electric generators*. Here variations in Field pressures around conductor are created by passing the conductor along magnets so that their "pathways" hinder or vary pressures of the Field along the conductor. The variations in the Field pressures along the conductor automatically lead to electron-enrichment differences in it, which produce current.

Force is required to move the conductor in ways that create as many such variations as possible, contrary to the equalizing Field pressures. Each equalizing effect has to be followed, again and again, by a condition of unequal Field pressures requiring more equalization.

The equalization, of course, is current. The technical problem is to create a continuous "need" for the Field to effect the equalization repeatedly, so that it can be accumulated as current.

Our explanations of electricity and magnetism agree with the more detailed and precise observations by physicists about electric and magnetic forces or their lines and fields. The greatest authorities, Faraday, Maxwell, and Lord Kelvin, had to assume very complex lines, vortex filaments, tubes, whirls, spheres, or wheels of ether to have some causal explanation.[6]

It is even worse not to see any general causal sources. Then skillful intelligent creation and maintenance—by angels—would have to be assumed for each one of the precise and complex electric or magnetic phenomena everywhere.

Physicists know that something in the "empty" space, or the ether, is the source of electric and magnetic effects.[6] But the universal human prejudice against the "negative," causal sources of our "positive" universe precludes even physicists from recognizing the "nothingness" as reality.

Otherwise it would not be too difficult to accept that a totally universal causal medium of force can be as undiscoverable as nothingness, yet can have all the necessary properties of immense strength or density. We may repeat here that all force is a nothingness for man but is as strong or dense as the matter which it clearly controls.

Of course, what we have indicated, only in principle, in our rudimentary, pioneer explanations, could be demonstrated incomparably better by expert physicists if theoretical physics recognized the otherwise simple fact that "nothingness" as the field of force can be a concrete, strong causal source.

This would imply an impossible acceptance of nothingness as reality. But actually it would amount to merely overcoming the generally obvious prejudice of man against recognizing the causal, negative sources of his positive values, cognitive as well as affective.

MYSTERIES OF LIGHT. We may as well start with the speed of light. It has become confusing causally and has led to endless mystifications, even about astronauts becoming younger when traveling at cosmic speeds.

Only a transmitting medium can make light travel always at the same speed. Otherwise the speed of light emitted from an approaching system would be increased and from a receding system decreased by the speed of such movements. When physicists had to abandon the incongruous ether as medium, they eagerly espoused Einstein's theory of relative speeds for different systems.

Einstein, as a mathematical genius, could work out his predictions without naming the "impossible" reality he was dealing with; mathematicians do not have to visualize the things their formulas apply to. His theory derives from a simple, basic principle, as all great discoveries do. This principle is the uniform speed of light—possible only with a transmitting medium.

Naturally, physicists wanted to add a visualized reality to the mathematical formulas. The curious theory of H. A. Lorentz and

G. F. Fitzgerald on the contraction of moving systems has been adopted. On fast-moving systems everything, including measuring sticks, is assumed to shorten and time processes to slow down. This theory—mostly recognized as a mere assumption—is not helpful.

Two *opposite* changes would be required to explain how the approaching as well as retreating systems compensate for the assumed changes in the speed of light. Thus both the slowing down and speeding up of time processes on moving systems would be required.

Of course, a mathematical formula can give both plus and minus at the same time, with a factor like the square root used in the equations of the speed of light. In the world of reality, however, the same factor or cause cannot have a greater and smaller, or a positive and negative, effect for the same event.

Nor can a system be assumed to be moving or standing still at the same time. Such assumptions have been used to obtain the same relative time effect with both approaching and receding systems as they supposedly contract.

Thus, it is argued that in the world of the Relativity Theory you can assume that system A is standing still and system B is moving or that the former is moving and the latter standing still. Then, in the case of approach, under the first assumption the time will be slower on system B; but in the case of retreat, under the second assumption the time will be slower on the system A. Since the times and speeds derive from relative comparison, the same speed of light thus can be shown to result in all cases.

But in reality, again, a system cannot be standing still and moving at the same time. Also it is not true that a system can be equally well viewed as moving or as standing still. A moving body is definitely different causally from a body that is standing still. In a moving body atoms and quanta operate, by the use of excess energy, in particular ways. In the body standing still they do not operate in such ways, or do not have energy to do so.

Yet the contraction assumption and, particularly, the slowing down of time processes on moving systems have been widely speculated about. This makes the theory appear mysteriously interesting, and men love mystery. Thus, science writers have speculated, extensively, about hypothetical *astronauts becoming younger* or aging little when traveling at speeds of light.

Certainly, such astronauts could catch up with a ray of light that passed us a time ago. They would thus recapture a tiny past effect. Pilots of supersonic planes can do the same with sounds, which are a bit more substantial. Yet the pilots do not regress in time or become younger.

Rays of light or sound waves are only tiny facets of reality, while the whole universe, with every atom in it, would have to be changed back to attain regression into past. Time is merely the relationship of changes, which are infinitely many.

By the way, time is often thought of as a spatial reality. This is a natural human delusion. Writers and philosophers have talked about permanence or continuity of time.

Even scientists have not escaped such notions, as can be seen from ideas such as time dilation or time as a fourth dimension. Actually time is never anything else than relationships of changes. If everything stopped changing for the equivalent of a thousand years, no time could be known as having passed. The only way to go "back in time" in regard to something—say, your room—is to change it back to what it was before.

Anyway, the fact is that *with a medium* the uniform speed of light, as everything else about radiation, is *automatically explainable.* Sound moves uniformly through the air as a medium, and no dilation or slowing down of time processes on moving systems—airplanes, for instance—has to be assumed to explain the uniform speed of sound emitted from such systems.

Only the frequency of sound changes, with an approaching or retreating airplane, under the Doppler effect. So does the radiation frequency from moving stars or galaxies. The Doppler effect is a key rule in astronomy. It works exclusively for waves, which are products of a medium and would be nonsensical without it.

An equally wide mystery about light is the dilemma of how light can be merely waves of empty nothingness and yet constitute matter quanta, the photons.

We have seen the simple, automatic explanation of the dilemma. Wave propagates a discontinuity as emptiness, in any medium. But bits of "emptiness" of the Field are automatically quanta of matter, of its opposite.

An additional mystery of quanta radiation is that its waves never lose their force. The waves conserve fully their energy quanta. Sir William Bragg has said it is as if a wave, created by dropping a plank 100 feet, having traveled 1000 miles, makes a plank out of another ship fly 100 feet high.[6]

The reason here is that matter, in the form of photons, can never be diminished by the Field. Matter and the Field are two terminal opposites that can resist each other forever; otherwise one of them would have long disappeared.

Also, the radiation waves do not change much structurally. The Field is so immensely strong that its waves slow down, become weaker or longer, only through cosmically immense distances. Practically they seem not to change at all. The simplest transmission of waves, as pressure differences, is by repeated pushes. Now, if you push a column of mercury at one end, you get equal, almost instantaneous push at the other end. The Field is, of course, more compact as well as more fluid than mercury or any substance.

Radiation is created when the Field squeezes off surplus matter quanta from an atom or thrusts into it to the same extent. As it does so, it leaves a discontinuity as emptiness or loosening behind, which is then filled in by a further thrust-in of the Field, creating a further discontinuity or loosening and so on, as in all waves. Of course, a discontinuity as emptiness in the Field is its opposite, matter—the quantum of matter, the photon.

A causally important fact here is that, unlike in other waves, there is no dispersion or loss in the waves of the Field. With its enormous pressure the Field holds tightly together the photons, the quanta of matter, but it can never diminish or annihilate them through absorption. For, in its every form, matter is the everlasting opposite of the Field.

Scientists have calculated that only an immense pressure, of millions of pounds per square inch, can propagate radiation waves at the speed of light.[9] The immense, cosmic force and density of the Field merely confirm that man's measurements in comparison with cosmic measures are minuscule—which is known to scientists already.

The enormous pressure of the Field as medium here is confirmed by another scientifically ascertained fact. Only a medium of this immense pressure or density can produce the transverse waves that constitute light radiation. An "elastic solid" transmits such waves.[9] Solids may have also longitudinal waves, but these decrease as the medium becomes softer and more elastic.[6, 9]

Here we should understand that the Field can have all the properties of solidity while being perfectly fluid. For there are no particles or divisions to interrupt its solidity. This has been excellently explained by Isaac Asimov, the noted master of clear, synthetic science, in his description of the "assumed light ether."[9]

The enormous pressure of the Field also explains *why radiation goes in a straight line.* In the process of repeated Field thrusts, each thrust comes by way of the closest, most "economic," or shortest distance—that is, from directly behind every loosening. The result is a straight wave path.

Waves act in this way in any medium. The immense pressures and total homogeneity of the Field insure that the path of light is inexorably straight.

Here we may mention again that prominent theories often fail to explain or note what is most commonplace and therefore most universal and important. The straight line of radiation seems too ordinary to need any special explanation. The same can be said of the straight path of the movement of bodies. All movement goes in a straight line. This is so obvious that a particular, causal explanation of it is not seen as necessary or worthy of consideration.

The same is true of all movement in general. What causes anything to move? We shall see in a moment that the Field creates movement in a way similar to that in which it creates radiation.

The strangest, most essential phenomena revealed by *quantum mechanics* are due to the standing-wave nature of "particles" and to the interaction between the Field and matter as opposing fluid media.

The standing-wave system within the atom, measuring in whole numbers, can change into another system of such waves, with a different set of such numbers, only by a jump or discontinuous transformation. No gradual transition is possible here. Each succeeding system can have only a distinctly different and precise order. There is no other form than the standing-wave system that the nucleons as waves can have within the confines of atom. And that entails all the precise ratios of integral numbers, which acquire squared relationships because these waves are spherical.

Also, the radiation created by wave systems can consist only of separate quanta. Waves by their very nature create separate, alternating oscillation beats. You can think here of the pounding by ocean waves against the beach or by sound waves against your eardrums.

Nucleons within atom are spherical standing waves. Matter surplus from them creates radiation, as the Field takes the surplus away. The surplus of the standing spherical waves is, naturally, spilled out by way of spherical subwaves having the same standing-wave patterns. The radiation, therefore, consists of discontinuous quanta, and its waves measure in the definite ratios of integral squared numbers typical of standing spherical waves.

The taking away of matter surplus by way of radiation waves results from interaction by the Field and matter. Here we may keep in mind that the Field and matter are two opposing fluid, though dense, media. Practically, *two such elastic opposites can interact only by way of oscillations or waves.*

The spherical wave within atoms, when it starts gaining matter enrichment, accumulates it, under intermatter gravitation, to the extreme at which it cannot further resist the pressures of the Field. At that point the Field moves in and takes away the matter enrichment. Both these processes are actually chain reactions, similar to those that operate during the creation of stars. We shall see, in explaining that creation, that it is inherent for matter to accumulate and to be dispersed in chain reactions.

Anyway, these opposite processes become oscillations that are exactly uniform because the strength of the counterpressures between matter and the Field is always the same. Each uniform wave or quantum resulting from such oscillations is the universal "quantum of action," known as Planck's constant. It is the ultimate energy grain of the universe.

These oscillations or reversals between extreme limits can be compared to the ways in which an elastic ball, musical chord, or surface of a drum oscillates between opposite extremes. The comparison of radiation with the vibrations of a drum was used by Einstein.[1]

In the end, this interaction between the Field and matter explains the *central facts of quantum physics*. Every quantum of radiation consists of the Planck's constant as the universal quantum of action. In fact, so do all quanta in the phenomena to be dealt with in quantum physics and constituting all action in the universe.

Quanta radiation derives from spherical waves inside the atom, because in this interaction the Field surrounds and compresses matter. These waves are also stationary waves, since they are contained within the atom by the compressing Field. The *stationary* and *spherical* structure of these waves explains the chief causally unexplained, virtually mysterious facts of quantum radiation.

Because of this structure, the radiation waves vary in length while still carrying the same quantum of matter, as we have explained. The measurements in whole numbers of radiation by an atom is due to the stationary form of its waves. And the sqaured-number ratios in this radiation are due to the spherical form of these waves. All spherically caused effects, in whatever medium, measure in these ratios.

A process which is the reverse of that of radiation is the *absorption of radiated quanta* by atoms they encounter. Evidently, the same relationships must apply here since the absorption process, as generally accepted, is that of *resonance* between similar harmonic systems.[1, 9]

The enormous strength and density of the Field make the resonance between systems, even at vast distances, perform as effectively as if there was no distance at all between them. That strength and density make the radiation wave conserve its force and structure, whatever the distance it may travel. Waves that find corresponding vacancies in an atom they meet are absorbed by it. The "resonance" here has been compared with that of musical instruments.[1, 9] Of course, the Field is immensely denser than the air which transmits musical waves.

Before we conclude, we have to explain how not only radiation but *all movement* results from quanta interaction of "periodic material waves."[2] Quantum theory recognizes that all movement is ultimately caused by quanta waves.[2, 11] Radiation ensues only when movement is stopped and the quanta have to be given off to the Field. Otherwise an energy-enriched particle moves endlessly, and the surplus never leaves it.

By the way, *movement* requires causal explanation more than anything else does, since it is the very first principle of action in the universe. But precisely because of its universality, movement seems to lack particular meaning and is too commonplace to evoke special interest.

Movement can be visualized as starting when the Field begins to "squeeze" away matter surplus from a particle. Before the surplus can be taken away, the particle naturally moves toward the separating surplus quantum, under "gravitational," inter-matter attraction. But as they start reuniting, the Field repeats its "squeezing" action, at the same side where the surplus hovers; and the movement by the particle is repeated.

In brief, *movement results from interactions between the Field and matter around surplus quanta*. These interactions create the "periodic waves" which do not leave the particle to become radiation waves unless the movement of the particle is stopped. The path of all movement goes in a straight line for the same reason that the path of light does, since movement results from action by the Field in the same, "most economic" way that governs radiation.

To conclude, we may note that light and all radiation particularly reveal the existence of the Field. Only a medium can have waves. Without a medium a wave is nonsensical; it becomes utterly inconceivable causally. Hence the admitted causal mysteries of modern physics facing a universe consisting of "waves of emptiness" revealed by quantum and wave mechanics. Understandably, explanations by concrete causes have been abandoned, in favor of mere mathematical descriptions.

The Field as the concrete, universally determining, invisible medium of force makes explainable the universe of all waves as well as the causally mysterious fundamental phenomena of quanta radiation, in simple ways.

We have seen this most significantly for the uniform speed of light and the strange revelations by quantum mechanics, or for the uncanny relationships between the lengths of waves and their energy levels, as well as for the radiation measurements in squared integers. Other causally mysterious aspects of radiation and quanta action also became explainable.

But the obviously erroneous common-sense view of the "empty" space as nothingness prevails. Men still believe that they can see clearly or move freely because the space is empty, though seeing requires waves, in a medium, and movement of any molecule, say in your arm, requires a moving action by the always unperceivable force, the Field.

Physicists do not seem to have escaped from this commonsense prejudice. Otherwise they would have immediately recognized the "nothingness" to be the universal causal reality, a medium of the unperceivable force that determines matter everywhere and uniformly in the cosmos, which is filled only with "nothingness."

Above all, it has been definitely established in modern physics that most physical phenomena are or consist of waves. And waves without a medium are simply not possible.

Physicists would recognize such a medium as present everywhere if they considered the obvious facts about the phenomena of force. They know that force determines everything in the universe while remaining for men a nothingness. Force is a strong or "dense" medium, since it governs and changes matter. And it can interact with matter by way of waves, since matter, as energy reveals itself to be dynamically similar to force; they are two fluid media acting as wave-creating opposites.

Unified Causality, Polarity, and Continuous Creation in the Cosmos

Probably the clearest proof of the concrete reality of the Field is a fact so universal that it is hardly noticed. It is the *unified causality* in the cosmos: the uniformity of causal laws and the causal interconnection of phenomena throughout the universe.

Everywhere in the universe, physicists find only the same forces, such as gravitation or electricity, and the same forms of matter, such as atoms or nucleons. Moreover, a happening at one point in the universe can have its effects at another; all points in the cosmos are connected.

The causal uniformity would be a supernatural, unimaginable miracle if a unified and universal causal medium did not exist. How could unconnected phenomena light years away exist and perform in always the same precise, multiple ways? Legions of angels would be required to operate and maintain continuously in exactly the same definite ways every single physical event or particle. For everywhere the forces and atoms are performing according to precise, complex mechanics or prescriptions, including the numerous "electron orbits," nucleic "shells," electric lines of force, and quantum numbers.

And events or phenomena on one star can have causal influences on another light years away. Obviously, everything in the universe is caused and connected by one causal medium. Only the Field as "nothingness" extends throughout the endless space and acts, as a uniform field of force, in the same way everywhere.

Indeed the *Field* as the medium of force that clearly governs everything while being the universal "nothingness" is *the only, fully sufficient explanation* of these otherwise inconceivable miracles. We have seen how all forces and forms of matter or "particles" are created and operated by the Field in automatically simple, uniform ways.

Any capacity is inherent in force, which clearly determines everything physical and is a nothingness for man. As clearly this "nothingness," the Field as medium of force, is everywhere in the universe and always the same. It is inevitable for the Field as force to become universal and homogeneously uniform.

The Field is thus the causal source and explanation of the greatest universal miracle of our cosmos, its unified causality. Physicists have followed their best scientific insights when they have continuously sought for a unified causal source, the unified field.

Philosophically, we can view the *Field as the ultimate, single essence* of physical reality. This offers a philosophically perfect explanation. No further questions remain, since the Field itself as the ultimate essence has not to be explained. Indeed, the Field can be held to be a fitting ultimate essence, while everything else, such as the material world, becomes only a slight imperfection or impurity in the Field. Is not *matter a mere impurity*, mere dust in the universe? The amount of matter is infinitesimal in comparison with the "nothingness" in the universe measuring in billions of light years.

In a word, the Field can be viewed as the ultimate reality, with essentially insignificant impurities in it, which constitute matter. This should make happy all philosophers and scientists seeking for one, final reality.

But for man the only reality is that of matter. Consequently, he views many of the effects coming from "nothingness," from the Field, as phenomena of matter having qualities opposite to the primary qualities of matter. Antimatter is a good example. Where the effects of the Field show up conspicuously they are merely seen as material phenomena of a negative kind, opposite to those of the more purely "positive" material world of man.

Opposition or polarity thus becomes a general feature of the physical cosmos that man knows, since the various effects of the Field appear indeed generally together with most material phenomena.

The main example here is the way scientists arrive at *negative particles* and *negative radiation*. Moves between the Field and matter constitute all effects of forces and of particles as waves or wave systems. But each move by the Field or by matter creates a similar, opposite move into matter or into the Field, each thrust producing an equal yield. Thus opposite, similar effects are inevitable.

Since physicists still assume that phenomena such as nucleons or electrons are particles, they have also to assume that their opposite effects, in the Field, are equally particles—*negative par-*

ticles. For certainly such opposite effects in the Field are as real and precise as are the effects in matter, and correspond to them in every way. No wonder that physicists discover what they believe to be antiparticles for all the more than two hundred currently known kinds of particles.

Here we may have to say a word about *the many newly discovered particles*. The number of such particles is increasing as physicists are using more powerful tools or huger cyclotrons for "smashing" atoms.

Such particles are the irregular and transitory, broken or disfigured forms of matter. They may be somewhat uniform if they are broken off under similar conditions, by cyclotrons of similar power. Yet they are viewed as fundamental, eternal particles. This is to be expected, as long as it is not recognized that various irregular, accidental, and transitory bits or quantities of matter are continuously formed into regular particles by the Field.

But should not physicists start questioning how nature, incredibly, can have so many complex, fundamental principles to create the hundreds of kinds of fundamental particles?

In a further, logical step, physicists have calculated that there is *antimatter* existing in the universe as generally as matter.[4, 5, 12] Antimatter or antiparticles are to be of the same particulate structure as matter. Antimatter should therefore be differentiable or knowable, as well as generally accessible. It should be as regularly observable as matter is. Actually, it has never been discovered as a separate reality—because it does not exist.

Only effects opposite to the material, "positive" effects are actually discovered in the observation of the various "antiparticles" or other "negative" phenomena.[4, 5, 12] Evidently, physicists are dealing here with the causal opposite of matter, without recognizing it.

Negative radiation results from interaction between the Field and matter in ways opposite to those of normal, photon radiation. In the radiation of light the Field thrusts into matter and creates in itself a ray of loosenings or waves. But under extraordinary conditions the usually dominant Field may, instead, have to yield or retreat.

This happens when compensations between various Field pressures require that, or when a new matter particle springs into existence, through the accumulation of matter quanta. Physicists have connected negative radiation with the creation of new atoms.[9] Here we may recall the explanation that the Field can be totally solid or compact while being perfectly fluid. Therefore, any cosmic wave, whether created by the Field's thrust or by its yield, travels through it perfectly, without dissipation.

Negative rays can also travel through matter, which acts as a medium in its own, particular way. A matter particle yields to the thrust of the negative ray, momentarily loses matter quanta, and compensates for them by absorbing matter quanta from the next particle, which does the same. Thus, matter here serves as a medium somewhat in the way the Field does in normal radiation.

In sum, *polarity of opposites* is a general, universally observed aspect of cosmos, because the Field and matter interact as two causal opposites in creating all physical phenomena.

The dominant opposite, the Field divides and deprives matter everywhere. The universe thus *seems to be governed by entropy* alone. But the opposite also is evidently happening. Otherwise the cosmos would have become lopsided, deprived of the renewal and variety which keep it continuing and acting, by uniform, opposite variations, in the same ways forever.

The physical universe has remained the same for billions of years. Light from galaxies billions of light-years away brings us evidence that this is so. Matter and the Field merely alternate in their permanent forms. We have indicated how the primordial, hydrogen atoms are created by photons or quanta of matter resulting from dominant, "destructive" action by the Field. This destruction and creation follow each other, in a world without end.

Creation in the universe is *endlessly continuous*. This is difficult for limited, finite man to accept. Endlessness is hardly thinkable for men, though it is the universal principle everywhere.

Men prefer to think of creation as of one act or one event. However, we should know by now that anything we can think of is causally endless, humanly ungraspable, and unsatisfactory. The universe is inconceivably infinite in time as well. If there were no renewal, no continuous creation, of new particles, the entropy and chaos in the universe would have annihilated all particles, during some astronomically long period of the cosmic infinity without end. Above all, who or what created eternal particles, once and forever?

The theory of *creation by the Big Bang* corresponds to the delusory human pursuit of definite, final knowledge. Men have to find a definite beginning of the world.

The main argument for the Big Bang is the assumed expansion

of the universe. Arguments, of course, are easily found for attractive solutions. In fact, the expansion of the universe is a mere scientific assumption, arising from the general source of mystification in physics, the failure to recognize the universal causal medium.

The lengthening of waves in a medium offers explanations here without the problematic, delusory assumption of the expanding universe. We have indicated that even billion-year-old light waves provide no evidence of fundamental cosmic changes. This could hardly be true of an expanding, evolving universe.

The expansion of the universe is assumed from the observation that light spectra from faraway galaxies shift toward longer wave lengths. The shift is attributed to the Doppler effect of such galaxies moving away from us. But *waves in any medium progressively lengthen while they travel long distances.*

This lengthening is very slight in the Field because of the enormous strength or density of the Field. But with immense distances waves lengthen even in the Field. Matter, as photons, though, remains undiminished by the Field. Only the mode of the Field action changes, as it slows down, infinitesimally, in its own performance.

In every medium, a similar slowing down creates the progressive lengthening of waves with distance. Extreme results of the wave lengthening in the Field are the radio waves, now increasingly discovered as coming from cosmic bodies of matter. (Of course, the lengthening of waves, in the Field, also results from the Doppler effect of some stars really moving, whatever their distance from us.)

The assumption of an expanding universe supposedly due to the Big Bang is untenable for various reasons.

It has been established that light waves from any source in the universe progressively lengthen precisely with its distance from us as observers. This confirms that all light waves, traveling through the Field as medium, lengthen simply in dependence from the distance they travel. Otherwise, with the assumption that this lengthening is due to the expansion caused by the Big Bang, we would have to believe that we are precisely at the central spot from which the Big Bang started.

For if we were on any side away from that spot, then stars and galaxies would be moving away from us at various rates. Physicists, certainly, do not believe that we are at the central spot of creation. Of course, *various explanations are offered* for our apparent centrality. They are specious and mystifying.

First, it is argued that a new logic or parameters from a fourth dimension should be used. The time-space dimension of the relativity theory is invoked, though Einstein was careful to explain that his use of the fourth dimension was not different from the general use of time data in weather maps or in train schedules.[1] Anyway, it is argued that in terms of the fourth dimension our universe would be like the surface of an expanding balloon. When such a surface expands, any point on it has indeed this centrality: all other points around it run away from it at uniform, progressive rates.

But why should the four-dimensional parameters conveniently have this balloon effect, and only for one phenomenon needing explanation? Instead, a change in dimensions would logically have strange effects as multiple and varied as events and things in the world. Also, we have seen that this assumed new geometry of a curved universe is pointless. Moreover, any actual, three-dimensional curvature of our universe would be irrelevant for a four-dimensional universe.

The whole argument is inconsistent. The proposed parameters of the fourth dimension are still to be of our three-dimensional world; they are even viewed as deriving from a three-dimensional construct, in the form of a balloon.

Our universe is three-dimensional and never anything else. But the four-dimensional argument, while admitting this, suddenly requires that we view our universe as being in a different dimension for only one particular, assumed phenomenon—just because physicists need a specific, strange explanation for it.

Other inconsistencies result from not recognizing that light waves travel through a medium and therefore lengthen automatically. For instance, the mysterious quasars seem to generate energy at inconceivably high rates and, incredibly, to emit jets or formations of mass at speeds higher than the speed of light.[12]

Evidently, quasars are systems that really are moving away from us. Therefore, light waves from them become longer, even turn into radio waves; quasars are, mysteriously, emitting unusually high amounts of radio waves. Here the wave-lengthening caused by the movement adds to the universal wave-lengthening due to distance, to a long passage of waves through the Field as medium.

But this strong, actually cumulative lengthening of waves is supposed to be due to the expansion of our universe, and to the balloon effect of points further away from us moving at cumulatively increasing speeds. Consequently, physicists calculate that quasars are extremely far away from us.

Then, since the quasars are so immensely distant and yet send us so much radiation, they are seen as generating energy at incomprehensibly high rates. Moreover, the movements of the jets of mass from quasars must have superluminary speeds if the quasars are assumed to be so immensely far away.

Such mysteries about quasars, as well as about radio galaxies and similar phenomena, are increasing.[12, 13] They become explainable if it is recognized that radiation waves travelling through the medium, the Field, lengthen automatically. This lengthening, added to the Doppler effect of galaxies that are actually moving, then explains what must seem impossible and mysterious to believers in an expanding universe.

Expansion of the universe has to be assumed if space is seen as empty. Radiation, whether it is accepted to be of particles or waves, could not be affected in any way by emptiness and would always remain the same. Only a medium, the Field, can have the effect of waves slowing down, and therefore lengthening, with distance. Anyway, if there is no medium, then the Doppler effect of an expanding universe is the only possible explanation (though the Doppler effect applies only to waves, which are impossible without a medium).

Then also, to explain the assumed expansion, a further assumption, of an explosive creation of the universe, has to be accepted. The assumption of *the Big-Bang creation* was easy because it is humanly appealing to think of creation by one act. But this assumption is inherently incredible as causal explanation.

Before you can have a bang as an explosion you must have a force or forces, and a medium with certain properties for the forces to act in the form of an explosion. Above all, you must have a mass or energy as great and as extensively ordered as is the creation resulting from the Bang.

Here the speculations of physicists become unreal, to the same extent that the always convenient mathematics can make them seem precise. Mathematically, the Big Bang creating our universe can be shown to have been generated by an infinitesimal point of mass, smaller than a proton or, in other calculations, as small as an apple. But even the most incredible mathematics can not help much.

Physicists recognize that the balance and precision of forces and forms of matter in the universe require incredibly exact predetermination.[4, 11, 12] What they overlook is that *even every atom and any other ordered form or effect* would have had to be *predetermined* in the Big Bang as a one-act creation. Whatever a created form or effect of force, it can emanate in a *one-act creation* only from equally extensive and precise causal predeterminants in it.

No creation by one single act, such as the Big Bang, can lead to precise, uniform particles—or to precisely, uniformly ordered anything—unless each of them was miraculously preformed or predetermined causally in the source of such a creation.

Of course, this miracle cannot be explained by any of the continuously varying Big Bang models, including the "inflationary" model. Just reflect how, under any possible *creation by one single event*, the myriads of ordered, uniform phenomena in the universe would have required equal *myriads of precise determinants* within the source of such a creation. This is inevitable whether that source is called a Bang or a metaphysical First Cause with an infinite number of Monads in it.

Here we may contrast the assumed creation by the Big Bang with action by the Field (predetermined as a simple causal principle). We have seen how every uniform particle or effect of force derives from the simple mechanics of the Field's action, and how the creation of new particles continues forever. (Causal principles or laws, creating all the endless phenomena in the cosmos, are always simple, for the reasons we have explained.)

The cosmos is infinite in its creation as in any other aspect. Everything in the universe is causally infinite, inherently contrary to non-infinite man and his categories of mind. A finite and dramatic single-act creation would be congenial to the human mind; but the reality is infinite, humanly strange, and eternally monotonous.

Matter is indestructible. Otherwise, it would have disappeared through one of the limitless possibilities during infinite time. Matter is essentially unchangeable. Only its forms change, diminishing or dwindling at one place and increasing or creating themselves at another, mostly through the creation of hydrogen atoms in the way we have indicated. As everybody knows, matter never comes from nothing, nor changes the size of its mass fundamentally, though the Big Bang creation implies otherwise. Matter only changes its forms, under dominance by the Field—in which it is a mere impurity.

The perpetual interaction between the Field and matter as opposites explains various features of cosmic creation. Opposite changes, pulsations, and oscillations are typical of galaxies and stars as well as of atoms.

The "pulsation" can be fast, in atoms or even in pulsars, and slow, in the life of stars as they develop and age. Here we may mention the simplest facts of the *creation of stars and planets.*

Stars grow by the process of matter happening to accumulate and thus acquiring greater gravitational attraction, which makes it accumulate even more matter. Such a chain reaction creates an abnormal condition sustained by continuous increase in the process. Therefore the first accidental stop in it starts a reverse chain reaction. As the Field pressures start dispelling the accumulation this increases their effectiveness, which dispels matter even more.

Supernovas are the most spectacular results of such opposite chain reactions. Novas, pulsars, or pulsating galaxies and quasars exhibit more regularly the effects of such reactions. Quite frequent, evidently similar, and causally unexplained phenomena are the "high energy transients" recently observed as ten-second outbursts, coming from our galaxy and from space at the rate of 150 a year.

Opposite chain reactions are universal ways of action in the cosmos. Atomic reactions or fire—even life, as we shall see—act by way of chain reactions. Above all, the ultimate quanta events, which create all other actions as waves, operate by way of opposite chain-reaction oscillations constituting the "universal atoms of action," as we have already indicated.

In fact, a chain reaction is the only possible form of action between two opposites that are equal in force. The counterbalancing equilibrium of immobility between such equal opposites can be interrupted only by some chain reaction, big or small.

But if the interaction between the two opposites is not recognized, the universality of opposite chain reactions is not easily thought of. Even Planck's constant, the universal quantum of action, is not causally understood; we have seen how it results from alternating chain-reaction gains by the Field and matter. Planck's constant is the main factor in quantum mechanics, which have remained a causally unexplained and only mathematically descriptive theory.[3, 11, 12]

In the pulsars or pulsating quasars and galaxies, or in nova action, one can easily recognize opposite chain reactions at work. But even here *physicists have sought different explanations*. Pulsars have been observed to pulsate at the rate of 30 or even 642 times per second. This would be consistent with oscillations between opposite forces. Yet physicists explain that the pulsation here is only an illusion created by rotation of a pulsar that has a shiny spot on its rotating surface.

How could a pulsar rotate 642 times a second? A pulsar, as well as a pulsating galaxy or a quasar, may be compared with suns or galaxies judging from its energy amounts. Anything of that size rotating even once a second would be creating motion with speeds higher than the speed of light.

Also, the explanation of novas has become specious. It is argued that novas result from stars exploding under their excessive pressures of gravity. But actually, a tendency by itself can never create an opposite tendency. Gravity pulling matter together cannot explode it. The opposite phenomena, encountered everywhere in the cosmos, are due to the opposite chain reactions created by the Field and matter as opposites.

The theory of black holes, as it is presently expounded, is not more consistent. If it were true, then every accumulation of matter, would continue contracting endlessly and would create a black hole. Actually, a limitless, concentric, gravitational condensation of a star can never happen, whatever the assumed size of the star.

In a star big or small, the matter at points close to the center is, in fact, attracted outward as well. For at such points there is proportionally more of mass in the outward direction and it provides much of the "shielding" effect. Physicists should include that "shielding" factor in writing their formulas for black holes. As it is, one may rely on the common sense which clearly points to this outward attraction inside any star or accumulating mass.

It is not by accident that we have stars and atoms everywhere instead of black holes. Matter is not compressible limitlessly—except in mathematical equations. In reality, matter is always a hard, never diminishable, forever fully resistant mass; it resists the Field perpetually.

That is why we have continuous, permanent-size matter particles everywhere. If matter could potentially contract with any ease, it would inevitably create, under inter-matter attraction, nothing but black holes. (Matter always exists as small particles because the Field breaks up any larger solid accumulations of mass.)

But theories about black holes are convenient. A black hole can be claimed to exist anywhere, since it is invisible. Then all kinds of gravitational and electromagnetic forces around the supposed black holes can be easily assumed to be causal factors. Physicists often badly need such assumptions.

Physicists frequently attribute to the forces of gravitation and electromagnetism various cosmic phenomena created in "empty" space, since such phenomena seem to have no other possible causal source. Actually, the causal mysteries here are merely covered up by more general causal mysteries. Electromagnetism and gravitation are still mysteries causally. Their causal source in "empty" space is still unknown. It should be a concrete, strong, or dense causal medium, residing in space, curved or not—a medium more compact than matter, which it controls. But for physicists no such a source in space exists.

Generally, a very important effect of the opposite chain reaction is the *creation of larger atoms*. When matter accumulates in chain-reaction ways during the creation of stars and planets, opposite chain reactions occur alternately. As the Field pressures move in to disperse an excessive accumulation of matter, their effectiveness increases and they acquire even more force. The results are implosions, of extraordinary force, around masses of accumulated matter.

Such implosions have above-normal compression strength. They compress into larger atoms the standard atoms of hydrogen, and then further compress the new atoms created by such compressions, as the Field gains the "packing fraction" at each compression. Thus, heavier and heavier atoms are created, with gains for the dominant Field. This process, though, has a limit.

For, concurrently with this compression action, the Field acts under its general drive to divide matter. Where the two actions reach their full impact, a middle ground is met and the more stable atoms of the middle of the element table are created. The lighter elements can be still compressed further, by fusion, and the heavier ones divided up, by fission.

Another important effect of the Field as the medium in cosmic creation is the *formation of planets*. In any fluid medium, a movement of mass in one direction creates secondary movements of it in opposite directions. The simplest example is a drop falling into water and creating splashes upward. The "splashes" from matter dropping into a forming star are, naturally, of cosmic proportions. As such outward splashes of matter accumulate, they start forming "suns" of their own, the planets.

Such matter radiating out of the star has much energy, as great as the atoms in the star have. This energy finally makes this matter orbit. Through a myriad of interactions and clashes this matter and its energy are finally consolidated into an orbiting planet. Energy as well as mass here accumulate in chain-reaction ways. An accidentally increased momentum in one direction changes movement of further encountered matter into the same direction, which further changes the movement of still other matter into that direction.

The orbiting planets form themselves in *definite regions* away from the sun. The regions are determined by their spherical distances from the sun. The process here is similar to the formation of nucleons as spherical layers, because in both instances the creating forces are the Field pressures. In fact, the distance patterns of planets are similar to those of formations of nucleons as spherical standing waves.

The distances of planets from the sun increase in these patterns, by a geometric progression, in the outward direction from the sun, as if by predetermined ratios of squared whole numbers of the astronomic unit. The well-known *Titius-Bode Law* expresses this.

But the cause of this orderly geometric increase has remained a mystery. This increase has a pattern partly similar to that of spectra series, with their square relationships of whole numbers. As we have seen, that pattern is due to the spherical structure of nucleons as standing waves. The above mystery has to remain unexplainable if it is not recognized that the Field is creating the planets in ways similar to those in which it creates the nucleons.

Whatever the details, the self-creation of planets is an automatic result of a fluid medium, the Field, creating countermovements to the accumulation of matter into a sun.

The present hypotheses for explaining the creation of planets are not helpful. They are mostly found untenable, as are the nebular, Kant-Laplace, and the binary star hypotheses. Or they imply that planets are created by some unusual occurrences. According to the close-encounter hypothesis only one star in a billion may happen to have planets. This is contradicted by the stark fact that in our solar system six out of nine planets have moons or "planets" of their own.

In their spherical regions, around the sun, *planets accumulate their mass much in the same way as suns do*. Each such a region is for the planetary mass its "normal" space, since that mass has the corresponding level of energy that keeps it orbiting in its totality. This has the relative effect as if that mass, in its region, were acting in its own space "normally," unaffected by its spherical orbit. The result is not different from what happens in a spacecraft orbiting the earth.

Naturally, in its "normal" space a planet forms in the same way as a sun does. It creates the same kind of outward radiation of mass, which again accumulates into "planets" of the planet, or into moons.

A ring of mass around a planet is a phase of development between the initial outward radiation of mass and its final accumulation into a moon. The radiation features are particularly clear in the ring of Saturn. The ring consists of ripples as subordinate rings in it. Such ripples are to be expected in an outward radiation of mass, in the above regular patterns, created by the Field as a medium.

Finally, we may mention that galaxies, suns, and planets *spiral, twist, whirl, or spin*. This reveals that they are under constant pressures by a surrounding medium—which also compresses them into spheres.

The Field pressures here act not very differently from what can be observed about pressure in any medium. The simplest examples are the whirls, twists, and cyclic movements in streams, storms, tornadoes, and cyclones. They are created and operated by universally acting pressures of air and water. A medium of pressures that tries to dispel a formation while at the same time confining it from all sides has to create whirls, spins, and spirals.

To sum up, force determines everything in the universe but is a nothingness to man. No man ever perceives force in itself. Man's universe is that of matter. It is also the universe the way he knows it. But anything can be known only through differentiation against something opposite. Man knows matter, by differentiating it against its universal opposite, against force, which thus remains for him the nothingness, the proper opposite of matter.

This opposite, the Field, is the universal field of force that determines everything that matter is or does. Statically as well as dynamically, matter derives its meaning for man through this opposite. But man sees or recognizes only matter, by virtue of which he exists. Its opposite is for him unreality itself, a nothingness. That is why the very source and cause of all material, physical phenomena—the universal field of force—is nonexisting, unperceivable by man, as are all forces, which come from this field.

The Field, as the universal field of force, remains a nothingness for man in its every aspect, particularly because of its universality. It is inherent in a field of force to fill all space homogeneously. The Field must be immensely strong to do this throughout the universe. But all cosmic forces are immense in human terms. Which is clear already to everybody.

We have seen how the totally universal, homogeneous Field must remain unperceivable in itself, much more so than the atmospheric pressure. Or how it cannot cause hindrance or drag to movements by material bodies, just as a stream moving a boat exerts no hindrance to its movement.

No instrument can discover the Field in itself or its drag. Instruments as well as what they deal with consist of matter or effects in it. And it is the Field itself that creates all effects and phenomena of matter, by moving matter particles or quanta. Therefore the instruments can register the Field even less than the boat can experience the stream that carries it.

But physicists have always thought that even a causally universal medium would interfere with movement of bodies. The experiments on ether drag were causally as shortsighted as was the concept of the ether itself. Physicists could have easily considered that a totally universal causal medium could be stronger than any substance, yet still be as unregistrable as nothingness, a clear opposite of matter.

Physicists have not been ready to appear absurd in terms of the common sense which shows space to be empty, free for our movements or clear vision. Physicists continued to think of ether in terms of matter, a very thin matter, rather than of its opposite. The concept of opposite causation has remained unrecognized in physics as well.

In its every aspect the Field is diametrically different from ether. The Field is the opposite of matter—a field of force as "nothingness," opposite to matter in every sense. Again, this corresponds to the central universal fact that force determines everything but is nothingness to man—as the causal, opposite, and "negative" source of his reality values.

Evidently, the Field, by whatever name, could be easily recognized as the causally unified field of force that makes everything causally explainable, just as force usually can cause anything.

Physicists have always been looking for such a field, as scientifically necessary and evident causal fact. We have indicated how the Field makes explainable, in simple ways, all the presently admitted causal mysteries of theoretical physics.

Of course, our explanations may be incomplete. Physicists with their phenomenal skills could do incomparably better with a concept like the Field. For such a Field can provide every necessary, concrete, and intense property, as strong as all force. The Field is "denser" than any matter, because it as force controls matter, in all its forms and effects. Moreover, the Field is nothingness as the field of force. Physicists, therefore, would not have to discover or postulate anything new.

Here we come to another important point. The concept of the Field requires no new hypothetical assumptions. It only requires that men abandon the already clear human prejudice against recognizing the negative, causal sources of man's positive values, including his cognitive values, which constitute his reality as he knows it. Once the universal, negative causal source, the "nothingness" as force opposite to matter, is recognized, every explanation follows easily, since force can create everything while being nothingness to man. Physicists now have to "discover" force as Newton discovered gravitation, which had remained unknown while being evident everywhere.

Our explanations are simple. Modern professional, theoretical physics is unbelievably complex. But it admittedly lacks causal, scientific understanding of the principal physical phenomena. The sciences have often become extremely complex when they have reached an impasse of understanding. Actually, the more generally significant a causal, scientific truth is, the simpler it is. The fundamental principles of nature can be only simple.

It can be said that no concept of a fundamental causal principle is true if it requires complex explanations or can be formulated only in some unusual language such as mathematics. The most universal or fundamental physical mechanisms should be explainable by simple, universal terms, such as those of movement or "push" and wave or "layer." Physicists themselves recognize causal simplicity as the criterion of scientism.

John A. Wheeler states that "we will first understand how simple the universe is when we recognize how strange it is." Coincidentally, the criteria of simplicity and strangeness are the very gist of the Field concept. Everything is totally simple and clear causally if the Field is recognized. And hardly anything can be stranger to men than the reality or the properties of the Field.

The use of mathematics by modern physicists confirms the underlying simplicity of causal bases in physics. Mathematics can be used here, and mathematics is the same for every man, as only natural, simple principles can be.

Of course, a physical event, such as a whirlpool, may be as simple visually as it can become unbelievably complex mathematically. Such complexity is bound to increase to extremes if the cause of the events is missed, and particularly if it works in ways contrary to the usually accepted causal logic.

In a wider, historical view, modern theoretical physics is so complicated for the same reason that the Ptolemaic explanations were esoterically complex. A fundamental, necessarily simple causal understanding is missing now as it was then. The simple insight that planets go around the sun was all that was needed to dispel the Ptolemaic esoteric complexity.

Modern physics is far removed from Ptolemaic metaphysics. But it clearly, admittedly, lacks fundamental causal understanding, as Ptolemaics did. Mathematics now serves better than metaphysical esotericism served then. A skilled mathematician can write a formula, even make a correct prediction, without revealing or knowing what it is he is dealing with. Indeed, physicists can say that they do not need to know the causes of physical phenomena.

Unfortunately, the missed causes exist, and work in ways contrary to the very way of thinking of physicists, who are avoiding what seems absurd in common sense but is true. Therefore, merely mathematical, even incidentally correct, systems of concepts are bound to be causally misleading.

Modern physicists are too sophisticated to hide behind noble metaphysics. Rather, they whimsically find a proper humorous tone for the underlying uneasiness. The act of Creation becomes a mere "bang" or an ultimate Monad a "bare-bottom" quark. Our physicists are also too sophisticated to venture into what seems simplistic and absurd—to accept relative value causality, which reveals the causal, "negative" sources of man's "positive" universe.

VII

HOW CAN LIVING NATURE BE SO UNFATHOMABLY CLEVER?

The human mind can deal only with one thing at a time. In contrast, a living mechanism works, purposively, with innumerable elements at every point and instant. Consequently, it is unreasonable to try to understand the mechanics of living nature in the one-by-one way in which our mind works in studying non-living, physical phenomena such as atoms or man-made machines.

Yet the modern sciences of biology or genetics are trying to do just that. They use only the methods of our exact physical sciences. The result is incongruities, such as the model of the gene as a separate atom or the virtual anthropomorphism of studying living phenomena in the "scientific," one-by-one terms of human mind.

However, living nature is elementarily simple in the principles or causal laws of its purposes and methods. Philosophically, this is so because we exist in the same way as all organisms do. Thus, we can understand, perfectly, causal principles such as organic integration or the subordination of lower organic mechanisms to higher ones.

As a result we can understand and deal with living nature causally—that is, scientifically—by dealing with such simple principles as they apply to the incredible multiplicity of living nature. Trying to deal with isolated elements of that ungraspable, organically interrelated multiplicity is not only futile, but also anthropomorphic. It amounts to assimilating, cognitively, the ways of nature to the way the human mind works—with one thing at a time.

Unfortunately, our current scientism, imitated from the exact, physical sciences, permits only such methods. It requires that each causal element be strictly isolated, separated out, if it is to be studied scientifically. This corresponds to the one-by-one method of the human mind, which makes the exact, physical sciences easy. Such ease is possible because physical atoms, or wheels in machines, are not causally interrelated in myriad ways as organic mechanisms are.

In addition to discussing these problems of a misapplied "scientism," we intend to explain the presently unsuspected causal source of life, and "inner selection." These two explanations are necessary to understand how life can work like an intensely self-perpetuating fire, and how the inner organic mechanisms become purposively perfect through competitive selection. Darwin's explanation of purposivenesss resulting from simple selection is thus extended to all living mechanisms.

The explanation of the causal source of life becomes possible through the insight into the opposite interaction between the Field and matter. In view of that opposite action, life becomes clear as a "negative" fire, opposite to normal fire.

As to inner selection, it is a natural result of inner mechanisms—acting with the vitality of a fire—competing at every level, within organic subordination, for stronger or fitter, more purposive self-realization. For, ultimately, the law of selection is the universal principle governing all existence, since only that exists which is able to persist.

In fact, the explanation of inner selection can serve as a general example of our proposed method of understanding the miracles of living nature by way of causal principles. For instance, it is ungraspably miraculous how every molecule in your fingertips or muscles is so purposively placed or performs with such a perfect coordination while creating movement or any living act. The miracle becomes causally explainable if you think of how even the tiniest organic mechanism evolves purposively by inner selection, within the organic subordination.

Any lower mechanism, amidst myriad potential living processes, attains automatically, by competitive inner selection, its strongest or fittest performance. Yet it does so only when its subordinating, higher mechanism also acquires a stronger or fitter performance from this competitive action. At each such a step the process is simple, understandable according to a simple model.

But as the same process is repeated on and on, along uncountable steps of subordination, the integrated organism as the highest subordinating mechanism also acquires the fittest, most purposive performance automatically, as does every lower subordinating mechanism within it.

The end result is that, due to this subordination, controlling inner selection, the organism as a whole becomes a purposive determinant that can be fully understood and dealt with causally or scientifically. Everybody can understand how the organism exists and acts as one integrated whole. The organically integrated reactions, such as feelings or pleasure, are always causally clear and simple, as we have explained repeatedly.

In contrast, it would be senseless to try to understand the purposive performance of the organism by analyzing "scientifically" how its separate mechanisms are acting. This would require following, instant by instant, almost all the countless mechanisms of the whole organism, since they determine each other causally. It would also, necessarily, require the understanding of the purposive drives of each mechanism as they have evolved, during millions of years of adaptations.

Yet scientists use only the "scientific" methods. For instance, the explanations from genes, as atoms of inheritance, are as general as they are untenable. How did the genes acquire the necessary, unfathomable purposiveness, since it cannot come from the physically accidental mutations, so overwhelmingly destructive that selection cannot work with them?

As organic determinants, genes must purposively determine every molecular connection within the organism. Each such connection has to be purposively coordinated causally with nearly every other molecular connection within the perfectly integrated organism. Evidently, the genes would have to be unimaginably clever in their purposiveness as well as astronomically numerous; but there is no natural source for making them so.

Living Nature Immensely Superior to Mind

Mind is able to deal only with one thing at a time. Thus men have to generalize or form everything into "ones," into things, before it can be grasped or dealt with. This is so, ultimately, because the conscious capacity is one of reliving past experiences and man always lives as only one organism. Thus, each act of such reliving is, in its final terms, always something one.

Whatever the reasons, the human mind deals only with one thing at a time, whereas living nature works with myriad elements at every instant and every point in the organism in perfectly purposive ways—under inner selection and organic subordination.

In truth, this limitedness of the human mind is the most important fact in our mental life and in the human universe, existing for man in the way his mind defines it for him. This universe is dealt with by sciences which do not yet recognize or account for that universally incapacitating limitedness of the mind when it has to deal with living nature. Under this limitedness man is virtually blind when he faces living nature with his usual method of thinking, in "scientific" ways.

The very universality of this limitedness of the mind is the reason it is not recognized. We all know that we can think only of one thing at a time. This fact is so general or commonplace, known to everybody, that it is never deemed worthy of noticing in any particular way. Man's disregard of this universal limitedness is due also to his self-centered, conceited views of his values and capacities.

Men value what is human above everything else; and the mind makes men human. Moreover, the mind as consciousness is inevitably mysterious in itself, as is any last and therefore unexplainable term in knowledge, which works by differentiation. Also, the mind as a complex living process is incomprehensible to the cognitive mind. In any case, for man the mind is the supreme, incomprehensible capacity, extolled in all human thought and philosophy.

Yet, this limitedness of the mind is decisive and all-inclusive when man views living nature. Even if man could see, miraculously, how a molecular living process goes on, he would see only one event at each moment. But in a living organism the determining factors are interactions by billions of purposefully integrated processes, determined each billionth of a second by still further innumerable processes. Indeed, the limitedness of man's mind here amounts to a practical causal blindness.

The decisive fact is that science has accepted the normal human method of knowledge, doomed to this blindness, as the way of studying even living phenomena. The sciences of living nature accept as scientific only the experiments and observations in which one phenomenon is isolated and studied for a single causal factor.

This method gives excellent, causally exact results in the physical and mechanical sciences. A non-living molecule or piece of matter behaves always in the same way whether it exists in isolation or intermixed with many other molecules.

But in living, organic matter each molecule or piece of tissue behaves in ways determined by almost every other molecule in the organism. Causally, you would have to see how all cells or molecules in the organism interact before you could understand or predict what happens to one of them.

The causally non-multiple, physical, non-living world can be understood and dealt with by the mind without difficulties. There science can advance perfectly. Man creates machines with separate parts or wheels and cogs that he can deal with by thinking of one thing at a time.

If man were able to deal with multiple processes simultaneously, as living nature does, he could create living tissues or a new animal as readily as he makes machines. In reality, everything living, even the life of a fly, is for man a miracle implying a living soul as much as his own life does.

Unfortunately, though predictably, the modern life sciences have adopted the methods of the physical or technical sciences. They have accepted the concept of genes, of hereditary atoms, as eagerly as they have espoused the experimental method of dealing with one separate trait at a time in studying all living behavior.

For instance, in studying the migration of birds scientists have tried to establish how birds follow stars or contours of land. Actually, the birds orientate themselves by countless responses, in the same way as a bird selects its food according to countless requirements in almost every cell of its organism. It is anthropomorphic to assume that, for instance, the birds will follow separate contours of land. Man would do that in his conscious orientation. Scientists know how misleading it is to attribute human ways of behavior to animals.

It is not realized, however, that a similar error is perpetuated every time organic behavior or an organic process is viewed as being determined by some separate response isolated from the rest of the countless organic interactions. Which is exactly the method inherent in the experimental scientism imitated from the exact sciences by natural scientists.

As to the genes, we shall explain later how incongruous it is to view them in the easy, "scientific" terms of atoms of inheritance. Here we may only emphasize the causal interdependence of every organic element or factor with other astronomically multiple factors and their interconnections in the organism. Think of the response by a taste bud. That response is determined by nutritional requirements in countless kinds of tissues and cells throughout the organism.

The same is true for genetic factors controlling any event in organic growth, reproduction, or some other function. A cell grows or an animal reproduces by choices determined by the requirements of the whole organism, by the interaction of all its cells, embodying an infinite number of evolutionary adaptations. And each of them would have to be determined by a gene.

Of course, the complex interdependence here is humanly inconceivable. This is exactly the point. Living nature thrives on unfathomable multiplicity as easily as the mind proceeds only by dealing with something one at a time.

Furthermore, every factor or element in that multiplicity is purposive. We have already indicated how this purposiveness automatically results from inner selection and organic subordination, under which every mechanism selectively self-enforces the strengthening of its higher, governing mechanism, and thus finally the organism itself; we shall see later how this purposiveness becomes inheritable through generations.

No such automatically simple explanation is possible in terms of genes. To be purposive any one of the organic elements would have to be determined by purposive genes. So would the interactions between the organic elements. Since such elements and interactions are literally infinite, there would have to be an astronomic number of purposeflul genes. This would require supernatural creation.

We admit that there is no other way of human or scientific thinking than in terms of "ones." But scientific understanding becomes quite different if the inexorable multiplicity is recognized. Then concepts can be chosen that permit taking into account that multiplicity even while thinking can proceed only in terms of ones—of simple causal principles.

Our tentative concepts of the principles of inner selection and organic subordination can serve as illustrations. We can understand how by inner selection any one mechanism "purposively" prevails by being strongest or fittest and thus most purposive, for itself. We can further understand how under the principle of subordination each such mechanism is permitted to work only to the extent it enables its higher, controlling mechanism to become stronger or fitter.

In this way it becomes causally clear how inner selection, working under organic subordination, finally provides the organism as the highest mechanism with the strongest, fittest, and most purposive adaptations.

We may note here that the organism itself, as the highest mechanism, is a self-evident fact but cannot be properly grasped cognitively because it is a multiple living process.

Only when man reacts in more than his mental capacity, as a living being, through his feelings or pleasure, can he understand his own organism. Then we can see that indeed the organism is the highest integrating mechanism controlling lower mechanisms in its pursuit of a stronger, more effective, more pleasant performance.

This is all that we need to understand how inner selection working under organic subordination can create an infinite number of "purposive" adaptations for the organism as a whole. This makes organisms causally understandable.

And a science can start only when causal understanding is reached. Once started, any exact science can become as miraculously effective as the technical sciences now are. Practically, this understanding would make it possible to condition or "educate" living mechanisms through their organically integrated responses, which are feelings or pleasure drives in human terms.

For inner selection is also a learning through conditioning. This is a decisive fact.

All organisms could be "educated" by conditioning through inner selection. Men could even plan their genetic future by, say, changing their enjoyment habits; we have indicated that organic adaptations can become genetically inheritable.

The gist of inner selection is that mechanisms strengthen themselves automatically by finding a stronger, environmentally better self-realization. It is like a channel of energy widening itself by its own stronger flow. Above all, this is the way all *learning* in living nature is achieved, through conditioning by environmental conditions.

Learning or conditioning proceeds under the Law of Effect, convincingly established by the great authorities Pavlov and Thorndike. According to this law, conditioning and learning result from organic satisfaction pathways deepening as more satisfaction is enjoyed. One can think here of a water flow forming an effective river by virtue of the strength of the flow.

Evidently, *inner selection and learning work in the same way.* It can be said that inner selection becomes a learning process. Moreoever, this learning is limitless because living mechanisms provide an infinite number of choices.

Generally, life is similar to fire, ready to extend in every possible form or way. Thus, the potential living mechanisms possible in life are endlessly many. Consequently, inner selection, also in its function of learning, can be limitlessly successful in promoting the strongest possible, or fittest, most purposive organic mechanisms.

The principle of subordination ensures that inner selection-promotes only those mechanisms that are fittest for the organism as the integrated whole. We may as well look closer at this decisive principle.

Without the subordination every mechanism would selectively increase only itself, and the overall result would be chaos within the organism. As we shall explain in detail later, the subordination insures that any lower, subordinated mechanisms are permitted to continue or increase *only to the extent that they enable their higher, subordinating mechanism to continue or increase*—to become stronger or fitter.

This subordination works in the same simple way on every level, at every integrative connection between a lower mechanism and a higher mechanism governing it. Yet this simplicity results in a humanly ungraspable marvel of purposiveness as the simple subordination integrates all the myriad organic processes while they selectively compete, automatically, to serve the subordinating controlling mechanism in order to survive.

For, to the extent that a mechanism does not favor its higher subordinating mechanism, it is not permitted to continue. This *competition for subordination* insures a fully purposive, selective organic integration. As the Darwinian insight reveals, competition in selection automatically translates into purposiveness.

Of course, the principle of organic subordination itself has been turned into a universal law by natural selection choosing the organisms capable to survive. Certainly this principle of subordination enhances the survival of better organized, fitter organisms. The organic subordination is of course a fact evident to everybody.

A decisive result is that, under inner selection and subordination, every organic mechanism succeeds in much the same way as the organism itself, the highest controlling "mechanism." In other words, inner *mechanisms learn by conditioning*, the way animals learn. This is nothing new. Scientists know that inner mechanisms learn. Your stomach learns to know the lunch hour.

But an ungraspably vast and intricate adaptation is the total result of the learning of the countless subordinate inner mechanisms. The mechanisms here are infinitely many. So are their integrative interactions, each evolving purposively under the selection that promotes those mechanisms that competitively become better subordinated as well as stronger.

Naturally, the mind cannot follow what is actually happening under inner selection. The organism becomes a purposive miracle. As the highest controlling mechanism the organism profits from every one of infinitely numerous selective adaptations and results of "learning." In the end, organisms must seem to be creations of a supernatural intellect. Even a sober mind would have to accept this view under the presently available explanations.

We should understand that generally learning through conditioning leads to *results comparable to the effects of foresight, planning, judgment, or even abstract reasoning.*

Such results are explained by scientists as purely mechanistic effects created by mere reinforcement and connections of satisfaction pathways, under the law of effect. This should be equally true for the results of inner selection, which also works under the law of effect.

Let us look at the "foresight" or "reasoning" resulting from conditioning.

A dog can be conditioned to salivate ten minutes after a bell has rung—to anticipate food in ten minutes. A physiologic mechanism here has learned to foresee a course of events. A hen can learn to peck a lever or to perform a dance in order to obtain a grain of feed. She thus acts with a purpose or "plan," somewhat like a person planting seeds and expecting harvest. A sheep can be conditioned to perform a shock-avoidance response upon merely seeing a switch turned. She has thus learned the meaning of abstract signs.

All animals learn to generalize, to respond to signs that can become less and less similar to the original stimuli. The mechanisms inside the organism learn in the same way. They work, through inner selection, under the law of effect in the same way in which an animal works and learns, by being conditioned as an organism, as the final, highest subordinating mechanism.

Imagine what such inner-selection learning can do, with this "foresight" and "reasoning" when the learning extends in purposive, integrating ways to an infinite number of mechanisms and their interactions, through countless levels, and for millions of years. The learning by organisms and their inner mechanisms thus becomes immense in extent and intricacy.

The result is the emergence of an infinite number of purposive systems of "insightful" learning and of "planned' or "reasoned" adaptations inside the organism. Yet it all requires merely the simple principles of inner selection and subordination. But because the mind cannot deal with more than one thing at a time, the end result is a humanly unfathomable miracle. Any final performance by organisms, or mechanisms inside them, has to remain *such a miracle merely because of its multiplicity*.

Think of a robin building its nest. Analyzed into the one-by-one terms of the mind each bit of the robin's performance is simple. Placing a twig crosswise on two other twigs or in a simple interlocking position would be seen as a result of simple learning even for a bird.

But the robin acts by simultaneous responses to countless systems of learned "memories" of such simple interlockings from the whole evolution of nest-building by robins. He "knows," at each point, how the myriad simple interlockings will have to be set together. He knows or "understands" it all at every moment, at every single act of response. He has in his mind, as it were, the whole nest with all its requirements while he sets each twig in its proper place.

We always have to keep in view how immensely superior are the learned sytems of "memory" and "understanding" of living mechanisms in comparison with those of the mind.

In the example of tasting a food, your organs and tissues exhibit an infinite amount of memory and understanding, embodying uncountable requirements, from your evolutionary past as well as from your present adjustments, for every cell in your body. You are reacting here non-mentally, as a living organism. In comparison with this, your mental memory and understanding are ludicrously small.

It can be said that much of the *whole past of life on earth is recorded in your cells*. As the Nobel laureate Albert Szent-Gyorgyi writes, "a cell resembles a site of archeological excavation...with the deepest strata representing the oldest evolutionary adaptations."[5] The human embryo goes through primitive forms, that at one stage look reptilian. Organisms live by repeating what they have learned through eons of evolution.

We admit that organic mechanisms cannot live through past experiences mentally, changing them or experimenting with them as in the "rehearsals" that make possible mental foresight and planning. But the organic, nonmental "memory" of conditioned adaptations is immense in comparison with that of the conscious mind. And as we have seen, conditioning can have effects that resemble those of foresight, planning, and abstract generalizations.

As opposed to mental learning, organic mechanisms "learn" by enacting the reactions factually, and thus risking physical harm or destruction, whereas the mind can work with abstract rehearsals without such risks. But the number of available forms of organic reactions is infinite and potentially always expanding in the "learning" through inner selection.

Therefore, the inner selection too can offer endless possibilities of "rehearsal," of trial and error. The trials and errors here do not necessarily become fatal, because they are minutely sorted out at the lower levels of inner selection, before they reach the higher levels or the organism as a whole. Further, the time available for reinforcements as well as for trials and errors, by environmental conditioning, is millions and millions of years.

In short, the mind is a unique capacity in its own particular way, but is incredibly limited in comparison with the myriad organic adaptations, by "learning" and "understanding" as well as "memory," that are available to living mechanisms and can have final results similar to those of the mind.

Let us consider the vast possibilities offered to organisms by such "memory" factually embodying guideline mechanisms from the past adaptations of species during the long history of life on earth. Every species has its beginnings in the early eras of organic life.

Thus, an organism can try out countless mechanisms, even those once used by its primeval evolutionary ancestors. It is like having a reserve of an immense number of tools. And inner selection is, in fact, incessantly trying out every possible useful mechanism available within the organism.

Interestingly, it has been now discovered that cells contain much more DNA than seems to be needed for normal coding in the organism. *Only 1 or 2 percent of the DNA appears to be actually used*. The rest seems to be doing nothing at all, through millions of generations, as has been described by Francis Crick[5] and Stephen Jay Gould[4] among other scientists. This "excess baggage" has been viewed as "parasitic," "junk DNA," or "nonsense DNA."[4, 5]

Considering how extensive is the coding by the 2 percent of DNA actually used, that "excess" 98 percent may contain immense reserves of genetic codes. DNA is the genetic code system for all organisms, and nothing in living evolution is nonsensical or purposeless.

Seeming miracles of organic adaptation become explainable if it is considered how *inner selection can choose and combine codes* for all kinds of mechanisms or forms *from the whole eonic past of the species*.

Inner selection is competitively resourceful and extensive in using any adaptation possibilities, even from the "environment" inside the organism including the "excess" DNA codes. Thus, a seemingly new, already perfected adaptation may emerge suddenly. Sir Peter Medawar has observed such adaptations and compared them to records being played on a phonograph, each of them already completed.

To take a couple of examples, the apparatus for poison injection by snakes or the angling device of the angler fish resembles imaginatively planned inventions. How could they be created by a nature having no mental foresight?

We cannot visualize the multiplicity involved in such creations. But we can think, in the one-by-one ways of the mind, of some causal principles governing possible inner "learning" by organisms from past adaptations and their codes, accumulated during the past history of species. Imagine, for instance, the primeval evolutionary ancestors of snakes as preying animals.

Schematically, preying animals find better, fitter ways of nourishing themselves when they can inject juices into a prey that destroy its tissues quicker. The DNA codes for various kinds of such injection mechanisms used by animals in the past may therefore be available, also through the excess DNA, to species of snakes.

The miraculous DNA is in effect the genetic self embodying infinite numbers of mechanisms and codes from the evolutionary past of the species. Organism can use, under intense and vast inner selection, any fitter mechanisms or their codes, available in the genetic self, even if they are in a dormant, merely potential state, as remnants from the historical past of the species.

Thus, we can understand, in terms of causal principles, how inner selection can reactivate various kinds of past mechanisms for the snake as they serve the injection of destructive juices into a prey. Such mechanisms may be primitive at the beginning. Here the unique role of inner selection becomes decisive.

However primitive an initial organic mechanism may be, inner selection perfects it, through endless adaptations, selectively added at every instant. The fittest form or function for the mechanism is inevitably and automatically found. All natural selection has such "purposive" effects. Moreover, inner selection works with innumerable mechanisms every moment and adapts them in accordance with requirements of the whole organism, under the principle of subordination. Of course, organically, fitter adaptations are felt as pleasures, in human terms.

We can therefore understand how even such primitive mechanisms for snakes can be perfected into a complex organically, integrated system of poison glands and tooth-like injection channels, through guidance by the "clever" pleasure reactions.

The point is that every time the mechanisms for the injection of destructive biochemicals are used, they are adapted selectively to provide increased fitness, which in human terms means increased pleasure. What is successful, therefore pleasant, is automatically promoted by inner selection.

Similarly we can understand how inner selection can create a perfect angling device for the angler fish. The creation can start with some primitive appendage, used by remote genetic ancestors of fish, far back in the evolution of primitive animals. Various mechanisms of appendages or protrusions for the gathering of food by such animals would be common.

By the way, biologists generally recognize what they call atavism, a recurrence in an organism or in its parts of a genetically historic form. This can potentially bring evolutionary changes, by way of the "hopeful monsters" propounded by Richard Goldschmidt.[4, 8]

In any event, once the fish reactivates some atavistic protrusion for obtaining food, inner selection can perfect it into a wondrous angling device. The decisive factor is, again, the competitive creation of fitter adaptations by inner selection in the new device during its long use. All natural selection provides fitter adaptations. Inner selection merely extends the principle of adaptation to inner mechanisms.

By countless steps, through long ages, slight improvements are thus added in the mechanisms of the angling device every time a prey is more easily attracted and pleasure felt, by the organism as a whole. This is possible because of the principles of subordination as well as endless mutltiplicity of trials available in inner selection.

Inventions by living nature are miraculous beyond comprehension because nature adds its inner-selection improvements at each one of the infinitely many occurrences, at every instant, through billions of years; we shall explain later how the acquired improvements are inherited through generations.

In the inherently clumsy terms of the mind, the improvements thus can become mysteriously, ungraspably purposeful in any possible aspect or to any degree of perfection of adaptations. The philosopher Bergson could, understandably, work out a famous and very convincing theory about the superiority of instincts. Similar ideas are frequent. Any thinking person has to be astounded by the perfection in nature.

However, men, and particularly scientists, try to explain the adaptations in living nature by viewing each of their causal factors separately, "scientifically," as the usual experimental method requires. Our minds inevitably work in this one-by-one way. But to view nature as working in similar ways amounts to anthropomorphism, a naive, scientifically intolerable way of imputing human characteristics to natural phenomena.

Yet experimenters as well as theorists in the life sciences treat nature as if it worked in the same one-by-one way as our minds do. By its very definition a "scientific," experimental observation has to *isolate each variable* as well as each causal factor affecting it. Theoretical "scientific" studies hold to the same method.

For instance, the instinct of salmon to return to their breeding grounds has been researched as a reaction to water temperature, in some studies, or as a response to some chemical property of water, in others, and so on. The uncanny abilities of other animals to find their way around have been studied in similar ways.

The "talk" of bees or apes is studied by searching for separate signals similar to words in human speech. Communications between ants are similarly studied by looking for some separate signal such as a particular scent. Actually, living beings use *countless* signals or "words" *simultaneously*.

Furthermore, mechanisms or cells inside the organism communicate with each other in their interactions even more extensively than do bees or ants. Scientists, again, look for one separate neurotransmitter or hormone as the means of such communications.

But the interactions as well as the signals or means used in such communications are innumerable, and proceed simultaneously at every spot in the organism. They could be causally understood only through responses by the organism as a whole, by what man knows as pleasure reactions. Pleasure is the only bridge of understanding between mind and the myriad inner organic reactions. But scientists are, simply, not prepared or trained to take into account the infinite multiplicity in organisms by accepting principles such as that of pleasure.

Indeed, scientific study stops wherever scientists do not find one separable factor, like a hormone or neurotransmitter, in the organic interactions. Similarly, in animal studies scientists proceed with communication research only when they find and can follow one, separate kind of signal as a means of communication. In reality, the means of communication are always there, endlessly many and inseparably interrelated, in animal interactions as well as in inner organic reactions.

In brief, scientists methodically deal only with the exceptionally few, "scientifically" analyzable living phenomena while overlooking the bulk of them in their inseparable multiplicity. Of course, what is "scientifically" analyzable is what works according to the one-by-one method of the human mind.

The result is similar to that of the old *anthropomorphic and anecdotal* nature studies, which found as significant only the few traits in animals that resembled those of man. Our scientists similarly deal only with the phenomena that work in the ways our mind does or all men do when they proceed mentally, according to the method of the mind. This one-by-one method is applied in science as well as in all of man's technical and rational work.

We should keep in mind that animals, such as salmon or migratory birds, respond not only to a multiplicity of outside influences at every moment but also to an equal number of inner "records" and instructions. When we behave instinctively we are acting similarly, whether the satisfactions are nutritional, sexual, or merely orientational.

The instinctive behavior of animals or men is incomparably superior to conscious reactions because in it organisms respond to countless stimuli in accordance with multiple organic purposes and instructions evolved not only during the lifetime but also through ages of evolution.

Scientists have observed that animals foresee earthquakes; in China earthquake predictions have been made from animal behavior. Animals regularly anticipate seasons, through environmental and inner "instructions." Bears accumulate fat for winter, and fur animals change their coats, through such varied and complex influences and responses that scientists cannot understand them.

Again, the *multiplicity* of living nature makes it so superior. *Computers are superior* to the mind for a similar simple reason—their increased multiplicity of transactions. Animals can do incomparably better than computers. Even a protozoan has more "circuits" and "memory chips" than the best computer. Moreover, animals are "programmed" for incomparably more complex, simultaneous, and multiple performances than computers are.

Computers are limited because they are built by and for the human mind, with its limited, one-by-one method. Computers have added multiplicity within this method. Thus, they can be superior to mind. It is not a major accomplishment, comparatively, to surpass the limited, purely intellectual capacities of the mind—to have artificial intelligence. Computers can beat chess players already.

The mind will remain superior to computers only where it can, additionally, use the instinctive mechanisms such as the multiple reactions in feelings, determined by myriad present and past experiences. Evolutionary "learning" as an instinctive organic record can be as immensely multiple as all living nature. But it lies beyond the limited, strictly intellectual capacities of the mind—beyond intelligence as such.

The frequent discussions of artificial intelligence would be clearer if the limited action of the mind as intellect was studied separately from the instincts or feelings and value reactions which work with ungraspable multiplicity. Computers can easily have intelligence as such. They can never have the endlessly multiple affective or value reactions.

Computers will always remain inferior to nature. If they can predict weather, so can animals and plants. Observant people know this. Foxes have been reported to save their young from low-lying dens before flooding rains come. Understandably, people start expecting too much from animals. Animals cannot foresee the severity of a coming winter or similar weather changes, but only because in this case worldwide data would be required that are not fed into the otherwise excellent animal "programming."

Generally, the programming in computers cannot begin to compare with that in organic mechanisms, which embody countless, perfectly integrated purposes. Each such purpose is a precise program for directing numberless processes and their interrelations. In computers the programs are limited in numbers and to the one-by-one method of intellect.

Still, the modern use of computers may help to show how superior to minds nature can become through its mere multiplicity. A computer for landing aircraft may interrelate only a couple of simple variables such as distance from the ground, fuel burn, and wing angle. But the resulting multiple, instantaneous computations are more "intelligent" than anything a dozen mathematicians, working for hours, could calculate.

By the way, the often-astounding mathematical feats by idiot savants are explainable if it is realized that organic mechanisms easily deal with enormous multiplicity. In the brain of an idiot savant this instinctive capacity may be simply abnormally interrelated with the conscious capacity of counting numbers.

Other astounding capacities of idiot savants may be due to similar mixups of consciousness with some instinctive behavior providing infinitely many responses. Or under hypnosis a person may acquire unusual capacities, such as the ability to make his warts disappear, because his conscious reactions have been mixed in with his multiple living processes.

In any event, we can understand how unfathomably clever living nature can become when even computers appear superior to mind. Computers operate by using the one-by-one method, according to one program at a time. In contrast, living mechanisms work with infinitely many programs simultaneously.

If a very advanced computer can be programmed to learn from its own experience, living mechanisms can learn in ways that are immensely more efficient. And their innumerable simultaneously operating programs are perfectly purposive because the organically useful subordination is the method followed in the inner selection.

In conclusion, we may emphasize that only its great multiplicity makes living nature appear unfathomably miraculous to the mind. Any single organic response, if we can isolate it, is totally simple in its purpose and performance, as we saw in the example of nest-building. But in the organism every purpose and performance is determined by interactions that are infinite in number and in the complexity of relations that results from such a multiplicity.

Also, all this happens simultaneously, at every instant and every point in the organism. The mind cannot even begin to grasp what is occurring here. The living performance even of a tiny insect has to remain inherently miraculous to the mind.

Actually, the only thing we really had to explain in this whole discussion is the immense multiplicity of interactions in organisms contrasted with the extreme limitedness of the mind dealing with only one thing at a time. Both are evident facts. The conjectures we used are only illustrations. You can find better examples. But once that extraordinary, all-inclusive contrast between living nature and the mind is clear, the causal, scientific insight can be expanded.

Then we can see how misleading and anthropomorphic, even merely anecdotal are the present methods in the life sciences without that insight. The concepts of limitless inner selection and of organic subordination indicate new possible approaches to causal, scientific explanations. The ungraspable multiplicity of nature here is accounted for under simple causal principles.

Living nature works in ways totally different from the one-by-one method of the mind. But the present experimental scientism allows one to deal only with isolated causal factors—to use only that one-by-one method.

This inevitably leads scientists to choosing only rare, exceptional aspects of living behavior from its actual immense multiplicity. And these aspects are only those which correspond to the peculiar, limited ways in which the human mind works. Is this really different causally, scientifically from the old selectedly limited anecdotal studies?

Scientists should account, in the ways we have indicated, for the virtual blindness of man when he tries to view living nature "scientifically." Otherwise, the natural sciences are bound to remain scientific distortions. But that blindness, as well as the immense, scientifically relevant superiority of living nature over the mind, has not been even mentioned in the natural sciences—because doing so would entail renouncing their present scientism. It would also degrade the mind in man's view.

The Unsuspected Causal Mechanism of Life

Living processes are causally uniform. Life in nature is everywhere the same. Evidently, the causal principle or mechanism of life is one and simple, since nature does not invent complex causal principles. Then why has not science discovered what the mechanism of life is? The reason is the failure to see the Field and its interaction with matter.

Life is *"negative" fire*, opposite to normal fire. The two opposite fires are inevitable as effects of the two universal opposites, the Field and matter. Normal fire is a chain reaction by the Field against matter; it destroys matter enrichment, under universal entropy. Life is a chain reaction by matter against the Field; it enriches matter, in a way opposite to entropy.

Scientists have compared life to fire. In the words of Philip Handler, "flames not only reproduce by means of sparks, but also show metabolism and growth."[6] At the same time scientists know that life proceeds by "negative entropy," which is the exact opposite of what fire does.

In fire the Field, as the dominant opposite, destroys matter enrichment with explosive promptness or simple ease. But the living matter, as the dominated, "oppressed" opposite, can proceed with its chain reaction only by circumventing the Field, in "surreptitious," involved, endlessly complex, and extended ways.

This is what makes life enormously complex, penetratively flexible, long-lasting, extensive in all its forms, and endlessly "inventive."

The causal source of the chain reaction of life is the *giant size of living molecules*, which is the most evident, universal, and striking property of living matter. Whereas a non-living molecule may consist merely of dozens of atoms, living molecules contain hundreds of thousands of atoms. Proteins, the determining forms of living matter, can have a molecular weight of four million.[3] Also, the number of free electrons to be shared in living bonds can be similarly vast in the giant molecules, enriched in chain-reaction ways.

A giant living molecule, arising like a negative spark—under conditions that we shall explain later—offers a *protective* "gravitational" area against the pressures of the Field. We have seen how gravitation amounts to protection against the Field's pressures and attracts matter.

These effects are incomparably stronger inside matter, where atoms and molecules are attracted or "protected" in the extreme closeness of each other. Evidently, a giant molecule can increase that protection and attraction enormously. This extraordinary effect of a giant molecule has a far-reaching, revolutionary result, contrary to the usual physical events dominated by the Field.

In the protective areas of a giant molecule more matter can accumulate and thus create even more protection. The result is a *chain reaction*, since accumulation of matter and energy here leads to a further increase in their accumulation and enrichment.

Energy, coming mostly from the sun, and matter in absorbable form are required to sustain the chain reaction of life and to keep it from collapsing. Atoms always absorb energy or electron enrichment, but under the Field's pressure they immediately give up such momentarily absorded energy. They can keep and accumulate the enrichment in the protective field of a giant molecule. This enrichment makes possible a further accumulation of matter by bonding, through increased free electrons.

The increasing accumulation of electron-rich atoms can evolve all kinds of bonds that grow into formations of endless combinations. It is known that "the large numbers of electric charges" as well as the great size of living molecules enable them to form the multiple "crystals" that living forms are.[10]

According to A. I. Oparin, a leading international authority on the theory of life, "energy-rich bonds" form the "aperiodic crystals" or *protein cyrstals* of living matter.[7]

All crystals are formed by the attraction of molecules under the "gravitational," protective action of crystal cores, amidst invisible pressures. Evidently, the pressures here are those of the invisible Field. (That is why scientists have difficulties in understanding the dynamics of crystallization.[10])

The protective-area effect is evident from many living processes. The formation of living compounds requires the presence of giant living molecules. Enzymes are such protein molecules, and enzyme action shows that the presence of enzymes makes the formation of other living molecules possible. In fact, enzyme action determines even the division of DNA, as has become well known from gene-splicing.

This raises an interesting question. If proteins can divide DNA, would not they be causally determining for it and thus be the ultimate causal, genetic source of the continuance of life? This would explain other puzzling facts about the dependence of DNA and RNA on proteins.[2, 3] DNA might be only the means of the generally complex processes of reproduction, including that of proteins. DNA is a mere polymer, not a fully consolidated molecule,[3] though it is enormously vast—as the reproduction function requires.

Anyway, *crystallization* concepts make living forms more easily explainable. The first functions of a living formation are *nutrition and growth*. They can be causally explained by processes similar to crystallization, which is often seen as a prototype of living growth.[6, 7] Scientists have repeatedly pointed out how cyrstals selectively assimilate matter from the environment and grow in orderly ways much as living forms nourish themselves and grow.[7, 9]

Everything is predetermined in such "crystallization" because the universal pressures of the Field do not permit deviations from the ways in which molecules find their best protection or balance. These ways, of crystallization, are determined by the composition of the crystal cores and by the elements in the environment. Genetic material would correspond to such cores. Naturally, inner selection permits only the organically useful processes to continue and thus makes them purposive.

The possible forms of living "crystals" in an organism are astronomic in numbers. This is inevitable with the endless multiplicity of bonds and of combinations of their interactions made possible by the numerous, free electrons accumulating during the "protective," chain-reaction process of life. (Even incomparably fewer elements, as in Rubik's cube, make immense numbers of combinations possible.)

Through countless stages, further and further combinations of electron-rich bonds of living compounds, and of all their possible forms of "crystallization," create the myriad details of the organism. Understandably, crystals with an infinite number of interrelated facets lose the inherently simple crystalline appearance. Viruses or diatoms may still look crystalline. But organic structures formed by more multiple, endlessly involved "crystals" necessarily resemble amorphously organized matter—become "protein crystals."[7, 10]

The enormous expansion and proliferation of living forms is, ultimately, a result of life acting as a chain-reaction fire. Life is spreading or "burning" through every possible condition and creating infinite forms. The extraordinary proliferation of forms of life enables inner selection to be exceedingly successful, much more so than is the general, Darwinian selection—which similarly requires a reproductive proliferation of organisms.[2]

The decisive factor in the formation of living structures is the *universal presence of the Field's pressures*. They determine with cosmic force that each "crystal" and molecule find its exact form or position in the best protective, way. That is why living forms are so precisely and endlessly "predetermined." They are governed by unbelievably *multiple causal laws*.

Correspondingly, living forms seem to be predestined for equally many and complex purposes. Of course, it is selection that establishes the "purposes," as it permits only those forms to continue which are most fit to survive and to reproduce themselves exactly, with all their "purposive," most survival-worthy capacities preserved.

Biologists have, hopefully, turned to concepts such as tropism to explain how, for instance, roots turn downward under gravitation. But such forces or laws attributed to them are only few, whereas the laws governing living phenomena are innumerable.

The control of living matter by the Field at every point and instant is the simple, unseen source of the myriad of laws and "purposes" for every living form or function, big or small. Otherwise, the infinite order in the living world would be a metaphysical miracle.

The final function of living forms is *reproduction*. It is equally an automatic result of the pressures of the Field acting on the accumulation of living matter.

Any accumulating or growing mass finally divides, in various ways. But living matter divides only by growing into two equal units at each division. This is due to the opposing tendencies in the unseen interaction between the Field and matter. The Field tries to break up any matter accumulation. But living matter, accumulating in a chain-reaction way, tends to hold together. Under two such opposing tendencies a living formation starts dividing at one point of its growth but does so by keeping as much mass together as possible. The inevitable result is division into only two units, which hover within each other's "gravitational" forces until each grows to its full size, ready for further division.

During such a division the two units become exactly equal. For if one is smaller it attracts more matter from the other with which it is joined. Any other dissimilarity is equalized in the same way, between two competing, yet joined units, under the same pressures and forces. The result is a precise similarity of reproduced units, particularly since the mere size of giant living molecules is the central determining factor.

The double-helix concept offers a molecular explanation of reproduction by joined units. It confirms how such a reproduction in simple, primordial ways, at the deepest levels, can account for all organic reproduction. The spiral-staircase model, though, may be closer to the modes of human thinking[12] than to nature's way of creating its symmetries and ordered effects, through endlessly varied and intermixed forms, which are confusing to mind.

Generally, life is causally uniform, in the same way as fire is. Life is a universal, natural phenomenon, necessarily deriving from one simple causal principle. Yet the universal force or mechanism that makes all living processes grow and reproduce has remained a mystery.

The present *theories about life* are no less conjectural than is our explanation, but they are clearly untenable. They have never arrived at one universal and uniform causal principle, the very essence of the living process, as a unique phenomenon.

However varied the forms of matter may be, they are either alive or not. And that single, always similar "negative fire" that life is makes the whole difference. As some scientists have pointed out, life is a unique process contrary to the general laws of entropy; it remains always the same; and it acts like a special kind of yet-undiscovered charge or "special form of movement of matter."[6, 7, 10]

But what that principle or force of life is has not been discovered. Scientists try to explain living phenomena without it. All scientific speculations about life perpetuate the belief that life evolved cumulatively and gradually by complex, unique chance combinations of matter, without a special causal principle or force.[7, 10] If this were so, every one of the innumerable and unique living forms or mechanisms would require a similar uniquely rare combination. But living forms evolve and grow in countless, regular, yet virtually miraculous ways all the time and everywhere. They do so under the singular cosmic drive or force of living process which is comparable to fire.

Without this universal drive or principle, the accumulation and corresponding complexity of living matter would be impossible. For, everywhere, our physical universe is governed by the destruction and dispersion of any accumulated enrichment or organization of matter.

Scientists, beginning with Oparin, have argued that *natural selection* could have created complex living compounds from simple chemicals.[7, 11] Indeed, this would seem to be the only possible explanation since living forms are purposive in their miraculous complexity.

But natural selection would actually work *against* this assumed evolution of life. For, evidently, compounds increasing in size, or in complexity and enrichment, are *least fit* to survive in the universe, governed by entropy, by the destruction of the accumulated energy or organization in matter—unless a special drive or principle enables matter to work against entropy.

Only the principle of life as self-increasing chain-reaction "fire" enables selection to make living processes endlessly rich and purposive. This fire drives living forms to grow and reproduce prodigiously, with explosive effect. Then natural selection chooses, from the limitlessly offered forms, those that are most excellently fit to survive—the most "purposive" ones.

Finally, we have to try to explain *the origin of the spark of life, of the giant molecule*. Very peculiar conditions would be required for such a molecule to arise.

Under ordinary conditions the Field precludes or destroys any unusual increase in size or in the energy enrichment of a molecule. But the peculiar, ambivalent conditions during the cooling-down period of a planet should be considered here.

First, such cooling down is still a continuation of intense burning or yielding to the pressures of the Field. This also produces the momentary loosenings in the Field which constitute all radiation. Thus, if the cooling down is universal and intense, the loosenings in the Field can reach extreme saturation. In such a saturation it can happen that the loosenings accidentally concentrate, at one cross point. This can become a momentary spot where the Field pressures are instantly absent, and a giant molecule can implosively spring into existence. Secondly, the cooling down may provide conditions cool enough for the incipient living formation to survive immediate destruction by burning.

This conjecture agrees with findings in experiments that have produced compounds resembling living matter.

In the well-known experiments by Urey and Miller, shocks from high electric charges were used.[3] This can create momentary saturations of loosenings in the Field, to some extent, without the destruction of the accumulating compounds.

In other noted experiments by Sidney W. Fox and the German biochemist Gerhard Schramm, high heat was used, in ways that prevented it from breaking up the resulting compounds. Shock waves, which can create high temperatures for short instants, are found effective in producing various compounds similar to biochemicals. Here can be mentioned the experiments performed by Akiba and Nurit Bar-Nun under direction of Carl Sagan.

In sum, life is a universal but uniquely peculiar causal mechanism or principle, comparable to fire, of which it is a causally equal opposite. Life becomes understandable as "negative" fire when the Field and its interaction with matter as its opposite are recognized. The interaction of these two opposites makes even non-living atoms vibrate with an intensity similar to that of life. In living process this opposition becomes vast and rich in forms.

Scientists have compared life to fire. But no further causal explanations have followed, because life is actually opposite to normal fire in its effects and properties. The opposition between the Field and matter is the key to understanding the essential causal facts of the living process. We have seen how life becomes an extremely delayed and "inventive" process, governed by countless laws, under the restrictive dominance of the Field.

Scientists also know that giant molecules are sources of the processes of life. Here again, causal explanations would require insight into the interaction between matter and the Field as opposites.

The giant size of a living molecule makes possible a chain-reaction opposition to the Field, a protection against it. But inevitably, the Field as the dominant opposite imposes an infinite number of constricting laws as if purposively predetermining even the tiniest living process.

The insight about life as a fire reveals particularly clearly the extreme intensity or expansiveness of life and its prodigiously multiple variability. This tremendous drive and proliferation of living mechanisms make inner selection inevitable and effective. Life is indeed a fire, opposite to normal fire.

The Science of Genes as Atoms—and Organic Interdependence

Genetics, as all modern sciences, proceeds by the methods evolved in our exact, physical or technical sciences. In these causally clear, true sciences, causal elements can be studied in the simple one-by-one way in which our minds work. Here scientists do not have to face the humanly ungraspable, causally interdependent multiplicity of organic processes.

An isolated molecule of iron or salt would act causally in the same way as would molecules in a chunk of it. A wheel in a machine is not moved by countless drives and mechanisms acting variously at each instant. But in living organic processes a molecule or mechanism acts in dependence on countless other molecules or mechanisms causally connected with it, which in their turn are similarly determined by virtually the entire organism responding to various conditions.

Evidently, the methods imitated from the exact, physical sciences are bound to be misleading in genetics. Those methods require dealing, in each case, only with a single factor, with one causal property of an atom or molecule, strictly isolated and causally limited to the effects of some single similarly isolated causal influence.

This is diametrically different from the concepts necessary for understanding the myriad causal interdependence and interactions of molecules or cells and tissues in an organism. The same is true for genetic factors that determine and guide this interdependence and interaction.

Genes as genetic atoms are the concepts that enable geneticists to comply with the "scientism" which deals with isolated causal factors. Correspondingly, *isolated gene mutations* are accepted as sources of genetic adaptations. This is unfortunate and unbelievable, in view of the truly miraculous, purposive *interdependence of everything in the organism* with most everything else in it. The gene mutations are assumed to come from physical or chemical accidents creating molecular changes in genes. Now, consider the multiplicity of the causal interdependence of cells and even of the molecular connections in the organism.

The human organism supposedly consists of quadrillions of cells.[3] Thus, we have to think of billions of cells even for a tiny organic formation. Each cell would contain incomparably greater numbers of molecules. And each molecule is determined, as to its place and action, by the cells and molecules connected with it, which are similarly determined, further and further, by the cells in the whole organism.

When a scratch on your finger heals, every organic function, of circulation, breathing, or nutrition, is causally connected with it. Whatever is done at one point in the organism depends, purposively, on the whole of it, on what happens at any other point in it.

In sum, each gene mutation, to be adaptive, would have to create a molecular change precisely, purposively agreeing with at least billions of other molecular formations in the organism.

In practice, this could never happen as a result of the mere physical accidents that assumedly create mutations. The probability against this happening would be of a magnitude beyond human imagination; think of a "Rubik's cube" having billions of sides, all to be precisely combined.

Immense numbers of non-purposive or deforming changes would occur first before one purposive, adaptive change could happen. But the cells or molecules on your skin or in the tissues of any organ within you are so smoothly, adaptively evolved that almost none of them are out of place. Above all, adaptive improvement by selection could not work where myriad deformations inevitably and inseparably have to accumulate for any possible improvement.

These are obvious, simple facts. Why is modern genetics not

recognizing them as relevant? Because these facts do not fit the "scientific" methods or our human way of thinking. The concept of genes as atoms that are not endlessly interdependent is the only one that fits the experimental methods imitated from the exact, physical sciences.

It is a generally known truth, among scientists themselves, that historically scientism has served contemporary prejudices or has been distorted by the dominant scientific ways of thinking. We are not different. The dominant scientific concepts of our times are those of the physical and mechanical sciences, our only exact sciences.

Modern genetics has inevitably gravitated toward the theory of the *Mendelian "particulate" inheritance*, of isolated traits because this theory conveniently serves the concepts of genes as atoms.

Actually, the Mendelian inheritance proves merely that genetic traits are generally permanent; if intermixed they separate out unchanged in later generations. But the unchangeability or conservation of organic sameness is the universal law of organic existence. Its demonstration in genetic inheritance proves nothing new.

And the old, universal fact is that, in preserving their sameness or normalcy, organisms adapt, or change through evolution, by virtue of environmental conditioning. But this happens in ways so gradual and endlessly subtle that genetics do not perceive it, as we shall see in a moment.

Further, modern geneticists have conveniently moved toward accepting the *theory of particulate gene mutations* to sustain their assumptions about genes as separable, atomic determinants of genetic evolution. Findings by De Vries that traits of primroses changed suddenly became the starting-point of the theory that genetic changes occur through accidental mutations of isolated genes.[2, 3]

However, it was later realized that De Vries had "witnesed nothing more than the expression of recessive traits through recombination."[3] Of course, such recombination of previously adapted traits can create a viable, adaptive change. Which could never happen with the purely destructive gene mutations.

In working out the theory of mutations, modern genetics has been drifting further toward convenient misinterpretations of observed facts. The theory of mutations was established on findings by T.H. Morgan and his co-workers in studies on the drosophila fly and on corn. Again, it was later recognized that the mutations here "were intergenic rather than point mutations."[3] Naturally, intergenic mutations, coming from combinations of previously adapted genetic traits, can create viable changes.

In contrast, the mutations by purely accidental, molecular disruptions in genes can never create adaptive organic changes. The destructions and cripplings coming therewith would be so endlessly many that no selection could create anything adaptive with them, as we indicated above.

Yet in modern genetics such mutations are accepted as the only original sources of genetic evolution. Of course, this is necessary to preserve the "scientific" concept of genes as the atoms of genetic inheritance that do not have to be endlessly coordinated causally with innumerable organic factors.

Modern genetics is a vast, superbly inventive science. It has, understandably, found various ways of demonstrating its theory of mutations. But it has done so by limiting its findings on mutations to the most primitive forms of life, bacteria and viruses.[3, 12] The argument is that only here can the probabilities in terms of millions be observed.[2, 3]

Actually, the world of totally primitive forms of life, such as bacteria is least representative of organisms. A bacterium may have only a couple of functions, for primitive syntheses of compounds, compared with the millions of intercellular functions working under endless interdependence in any true organism. In practical terms bacteria are not organisms.

More probably, the stresses from such mutations indirectly affect all the genetic material in the one-celled bacterium. We shall see later how some viable intergenetic changes can result from such stresses.

Thus here, as in the Morgan experiments, intergenetic adaptations rather than mutations may be the sources of the few viable genetic changes. Not mutations themselves but their general, indirect stress effects create such intergenetic changes.

Indeed, the experiments show that the increase in radiation which brings the mutations does not directly relate to the increase in adaptive changes.[2, 3]. The argument is that strong radiation brings destruction.[1, 2, 3] The relevant argument should be that all such mutations can be only destructive and can never serve the infinitely refined genetic adaptations.

The dominant themes in explanations of genes at work are usually descriptions of all kinds of possible combinations of traits or genes. As most significant are viewed rare findings that, supposedly, a change in the position of one of the four DNA bases has been the cause of a genetic change.[2, 12] It is argued that the four bases are like letters of the alphabet which can combine for any possible organic compound or trait.

Marvelous speculations are regularly advanced about the *alphabet* of such a *few bases* as genetic components forming a whole library of organic encoding. The concept of atomistic genes as causal determinants then may seem convincing. But the thinking here is unbelievably, though conveniently, shortsighted.

It is overlooked that there must be a genetic determinant or code for every *connection* of organic elements as well as for *further connections* of their connections, in the endless, organic causal interdependence.

Some 100,000 genes have been assumed to control the human organism.[12] These would be the "words" or codes in the "library." More frequently, scientists assume that the kinds of the codes in this library number in millions.[1, 2, 3] Whatever the number of genes or codes, the organic *interconnections* are still overlooked. Each of them in turn requires genetic determinants, to form corresponding organic "words."

In truth, these interconnections are as many as there are causal relations in the organism, of every cell or molecule with almost any other cell, entailing further interconnections of such infinitely numerous relations. For in the organism everything has to be purposively, precisely related with everything else. This is so essential that it has to be repeated here as well.

Now consider that ten numbers related in all their possible ways give ten billion combinations. The million or hundred thousand organic "words" would also have to relate, by chance, in about half of all their possible ways before creating the unique sets of organic, precise interconnections of everything with everything else. Therefore, the necessary genes as determinants of the causal *connections* of the organic "words" and "letters" for the human organism would be literally astronomical in quantity. The number would likely have hundreds of thousands of zeroes—far above the possible number of atoms in the universe.[3]

It would be preposterous to try to understand or manage organisms by attempting to deal with such numbers. On the other hand, the inner-selection concept offers sufficient causal explanations for the entire myriad purposiveness of the organism.

And this enables us to understand, predict, or control the organic, and finally genetic, effects causally, through integrated organic reactions such as the pleasure drives, overenjoyments, habits, or acquired new adaptations "learned" through inner selection under environmental conditioning.

Genetic explanations can be made sophisticated. But the above multiplicity of purposively interdependent organic elements and their connections are facts that cannot be theorized away.

Yet geneticists proceed only with the concept of genes as atoms of inheritence, causally separable and numerable, as scientism requires. The central argument in modern Mendelian genetics is the permanence of genetic traits. The main part of genetics becomes the study and demonstration of the effects of isolated, unchanging traits and their various possible combinations.[2, 12] The Mendelian inheritance is, indeed, known and applied as "particulate" inheritance.

Of course, the conservation of organic sameness is the universal law of organic existence. But a change of mechanisms or traits becomes necessary precisely to conserve that sameness as normalcy under changing conditions. Thus, change results from conditioning or "learning" imposed by environment. Inner selection makes such learning possible and, as we shall see, genetically inheritable.

But, experimentally or *"scientifically," this conditioning* and the changes it brings *cannot be discovered* or causally related.

First, such changes are imperceptibly slight. The etablished and tenaciously preserved organic sameness is evolved and deepened through millions of generations. Conditioning during one or a few generations can bring only a barely perceivable change. Where a succession of thousands of generations can be observed, with fast-reproducing organisms, geneticists find distinct new adaptations to a changed environment.[1, 3]

Secondly, the conditioning is causally paradoxical, contrary to direct, experimental observations. In any conditioning, organic drives have to be used in order to suppress something in them, to restrict them in the end.

Any change affecting an organism is resisted or opposed at first by the organism. Even in educational conditioning, the first reaction is resistence to it. Only after long exposure of the organism to changes are they finally accepted. A physiologic conditioning, such as imposition of one customary food, brings rejection of it or the desire for other foods, before a general preference for the imposed habitual food finally develops.

Thus, organic conditioning may show effects which, at each

phase, are contrary to the final result, or seem causally unconnected with it.

Thirdly, and most importantly, conditioning results from subtle, "tricky," causal influences that cannot be measured or related merely in straight experimental terms.

Even for the conditioning of simple organisms such as plants, it is better to think in terms of their inner "evaluations." If you merely obstruct a root, it will only persist to overcome the obstruction. But if the obstruction favors the deviation of the root toward some water source, the result will be a conditioned or "learned" adaptation. Such "tricky" inducements become decisive genetically as well, because adaptive traits are inherited, however gradually.

In the famous experiments by August Weismann, tails of cats were cut, for several generations, but no shorter tails were found in offpsring. This was considered another decisive proof against genetic effect from conditioned organic changes. Actually, no conditioning resulted here for the cats, considering how subtle and tricky the "pleasant" inducements required in any conditioning have to be.

In different experiments, such authoritities as Pavlov and McDougall, the founder of Hormic Psychology, demonstrated that learning by conditioning can be genetically inherited. This is at least arguably possible. Such learning can involve changes on organically deep inner levels. Pleasure drives are conditioned here. They are organically the deepest influences, and organically deep events can have genetic effects.

In any case, modern genetics with its physical-science experimentalism can not discover the imperceptibly slight, paradoxical, and "tricky" effects of genetic conditioning.

Consequently, genetics can only reaffirm the general, gross preservation of genetic sameness, evident from the primitive Mendelian experiments. Mendel's findings can be repeated in all similar experiments, and a modern scientist would have to be very reckless not to accept experimental proofs.

Recently, however, scientists have begun to *discover that the Mendelian dogma of unchanging genes is deficient*. Typically, the latest Nobel prizes in the field of genetics have been awarded for such discoveries—to Barbara McClintock; to Francois Jacob, Andre Lwoff, and Jacques Monod; to Howard Temin, and to Sir Peter Medawar.

McClintock discovered that genes change in their action, and she did so by studying "whole organisms."[13] Her discovery was contrary to what geneticists believe. She said, "they thought I was crazy, absolutely mad."[13] The French Nobelists Jacob, Lwoff, and Monod have discovered that genes can be changed by "regulatory genes," or by the operons they create.[5] Howard Temin has demonstrated in his research on retroviruses and on "reverse transcriptase" that DNA can be changed by RNA, according to changes in the immune system—which are environmentally induceable.[13] Sir Peter Medawar has written about similar changes.[13] The Nobelist James Watson found the gene-change discoveries of McClintock significant and supported her research.

Discoveries of such gene changes multiply as new knowledge in genetics accumulates. But the "scientific" method cannot be easily abandoned. The gene changes are still explained in terms of other genetic atoms, like the "activators" and "jumping genese" of McClintock, or the operons. Similarly, "rate genes," "regulatory" genes, or "transposons" have been proposed as causes of genetic changes, by Sir D'Arcy Thompson and Sir Julian Huxley.[5, 13]

Explanations by such genetic factors as separate genetic atoms are certainly the only possible ones in the present experimentalism imitated from the physical sciences. But the concepts of such "atoms" are misleading for obvious reasons.

Organisms and organic mechanisms are wondrously purposive in their genetic adaptations. This is the most obvious fact about them. And it is only *the organism as a whole that adapts* or becomes purposive. The same is true of mechanisms or organs inside organisms. They also integrate their countless subordinate mechanisms, under the law of subordination, while serving the organism as a whole. Everything in the organism—we have to repeat—has to agree with everything else in it.

This, of course, cannot be grapsed or dealt with in terms of "scientific," separable causal elements. But it is a fact; and explanations using separate genetic factors are causally fictitious. It is comfortable to explain that a regulatory gene or activator induces gene changes. But how can the regulating gene be so miraculously purposeful that the changes are coordinated with the countless mechanisms responding adaptively as one organism to environmental conditions? Scientists should recognize the organic integration and the action of the organism as a holistic system.

If they did so, they would find that the proper organic factors to be dealt with are *organic drives* and satisfactions as reactions by *the whole organism*. Particularly because these reactions are the only ones that can be grasped or treated by the mind causally, or scientifically, in full. We have seen that the best, or rather the only, way to understand the complex organic causation, mechanically and causally, is *in terms of pleasure*, which indeed determines and "explains" how the whole organism behaves and adapts, or becomes conditioned by environment, through endless experimentally ungraspable influences, past or present.

Genetics could be an important science providing direction even for human genetic improvements. Men, as all organisms, develop their habits and adaptations, vices and healthy customs, according to their drives and satisfactions—or, simply, pleasures. And our ways of living, particularly our "sins" or over-enjoyments, have genetic effects for the following generations.

This is clear from age-old moral wisdoms as well as from findings about chromosomal changes brought by various habits such as the use of narcotics. Such changes are confirmed by the genetic research of the above Nobel laureates.

Revealingly, the Nobel Prize to Barbara McClintock was awarded in the field of medicine. The importance of *genetic changes through habits* affecting health has become too obvious. Malignancy is clearly caused by changes in chromosomes. Such changes are inheritable. The findings by the Nobel laureates Temin and Medawar on retroviruses also reveal that environmentally caused chromosomal changes—brought about by habits—genetically affect the immune system and can be causes of inheritable malignancy.

Understandably, research on gentic influences from habits, such as drinking is rare. A scientist would have to be very imprudent to proceed contrary to the truths proved in experiments concerning the Mendelian unchangeability of traits. Still, Dr. Louis Bartoshesky found in his research studies that heavy drinking by a father had the effects of fetal alcohol syndrome on his child.[13] Experiments on rats by Lester Soyka and Justin Joffe showed that various drugs administered to male rats had adverse effects on their offspring.[13]

Such findings, showing genetic influences from habits of parents, are of unique importance. They reveal the gravest genetic facts that people have always intuitively known. But modern genetics is not interested in such facts, which are contrary to experimental Mendelian tenets; research on these most important problems is rare and gets little attention.[2, 12]

We may as well look more closely at *how impossible the mutation concept is in practical reality*. This concept is necessary to sustain the dogma of genes as atoms of genetic inheritance. But, if mutations were causes of genetic change, any possible adaptive improvement would come together with billions of potential cripplings or deformations for mechanisms everywhere in the organism, on the surface of the skin or in the muscles of the heart.

If selection were to promote adaptations here, it would have to kill a species a billion times over for every tiny adaptation to eliminate the deformations. And such adaptations are infinitely numerous for every mechanism.

Actually, inner selection must work so that the overwhelmingly destructive mutations are always counteracted. Protection here is necessarily offered by multiple provisions for renewal and repair, as in every important organic protection. We may recall that cells have proportionally huge amounts of seemingly unneeded DNA, presently considered as "junk" DNA. It must contain an immense amount of gentic codes, a plentiful reserve for providing duplicates as replacements for damaged genetic material; a most important genetic threat here requires such measures.

Generally, mutations are assumed to bring *changes that are sudden and disruptive, unrelated to previous adaptations*. This could not be different because mutations come from the outside as pure accidents. In contrast, natural adaptations are always imperceptibly gradual improvements of previously evolved functions. Such improvements are brought by the inner selection working under organic subordination.

The gradualness of adaptations is the main fact noticed about natural evolution. It is required by the genial theory of Darwin, which still serves as the basis of our understanding of evolution. Darwin did not believe in evolution through the emergence of sports. The whole body of findings in natural history illustrates gradual transition of forms. Paleontologists and biologists always look for and find small, incipient beginnings as well as vestigial remains of evolving organic structures.

Even when sudden changes occur during the evolution of a species, they have to be functionally integrated and streamlined by gradual adaptations. Sudden, accidental changes are inevitable in our chaotic universe, inherently disruptive for living processes. That is why evolution is sometimes not perfect in its gradualness, as is pointed out in the punctuationalist theories. But the sudden changes are exceptions to the rule and are duly taken care of by detailed adaptations through inner selection.

The universal principle of genetic adaptations is the functionally integrated change, and this cannot be sudden. Adaptations in one generation cannot prevail much against mechanisms purposively deepened during millions of generations and integrated through the whole organism. A sudden genetic change is left in by selection only to the extent it becomes organically integrated, made useful through inner selection.

As to the necessarily disruptive nature of the mutations, it makes the mutation theory unbelievable.

The miracle of purposiveness in living nature is possible only because each new adaptation is always an *added refinement or expansion* of the myriad previous adaptive improvements of some *vital organic function.* Every organism is a perfection of integration and streamlining, in which not one structure or function, large or small, is out of place. Each adaptation has required unimaginably many changes, but not once has its streamlined perfection been disrupted by a change unrelated or unadjusted to previous adaptations *conserving a function.*

Only this undisrupted, perfectly integrated continuation and expansion of infinitely numerous and varied improvements of previous functions and their adaptations make the miracle of living nature possible.

You can see this from the unbelievably complex and varied, yet uninterrupted, perfectly purposive adaptations of organic structures and functions everywhere. Think, for instance, of the extremely strange and extensive, yet *functionally conservative,* sexual and reproductive specializations, of say, spiders or nonaquatic frogs, as well as of the endlessly extensive organic perfection of your body or of a beehive.

All in all, it is almost self-evident that the inherently *destructive* and *sudden* mutations can never account for the miraculous, exquisitively refined and gradual adaptations for *conservation* of organic functions. Particularly since selection cannot work where billions of mutational cripplings would necessarily accompany each tiny adaptation.

But mutations are a "scientifically" inevitable corollary of genes as genetic atoms. Genes conceived in terms of the physical sciences can change, randomly, only by physical accidents, by mutations that are never connected with organic integration or previous adaptations.

A very different science is needed to explain how random changes bring organic purposivenes. Concepts like that of organically integrated adaptation through inner selection would have to replace the concept of mutations of genes as genetic atoms.

Generally, what is offered as *evidence of genes* actually results from the mode of location of genetic material in chromosomes. It is only natural that a major part of the genetic material for a particular trait is located close together on a chromosome. It is a matter of preference to view such a concentration of genetic material as a separate gene.

All organic structures can be either viewed separately or recognized as the mere parts of the organism that they are. An organ such as the nose or mouth can be viewed as controlling the separate functions of smell or eating. We know, of course, that the mouth or nose in its function is causally incongruous if separated from the organism as a whole, though the function of eating or smelling is clearly centered around the mouth or nose.

Geneticists may, for instance, claim the presence of a gene for eye color after discoveries that genetic material centered around a certain spot on a chromosome of a fly affects its eye color. Such a claim is as incongruous as the view that the mouth determines the function of eating. But the connections between such centers of genetic material and genetic traits are fully sufficient to construct gene maps or similar systems showing linkages and interconnections of genes.

To explain the resulting endless inconsistencies from such constructs, geneticists have conveniently worked out numerous rules of exceptions. They have various explanations, not only from the limitlessly unpredictable mutations, but also about a series of gene mutators, suppressors, enhancers, regulators, operons, epistases, hypostases, activators, and other unlimited gene modifiers or controllers.[2, 12] With such limitless possibilities of exceptions, particularly the totally random mutations, anything can be explained—after it has happened.

The central problem, however, remains. A regulator with any range of properties can be easily claimed or "discovered" amidst the multiplicity of organic interactions. But only a supernatural intelligence could make the mutation regulators so ingenious that they can provide the multi-faceted purposiveness throughout the infinite interrelated organic, cellular and molecular connections. However sophisticated the present explanations may be, that holistic purposiveness cannot be dismissed. It is present in any conceivable organic causation and the myriad causal connections of organic integration.

A true explanation here has to account for organically integrated action by all tissues and molecules operating simultaneously as one purposive organism. The explanation from inner selection working under the integrating organic subordination accounts for that. But no such explanations are possible through the study of separate elements or atoms such as genes—nor through the use of physical-science methods generally.

We admit that genetics is enlightening and interesting where it deals with "genes" as with already evolved, purposive bearers of traits. For instance, useful insights are offered by explanations of chromosome rearrangements, breakages, crossing over, inversions, translocations, euploidy, poliploidy, genetic drifts and isolations or population genetics.[2, 12]

These are vast, and the most relevant fields in genetics. But they deal only with combinations of *already evolved, wondrously purposive traits*—which have resulted from Darwinian and inner selections but can never be created by the massively crippling mutations.

Genetic engineering also works by merely using already evolved, purposive genetic traits. "Recombinant DNA" engineering, as it is called, describes this properly. No separate genes could be engineered or even isolated from the whole genetic system. A trait such as the resistance to cold by wheat consists of properties that affect the whole organism. Correspondingly, genetic engineering deals here with a significant part of the whole DNA.

It has been calculated that some three billion base units are contained in the whole DNA of a cell. Their genetically relevant interconnections, causally corresponding to the infinite number of molecular organic connections, would be even more numerous. Each such interconnection factor would be a gene as a genetic determinant. Thus any imaginable, submicroscopic speck of material that genetic engineers can deal with contains necessarily innumerable "genes," whole systems of the integrated DNA.

The decisive fact is the interdependence of all genetic material of the DNA in controlling the traits. Certainly, a "gene" connectable with some abnormality—say, a genetic disease or mongolism—may be found on one chromosome or part of it. But a "gene" is always only some central portion of the genetic material for a trait.

In fact, each "gene" is an inherent part causally of all "genes" found on the other chromosomes as well. The triploid chromosome of mongolism interacts with other chromosomes, as all chromosomes always interact, under the purpose of total causally interdependent, organic integration.

In sum, the recombinant DNA engineering or "gene-splicing" is actually always dealing with whole systems of genetic material, sufficient to have organic effect, requiring action by the whole organism.

Of course, sometimes the "gene" as the central part of genetic material for a trait may indeed be sufficient for engineering a useful product. This is the case in engineering organic mechanisms such as antibodies, which can be effective even if they destroy or affect only a part of a harmful intruder or of a living process.

Generally, nobody can dispute that the Mendelian findings are correct as they illustrate the principle of the unchangeability of genetic traits. But the "scientific" theory supposedly proven by the primitive Mendelian experiments is untenable. The *Mendelian particulate inheritance* is incongruous in view of the actual, complete, causally interdependent organic integration. The organic mechanisms are as infinitely interdependent in their intricate and exquisite purposiveness as the gene mutations can always be only totally unrelated to organic integration and overwhelmingly disruptive for it.

Thus we have in genetics, on the one hand, endless repetitions of the facts of genetic unchangeability, which needs no proofs or demonstration. On the other hand, we have genetic "scientific" explanations leading to obvious causal incongruities. The *practical result* of the confusion has to be emphasized.

Orthodox genetics cannot help us in our main genetic concerns. We are to wait, helplessly, for the uncontrollable and destructive mutations as sources of genetic improvement. Geneticists remain "scientifically" unconcerned with degenerative changes that we may be accumulating with our ways of life for future generations. We actually can determine our genetic destiny, by controlling our habits of living. This requires effort. Science could help here, in our scientific era. But genetics, in its scientism, would rather assure men that their ways of life do not matter.

Practical geneticists, in fields such as cattle-breeding *disregard the theory* of unchanging genes. They proceed just as practical breeders have always done. New, improved, permanent traits are obtained in practical breeding, contrary to genetic theory.

According to the theory of modern Mendelian genetics, cross-breeding does not produce changes in genes, and organisms revert to their previous traits in future generations. But in practice cross-breeding, and all sexual reproduction, create permanent improvements and decisive changes in "genes" as more varied genetic material is brought together for inner selection to work on. That is why sexual reproduction is so strongly promoted by natural selection. The mixture and enlargement of genetic material enhances adaptive changes in traits.

Such changes evolve in the way all adaptations do, by inner selection, which works during the formation of the reproductive cell as well as at every instant afterward. We have seen how genetic codes even from the remote past of species may be used for improvements, by inner selection. Hybrid vigor comes from the use of added genetic material.

In sum, improved breeds can result through the self-strengthening of better traits by inner selection using an expanded mixture of genetic material. Thus, "genes" are changed by inner environment. Of course, changes in one generation can prevail only partially against established traits.

The Mendelian theory is contradicted every time improved breeds are produced through cross-breeding, by practical breeders, and by geneticists in their practical achievements, as well as by the natural sexual cross breeding.

Theoretically, such permanent changes could not happen. Every textbook on genetics demonstrates how, upon cross breeding, after a dozen generations, only the pure, homozygous traits are left by the segregation; or how the mixed, heterozygous traits progressively disappear.

According to the founder of the "gene" terminology, W. L. Johannsen, "artificial selection can do nothing but disentangle a mixture of variations, and a continual elaboration of characters as it was postulated by Darwin is impossible."[2]

Indeed, under our Mendelian genetics, breeding and cross-beeding, natural and artificial, would only lead back, in the end, to pure lines of traits. In the theory of unchanging traits this is a basic certainty—glaringly and continuously disproved by what nature and practical breeders achieve.

According to the theory, genetic characters can only decrease, as all variation, by occasional cross breeding, would be effaced in the end. The genes would remain forever the same, in their effects and numbers. Genes are true, eternal, unchanging atoms.

Reality is, however, different. The organism has an infinite number of characteristics even for each of its tiniest stuctures and functions as they relate to the rest of the organism. And every one of the characters must, necessarily, have a determinant, a "gene," as purposive a is the character.

Now, the eternally unchanging genes do not vary or evolve. We have to ask again what supernatural creation established the infinite numbers of miraculously purposive, unchanging genes.

Living nature varies and evolves endlessly. It meets any relevant environmental condition with infinitely refined adaptations. Organisms and their mechanisms are shaped by the environment as if a skillful craftsman here was continuously at work. We have seen how this humanly ungraspable perfection results automatically from the organically subordinate inner selection promoting adaptations in accordance with external and internal environments at every point, every instant.

This is totally different from the theory of unchanging genes, forever fixed in number, mutating only through disruptive, sudden accidents and never even thought of as being related to the changing environmental requirements on an organism or with the infinite, miraculously purposive, organic interrelatedness.

In sum, modern Mendelian particulate genetics is an inevitable result of the imitation of the methods of our exact, physical sciences. These methods require dealing with separate elements or isolated causal factors, with genes as atoms. But the living, organic phenomena have causal, scientific meaning only as results of organic integration through causal interdependence of humanly ungraspable multiplicity. And this should be true also for the genetic factors, which determine organisms.

The causal interdependence of any element in the organism with almost all other elements in it is the very gist of organic existence or action. It requires the coordinated interaction of myriad elements simultaneously at every instant.

This automatically results from the organically subordinate inner selection, but is totally incompatible with concepts of scientism from the physical sciences, requiring the separation of causal factors so that they can be treated as isolated elements or genetic atoms. The role of the inner selection in genetic causation is decisive, as will be explained later.

Inner Selection a Source of Infinite Adaptations

Selection is the universal law of existence, since only that exists which is able to persist. Matter and atoms exist by being able to resist destruction by the Field. Organisms evolve as they acquire, accidentally, changes that happen to help them survive. In continuous competition only the fittest survive.

Opposition or destruction, a negative cause, thus brings perfection. This is inconsistent with human value beliefs. Darwin was a genius, able to break free from generally held beliefs.

Naturally, selection governs all forms of life, whether they are organisms or mechanisms inside them. Those inner structures and processes that happen to become stronger or fitter prevail—provided they enable each higher inner mechanism that governs them to become stronger, which does the same, and so on.

Thus, finally, the highest controlling mechanism, the organism as the organic and genetic self, acquires the advantages. This is how inner selection promotes fitter organisms. Darwin's theory probably permits such considerations. But as it is understood now Darwinian selection is so limited that it becomes insufficient as a general principle.

According to Darwinian selection only that individual, or his progeny, survives who acquires a better specific adaptation. The rest of the species must perish. To the extent that this does not happen the better specific trait is lost by disruption or dissipation within the species, through mixture with existing traits.

But could not that trait be preserved within a group of a few individuals, say on an island? This would require that even for each tiny improved trait, a separate group should evolve which does not interbreed with the rest of the species and thus becomes in effect a separate species. And the number of such traits is infinite. Moreover, the separated improved traits still would not be joined in the one given species. Whatever the conceivable conditions, the Darwinian selection works only to the extent that all or most individuals in a species perish except the one who happens to acquire the better specific trait.

The critical fact, however, is that *the number of better traits* for each species is virtually unlimited, *inconceivably vast*.

As we have repeatedly explained, almost every molecular connection within an organism requires purposive determinants for proper integrated adaptations so that it is formed in accordance with other molecular connections in the organism. Thus, the better adaptive traits for each species must be infinite in number. And the minutest organic process in any adaptation has to be causally determined in the same way as a great one is.

Consequently, even for a small adaptation, *each species would have to perish*—all of it, except for one individual—*an infinite number of times* under Darwinian selection. Evidently, this selection cannot be the only, exclusive rule

In contrast, inner selection provides adaptive improvements and eliminates non-adaptive mechanisms at every point in the organism every instant. We shall see later how the organic adaptations, brought about by inner selection, become genetically inheritable.

Moreover, the selective promotion of better traits and elimination of maladaptive changes are completed by inner selection on the levels of the lower mechanisms, before the changes reach the highest mechanism, the organism as a whole.

Organisms and species thus are affected only by the selectively promoted improvements but not by the maladaptive or disruptive influences. These are eliminated at the lower levels of organic integration. The extinction of all members except one of the species is thus never required. Promotion of the better traits, as well as protection against nonadaptive changes, becomes automatic for each individual. This is a very important fact.

The universe, governed by the law of entropy, constantly destroys organized or accumulated matter and energy. Organisms have little chance to be favored by the outside world, but incomparably more chances to become disrupted and disorganized.

Without the early inner elimination of maladaptive influences organisms, and their genetic traits, would soon become accumulations of cripplings and distortions. Organisms then would have either to perish in masses at impossible cumulative rates, under Darwinian selection, or continue gathering more and more cripplings organically and genetically through generations.

We have to explain here in more detail the basically simple *way in which inner selection works*, under the rule of organic subordination.

Every living process, as a "negative fire," tries to expand and vary endlessly, intensely. Those processes within an organism take over which are stronger, more effective. Inner selection starts here. But if it were not controlled, the organism would fall apart, as each process inside it would work only for itself. The rule of organic subordination prevents this.

Now, the principle of organic subordination is a fact. Everybody can see how tinier, less decisive organic processes serve the more decisive organs or tissues. It is not difficult to understand that this is the only way the integrated organism can work. As a natural causal principle organic subordination is simple.

We can even think of simple models of the subordination by separate organic mechanisms; such models are to serve as mere causal illustrations of what has to remain, in terms of interacting processes, a mentally ungraspable interrelated multiplicity. We can think of tiny, subordinate organic structures or mechanisms being connected with a controlling larger one in such a way that they can become stronger only on the condition that the larger one becomes stronger.

Such connections would not be difficult to have in nature. Small electric conductors, comparable to those in neuron action can be easily, simply connected with a larger one so that they can function only when this enables the larger one to work. A river system, developing somewhat like an organized network, can evolve as such only if the workings of small rivulets enable a greater stream they are connected with to work efficiently. Otherwise the result would be ineffective water pools but not a well-organized river system.

We may keep in mind that the universal rule of all, general selection promotes the principle of subordinate connections between organic mechanisms. For this makes possible the formation of larger, well-integrated organisms and such organisms are fitter to survive.

Anyway, it is evident that the rule of subordination governs throughout the organism and that the enactment of subordination between living processes or mechanisms can evolve in simple, natural ways. But the result is a humanly unfathomable miracle, because of the incredible multiplicity of the subordinate mechanisms competing for stronger self-realization as well as for greater self-subordination. For they are permitted to survive only to the extent that they serve effectively the higher and higher subordinating mechanisms. And all competitive, continuous selection becomes purposive; this is the central discovery in Darwin's theory.

Thus the organism, as the highest subordinating mechanism, and every infinite process within it automatically become purposive or stronger and fitter, through competitive inner selection.

The insight into life as a "fire" is important for understanding competitive inner selection. Life as such a fire expands with burning, intense persistence to every possible source of available energy in every nook and cranny of the external and internal environments. The living inner forms thus tend to proliferate with explosive intensity.

Darwin, supposedly, saw selection as possible because orgnisms reproduce offspring in huge numbers. Living forms as inner mechanisms, which life tries to create in every possible way, are potentially far more prolific. A living molecule is a source of endlessly expanding chain reactions of living processes, as we have seen in explaining life.

Thus, unlimitedly numerous and varied ways for exploiting the environment by organic mechanisms are competitively promoted by inner selection. Moreover, each of the endless ways becomes purposive with equal competitive intensity and multiplicity, under the criterion of better survival for any mechanism through its greater self-subordination. In the end, every possible purposive benefit obtained from the environment accrues to the highest subordinating mechanism, the organism as a whole.

Here we may recall that the organism as a whole is a concrete entity or self but is humanly hardly understandable in its multiplicity. It is, however, sufficient to realize that the countless constituents of the organism do interact so that one unified response results for the benefit of all of them. Your pleasure response to the right food is a good example.

Nature knows how to make countless mechanisms cooperate, as easily as two or three under the simple criterion of better survival or continuance for better cooperating mechanisms.

Now we may look at the causal relation between the purposively adapting whole organism and the similarly integrated genetic self as the genetic material that determines the organism's progeny. Does the marvelous purposiveness of traits of each species derive *from the purposive lifetime adaptations* of its past members? What other source could that purposiveness have?

Destructive mutations as such a source would be unthinkable, particularly because selection cannot work where every possible improvement would have to come together with an infinite number of cripplings. Selection as the universal law of existence promotes living forms with fitter, more purposive adaptations. Such adaptations are evolved only by and for whole organisms, as members of a species, mostly through inner selection. Darwinian selection is a superb concept, and it has to be extended to include selective improvement by the inner mechanisms of an organism.

Darwin, apparently, understood evolution by natural selection better than his interpreters do. He held that the inheritance of acquired traits was necessary and that it resulted from inner, cellular processes. He knew that the gradual evolution observed in nature was possible only through this inheritance of acquired adaptations by imperceptibly small steps.

In his theory of pangenesis, Darwin reasoned that each cell in the organism releases gemmules which collect in the reproductive cells, so that the offspring have cell structures similar to those of the parents' organisms.[14] Genetic gradualness would be insured here because cells within the inherently self-preserving organism are protected against sudden changes.

Darwin was a genius in his insights. He recognized that the reproductive cell must be a product of the whole organism, of all the cells in it. Everything that the organism creates or does results from the interaction of practically every tissue and cell in it. But Darwin, careful scientist that he was, presented his theory of pangenesis in terms of the exact, physical sciences. Accordingly, he resorted to the concept of gemmules as kinds of atoms.

In reality, however, organisms do not act through separate units or mechanisms as distinct atoms or wheels. What the mind sees as one organic function or causal factor is actually an interaction of countless elements throughout the whole organism.

For instance, the function or factor of growth is causally intermixed and dispersed through all tissues or cells of the organism. So is the function of nutrition or any other organic function or causal factor, though we usually think of them as single functions or factors. In doing so we try to identify a causal factor with one organic locus or center. The function of growth may be attributed to the action of the pituitary gland, though this function is clearly determined by the whole organism—while the pituitary hormone serves only as signal or triggering mechanism for the integrated organism.

With this in mind, we can say that the genetic self as the integrative genetic material, embodied in the reproductive cells, becomes *diffused or integrated through every organic cell,* yet still remains the genetic self or center, from which and to which every organic influence flows, and which reproduces itself in countless, subsequent reproductive cells.

Of course, this is ungraspable to the mind. Only pleasure reactions can explain to the mind how it all works. We have indicated repeatedly—because it is decisive and true—that pleasure reactions make understandable to the mind what causally happens inside the infinite organism.

Indeed pleasure reactions show that the genetic self is integrated and diffused through every cell or mechanism in the body, yet still acts and exists as one central self. This is clear from the genetically controlled processes in eating, sex, or any other function. Especially since the DNA itself, as the genetic material, directs all the interrelations of this integration throughout the organism. And the pleasure responses, say in eating, show that these processes are diffused throughout the organic cells, whose needs create the pleasure, for evoking a centrally-controlled action.

Furthermore, an organism is only the latest "shell" for embodiment of the genetic self which is the real, continuous, and determining existent. Scientists know this.[14] In sum, the genetic self, embodied in the organism, exists and acts diffused or integrated in every mechanism or cell in the body while performing as a controlling central self. It acts in the same way while reproducing itself in millions of reproductive cells.

This concept of the genetic self is very important, though it may seem only philosophical because of its "scientifically" ungraspable multiplicity. The genetic self with these attributes is a fact, as is that multiplicity.

We know that one reproductive cell, as the genetic self creates even the smallest traits throughout the developing organism. This includes not only the shape of the earlobes or the pigments of eye color, but also all the other, innumerable, microscopic yet decisive traits, genetically controlled through their whole growth and development.

Where in the body is this genetic self? Evidently it is everywhere in the organism, in all its cells and their molecular connections with other cells and molecules. It is significant that all cells in an organism always contain DNA, mostly in its full complement of chromosomes. Of course, the mind can never grasp the endless interactions of such cellular DNA between the cells.

But this interaction would not be less extensive than that of the cells, which follows the universal organic principle of total organic integration. Particularly since the DNA itself, as the genetic material, creates all the interrelations of this integration throughout the organism. A fully integrated genetic self "diffused" throughout the organism is therefore causally as inevitable as is the organic integration.

Generally, *as a part of organic cells, the genetic self*, would be exposed to what happens in the cells, and thus in the whole organic self. Under all the forms of the embodiment of the genetic self throughout the organism, somatic influences on the genetic material are inevitable. The genetic, indiscernible self as the center and the cells in which it is diffused influence each other continuously.

Practically, the somatic organism is merely the expression or the shell of the genetic self. All the controls in the organism ultimately come from the genetic self.[14] Thus, everything we have said about organic subordination in inner selection is brought about by the subordinating or governing genetic mechanisms.

Each genetic mechanism is therefore favored or strengthened and sustained by the lower, somatic mechanisms which, reciprocally, depend for their existence, and strength on the higher genetic mechanism that controls them. This *interlocking, reciprocal interdependence* is the very gist of inner selection, as we have repeatedly explained.

The final result is that each genetic mechanism purposively changes, expands, or retracts, in accordance with corresponding purposive changes in the somatic mechanisms, which thus constitute its inner environment.

We saw how the subordinated mechanisms always act as the environment for the subordinating mechanisms—and how the two *interdepend purposively* under inner selection. Naturally, each such inner environment depends, in the same causally interlocking ways, on a more external environment, and so on. The final, ultimately decisive environment is the one around the organism, the outside, natural conditions.

Of course, the interactions here are not humanly graspable in their multiplicity. But they can be understood causally through the simple principle governing them—the *reciprocal purposive interdependence in inner selection* between the genetic controls and the somatic mechanisms.

This causal interdependence should not be difficult to accept. Think of how the genetic self, from the reproductive cell, shapes so perfectly and minutely every form or property throughout the subsequent organisms. It is far easier for the organism to affect the genetic self, which copies itself in reproductive cells. It is easy because that self is part of every cell and molecular connection in the organism.

Organisms do adapt to the environment. Muscles grow stronger when they are needed. Limbs or tissues that are not exercised dwindle. These are easily observable facts. And such adaptations are maintained by the organism even during its periodic renewals in which all tissues or cells are regrown, as if created anew. Evidently, such changes are deep enough to determine organic controls. And if these controls have changed on one level, they correspondingly affect the higher, subordinating, genetic controls, under the *interlocking, reciprocal* action through inner selection.

The overall effect is that the final, ultimately decisive external environment, around the organism, changes the genetic self, however slightly, just as it changes the muscles and organs, adaptively, during the lifetime of the organism.

The decisive facts are, of course, inner selection and the "diffusion" of the genetic self through every cell in the organism. The subordinative inner selection provides the purposiveness on all levels of the somatic and genetic, reciprocal controls. The "diffusion" of the genetic self insures that environmental changes reach it even if they effect primarily only the cells or something in them.

Naturally, the genetic controls, maintained and deepend through thousands of generations, cannot be changed much by environmental influences during one generation. The levels of subordinating controls and the inner environments are too numerous here for such influences to reach the genetic self more directly. (We use terms such as "levels" or "environments" to have some humanly comprehensive explanation; in reality the living factors work through endlessly involved and countless, humanly ungraspable transitions.)

In fact, the environmental influences on the genetic self are generally so weak as to be unnoticeable. Yet every one of these influences inevitably has its tiny effect, because the genetic self is everywhere in the organism all the time.

That is why the *genetic adaptations can be so decisively useful yet so infinitely refined*, or smooth and streamlined, like rocks shaped by winds through the ages. Environmental influences, working through millions of years, leave their average purposive impact, with even the tiniest environmental changes contributing to it.

This is how animals are so purposively and minutely shaped by the environment, which works here as a craftsman with exquisite skills. The end result is incomprehensibly detailed or smooth purposiveness and streamlining.

For instance, the wings of birds, bats and butterflies have been formed with minute, streamlined perfection by the requirements of flying. These wings have been, revealingly, created into surprisingly similar shapes in spite of the total genetic unrelatedness of the species. Many mammals have been shaped with equal skill into "fishes" by the sea. Conspicuous examples here are whales, porpoises, seals, manatees, various reptiles, and even penguins to a degree.

Further, we may recall that *organisms as well as mechanisms within them "learn"* by way of environmental conditioning. The living mechanisms deepen themselves, become stronger, under inner selection, wherever environmental conditions permit such self-deepening. Thus, the organic and genetic mechanisms evolve here under the same law of effect which governs inner selection and all learning by conditioning.

Moreover, learning through conditioning, though mechanistic, can have effects similar to those of foresight, planning or even abstract symbolic understanding, as we have seen, The possibilities of seemingly ingenious planning in genetic adaptations are therefore limitless. But they are available only through inner selection, which works under the law of effect, the law of all learning.

Darwinian selection, as it is usually understood, offers no possibilities for such genetic learning and adaptations by "foresight" or "planning." The fittest individual survives—while his whole species perishes—because some purely accidental change has increased his fitness.

Inner selection, similarly, depends on pure accidents and on the survival of the fittest mechansims, but it does not require the critical perishing of the organisms that do not have the adaptation in question. On the contrary, endlessly multiple, competing inner mechanisms always remain. They constitute the organism, which then can go through numerous other accidents, trials, and errors, by which its mechanisms learn other adaptations.

The possibilities of new trials here are so multiple that they may have an effect similar to that of the abstract, unlimited "rehearsals" by human mind for gaining foresight which makes planning possible. Inner selection can offer almost unlimited possibilities of "rehearsals" as it works for eons with endlessly multiple and minute inner mechanisms.

Also, a subtle, *inventive drive comparable to the human pursuit of pleasure* results from inner selection integrated for the whole organism. Inner selection chooses, under the principle of subordination, what is most favorable to the whole organism, to its survival. This choosing is thus identical with the human pleasure drive, which also merely serves survival.

Man understands simply and perfectly the pleasure drive, in all its multiple causal implications. He can therefore understand simply, yet thoroughly, by thinking in terms of pleasure, how organisms purposively act and evolve—through inner selection—by pursuing pleasure as simply as man himself does.

This can be important for the causal, scientific understanding of evolution by man. For instance, he can properly conclude that the "pleasure" which spiders experience in trapping insects is for spiders a causal factor as decisive as would be, say, a change in the geophysical conditions surrounding them. It can be said that the "pleasure" drive shapes, in every action by the animal, the most suitable forms in the organs, in the claws or mouth, which he uses in the action.

Biologists and paleontologists often look for physically great geologic changes in the environment, or new niches in it, as the causes of new adaptations. Actually, the decisive changes and niches of adaptation sought by the animal are the inner "pleasures" shaping even the tiniest organic mechanisms.

Combine this with the reserve of inner *genetic codes from the past of the species*, and you can see the limitless possibilities for the species to select expanded, more "pleasant," adaptively richer evolutionary changes.

Organisms can use, as it were, the memory of the species accumulated through eons. Man repeats from the embryo on, his genetic past, the source of the instincts by which he develops and survives. The multiplicity necessary here is as unfathomable as it is everywhere else in living nature.

When a cat stalks a sparrow, he uses ingenious, physiologically complex movements and hiding tactics. They are genetically inherited, and consist of innumerable biochemical processes. Could each of these infinite processes have evolved through Darwinian selection? This is hardly conceivable.

But the explanation is simple with the multiple inner selection working under the guidance of pleasure and the infinite genetic memory. That memory can extend, under stressful conditions, to the reserve of genetic codes from the whole primeval past of the species. With this in mind we can think of causal explanations even for sudden, seemingly planned, "insightful" evolutionary adaptations.

For instance, the use of camouflage by animals is a universal trait and has been most often pointed out as a miracle that it is. The pleasure of successful hiding here can combine with the limitless codes and memory from the genetic past. The pleasure here is unique, organically overwhelming, because it derives directly from survival mechanisms decisive for life and death. Correspondingly, the "memories" and codes from the genetic past can be easily revived here under the pleasure drive.

As to that genetic past, a primitive animal consisting of few cells would respond to outside conditions with its whole body, with its outer layers. And it may "learn," become conditioned by inner selection, to keep these layers in the same color as the environment. This learning would be purely mechanistic, under subordinate inner selection: each time one of the potentially countless living processes happens to match those colors, it prevails, because it favors the higher mechanism of survival.

Further, mechanistic learning by conditioning can lead to its "insightful" generalization if it involves mechanisms general enough, such as those of survival. Animals having learned a trick in one context may use it in another, under pressure. Pscyhologists and physiologists have a purely mechanical explanation for such a transfer of learning. And mechanisms inside animals "learn," are conditioned, in the same way, through inner selection working under the same law of effect.

The end result is organic adaptations and, finally, genetic changes, by "insighful" learning and through its transfer.

Thus, a primitive animal may learn even genetically to copy the same color and then the same shape on its outside that the forms in the environment have. This may not be difficult with instinctive mechanisms, since they would react here by simple point-to-point responses to countless stimuli of light from the environment. No need here for a focusing lens creating the separate images required in mental perceptions.

Similarly, a multiple-reaction method makes sonaring by bats easy to explain. The bat responds to innumerable points as easily as man would respond to one or a few. Or the parrot copies multiple sounds as easily as any organism can copy one sound.

In short, the ready capacity here to deal with multiplicity renders point-to-point imitations of the environment easy. Moreover, such "learning" consists of factual somatic and, finally, genetic changes of inner mechanisms. Inner-selection "learning" always consists of actual enactments of the "learned" adaptations.

Add to this the above generalization of camouflage, its extension from color imitation to shape or sound imitation. We have indicated that such generalizations can be mechanistic. But the end result can be ungraspably miraculous—because of the multiplicity of such "learning" and of its extensions by generalizations or transfers.

In sum, the imitation of the environment may first evolve into a universal genetic trait in some primitive animals. The pleasure of survival itself is shaping these adaptations. They may therefore have deep effects in the organism of primitive animals: the imitation mechanism deepens strongly as the pleasure of survival is felt every time the risks of death are overcome by successful camouflage.

The genetic code for the trait of camouflage therefore easily becomes an important part of the reserve codes stored in the "excess" DNA. The trait then can be resorted to by a later, somewhat higher animal, an insect or lizard, particularly under abnormal, stressful conditions.

Geneticists have observed that organisms sometimes regrow, *under traumatic, stressful conditions*, some ancestral forms. This often creates monsters.

Stephen Jay Gould has explained how homeotic monsters result from the "mimicking of an ancestral form."[4] With reference to Theodosius Dobzhansky he discusses reversals to previous forms as a possible general evolutionary method. The "hopeful monsters," as we have seen, can play a similar evolutionary role.[4, 8]

Particularly when organisms are exposed to stressful conditions, such forms of "hopeful monsters" may be automatically created by organisms. The search for new ways under difficulties is a universal organic drive. It is inherent in the nature of life as an inventive and flexible, relentless "fire."

Organisms are exposed to the greatest amount of such stressful difficulties in the experiments that induce artificial, lethal mutations. Indeed "monstrous" forms are produced in such experiments and are occasionally found to have potentially adaptive traits, as was shown in experiments by the Nobelist H. J. Muller.[1,3] Scientists now admit, as in explaining the De Vries mutations, that such traits result from "intergenetic" variations[3] rather than from physical and destructive mutational influences, such as radiation. Organisms under stress would naturally resort to new intergenetic adaptations, through inner selection, also by the use of codes from the "junk" DNA.[4]

The codes from the historical past, stored in the excess DNA, act in the way all living processes do, and therefore can extend or spread as intensely as the "fire" of life generally does. These codes go to work competitively, wherever this is selectively permitted by the whole organism, whenever the organism as the highest controlling mechanism gains advantage from their action. Thus the purposive inner selection governed by subordination becomes the working method for the stored genetic codes as well.

The whole past experience of life on earth then becomes potentially available for selectively intense, purposive adaptations by organisms. The possibilities here are enormous in their multiplicity and intricacy of combinations. It can be said that practically every imaginable adaptation thus becomes possible.

Such adaptation is always inventively purposive. Inner selection, competing for greater, purposive organic subordination, operates here; Darwin demonstrated how "ingeniously" purposive can become the effects of mere competitive selection. Moreover, learning by conditioning through inner selection is continuously at work here, at every point and instant, for ages.

Incidentally, we should note here that our explanations are so wide and unusual that they may seem farfetched. The reason for this is that we are opening wide new possibilities for explanations by proceeding in totally new, humanly repugnant ways—by turning against wholesome human prejudices.

In particular, we have revealed the extreme limitedness of the human mind and the virtual anthropomorphism of our life sciences as they use the one-by-one method with which the human mind works. This one-by-one method amounts to blindness in dealing with the multiplicity of any living phenomenon, and in overlooking the inner selection or organic interdependence.

Ultimately, this "blindness" is due to the impact of general human prejudices. The prejudice against opposite-value causality has allowed only the physical science to succeed. This has led to the dominance by the physical sciences. And these sciences work in the one-by-one way in which man's mind works. Thus, another general human prejudice is compounded: the unbelievable limitedness of the human mind is not accounted for in any formal science.

We also have brought in the concept of the Field, which is particularly untenable according to human prejudices but makes causally explainable the living process itself.

Understandably, we cannot fully confirm our explanations by references to findings in the present sciences, which are not aware of the above "blindness" and prejudices. But, as in most cases of general human prejudices, the objective causal truths here are so simple that they hardly need experimental proofs.

We are not, however, contradicting Darwinian theory, the real key to the natural sciences. We are rather imitating it as an unorthodox approach beyond contemporary prejudices which does not need experimental proofs; the facts of Darwinian selection are still not fully understood and are merely inferred from Darwin's genial theory.

The general natural selection and inner selection work cumulatively. Selection is a universal principle of existence. Sudden catastrophic changes affecting the evolution of a species can often occur. Then, by Darwinian selection, the whole species may perish except for the one individual, and his progeny, who happens to have a new trait enabling him to survive. We have seen that this is, in the end, the only way Darwinian selection can work effectively.

In any event, Darwinian selection can have its radical effects at isolated points, though any sudden forms it brings still require purposive refinements from inner selection to become adapted. Selection under such sudden changes makes explainable the "punctuational" evolution. Niles Eldredge and Stephen Jay

Gould have especially demonstrated "punctuations" in evolution. During difficult periods for a species, abrupt changes may become the only way to survive. Such changes may come by mere chance or through resorting to the store of past genetic codes. (The mutations, in their accepted sense, are however far too destructive to help any selection or evolution.)

The imperceptibly gradual and refined inner selection, though, remains the main causal source of evolution. Through it organisms "learn" under environmental conditioning to adapt automatically to each infinitesimal condition by adjustments that resemble planned behavior and are guided by "pleasure" drives.

The organic inner mechanisms "learn" in the way animals learn, by being conditioned. This learning becomes, as we have seen, similar in its effects to human learning, with foresight, planning, or reasoned inferences from the past. Also, the "learning" by inner mechanisms leads to factual adaptations, as far as this is permitted by the rest of the integrated organic system. Further, this "learning" becomes generally inheritable, however slightly or gradually.

Above all, the *past "remembered" here* by the mechanisms and exploited in their "learning" is *immense in its multiplicty and multiple complexity.* Human memory is ridiculously small in comparison with instinctive capacities; the simple example of tasting a food is sufficient for us to realize this.

Certainly, the human mind is superior in its particular way. But, as we have seen, inner selection makes possible so many endless trials and errors of learning, through the ages, that the effect is practically equal to that of our abstract, unrestricted mental "rehearsals" as sources of planning or of compliance with past experiences.

Thus, inner selection factually creates adaptations as if by purposefully chosen planning inferred from a memory that is enormous in comparison with human memory. The purposiveness here is always insured by the simple principle of organic subordination working at innumerable levels of the endless, integrative inner selection.

In sum, nothing more than the *multiplicity* of living nature turns it into a *purposeful miracle* that man could never imitate in peformance or even visualize in his mind. The *limitedness of the human mind* is the source of the mystery here. Recognition of these facts would widen the view in modern biology or genetics, which are now built on incongruous atomistic "scientism."

For instance, our concept of the genetic self makes causally explainable the central mystery of the acquisition of purposive genetic traits. This concept reveals how the *genetic self*, acting as a genetic center, is integrated and *diffused through every cell* in the organism, and therefore can acquire the adaptations that the organism clearly develops. But such a scientifically unanalyzable, multiple "diffusion" would never be considered by scientists. Is it unreal or unimportant?

In fact, it is the most general and causally decisive method of organic existence. Your functions of growth or nutrition are diffused through every cell in your organism. So are the other functions, of survival or fulfillment of your organic capacities. The same is true for actions by determinants such as hormones, and above all for the always fully integrated, universally decisive pleasure reactions or feelings.

In all these functions the organism acts as one self, in one way or under one principle that can be causally , scientifically dealt with. Similarly, the genetic self, treated under *principles such as organic "learning" or the pleasure drive, can be causally understood and controlled.* The genetic self, indeed, acts as one genetic center even while being diffused throughout the organism.

Geneticists or biologists, though, would never consider concepts like the myraid intermixture of purposive determinants throughout the organism. They still persist in dealing "scientifically" only with isolated, separate elements or atoms in explaining what happens organically and genetically, You can see this from any one of the textbooks on genetics or biology.

The present general fallacy of "scientism" can be resolved if the organism is viewed as a whole resulting from infinitely multiple interactions.

Only the organic, holistic causal principles can be actually understood. We have indicated those causal principles. They are not difficult to recognize, but this requires a *new, humanly and scientifically repugnant approach*, which demotes our mind and rejects a universal use of the method of our exact sciences.

To conclude, we should emphasize the effect of the prejudiced and anthropomorphic blindness of man as scientist when he deals with the living nature. His one-by-one method of thinking is sufficient in the physical and mechanical sciences, which have become our exact sciences. But this method can be only blindly misleading in the fields of living nature, such as biology or genetics.

Yet, even here, scientists persist in thinking in the "scientific" terms of separate factors and atoms, of genes and isolated experimental variables. Such terms are anthropomorphic for living nature because they derive from the one-by-one ways in which man thinks and consciously acts. These ways are contrary to those of the endlessly interdependent organic integration of living mechanisms.

Living nature will remain an inherent mystery if men try to understand it through isolated atoms or single factors of its astronomic causally interdependent multiplicity. But men can easily understand the causal principles of living nature. Man as organism exists by the same principles—which therefore should be perfectly simple to him.

Thus, we have here the dichotomy between the unfathomable causal mystery of living nature and its necessarily simple, natural causality.

The ingenious camouflage of a crab which places debris on itself can never be explained causally by genetic atoms such as genes or their accidental, massively crippling mutations. But inner selection and organic subordination, though self-evidently simple, can make explainable, with the use of causal principles, the organic and genetic learning and its seemingly intelligent purposiveness. Such a "learned" purposiveness can have effects resembling foresight or planning in the pursuit of pleasure, in human terms. Thus, the camouflage by the crab becomes causally explainable.

In a word, we can explain living nature causally by its simple, presently unrecognized principles, such as inner selection or the integrated pleasure response, which are causally, concretely true. And miraculous sciences can be built on causal understanding, in any field.

For instance, human genetics could be made as all-important as it is presently helpless, with geneticists expecting destructive mutations to be the sources of our human genetic improvements. Actually, by using the inner-selection "learning" through conditioning of pleasure reactions, we could scientifically engineer our genetic adaptations.

Inner selection can be a source of unlimited adaptations because it works by learning through conditioning. Such learning, by organism, is mechanically simple, as psychologists and physiologists have explained. It works under the law of effect. And inner selection works in the same way, with all the mechanisms inside the organism.

This learning, accumulated through millions of years by a species, can become incredibly ingenious. Particularly since it can resemble planning, in its effects, as all learning by conditioning can.

Even during the lifetime of an organism such learning can become extensively and richly "planned." B. F. Skinner, in his famous experiments on conditioning, demonstrated how limitlessly varied the effects of conditioning can become. In his cages of birds the conditioning was effected by grains of feed. When he allowed the grains to drop randomly during a night, in the morning he found the birds performing all kinds of stands and dances in their "planned" attempts to obtain the grains.

Now, think of organic mechanisms "planning," not only over one night, but during millions of years. Myriads of "dances" have to result, and systems of them become causally related to their other systems, on and on. Moreover, each system of systems here is purposive and adaptively integrated to infinitesimal detail, under the endless though simple inner selection and organic subordination.

The main, unfathomable miracle of living nature is the cleverness of genetic adaptations. It becomes causally understandable as a genetic inheritance of "learning" or adaptations acquired by individuals of a species. It is clear that individuals do adapt or "learn" organically. Inner selection explains causally how it happens. The only other needed concept is that for the diffusion of the genetic self through all cells of the organism.

Both these concepts are self-evidently simple; we have seen how the integrative inner selection and the "diffusion" of genetic material work in principally simple ways. But the multiplicity of living nature makes it all humanly ungraspable.

If you looked at an organism consisting only of a couple of cells, you could understand how the genetic material diffused in them would selectively improve or adapt together with the organism. Now, everybody can see that in a person as well, the genetic material from his parents must be causally diffused throughout his body, or that organisms change adaptively. But because it all is so ungraspably multiple, beyond the capacities of the mind, science leaves unexplained the central miracle of the cleverness of living nature and its evolution.

Living nature remains unfathomably miraculous to man not because of any superior qualities in it, but because of the extreme limitedness of the human mind.

Men, however, do not recognize that this limitedness makes them virtually blind in their viewing of living nature. Even scientists continue dealing with nature according to the one-by-one terms with which the human mind works. This method can only perpetuate a specially incapacitating "scientism," and a virtually anecdotal study of nature, since only in rare, curious aspects do living processes work in the way the human mind does.

In a final note, we admit that our explanations are mostly theoretical. Generally, theories are cheap while factual proofs are important. This, however, is not true when explanations have to do with some universal causal, scientific prejudice which distorts the viewing of facts or hides them. And the very gist of this book is an explanation of such a universal causal prejudice. (We indicated that our explanation does not require any superior insight; it rather comes from our humanly abhorrent rummaging in the "refuse heap" of ideas which are avoided in respectful, wholesome human thinking.)

Indeed, even the most important scientific discoveries often have been primarily theoretic achievements. They have been scientifically revolutionary and conclusively far-reaching, not because of their factual proofs, but because of their new ideas, new, simple theories opposing some existing prejudice, as we have indicated before.

The Copernican theory, which can be stated in a single sentence, was conclusive even though the factual mathematical proofs on which it was founded are now shown to have been erroneous.

Darwinism became the basis of a revolutionary new scientism because of its *simple* theory, not because of particular factual proofs. The facts about Darwinian evolution are still continuously revised, mostly through logical inferences from its fundamental *self-evident ideas*.

Typically, the discovery of gravitation was a mere insight beyond a general human prejudice. Nobody needs factual or mathematical proofs to accept the gravitational force or to understand its importance. But it required a discovery.

In short, theory, not factual proofs, is important in overcoming universal causal prejudices that prevent scientific causal understanding. The prejudice that we are explaining distorts, primarily, the sciences dealing with man. Additionally, this prejudice prevents man from understanding his one-sided and limited ways of viewing the material world as he knows it. This affects fields such as theoretical physics and the study of living nature.

The amount of factual, experimental findings in all these fields, dealing with man and his knowledge, is immense. We have used the best, most authoritative of them to have facts that prove our explanations.

But the "soft" human and social sciences, even the theoretical physics, are admittedly still lacking the most fundamental, necessarily simple causal explanations or causal laws. We have seen this for each of the sciences of man and of his universe. We have also seen that man as a creation of nature is governed by simple causal principles.

Apparently, the universal incapacity of all men to understand causally the human world must have a humanly universal, natural reason which cannot be too complex. We have demonstrated how this incapacity comes from man's prejudice against recognizing the causal, "negative" sources of his positive values. This prejudice is universally necessary for man, since he would not survive without it.

Our explanation of such a simple universal prejudice depends as little on involved experimental demonstrations as do the above really great discoveries. Even there theory has been primarily decisive, independently of factual, experimentally precise demonstrations.

REFERENCES

Chapter I (pp. 1-44)

[1] Kimble, Gregory, *et al., Principles of Psychology*. New York: John Wiley & Sons, 1984, pp. 61, 126, 273, 548, 611, 723.

[2] Smith, Ronald E., *et al., Psychology: The Frontiers of Behavior*. New York: Harper & Row, 1982, pp. 14, 59, 263, 417, 533, 671.

[3] Minton, Arthur J., and Shipka, Thomas A., *Philosophy: Paradox and Discovery*. New York: McGraw-Hill Book Co., 1982. pp. 53, 84, 153, 178, 249, 310, 405.

[4] Nozick, Robert, *Philosophical Explanations*. Cambridge, Mass: Harvard University Press, 1983, pp. 151, 237, 341, 518, 762.

[5] Kaplan, Harold I., and Sadock, Benjamin, *Comprehensive Textbook of Psychiatry*. Baltimore: Williams & Wilkins, 1984, pp. 247, 743, 1321, 1562, 2391.

[6] Gilman, Alfred G., and Goodman, Louis S., *Pharmacological Basis of Therapeutics*. New York: Macmillan Co., 1980, pp. 162, 358, 537, 719.

[7] U.S. Bureau of the Census, *Statistical Abstract of the United States 1985*. Washington, D.C.: U.S. Government Printing Office, 1984, pp. 74, 75, 112.

[8] Dunnette, Marwin D., *Handbook of Industrial and Organizational Psychology*. Chicago: Rand McNally Co., 1976, pp. 266, 438, 519, 1126, 1463.

[9] *International Encyclopedia of the Social Sciences*. New York: Macmillan Co., 1968, Vol. III, pp. 471ff.; Vol. VII, pp. 66ff., 522ff.; Vol. IX, pp. 113ff.; Vol. XIII, pp. 49ff.; Vol. XIV, pp. 409ff.

Chapter II (pp. 45-103)

[1] Harvey, A.M., ed., *The Principles and Practice of Medicine*. New York: Appleton-Century-Crofts, 1984, pp. 16, 135, 482, 712, 963, 1214, 1471.

[2] Nordenfelt, Lenart, and Lindhal, Ingemar, eds., *Health, Disease and Causal Explanations in Medicine*. Hingham, Mass.: Kluwer Academic Pubs., 1984. pp. 14, 81, 163, 274, 386, 409.

[3] American Medical Association, *Book of Heart Care*. New York: Random House, 1982, pp. 5, 8, 31, 68, 76, 81, 149, 189, 197.

[4] Surwit, Richard S., Williams, Redford B., and Shapiro, David, *Behavioral Approaches to Cardiovascular Diseases*. New York: Academic Press, 1982, pp. 31, 51, 79, 87, 96, 114, 129, 144, 179, 182, 201.

[5] Hurst, J. Willis, *et al.*, eds., *The Heart: The Heart, Arteries and Veins*. New York: McGraw-Hill, 1982, pp. 151, 328, 393, 948, 951, 1196, 1637, 1640, 1646.

[6] Fisher, Arthur, and Editors of Time-Life Books, *The Healthy Heart*. Alexandria, Va.: Time-Life Books, 1981, pp. 6, 17, 30, 54, 61, 84.

[7] Rapaport, Elliot, ed., *Current Controversies in Cardiovascular Disease*. Philadelphia: W.B. Saunders Co., 1980, pp. 43, 53, 70, 102, 129, 161, 199, 488, 506, 613.

[8] Holland, James F., and Frei, Emil, III, *Cancer Medicine*. Philadelphia: Lea & Febiger, 1982, pp. 39, 43, 74, 133, 191, 305, 322, 741, 956, 1174, 1745.

[9] Editors of Time-Life Books, *Fighting Cancer*. Alexandria, Va.: Time-Life Books, 1981, pp. 13, 15, 49, 103, 109.

[10] Simmons, Harold E., *The Psychogenic Biochemical Aspects of Cancer*. Sacramento, Cal.: Psychogenic Disease Publ. Co., 1979, pp. 6, 14, 31, 38, 41, 68, 107, 136, 151, 157.

[11] De Vita, Vincent, *et al.*, *Cancer: Principles and Practice of Oncology*. Philadelphia: J.B. Lippincott, 1982, pp. 34, 47, 187, 216, 264, 297, 301, 752, 788, 1291.

[12] Renneker, Mark, ed., *Understanding Cancer*. Palo Alto, Cal.: Bull Publ. Co., 1980, pp. 103, 106, 108, 126, 132, 139, 141, 297, 301.

[13] Ellenberg, Max, and Rifkin, Harold, eds., *Diabetes Mellitus: Theory and Practice*. New Hyde Park, N.Y.: Medical Examination Publ. Co., 1982, pp. 48, 61, 119, 135, 152, 179, 256, 290, 457, 473, 530.

[14] Ireland, J.T., Thomson, W.S.T., and Williamson, J., *Diabetes Today.* New York: Springer Publ. Co., 1980, pp. 9, 10, 40, 117, 164, 189, 202, 263.
[15] Brownlee, Michael, ed., *Handbook of Diabetes Mellitus.* New York: Garland STPM Press, 1981, pp. 19, 83, 172, 186.
[16] Katz, Howard M., and Mahler, Richard J., *Diabetes, Obesity and Vascular Disease.* New York: John Wiley & Sons, 1978, pp. 229, 231, 256, 266, 418, 682.
[17] Kelley, William N., *et al., Textbook of Rheumatology.* Philadelphia: W.B. Saunders Co., 1981, pp. 32, 61, 226, 721, 737, 887, 893, 1480.
[18] McCarthy, Daniel J., ed., *Arthritis and Allied Conditions.* Philadelphia: Lea & Febiger, 1979, pp. 12, 131, 138, 141, 146, 174, 187, 209, 213.
[19] Holtermuller, K.H., and Malagelda, J.R., eds., *Advances in Ulcer Disease.* Princeton, N.J.: Excerpta Medica, 1980, pp. 7, 23, 27, 34, 59, 128, 143, 172, 423, 531.
[20] Eisenberg, M. Michael, *Ulcers.* New York: Random House, 1978, pp. 6, 35, 38, 39, 53, 71, 80, 86, 91, 94, 113, 209, 211.
[21] U.S. Bureau of the Census, *Statistical Abstract of the United States.* Washington: U.S. Government Printing Office, 1984, pp. 74, 75; 1978, pp. 50, 51, 62, 64, 65, 68, 86.
[22] *Discover, the Newsmagazine of Science.* Dec. 1984, pp. 17-25; Mar. 1984, pp. 21-28; Nov. 1983, pp. 80 ff.; Mar. 1983, pp. 26ff.; Feb. 1983, pp. 30-32; Dec. 1982, pp. 15ff.; Nov. 1982, pp. 15-16; Sept. 1981, pp. 37-39; Aug. 1981, pp. 26-30.
[23] *Annals of Internal Medicine*, November 1974, pp. 700-701.
[24] Friedman, Meyer, and Rosenman, Ray H., *Type A Behavior and Your Heart.* New York: Alfred Knopf, 1974, pp. 48, 52, 84, 86, 109, 111, 115, 123, 161, 189, 230, 254.
[25] *Time*, June 6, 1983, pp. 48-62; Sept. 27 1982, pp. 83ff.; Aug. 16, 1982, pp. 40 ff.; Nov. 1, 1981, pp. 15ff.; June 9, 1981, pp. 51ff.; Feb. 16, 1981, pp. 57 ff.
[26] *Psychology Today*, April 1985, pp. 18-20; October 1982, pp. 28 ff.; February 1981, pp. 28-39; June 1980, pp. 66-76.
[27] Tushnet, Leonard. *The Uses of Adversity.* New York: Thomas Yoseloff, 1966, pp. 52, 61, 63, 64, 71.
[28] Suitor, Carol West, and Hunter, Merrily Forbes, *Nutrition: Principles and Application.* Philadelphia: Lippincott Co., 1980, pp. 6, 73, 141, 174, 192, 212, 214, 361, 362.
[29] Caliendo, Mary Alice, *Nutrition and Preventive Health Care.* New York: Macmillan Co., 1981, pp. 7, 12, 171, 298, 312, 326, 407, 486.

Chapter III (pp. 105-160)

[1] Kaplan, Harold I., and Sadock, Benjamin J., *Comprehensive Text-*

book of Psychiatry. 4th ed. Baltimore: Williams & Wilkins, 1984, pp. 247, 364, 496, 521, 743, 838, 1079, 1288, 1306, 1321, 1493, 1503, 1544, 1562.

[2] Menninger, Karl A., *The Vital Balance*. Magnolia, Mass.: P. Smith Pub., Inc., 1983, pp. 163, 254, 281, 357, 385, 399.

[3] Friedman, Claude T., and Faguet, Robert A., *Extraordinary Disorders of Human Behavior*. New York: Plenum Publishing Corp., 1982, pp. 7, 10, 167, 288, 316, 321.

[4] Cavenar, Jesse O., and Brodie, Keith H., eds., *Critical Problems in Psychiatry*. Philadelphia: J.B. Lippincott, 1982, pp. 12, 41, 58, 123, 131, 214, 237, 418.

[5] Dongier, Maurice, and Wittkower, Eric D., *Divergent Views in Psychiatry*. New York: Harper & Row, 1981, pp. 47, 96, 202, 245, 249, 277, 314, 319.

[6] Gross, Martin L., *The Psychological Society*. New York: Random House, 1978, pp. 23, 26, 33, 200, 236, 251, 277.

[7] Ingleby, David, *Critical Psychiatry*. New York: Pantheon Books, 1980, pp. 8, 17, 121, 183, 193, 214, 217, 241.

[8] Gilman, Alfred G., and Goodman, Louis S., *The Pharmacological Basis of Therapeutics*. New York: Macmillan Co., 1980, pp. 153, 186, 217, 223, 249, 391, 537, 629, 710.

[9] Tanner, Ogden, and the Editors of Time-Life Books, *The Prudent Use of Medicines*. Alexandria, Va.; Time-Life Books, 1981, pp. 19, 20, 67, 82, 160, 211, 215, 231.

[10] Gerald, Michael C., *Pharmacology: An Introduction to Drugs*. Englewood Cliffs, N.J.; Prentice-Hall, 1981, pp. 39, 96, 485, 551, 512, 523, 637, 651, 720.

[11] Kimble, Gregory, *et al.*, *Principles of Psychology*. New York: John Wiley & Sons, 1984, pp. 74, 126, 228, 378, 546, 611, 723.

[12] Morris, Charles G., *Psychology: An Introduction*. 5th ed. Englewood Cliffs, N.J.: Prentice-Hall, 1985, pp. 31, 56, 129, 312, 447, 538.

[13] Kline, Nathan S., *From Sad to Glad*. New York: G.P. Putnam's Sons, 1974, pp. 116, 119, 122, 127, 129, 141, 205, 218.

[14] Smith, Ronald E., *et al.*, *Psychology: The Frontiers of Behavior*. New York: Harper & Row, 1982, pp. 59, 137, 214, 336, 417, 436, 459, 513, 561, 672.

[15] Robert, Marthe, *The Psychoanalytic Revolution*. New York: Harcourt Brace Jovanovich, 1966, pp. 48, 68, 110, 111, 248, 249, 386.

[16] Dunnette, Marwin D., *Handbook of Industrial and Organizational Psychology*. Chicago: Rand McNally Co., 1976, pp. 266, 327, 438, 519, 1126, 1463.

[17] U.S. Bureau of the Census, *Statistical Abstract of the United States*. Washington: U.S. Government Printing Office, 1984, pp. 74, 112; 1978, pp. 62, 64, and 68.

[18] *Time*, July 30, 1979, pp. 70 ff.; Oct. 15, 1984, pp. 80ff.; Nov. 10, 1980, pp. 112ff.; May 23, 1983, pp. 60ff; Sept. 1, 1980, pp. 15-19.

19 *Psychology Today*, May 1982, pp. 41-59; Feb. 1981, pp. 28-39; June 1980, pp. 66-76.

Chapter IV (pp. 161-216)

1 Martin, Gary, and Pear, Joseph, *Behavior Modification*. Englewood Cliffs, N.J.: Prentice-Hall, 1983, pp. 12, 176, 194, 196, 381, 432, 469.

2 *International Encyclopedia of the Social Sciences*. New York: Macmillan Co., 1968: Vol. II. pp. 226ff; Vol. III, pp. 471ff.; Vol. IV, pp. 74ff., 286 ff., 430 ff.; Vol. VII, pp. 66 ff., 522 ff.; Vol. IX, pp. 113 ff.; Vol. XIII, pp. 49ff.; Vol. XIV, pp. 409ff.

3 Klein, S.B., *Motivation: Biosocial Approaches*. New York: McGraw-Hill, 1982. pp. 14, 218, 220, 344, 372, 546.

4 McKay, Matthew, *et al.*, *Thoughts and Feelings: The Art of Cognitive Stress Intervention*. Oakland, Cal.: New Harbinger Pubs., 1981, pp. 8, 141, 163, 208, 214.

5 Montapert, Alfred A., *Inspiration and Motivation*. Englewood Cliffs, N.J.: Prentice-Hall, 1982, pp. 16, 21, 183, 186, 274.

6 Mahoney, Michael J., *Cognition and Behavior Modification*. Cambridge, Mass.: Ballinger Publishing Co., 1983, pp. 11, 13, 128, 171, 249, 361.

7 Hamilton, Vernon, *The Cognitive Structures and Processes of Human Motivation and Personality*. New York: John Wiley & Sons, 1983, pp. 9, 63, 81, 174, 228, 235, 316, 318.

8 Reilly, Robert R., and Lewis, Ernest L., *Educational Psychology: Essentials of Theory and Practice*. New York: John Wiley & Sons, 1984, pp. 22, 121, 374, 428, 476.

9 Reynolds, Cecil R., *et al*, *School Psychology: Essentials of Theory and Practice*. New York: John Wiley & Sons, 1984, pp. 22, 121, 374, 428, 476.

10 Klausmeier, Herbert J., *Educational Psychology*. New York: Harper & Row, 1984, pp. 20, 71, 215, 218, 367, 375, 423, 457.

11 Lindgren, Henry C., *Educational Psychology in the Classroom*. New York: Oxford University Press, 1980, pp. 23, 29, 163, 294, 299, 377, 438, 466.

12 DeWolf, L. Harold, *Crime and Justice in America*. New York: Harper & Row, 1975, pp. 4, 6, 106, 173, 223.

13 *Time*, June 30, 1975, pp. 10-24; Aug. 27, 1984, pp. 42-44; Oct. 11, 1982, p. 61; Mar. 23, 1981, pp. 17-20.

14 Radzinovicz, Sir Leon, *The Growth of Crime: The International Experience*. New York: Basic Books, 1977, pp. 78, 81, 93, 187, 328.

15 Wolfgang, Marvin E., and Ferracuti, Franco, *The Subculture of*

Violence: Toward an Integrated Theory of Criminology. Beverly Hills, Ca.: Sage Pubs. Inc., 1982, pp. 24, 38, 141, 320, 327, 405.

[16] Jacks, Irving, and Cox, Steven, eds., *Psychological Approach to Crime and Its Correction*. Chicago: Nelson Hall, 1983, pp. 31, 77, 102, 116, 287, 325, 341, 574.

[17] Vold, George B., *Theoretical Criminology*. New York: Oxford University Press, 1980, pp. 62, 133, 181, 217, 247.

[18] Ray, Oakley, *Drugs, Society and Human Behavior*, St. Louis: C.V. Mosby Co., 1983, pp. 26, 203, 218, 421, 473.

[19] Leavitt, Fred, *Drugs and Behevior*. New York: John Wiley & Sons, 1982, pp. 127, 176, 271, 384, 403, 451.

[20] Smith, J.E., and Lane, J.D., *Neurobiology of Opiate Reward Mechanism*. New York: Elsevier Science Pub. Co., 1983, pp. 19, 184, 229, 318, 438.

[21] Garan, D.G., *The Key to the Sciences of Man*. New York: Philosophical Library, 1975, pp. 23, 66, 68, 72, 262, 264, 267, 272, 286, 287, 289, 291, 293, 302, 334, 335, 368.

Chapter V (pp. 217-278)

[1] Huxley, Sir Julian, *et al.*, *The Humanistic Frame*. New York: Harper & Row, 1975, pp. 25, 29, 188, 243, 445, 607.

[2] Tiselius, Arne, and Nilson, Sam, eds., *The Place of Value in the World of Facts*. New York: Wiley-Interscience, 1971, pp. 19, 52, 193, 207, 284, 305, 371, 416.

[3] Otto, Herbert A., ed., *Love Today*. New York: Association Press, 1972, pp. 27, 47, 151, 172, 183, 254, 268, 272, 273.

[4] Bronowski, Jacob, *The Ascent of Man*. Boston: Little, Brown & Co., 1976, pp. 127, 153, 159, 160, 163, 164.

[5] Fromm, Erich, *The Sane Society*. New York: Holt, Rinehart & Winston, 1975, pp. 206, 208, 310, 311, 357.

[6] Martin, F. David, *The Humanities Through the Arts*. New York: McGraw-Hill, 1983, pp. 18, 52, 226, 318, 460, 467, 483.

[7] Ross, Stephen D., ed., *Art and Its Significance*. Albany, N.Y.: State University of New York Press, 1984, pp. 61, 89, 163, 224, 257.

[8] Sparshott, Francis, *The Theory of Art*. Princeton, N.J.: Princeton University Press, 1982, pp. 14, 91, 271, 304, 415, 556, 618.

[9] Nozick, Robert, *Philosophical Explanations*. Cambridge, Mass.: Harvard University Press, 1983, pp. 74, 118, 273, 349, 432, 547, 610, 782.

[10] Solomon, Robert C., *Introducing Philosophy: Problems and Pers-*

pectives. New York: Harcourt Brace Jovanovich, 1982, pp. 67, 174, 176, 283, 372, 506, 542.

[11] Dubos, Rene, *A God Within*. New York: Charles Scribner's Sons, 1972, pp. 148, 193, 194, 206.

[12] Muller, Herbert J., *Uses of the Future*. Bloomington, Ind.: Indiana University Press, 1974, pp. 46, 87, 97, 98, 114.

[13] Toffler, Alvin, *Previews and Premises*, New York: William Morrow & Co., 1983, pp. 31, 72, 138, 174, 215.

[14] Garan, D.G. *Against Ourselves*. New York: Philosophical Library, 1980, pp. 193, 196, 199, 206, 207, 210, 215, 218, 219, 269, 275, 276, 277, 285.

Chapter VI (pp. 279-342)

[1] Einstein, Albert, and Infeld, Leopold, *The Evolution of Physics*. New York: Simon & Schuster, 1961, pp. 124, 141, 158, 196, 256, 303.

[2] Planck, Max, *The New Science*. New York: Meridian Books, 1959, pp. 97, 113, 170, 205, 264, 269.

[3] Davies, Paul, *Superforce: The Search for a General Unified Field*. New York: Simon & Schuster, 1984, pp. 22, 47, 68, 101, 136, 149, 183, 207, 244.

[4] Shimony, Abner, and Freshbach, Herman, eds., *Physics and Natural Philosophy*. Cambridge, Mass.: MIT Press, 1983, pp. 106, 188, 218, 249, 309, 374, 441.

[5] Pagels, Heinz, *The Cosmic Code; Quantum Physics as the Law of Nature*. New York: Simon & Schuster, 1982, pp. 16, 95, 113, 138, 143, 202, 271.

[6] Whittaker, Sir Edmund, *From Euclid to Eddington*. New York: Dover Publications, 1960. pp. 53, 82, 155, 178, 201, 247, 263.

[7] Bridgman, P.W., *The Way Things Are*. Cambridge, Mass.: Harvard University Press, 1959, pp. 157, 183, 188, 191, 206, 207.

[8] Schroedinger, Erwin, *Science, Theory and Man*. New York: Dover Publications, 1967, pp. 59, 131, 177, 195, 200.

[9] American Foundation for Continuing Education, *The Mystery of Matter*. New York: Oxford University Press, 1965, pp. 102, 109, 535, 539.

[10] Heisenberg, Werner, *Across the Frontiers*. New York: Harper & Row, 1974, pp. 16, 71, 184, 219, 221.

[11] Reichenbach, Hans, *Philosophical Foundations of Quantum Mechanics*. Berkeley, Cal.: University of California Press, 1982, pp. 40, 64, 116, 172, 183, 191.

[12] *Discover*, Dec. 1982, pp. 20-28; Oct. 1982, pp. 69-74; July 1981, pp. 29-32; May 1985, pp. 13-25.

[13] *Scientific American*, Feb. 1981, pp. 70-74; June 1981, pp. 163-174.

Chapter VII (pp. 343-403)

[1] Sober, Elliott, ed., *Contemporary Issues in Evolutionary Biology.* MIT Press, 1983, Cambridge, Mass.: pp. 18, 99, 117, 233, 310, 317, 462, 531.

[2] Gardner, Eldon J., and Snustad, Peter D., *Principles of Genetics.* New York: John Wiley & Sons, 1984, pp. 161, 177, 392, 431, 450, 513, 565.

[3] Korn, Robert W. *Contemporary Perspectives in Biology.* New York: John Wiley & Sons, 1971, pp. 65, 259, 265, 384, 387, 396, 457.

[4] *Natural History*, Mar. 1984. p. 20 ff; Nov. 1981, pp. 7-15; Oct. 1980, pp. 8-14.

[5] *The Sciences*, Mar. 1983, pp. 49ff.; Nov. 1981, pp. 3-4.

[6] Handler, Philip, *Biology and the Future of Man.* New York: Oxford University Press, 1970, pp. 20, 21, 165, 172.

[7] Oparin, Alexander I., *Life, Its Nature, Origin and Development.* New York: Academic Press, 1962, pp. 7, 14, 55, 65, 113, 159.

[8] Hitching, Francis, *The Neck of the Giraffe.* New York: New American Library, 1983, pp. 71, 190, 202, 236, 241, 243.

[9] Guttman, Burton S., and Hopkins, John W., *Understanding Biology.* New York: Harcourt Brace Jovanovich, 1983, pp. 107, 478, 653, 721, 806.

[10] Corliss, William R., *Incredible Life: A Handbook of Biological Mysteries.* Glen Arm, Md.: The Sourcebook Project, 1981, pp. 158, 236, 441, 539, 682, 976.

[11] Gottfried, Sandra, Madrazo, Gerry, Olenchalk, Joseph, *et al. Prentice-Hall Biology.* Englewood Cliffs, N.J.: Prentice-Hall, 1983, pp. 72, 151, 176, 211, 695.

[12] Lewin, Benjamin, *Genes.* New York: John Wiley & Sons, 1983, pp. 16, 23, 31, 134, 236, 395, 503, 587, 632.

[13] *Time*, Oct. 24, 1983, pp. 53ff; Nov. 30, 1981, pp. 84ff.; July 2, 1979, pp. 76ff.

[14] Gould, Stephen Jay, *Ontogeny and Phylogeny.* Cambridge, Mass.: Harvard University Press, 1977, pp. 97, 98, 199, 201, 206, 354.

[15] *Discover*, Jan. 1984, pp. 76-78; Mar. 1983, pp. 39-42; Dec. 1983, pp. 27-32.

INDEX